A Personal Note

More than a dozen years ago, two veteran newspapermen, excited about the world of journalism they knew so well, sought to share it with—as the dedication of their book put it—"Kathleen Anne and Kay-K, our teen-agers who looked over our shoulders as we wrote this book for them and their peers."

Those teen-agers went into journalism and shared a love for their profession with their fathers. One was tragically killed—but not before her photography was published nationally. The other, now the mother of perhaps a third-generation journalist, was a pioneering reporter on ecology and environment.

In those dozen years American journalism, professional and scholastic, has expanded its challenges, capabilities, and responsibilities. But the basic principles of technically excellent and morally sound journalism remain constant.

This book seeks to explore the new even as it cherishes the old. Writing it has been an invigorating and arduous project.

"Where do you begin learning journalism?" a student once asked a wise old editor.

"Everywhere at once," was the reply.

You will never doubt that observation if you ever try to write a book on the subject. For inevitably, the most simple, elementary statement must presuppose prior knowledge by the reader. You can't talk about newswriting unless you know something about circulation. You can't discuss headline writing unless you know something about typesetting. The interlocking of subjects is total and constant.

So your authors would urge you to ignore the apparent divisions in this book. For the section on newspapers has much information necessary for the editor of the yearbook; principles outlined in the chapter on Mimeographed newspapers apply equally to offset literary magazines.

This overlapping is necessary because the only alternative would be to repeat the same principles over and over as they apply to any specific kind of scholastic journalism. Such redundancy would make this book encyclopedic.

Despite this overlapping, any book that seeks to explore a subject as broad as journalism must be a big volume. This is. So take it in small bites.

Skim it first.

The stars that you'll notice every once in a while signal the most important axioms of journalism. (And they may make it easier for you to find just that sentence that will win an argument for you.) Italicized words signal those special terms that make it easier for you to communicate with your journalistic colleagues.

While it hasn't been mentioned specifically in the text, a constant reward of journalism is the warm fellowship that exists in all its fields. No matter where you go, you are an old friend. This can't be demonstrated better than by the friendly cooperation of the many, many individuals and companies who have contributed and shared material for use in this book.

We are particularly grateful to:

Viola Arnold and Kathleen Arnold Loomis for extraordinary services.

Dr. Joseph M. Murphy and Charles R. O'Malley of the Columbia Scholastic Press Association; Richard P. Johns of Quill and Scroll Society; Wally Wikoff of the National Scholastic Press Association; Thomas E. Engleman and C. Robert Skinner of The Newspaper Fund, Inc., and its former executive director, Paul Swensson; Stewart Macdonald of the American Newspaper Publishers Association Foundation; Albert W. Caron, Jr., of the Newspaper Information Service, American Newspaper Publishers Association; Ada Anne Chirles, Director of Publications, DeWitt Clinton High School, Bronx, N.Y., and advisor to New York City High School Press Council for the Board of Education; Maxwell Nurnberg, School of Continuing Education and Extension Services, New York University.

Tom Little and the *Nashville Tennessean;* Mead Papers, Howard Smith Papers, division of Domtar, Ltd.; Laurence B. Lain of Marion, Ind.; Arthur Van Allen of Indianapolis; William J. Keller, Inc. of Buffalo; R. Wallace Pischell, Inc., of Pasco, Wash.; John & Ollier Engraving Co.; Miss Jean Heller of Williamsport, Pa., King Features Syndicate; Marshall Matlock, director of Empire State Scholastic Press Association.

College English for permission to reprint an adaptation of an article by George W. Feinstein in the April 1960 issue; Houghton Mifflin Company for quotation from Archibald MacLeish's "Ars Poetica"; *Editor & Publisher;* Professors George E. Stevens and John B. Webster of the journalism program at Purdue University; Journalism Education Association, Inc.; Associated Press Managing Editors Association; Indiana State Department of Public Instruction; New York State Education Department; National Conference of Editorial Writers; and the staffs of student publications reproduced in this book.

Edmund C. Arnold
Hillier Krieghbaum

HANDBOOK
OF
STUDENT JOURNALISM
A Guide for Staff and Advisors

WITHDRAWN

Other books by Edmund C. Arnold

FUNCTIONAL NEWSPAPER DESIGN
Harper & Bros., 1956

PROFITABLE NEWSPAPER ADVERTISING
Harper & Bros., 1960

FEATURE PHOTOS THAT SELL
Morgan & Morgan, 1960

INK ON PAPER: A HANDBOOK OF THE GRAPHIC ARTS
Harper & Row, 1963

THE STUDENT JOURNALIST: A HANDBOOK FOR STAFF AND ADVISOR
(with Hillier Krieghbaum)
New York University Press, 1963

TIPOGRAFIA Y DIAGRAMADOS POR PERIODICOS
Inter American Press Association, 1964

THE GRAPHIC ARTS SERIES (5)
International Correspondence Schools, 1964

THE YEARBOOK
Richards Rosen Press, 1966

MODERN NEWSPAPER DESIGN
Harper & Row, 1969

INK ON PAPER 2
Harper & Row, 1972

EDITING THE YEARBOOK
Richards Rosen Press, 1973

Other books by Hiller Krieghbaum

AMERICAN NEWSPAPER REPORTING OF SCIENCE NEWS
Kansas State College, 1941

FACTS IN PERSPECTIVE: THE EDITORIAL PAGE AND NEWS
INTERPRETATION
Prentice-Hall, Inc., 1956

WHEN DOCTORS MEET REPORTERS
New York University Press, 1957

SCIENCE, THE NEWS AND THE PUBLIC
New York University Press, 1958

THE STUDENT JOURNALIST: A HANDBOOK FOR STAFF AND ADVISOR
(with Edmund C. Arnold)
New York University Press, 1963

SCIENCE AND THE MASS MEDIA
New York University Press, 1967

TO IMPROVE SECONDARY SCHOOL SCIENCE AND MATHEMATICS
TEACHING
(with Hugh Rawson)
Government Printing Office, 1968

AN INVESTMENT IN KNOWLEDGE
(with Hugh Rawson)
New York University Press, 1969

PRESSURES ON THE PRESS
Thomas Y. Crowell, 1972

HANDBOOK
OF
STUDENT JOURNALISM
A Guide for Staff and Advisors

Edmund C. Arnold

**Chairman, Graphic Arts Department
School of Public Communications
Syracuse University
Visiting Professor of Journalism
Mass Communications Department
Virginia Commonwealth University**

Hillier Krieghbaum

**Professor Emeritus and Former Chairman
Department of Journalism
and Mass Communications
College of Arts and Science
New York University**

New York University Press

1976

Manufactured in the United States of America

Library of Congress Catalog Card Number: 75-27047
ISBN: 0-8147-0557-X

Contents

HANDBOOK
OF
STUDENT JOURNALISM
A Guide for Staff and Advisors

BOOK

SCHOOL AND PROFESSIONAL JOURNALISM

VOGUE DIDOT Gara
Bodoni 6 Caso1
Bodoni Italic Be1
Ultra Bodoni Ext1
Bodoni 3 *Bodon*
Ultra Bodoni

Typefaces in Roman race

1

The Nature of Journalism

Journalists are almost the indispensable people. Whether professional or student, they have one of the most responsible and rewarding assignments that anyone can undertake.

The impact of what reporters do extends beyond simply making a lot of money or a business success, beyond personal prestige, fame, or power, and beyond winning ball games or other honors for a school's glory. Journalists witness history in the making and then tell it to the world. They supply background on which solid decisions must be made in a democratic society. They help people find the best buys through advertisements, the timing of their favorite television programs or motion picture performances, and the predictions of future weather conditions.

In any social structure, something has to hold the diverse segments from flying apart. In the complicated and complex contemporary world, that "something" is our extensive system of communication, a system that can aid in keeping things together. So journalism has become the mortar that cements social institutions into a viable society.

While this is imperatively true for professional journalists with community papers, broadcast stations, and magazines, it also applies to students with the thousands of high school publications and the hundreds of school broadcasting systems. The underground school press may be included, too, because it provides a possible escape valve for antiestablishment feelings that, if frustrated, might cause a far bigger explosion than battered emotions of administrators and other authoritarians.

Journalism is the most popular extracurricular activity in most schools. While more students may be involved in all athletics when considered as a whole, no single sport attracts as many participants as student publications.

Students who choose journalism as their outside activity are almost without exception the school's outstanding leaders. Alumni keep closer contact with their school journalism groups and associates in them than do those in other activities. Even those adults who enter careers far removed from communications look back on this school avocation as highly interesting and rewarding.

Many factors contribute to the appeal of journalism.

Newsmen and newswomen, whether dean of the White House correspondents, a foreign correspondent covering a faraway war, a specialist explaining the importance of a complicated breakthrough in experimental physics, or a staffer on a school paper, have the respect—and envy—of most of those who know them. They have entry to places banned to an average citizen. They talk with the great and successful—governor, Nobel prize-winner, popular rock singer, or star quarterback on a school's championship football team.

In addition, communications provide countless and ready opportunities for those who want to perform in the public service.

1

Journalism fills a fundamental need among humans. We all want to know what's going on, and we enjoy being able to tell our friends.

Everyone is a communicator of sorts. Think back over the past 24 hours.

You tell your best friend about an out-of-town visit that you have just arranged.

You notify your mother about a coming PTA meeting.

You confide to your father that the star dash man may not compete in the coming weekend meet.

You ask the student paper's editor if there is a possible feature in a discussion in your home room.

You learn, during conversation with a clerk at the supermarket, that candy prices will be increased.

You write a note to your buddy at summer camp telling what you have done during the past few weeks.

You tune in for an evening network news program to find out the world news.

You telephone your grandmother to thank her for a birthday check that just arrived.

Sometimes you were supplying news. Sometimes you were gathering news. In very basic ways, you were performing as a journalist.

Word of mouth was the first—and still remains a major—form of human communication. Probably the first example was when a primitive caveman grunted appropriately to his mate and she deduced that he had killed a tiger during the hunt. Medieval town criers performed a communication job for an entire community which was small and compact. In modern metropolitan centers, however, even with a giant bullhorn, no one could reach a whole city today. To provide general information for the contemporary mass audience is far beyond the capacity of any town crier. So the *mass media* arose. Included among them are newspapers, magazines, radio, television, books, trade journals, house magazines, newsletters, handbills, public address systems, bulletin boards—and on the list might go.

☆ Note—and remember—that the word "media" is plural and use of a singular verb, such as "is," is incorrect. The singular is "medium."

The typical American, according to recent calculations, spends more time with the mass media than doing anything else except sleeping and working. That is true whether an adult in a paid job or a student in school.

Radio and television fill four to six hours daily as individuals get news and entertainment from these media. The average television set is tuned on for more than 40 hours a week and a typical radio set—and there are more sets than there are individual Americans, including newly born babies—is dialed to some program from two to three hours each day.

For the entire globe, broadcasting has become an instantaneous mass medium. A record estimate of a billion people viewed at least some part of the summer Olympics at Munich in 1972 with a suspense story of hostages and death as well as results of international sports competitions.

Americans spend approximately half an hour daily (with much more on Sundays) reading a daily newspaper. More time is devoted to specialized journals for professional information, tidbits about hobbies, or just improving one's knowledge about the community or the world. All this is a development of the 20th century so unusual that social scientists are studying it in detail.

The 20th-century public, in an extraordinary way, has become news "consumers."

Basics of Communication

As a student journalist, you ought to understand at least the basic concepts of communication theory as well as the practical applications that will fill most of the pages of this book.

Thanks to modern communications equipment, a broadcaster in Africa or Asia can send news messages by voice or picture via outer-space satellite to a U.S. television audience and a foreign correspondent can telephone half way around the globe to talk with an editor and to dictate dispatches. Yet despite all this technology, the essential principle remains the same. This is how communication researchers have diagramed it:

For a publication, either in a community or in high school, the diagram would become:

Ideal communication depends on a perfect combination of all three components. A careless or inefficient "sender" or staff writer may introduce what students of information transmittal call *interference* or *noise*. A tired or distracted "receiver" or reader or listener may misunderstand the facts, despite their being entirely accurate, and thus get wrong impressions.

Some types of "messages" are more compelling than others. A photographer may present some facts more graphically and therefore better than several hundred words of description. For instance, the illustration of mankind's first footprint on the moon in July 1969 has become a classic and probably is better remembered by millions than is any writer's description. One reporter may compose a more dramatic story than another and thus be more effective in that instance.

Thanks to advancing technology during the past half century, mankind now has not only the printed word but television, radio, and motion pictures to help present the news of the world. The typical American depends on all these channels but pinpoints their utilization. Radio or television gets the news first. Daily newspapers provide additional facts and background. Magazines and books explore more deeply and provide interpretations and analyses that seldom are viewed in broadcasts. To get the full story, the public needs not only a quick summary of the highlights but *in-depth reporting, interpretation,* analysis, explanation, and *background.* These are found primarily in print media and their use varies frequently —according to the time available for their assembly. The more time until a deadline, the more time to write in depth.

For a variety of reasons, including the costliness of broadcast equipment and need for greatly sophisticated techniques, scholastic journalism depends upon the print medium in all but a few hundred schools.

☆ Every publication and broadcast station has a specialized job to do for its unique audience.

This is true whether the publication or channel is a metropolitan daily with national circulation, such as the *Washington Post* or *Christian Science Monitor;* a 5-minute radio summary of the local news; a monthly union periodical for carpenters; a national network's evening news television program; a small Montana weekly; a yearbook at a Pacific Coast college;—or your own school publication. This uniqueness explains, in part, the deluge of words for Americans today. A successful staff thus has to know not only the communication techniques and theory but the characteristics, attitudes, and even peculiarities of its own audience.

Some publications gather news about the important and interesting happenings around the world during the past 24 hours. They are properly known as NEWSpapers and appeal to the mass audience of a large community. Others gather news about a special segment, such as a limited geographical area of a metropolis and its suburbs; the restricted fields of a profession, such as doctors or accountants; the limited area of a trade, such as carpenters or tailors; or a business specialty, such as supermarket managers or chemical manufacturers. Still others provide literature and opinions for especially discriminating and sophisticated intellectuals.

To meet all these varied demands, a rush of words appeals to every possible segment of potential audiences. These vital statistics for the major mass media give you some idea of the magnitude of this flood:

Some 1,760 daily newspapers distribute more than 62.5 million copies.

Some 9,400 weekly papers have a total circulation of approximately 25 million copies.

Some 9,500 general and specialized magazines print an estimated 350 million copies of each issue.

Some 10,000 company publications or "house" magazines distribute 300 million or more copies to employees, stockholders, distributors, and buyers.

Some 336 million radio sets in homes, automobiles, and business establishments may be tuned to approximately 7,300 stations.

Some 88 million television sets may be adjusted to approximately 700 commercial or educational stations.

With this deluge, is it any wonder that a typical American sometimes feels as if he is drowning in words?

Functions of a Publication

Although each publication's staff may see its job as something different from all others, some generalizations are possible. For instance, functions of publications are:
1. To inform the readers;
2. To influence them;
3. To amuse them; and
4. To serve readers and the community.

The *information function* can be expressed through an account of last Saturday's football game or a picture of the valedictorian receiving a $500 scholarship. It might include an explanation of why the local school board is considering eliminating teaching of Russian and Spanish, plus a summary of arguments given for and against the proposal by student leaders, parents, and community spokesmen. Advertisements, too, carry helpful information, some of which may interest potential purchasers more than many of the news stories.

The *opinion function* is traditionally achieved through the editorial page. For example, comments might appeal for greater attendance at track meets or might give advice on how to study more effectively for final examinations. Arguments in editorials

should always rest on factual accuracy and sound logic. The effort to influence readers also may occur in "Letters to the Editor" or in many columns that express individual viewpoints and not the opinions of the publication.

The *entertainment function* carries into journalistic practice the familiar saying, "All work and no play makes Jack a dull boy." A paper filled only with straightaway facts and solemn editorial appeals would be dull, so staffs lighten their menus with humor, human interest, and other items that may amuse. For instance, a short item might report a slip-of-the-tongue answer that brought laughs in English class.

The *service function* could include information on co-ed fashion trends, a schedule of school dances or club meetings for the next few weeks, or advertisements that would bring buyers and sellers together in mutual benefit.

Staff members, especially those in high schools, sometimes view their jobs from still another viewpoint: That of the format and the audience reaction to their publication.

The newspaper or news magazine, no matter whether it is printed or Mimeographed, chiefly emphasizes what has happened since the last issue. What games were won, what honors given, what shifts made in faculty, what class and club officers elected, what assembly speakers heard—these are the bare bones for each issue. Most students read these enthusiastically, but, except for staff members, few will keep all issues through the years.

The literary magazine strives to provide recognition for good creative work, such as short stories, essays, poems, and play fragments. Most students want to see each issue but they keep only those in which their own work is printed.

The yearbook has been accepted by tradition as the memento to treasure for years. It has become the unofficial record that almost every student keeps to recall school years, the souvenir brought out when alumni get together to reminisce.

In the late 1940s, a group of educators and other distinguished nonjournalists participated in an evaluation of press performance and outlined ideals it might attain. Under the chairmanship of Dr. Robert M. Hutchins, then chancellor of the University of Chicago and later to be associated with the Fund for the Republic, this group was known as the Commission on Freedom of the Press. Its formal report, *A Free and Responsible Press*, should interest those starting into news work. The title's twin emphasis on freedom and responsibility supplies a meaningful focus for any journalist's thoughts about a professional career and duties. This is as true for staff members of a school periodical as for learned editorial board members of a scholarly professional journal. Included in this small book is the following valid outline of goals for a successful press in a democracy:

> Today our society needs, first, a truthful, comprehensive, and intelligent account of the day's events in a context which gives them meaning; second, a forum for the exchange of comment and criticism; third, a means of projecting the opinions and attitudes of the groups in the society to one another; fourth, a method of presenting and clarifying the goals and values of the society; and, fifth, a way of reaching every member of the society by the currents of information, thought, and feeling which the press supplies.

Most students and faculty members—and even many enlightened administrators—want their school's publications to be something more than just printed bulletin boards and propaganda ventures. Thus they recognize a need for organs of student expression or, to cite the Hutchins quotation, "a forum for the exchange of comment and criticism." Several of the national scholastic press organizations have paraphrased the Commission's words as goals for their membership's publications. All five parts have relevance for secondary school journalists and advisors.

Further showing the influence of the Hutchins Commission, an official position statement of the Journalism Education Association (JEA) stated that the roles of the secondary school media comprised (a) "educational tools"; (b) "means of expression for journalists and the public"; and (c) "instruments through which students, faculty, administration, and the public gain insight into student thinking and concerns."

What's News?

It is not entirely by accident, some journalists contend, that the letters that make up the word might properly stand for North, East, West, and South (N-E-W-S) but history shows that the spelling originally was "newes." Anyway, it's a good story and the idea fits because news may come from everywhere.

In another incident worth retelling, an American editor who insisted that the word "news" was plural since it comprised a bunch of news reports cabled his London correspondent, "Are there any news?"

Replied the reporter, "Not a single new."

Since news figures so prominently in any discussion of communication, let's take time now to define it. That isn't as easy as might, at first glance, seem. Even professional journalists don't agree among themselves. And then some of the traditional definitions have to be revised for the current world of outer space, science, a shrinking globe, and an expanding area of human interests.

In the post-Civil War period a century ago, a New York City newspaper editor originated a definition that has passed into journalistic folklore:

> When a dog bites a man that is not news, but when a man bites a dog that is news.

Another editor later in the last century put it this way:

> News is what the city editor says it is.

When journalism classes started in colleges more than 65 years ago, Professor Willard G. Bleyer of the University of Wisconsin evolved this definition:

> News is anything timely that interests a number of persons, and the best news is that which has the greatest interest for the greatest number.

These definitions neglected the increasing requirement for readers to be told about the significant and the important, regardless of how interesting such events might be. In the last quarter of the 20th century, readers want, and will need, not only the bare bones of a happening, not only the interesting, the unusual, and the startling but also an accurate, balanced, and informed account of what has taken place.

Thus, to remedy this defect, this definition is proposed:

> News is the reporting of anything timely which has importance, use, or interest to a considerable number of persons in a publication's audience.

For a high school paper, this might include telling of changes in the state requirements for graduation (important), a schedule of classes for the spring semester (useful), and humorous incidents that took place backstage during rehearsals for the junior-senior play (interesting).

For a metropolitan daily, it might mean reporting Congressional action on tax revision (important), the times and stations of radio and television shows (useful), and a short item on how firemen rescued a stranded cat from a treetop near City Hall (interesting).

For a trade publication, it might involve a story on recently established government tariff regulations (important), descriptions of new products available for the spring season (useful), and a personality profile of the new president of a big company or union (interesting).

In the process of reaching the public, all news items and feature stories are tested for six "angles" or handles to the news. If a story fails any of the six tests, it risks getting only scanty attention or of being eliminated entirely.

These angles include:

1. *Today angle.* Is this recent news or just a rehash from ancient history?

Papers and news magazines are geared to what has happened since the previous issue. Even background, interpretation, or analysis of the news implies a today angle that needs to have further explanation, elabora-

tion, or humanization. Almost no news writer considers it his or her job to educate the public—to be a public schooling facility —but an instructional backdrop of a contemporary happening may be needed to present even the today angle clearly. Reports from the advancing frontiers of science and medicine especially require this since much that is told was never taught in school; it hadn't been discovered then.

2. *Local angle.* Did the news happen here and nearby—or was it far away?

A fire in their own community will interest most of the residents there, but, unless there is something rather unusual, it will have minimum appeal for readers half a continent away. On the other hand, because the United States is a superpower and what happens abroad may involve its citizens, many events halfway around the globe may have local echoes. Vietnam is a classic example of how events abroad involved Americans; thousands of them actually died there. To give another example: If an AFS exchange student from Argentina is at your school this year, the distance between here and there automatically is decreased although traditionally reader interest is inversely proportionate to distance. Students might also be intrigued by what happens in schools in other states because the "local angle" involves common interests. "Here" in these cases concerns similarity in jobs, profession, trade, or specialty rather than just geography.

3. *Prominence angle.* Does it concern important or interesting people or places?

What happens to the president of the United States, the pope, or the governor interests readers. If any of them has a common cold, news items are printed prominently. Favorite broadcast stars, sports figures, stage personalities, and prominent writers receive the same treatment.

Widely known locations, such as Telegraph Hill, the Vatican, Arc de Triomphe, and the White House, enhance any event that happens there.

4. *Consequence or important angle.* Does this news have significant impact?

Some events—private or public—influence the lives of individuals as long as they live.

These are things which involve one deeply. An astronaut's landing on the moon got smashing news display, in part, because mankind's attitudes shifted about the universe in which we live. Revisions in the tax laws, technical though they may be, interest millions because these changes may raise or lower their payments to Uncle Sam.

5. *Human interest angle.* Does this news possess an interesting or unusual human sidelight?

People are interested in people. Even when they are not presidents, famous television personalities, or other prominent individuals, previously little-known persons may do things that are worth reporting to a large audience. A display of great heroism, an unusual freak accident, a humorous twist of events—all these may have the essence of news. If a human-interest angle concerns a prominent person, then the double bonus may send the news story onto front pages.

6. *Paper's policy and good taste.* Is this the sort of news one really wants to print?

A specialized publication, for instance, is not interested in events outside its particular field. A physicians' and surgeons' journal has no interest in the latest fad in women's clothing but such an item would have considerable appeal for a department store buyers' periodical.

Reporting some events may conflict with the moral standards of a publication's audience. Even the *New York Times*, which has been called a showpiece of U.S. journalism, concedes this point in its slogan of "All the News That's Fit to Print." Most papers have their own "fit-to-print" test.

This leads to an unresolved philosophical argument that has swept newspaper and magazine offices for generations: What news should be printed? Should one give the public what it wants or give the public what the staff thinks it needs to know?

Often this debate became a tug of war between the responsible ideal for a democratic society and the brutal reality that a publication must at least break even financially over the long run if it is to survive in the market place. Until fairly recently a considerable number of publishers favored

giving readers what they wanted—or what they thought the public wanted. Recently, more and more newsmen and newswomen have swung to the second philosophy.

Why?

The general public today is more educated and increasingly sophisticated. Readers and listeners make up their own minds. Editors and reporters are better trained, most of them prepared in college for communications careers through courses in the subject or work on campus publications or in broadcasting. Publishers and owners increasingly are concerned in the public good as well as in making a good profit. And part of the change arises from a recent popular philosophy known as the "new journalism." More direct quotations, anecdotes, atmosphere, and extensive descriptive backdrop were especially favored.

Beginning in the early 1960s, journalists in increasing numbers broke away from many of the tested and certified conventions of communication in a search for new ways to achieve greater readability. Among the innovations was a technique for writing nonfiction almost in fiction format. With this approach, news articles, supposedly strictly factual, were spiced with fiction blended into reporting. Some "new journalists," without any warning to their audience, took a series of experiences from a whole group of individuals and attributed them all to one person, who was given a fancy—but false—name. Their excuse was that the technique heightened the narrative. Once a news writer starts toying with fiction because truth is sometimes drab and frequently hard to dig out, that writer may have difficulties sticking with the facts in the future. And how are readers to sift facts from fiction in such copy?

Truman Capote gave the trend a swift boost when *In Cold Blood,* a fact book that read like fiction, became a sensational best seller. But Capote trained himself for the necessary interviewing until he attained close to total recall of what was told him. Thus his printed quotations were far more accurate than many taken down hurriedly in improvised shorthand by correspondents for articles appearing on newspaper front pages. Then the author built his story, scene on scene, as if it were a novel. It combined the authority of fact with the lure of fiction. And it was extremely popular.

Other "new journalists" threw themselves so completely into a cause which they covered that their copy quite properly was called *advocacy journalism,* an approach which went counter to the conventional ideal of objective reporting. While no rules, legal or professional, require a reporter to behave as an ideological eunuch, most individuals want at least some assurance that a news item they read or hear on the day's events is not presented by a pitchman for one viewpoint. On most publications that job is restricted to editorialists or columnists.

People with axes to grind can—and should —expect to be distrusted. For example, a player slides into second base. He and the shortstop start fisticuffs. Whose report would you be most apt to believe: The base runner? The shortstop? The coach of either team? The umpire?

Still other "new journalists" established themselves as spokesmen for the counter-culture. Absolutely nothing is wrong with that if ground rules for the technique are clear in readers' minds. But these writers should not pose as disinterested channels for pure and complete objectivity while peddling their wares. Even under ideal conditions, no one can be completely objective.

Qualms are expressed about the "new journalism" by quite a few professionals but the processes it uses certainly should be examined by students. All of the conventional approaches to reporting should be reassessed and some of them discarded as antiquated and ineffective. If the ways of the "new journalists" supply new and better patterns for conveying truthful information, you should not hesitate to experiment with them. However, if the "new journalists" are faking, fictionizing, or editorializing, then shun them. What news personnel need today is a realistic attunement to a world of rapid change—and quite a few of those changes will take place in the ways for communicating.

☆ Accurate and effective journalism always should be a news writer's goal, never a quest for the new when it is false and biased.

For most publications, the decision on what to print and how to do it may not be either-or. Rather, a choice may be whether the staff consistently leans toward one or another philosophy. Very few papers currently give readers only the vicarious thrill and the jazzy sensation. Certainly no newspaper or magazine of important circulation spreads out only legalistic and technical facts that might aid in making an informed decision about some complicated civic problem. Successful publications blend the important and the interesting—the significant and the sensational. This can best be done when the important is told interestingly and the sensational is related to the significance. And this applies as much for student journalists as any others.

The Function of Scholastic Journalism

Americans have a passion for the latest and the newest—the appeal of the current vogue whether it be in clothes, food fads, philosophies, or politicians. Yet this characteristic barely dominates a countervailing respect for that which is old and antique. What most persons do not know is that scholastic journalism or campus communication is older than the United States government itself and began less than a century after the first professional newspaper was printed in Boston in 1690.

Students of the William Penn Charter School in Philadelphia put out a neatly handwritten "publication" dated June 1777. This was only 11 months after the Continental Congress had adopted the Declaration of Independence in the same city and a whole decade before the U.S. Constitution was drafted. During the rest of 1777 and into most of 1778, approximately 60 copies of *The Students' Gazette* were written out in neat longhand by the pupils as the Revolutionary War swirled around them. Like their present-day successors, these junior journalists covered news wherever they found it, so they cited "the many Disturbances which have arisen in this State." Little imagination is required to visualize these student journalists gathering information as troops marched past their academy building and then writing it down meticulously with their quill pens.

The first printed school paper of which we have a surviving copy is *The Literary Journal,* issued by the Latin School in Boston, dated May 9, 1829. However, this obviously was not the originator because an article in that first issue explained that it was being launched because similar publications had been successfully started by others.

From these activities of long ago, a fantastically large harvest has grown. According to Charles R. O'Malley, director of the Columbia Scholastic Press Association, the best estimates on the numbers of high school periodicals today are:

Newspapers and news magazines—25,000;

Yearbooks—18,000;

Literary magazines—3,000; and

Departmental and foreign language publications—2,500.

The total approaches approximately 50,000, an average of about three publications for every two schools, public and private, in the nation. Some of the largest urban high schools have special papers for major departments and for representatives of major minority groups, including Spanish language journals in such states as Florida, Texas, California, and New York.

A rough estimate of production costs for all these school publications runs between $100 million and $150 million with escalation annually, due to increasing costs each year. Yearbooks alone, the most expensive print costs per book, are currently budgeted for more than $65 million. And remember that these statistics do not include any allocations for office space, supplies, and teachers' salaries paid by school administrations.

Oldest known high school publication was handwritten. This is 20th issue of second year, making it as old as our nation. (Courtesy Columbia Scholastic Press Assn.)

Operation of school radio and television stations has been building up tremendously during the 1970s but equipment for them has been so expensive that only affluent communities are able to enter this area of broadcasting, which has been particularly attractive to minority group students. As of the middle 1970s, approximately 700 schools had their own broadcast operations.

No matter how an observer looks at the school publications and the broadcasting operations, the gigantic scale they have attained in student participation and money involved has got to be impressive, indeed.

The Worlds of the Journalists

The central goal of any publication is: To mirror its world in its cycle. A daily paper tells of events in its local community, the nation, the world, and beyond into outer space for the past 24 hours. A specialized magazine may concentrate on what happened in research, development, and teaching of chemistry during the past three months.

For a school paper, the cycle varies and its "world" is hard to define. One approach might be to ask: Is this information that our readers and listeners want and need to know? If the answer is Yes, then gather it, write it, and distribute it. You are their surrogate witness.

In many ways, a school publication—its operations, its appeals to an audience, and its staff organization—is similar to a community daily or a nationally circulated magazine. The relationship may be described as "the same but different." Guiding concepts and general principles are rather close but details can vary widely.

Student and professional newspapers gather news of timely events in their special worlds. Both present these reports in overabundance, like a Swedish smörgåsbord, for their particular audience to pick and choose. A school paper or news magazine covers the school and all that happens there, places off-campus where students congregate or to which they travel, such as the out-of-town state capitol for a civics class visit or a public utility plant using atomic power, plus events that have direct impact on students and their lives. These last might concern lectures at a community youth center, national studies of drug use by students, or current books and records of special interest to teen-agers.

A student's world does not stop at the edge of the school yard or the boundaries of athletic fields. Today's students do not live in a social cocoon—even if their parents may have. Too many student editors forget that their readers are affected by events beyond the classroom. However, school papers are no substitute for the local daily. They don't have either enough space or frequency of publication to try that. Assignment editors must also remember that the local daily will cover a school board session whether they do or not, but appointments to the stage crew for a class play may go unreported if their paper neglects the news.

☆ Don't build an iron curtain for news coverage.

On the other hand, don't tackle the whole wide world as your news beat.

For the last issue of each term or of the entire school year, some editors review all that happened around the school. In effect, this strives to approach a mini-yearbook and presents a memento for students who would not preserve every issue for the four years they were in classes.

Increasingly, especially during the early 1970s, news magazines have become a trend for hundreds of schools. As budgets shrunk, time between publications has increased. Since this medium more easily adapts to coverage of events that occurred weeks or a month ago, its popularity has grown. News magazines break away from heavy dependency on the summary lead and even "stale" news seems less dated. Since the professional news magazines have set such high standards, editors of scholastic news magazines are forced to make comparable efforts in their preparations.

Other schools try to blend newspapers and news magazines into a single hybrid but this, too, is an exacting process.

The school literary magazine, regaining some of its former popularity in recent years, strives for a happy combination of short stories, poetry, and nonfiction. Its editors often work closely with English teachers and, with luck, they may come close to the adult *quality* and *opinion magazines* that cater to a restricted but elite audience. Such school magazines become exhibits of superior classwork or special assignments that are worthy of extensive display.

Since they experience most of the spectrum of human emotions and a wide range of experiences, students have something important to contribute. But they should not extensively imitate the writing styles and selection of topics favored by their elders. To print what a student thinks about the chances of World War III and a recommendation on what the world powers should do would be presumptuous and egotistical unless the author is a near-genius. A human-interest report on a summer spent working in Israel or in Washington as a congressman's page could be most interesting and rewarding reading. When a student discusses a teen-age problem or experience in either feature or short-story form, the chances are that it will appeal not only to students but to adult readers, too. Success does not come through mirror images of various journalistic patterns found in adult publications.

☆ The best literary magazines reflect student activities, thinking, and philosophy.

Compared with other school publications, the yearbook has a wider time span to cover. The previous issue came out 12 months earlier. The principal thrust of yearbooks strives to combine pictures and text into a pleasing whole that will be preserved for years to arouse memories. Although the graduating class, with its photographs, is featured, serious thought should be given to weaving in illustrations of interest to the other classes. Not only is this good journalism but it will help to sell books to others than seniors.

Student broadcasters, like those associated with publications, may gain basic experience in their field. Their message may not go out to millions as do the network news programs but the intensity of student interest in the lunch room or in their home rooms may be as keen as that of adults tuned in for an evening news show. Students, moreover, have to gather most, if not all, of their own material while some professional announcers have their scripts prepared for them by other station staff members. Hence the scope of their school experience may be far more wide-ranged and thus more helpful on the way to a successful career.

Rewards of Scholastic Journalism

"It takes all kinds to make up a world." When students apply for positions on school newspapers, magazines, yearbooks, or in broadcasting, that comment describes the many motivations for seeking the jobs.

Some students seek staff jobs because they dream of a day three years or so later when they may overhear some cute co-ed say, "That's Joe, the editor of the 'Central High News'." It may be the ego-whip of ambition and nothing's wrong with that. Individuals have attained some of the highest positions in the world because of just that drive. Remember, however, that the path to fame is not covered exclusively with roses without thorns. There is work, more work, and still more work—but it should be great fun, too.

Other students may join the staff because they want to learn journalism or business. Possibly their fathers, favorite uncles, columnists they admire, or respected investigative reporters have inspired a desire to learn more about "the writing game" or how the business of advertising, subscriptions, or circulation functions. High school journalism will have rich rewards for them. So will experience in broadcasting for those who want to go on the air or join radio or television business departments.

Such high school jobs can yield vocational background that will provide assets if a student wants a summertime replacement job on a local daily or desires to work on a college publication later.

Still others attend the recruiting session because they want to "do something." They may not have the rugged physique for the football team or the excessive height for basketball. They try out for communication assignments, which may develop chances to apply their idealism to be useful campus citizens.

Parents may urge their children to seek a publication or broadcast staff position for still another reason: They are thinking on to college and postgraduate careers.

In evaluating college application forms, most admissions officers review outside activities as well as academic records. A major job on a high school newspaper, magazine, yearbook, or broadcast station qualifies for extra marks here. While this motivation certainly tends toward the opportunistic, it won't prevent staff members from enjoying themselves just as much as any others who try out—if they'll relax and work hard for the fun of it.

For the student journalist, it helps to develop that "nose for news" that so intrigues the curious nonjournalists, an ability to spot the unusual, the interesting, and the important and then to dig out the facts even if the persons interviewed are reluctant to provide them. It stimulates a sense of accuracy, the unrelenting quest to get things right. It introduces students to a knowledge of journalistic techniques—organizing facts into logical news format, the rigid requirements of careful editing, and the exacting expertise of writing headlines. Candidates for the business staff prepare themselves as carefully in their special fields. Regardless of whether the work is on the editorial or the business side of a publication or station, it develops a sense of responsibility. Students rapidly realize that if they miss an appointment for an interview or for picking up copy for an ad there may be no other chance and they alone are to blame.

High school journalism stimulates regular work habits. Students have to be methodical and plan a schedule to maintain above-average grades to be eligible to perform their publication assignments. It develops respect for the sanctity of deadlines and the immeasurable value of time. Reporters and editors learn that only the copy that is submitted on time gets into print. It brings out initiative. Successful newsmen and newswomen search for novel facts and novel techniques, and successful space and subscription sales persons have to try new methods, too. It increases leadership qualities. Any editor-in-chief or business manager has to direct a staff efficiently if the project is to thrive. It teaches teamwork. No one can put out a publication or newscast single-handedly.

The student who heads a highly regarded school publication or station merits the recognition of classmates, and also receives many material and honorary rewards, including regional and even national awards, if the efforts are sufficiently outstanding.

One of the greatest rewards of school journalism has little to do with the initial reasons of a successful job applicant. This is development of a more mature personality, to become an individual who has grown while assuming major obligations. Almost as a by-product, but regarded by parents and teachers as important as learning journalistic or business practices and techniques, is a capacity to think more clearly and an ability to express oneself more lucidly. This grows with astonishing rapidity for most senior staff members.

☆ Working in scholastic communications is both rewarding and fun.

School Press Associations

Practically all high school publications belong to at least one of the various scholastic press associations—state, regional, or national. Membership provides a wealth of useful information on how to put out a better publication as well as regular evaluation of how judges think your efforts compare with those of other schools in the same general grouping. A truly outstanding newspaper, magazine, or yearbook may win fame and respect as it consistently ranks high in competition. Usually several senior representatives (plus others if the school's budget permits) will attend the press association's annual convention and will listen to famous professional and academic experts.

All of these scholastic associations seek to advance the cause of education generally, but they concentrate on competitions and evaluations of member publications to improve specific qualities of high school communications. Good papers consistently win top honors and special recognition, but a specific win or loss by your own publication in any one year may not truly reflect what that particular staff did. Placing low year after year does mean that something—possibly something drastic—should be done. Realistic staff members will consider the judges' comments and, along with the faculty advisor, decide as objectively as possible what should be done.

Schools differ greatly, especially regarding the backgrounds of their audiences, and thus publications seek to achieve highly varied goals. Placed in the same category because of comparable enrollment and printing process, two publications will be judged by a single set of standards although actually the staffs try to use different solutions for vastly different problems. This is not to blame the judges, however. No breakdown into categories could possibly include all the differences. And despite all efforts, contest judges somehow turn out to be human beings with different ways of reacting.

One high school publication staff still tells with wide grins how some years ago their predecessors managed to sneak two copies into the judging. One rated an "A"; the other got "D."

☆ Edit your publication for your readers, not for contest judges.

Oldest of the national high school press associations is the *National Scholastic Press Association (NSPA)*, founded in 1921 by Professor E. Marion Johnson at the University of Wisconsin. It started under the name of the Central Inter-Scholastic Press Association. When Professor Johnson shifted to the University of Minnesota in 1926, the headquarters moved along with him. When all of the then 48 states were represented in 1928, the name was changed to NSPA and Professor Fred Kildow, who had participated as a student when the group was set up, became director. He held the job for more than a third of a century as a Minnesota faculty member.

Membership is by publication rather than by school. Dues vary by publication but are approximately $18. NSPA also owns and edits the eight-times-a-year magazine, *Scholastic Editor Graphics/Communications*.

As part of NSPA membership, critical analyses of newspapers, literary magazines, and yearbooks are provided by judges who are active in high school journalism. An official NSPA guidebook is designed to assist both judges and advisors in noting strong points and weak points. While the main purpose of the evaluation is self-help, ratings are given each entry. The top rating is All-American and certificates are awarded to all publications that rate Third Class or better.

NSPA conducts a national publications conference every fall (usually in the central states area) and another each spring on the West Coast. These consist of up to 50 sessions and workshops on all phases of school publications. Other services include a *Helps* newsletter, publishing and distributing texts and film strips, and assistance in regional workshops.

The address is 720 Washington Avenue SE, Suite 205, University of Minnesota, Minneapolis, Minn. 55414.

The *Columbia Scholastic Press Association (CSPA)* was organized late in 1924 at Columbia University by Joseph M. Murphy. Its first newspaper and magazine contest was held the following year; yearbooks were added in 1935.

A publication attains CSPA membership upon entering an annual critical judging and evaluation. *The School Press Review*, CSPA official monthly, is published from October through May for all members. Special aids available for staff publication members through CSPA include a style book, proofreader's cards, and a series of brief, instructional pamphlets.

Faculty may enroll in an advisors association for a small additional fee.

A three-day annual convention is held in March and a two-day yearbook "short course" in the fall. Winter sessions have attracted as many as 5,000 from 35 states and overseas for 250 workshops on specialized school press topics. Nationally famous speakers talk at a concluding luncheon meeting.

Up to 10% in each category—type of publication, size of school, type of reproduction, etc.—may win a Medalist award and special certificate for "special qualities evident to the judges, characterized as the personality, spirit, or creative excellence of the entry."

All-Columbia Honor Ratings recognize outstanding publications although no special award certificates are given. The All-Columbia rating, CSPA officers said, exists "to encourage work in selected fields of publication work and not as an award for the publication." Established in 1972 for yearbooks and in 1973 for other publications are Trendsetter Awards, which spotlight "unique innovations or bold new approaches to responsible journalism which can add to the repertoire of the student press." These are presented, generally, for special elements and techniques within a publication which any other school staff could easily use, not for excellence of the publication as a whole.

Advisors who direct outstanding work may be awarded Gold Keys.

The address is Columbia Scholastic Press Association, Box 11, Central Mail Room, Columbia University, New York, N.Y. 10027.

Students with outstanding records in scholastic journalism may receive individual recognition through election to *Quill and Scroll Society,* an international honorary organization for high school communicators. Started in 1926 by Dr. George Gallup, a former college journalism teacher who later won world fame for his public opinion polls, Quill and Scroll seeks to encourage and reward achievements in creative writing, editing, and business management as well as to acquaint school administrators, parents, and the general public with the values of high school journalism.

The Society has 11,000 chapters in the United States and many foreign countries and has initiated more than a million students.

To be eligible for a Quill and Scroll charter, a school must publish a newspaper, yearbook, or magazine which is considered of sufficient merit by the Society's executive council. Schools where students gather and write news items under supervision for regular community papers also are eligible.

Membership may be obtained only through a local chapter. To be eligible for membership, a student has (a) to be a junior or senior; (b) to rank in the upper third of class scholastic standings; (c) to have done "superior work in some phase of journalism or school publications work"; and (d) to be recommended by the advisor or supervisor and approved by the Society's executive secretary.

Members pay a basic $4 initiation fee and the Society supplies each new member with a regulation gold badge or staff position pin and a 1-year subscription to *Quill & Scroll,* a quarterly publication.

Each year Quill and Scroll sponsors Newspaper Week Observance, national writing contests, an annual current events quiz, a program for granting ten college scholarships for $500, and a newspaper evaluation in which students and member papers may earn national recognition and awards.

The address is Quill and Scroll Society, School of Journalism, University of Iowa, Iowa City, Iowa 52242.

Future Journalists of America (FJA) was founded in 1958 to promote interest in journalism careers. Membership is not restricted to scholastic achievement but is open to any junior or senior high school student. FJA holds an annual Festival of Excellence and Creativity for school papers and yearbooks. A monthly newsletter, *FJA Communique,* is published.

The address is Future Journalists of America, H. H. Herbert School of Journalism, University of Oklahoma, Norman, Okla. 73069.

State and regional high school press groups hold much the same types of contests and conferences as the nationwide ones.

Colleges and universities offer workshops and conferences for those associated with high school communications. Some sessions during the school year run one or two days or a weekend, while others during the summer may last for more than a month and carry college credit for advisors and journalism teachers who join the students in training. Such summer work may be exclusively for newly appointed editors and business managers, exclusively for advisors and other teachers, or for the two groups working together as they would during the school year.

Thanks to The Newspaper Fund, Inc., a whole range of programs stimulates interest and enthusiasm for scholastic journalism and awaken high school students to opportunities in communications careers, especially with newspapers. Among its projects are workshops for publication advisors and students, pamphlets and films about high school communications, and reprints of superior articles and layouts from student papers across the country. Several urban journalism workshops for secondary school pupils and visitation programs for inner-city students were supported in the middle 1970s. Summer study by approximately 50 publication advisors and secondary school journalism instructors is funded, selection favoring those who lack previous training and experience. When these teachers return to their home schools, their students share vicariously in the training.

By the middle 1970s, The Newspaper Fund, Inc., had received approximately $3.5 million from Dow Jones and Co., Inc., which publishes the *Wall Street Journal, National Observer,* and *Barron's* financial weekly.

The address is The Newspaper Fund, Inc., P.O. Box 300, Princeton, N.J. 08540.

Students and teachers who have major responsibilities for a coming year's publication in a progressive high school should investigate the possibilities for training. If their time schedules and finances permit, they should participate and learn as much as they can. Many options are available and any of them should help make next year's paper, magazine, or yearbook better than last year's. And that is what progress is all about: Getting help from whatever source and then using it to perform a better job in the future.

3

Building an Effective Staff

No one, ideal way exists for organizing a student publication's staff. The same is true for hometown dailies, too. But there has to be a firm chain of command, much like a military operation but without the combat.

Although both students and advisors might be happier if a single royal road were the only map to leadership, too many factors enter in for one procedure to apply for all high schools, all papers, and all staffs. Among these variables are school size, publication frequency, and availability of competent, experienced students for a varied combinaiton of jobs. As with much else in communication, ingenuity and imagination may show the best way around difficulties.

Whether professionals on a metropolitan daily or students on a high school newspaper, news magazine, or broadcasting operation, staff members have special duties much like officers and employees in a corporation. The company president translates into the *publisher* or *general manager* of the hometown paper and the *editor-in-chief* on the high school paper or *station manager* for broadcasting.

A typical professional paper has four major divisions, each with a separate and different function to perform:

1. The *news department* gathers, edits, and displays news and features. The individual in charge here is the *managing editor* —M.E.—or the *news editor*. Immediate subordinates include the city editor, wire editor, sports editor, women's or lifestyle editor, picture editor, business editor, entertain-ment editor, and travel editor. In turn each of these has reporters who are sent out to gather news and features. *Copy editors* process the news after it is written. A graphic arts director puts the whole mix together for publication.

2. An *editorial page* staff provides a voice for the publication's opinions. This is done through editorials, background, analysis, or interpretation. In charge is the editor of the editorial page or simply the editor. The people who write for this page are editorial writers, columnists, or news specialists.

3. The *business department*, concerned primarily with circulation and advertising, looks after earning the money to pay salaries and bills. Its top executive is the *business manager*, who also is responsible for keeping the records in the accounting department as well as thinking up ideas to promote the paper so as to keep its name before the public.

4. The *mechanical department* actually manufactures the product that is sold: The paper itself. The *mechanical superintendent* supervises the *composing room*, which prepares the plates that actually print the paper; the *press room*, where the printing is done; and the *mail room*, from where papers are sent out to subscribers via newsboys or the postal service.

School Periodical Staffs

Basic organization of a school publication's staff is much the same as that of a commercial newspaper except that most do not have the equipment for printing an issue. So an outside business concern does the work of the mechanical department. This does not apply for Mimeographed papers, which will be discussed in detail in Chapter 19.

A student editor-in-chief has been called "potentially the most influential pupil in the entire school," although ultimate achievements depend on the business manager and senior editors to an extraordinary degree. Several staff setups are possible:

1. Page editors. Under this organization, a senior staff member is responsible for each of the four principal pages: Front page, opinion page, features, and sports. While this arrangement is generally effective, some students and advisors object that it is old-fashioned and imposes a rigid regimentation for telling what happened. When strictly applied, a paper ends up with no features on the front and sports pages, where they more properly might belong.

2. Central assignment desk. This setup depends upon a powerful assignment editor who parcels out all work to be done by individual reporters regardless of where the resulting copy will be displayed in the issue and then upon a *universal copy desk* that edits all kinds of copy. This staff organization functions best if all, or practically all, of the members can meet in the publication office during an academic class or a period earmarked for outside activities—or can assemble immediately after school hours.

3. Rotation of staff jobs. With this organization, all the senior people on a publication have a chance to work at most of the possible assignments. For one issue, an individual may be in charge of editorials and opinion and the next issue responsible for front-page makeup. Such shifting certainly provides broad educational experiences for staffers but it may prevent any one of them from becoming highly proficient in a specific job, thus contributing toward an almost perpetual state of turmoil when deadlines come due.

4. Dual staffing. Adapted for larger urban schools where more students turn out for the school's publications than there are jobs

to keep them busy, this system sets up two distinct staffs with each handling all the work for alternate issues. Of course, the two editors-in-chief must work closely together on planning both issues. In metropolitan high schools with thousands of students and papers published oftener than once a week, this setup allows students to have—with luck—enough free time to maintain their scholastic grade averages.

Regardless of which type of staff arrangement is used, the second-in-command who heads the staff that gathers, processes, and displays news and features is the news editor. On a medium or larger periodical's *editorial side,* as the news editor's bailiwick is called, there may be the following staff positions for subordinates:

1. *Feature and department editor,* who plans and supervises coverage of special background, interpretation, human interest, and historical articles and makes sure that good material is on hand at the proper time. Expertly done feature articles possess many qualities of great literature and usually permit a higher degree of achievement toward that goal than in the creative writing of short stories and poems. Often people do not think of great literature and journalism in the same breath but the accuracy of such pairing is well demonstrated in *A Treasury of Great Reporting,* edited by Louis L. Snyder and Richard B. Morris.

2. *Sports editor,* who arranges coverage of athletic events that involve the school's teams. Undue concentration on varsity squads should be avoided; many other contests deserve reporting, including co-ed and intramural games. Traditionally, sports editors have been men but no longer does this important job go automatically to a male. Just as on commercial publications, many school papers have female sports writers and editors who are doing fine jobs. Nor do they now cover only women's sports. The professionals have established expertise in everything from pro football to horse racing.

3. *Picture editor,* who is responsible for photographs and, even more important, for ensuring that photographers are at the right places at the right times to shoot pictures for the paper. It is difficult, sometimes

Flow of news through typical daily newspaper.

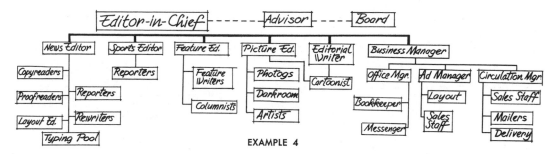

EXAMPLE 4

impossible, to re-create a situation for the benefit of a person with a camera who wasn't there on time. A tardy print reporter can always interview eyewitnesses, but no photographer can use that substitute for being late. A picture editor also is responsible for cropping, scaling, and identifying prints.

A recent trend among metropolitan papers is additon of a *graphic arts,* or *typographical, director.* This person is in charge of all *nonverbal communication*—the use of type in all its forms and of all art, photographic and hand—for editorial, advertising, and promotion departments.

4. *Editor of the editorial page,* who handles editorials and other opinion and comment, whether in columns or letters to the editor. Often an editor-in-chief will write the editorials, frequently after decisions by a board of editors that establishes the paper's policy. However, a subordinate editor should be named to take care of all the other items on an editorial page.

5. *Literary or creative writing editor,* who is more associated with the traditional literary magazine than with a newspaper. This person obtains and edits such work as short stories, essays, and verse. Where the paper prints these items, such a position should exist.

6. *Exchange editor,* who mails out each issue to schools with which your publication has "exchange" subscriptions and also checks the copies received in return for possible reprint material or for ideas that may be adapted for assignments in your own school community.

On the business side, aides of the business manager might include:

1. *Advertising manager,* who supervises selling advertisements, collecting fees, obtaining copy from advertisers, and supplying printed copies of the paper, or *tearsheets,* to those who purchased space. In schools where advertising is prohibited or curtailed, obviously there is no need for this job.

2. *Circulation manager,* who sells subscriptions and arranges distribution of issues to students, teachers, school administrators (including members of the local school board), alumni, parents, and other friends of the school.

3. *Office manager,* an individual or group, that keeps the records of money received and spent plus other information needed for efficient office operations.

Qualities of Staff Members

If a school publication were staffed by saints who did only the right things, what characteristics would they have in common?

This hypothetical question is helpful to contemplate.

Although graduated staffers and teachers do not always agree on the exact order of importance, these characteristics would be listed by any experienced group:

☆ Each staff member should be well trained for the job and, preferably, have risen through the ranks.

No substitute is available for good, old-fashioned, plain competence. If a staff member is going to do an interview, cover a football game, sell an ad, or edit copy, that person should know the technicalities of the job and should have enough practice to complete the assignment in reasonable time.

The best way to learn is to study what should be done and then *do it.* You learn by doing but you must always keep your eyes

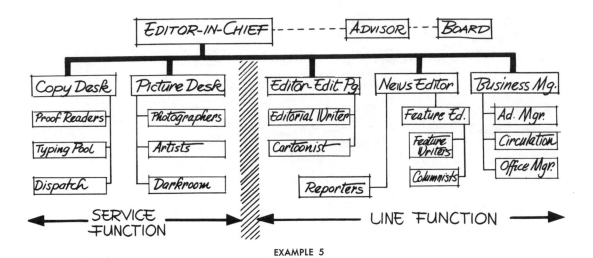

EXAMPLE 5

and mind open. There are some things that you cannot learn from books, even textbooks. These you pick up yourself by doing.

☆ Senior editors or business staffers should have executive ability and leadership qualities.

This means an editor's capacity to distribute work fairly evenly so that the news staff is not overworked while the editorial and opinion-page staff is sitting around doing nothing.

It also means that the business manager will send ad sales staffers out to seek advertisements when merchants normally will have free time. Senior staff members—who need not be in the senior class although most of them will be—must remember that they can't sit in every editorial chair at the same time. Delegating duties and responsibilities may be one of the most difficult things for a leader to learn. But it is just as essential as it is difficult!

Along with the teacher advisor, senior staff members have a further responsibility: To train their successors. Since most student publications shift their top management every year—sometimes oftener—a training program must be undertaken. Providing a steady continuity of competence is part of leadership on any publication.

☆ Despite crises and disasters, ideal staff members remain cooperative and willing.

When things start going wrong, as eventually they always do, it is most important to have willing hands and cool heads. This does not mean that staff members should cultivate a phony Pollyanna air, but it does mean that when tempers are short because of mounting tensions at deadlines, all the staff will realize that a certain curtness is not to be taken as a major break in friendship. A solution is not to bolt from the office and sulk but to offer your services to help relieve the burdens. If the staff confronts a major emergency, it is that much greater opportunity to perform services "above and beyond the call of duty."

☆ Staffers should concentrate on putting out a good publication, not on gaining personal praise.

This is stressed succinctly as one of ten points in the Indiana High School Press Association Code of Ethics, adopted more than half a century ago:

To work as a team, not for individual glory.

☆ Successful staff members are persevering; they have a quality of stick-to-it-iveness.

If a person to be interviewed is rushed and doesn't have time to see you until an inconvenient time for you, you will somehow arrange to meet the individual at that inconvenient time. If hours are ticking away, a copyreader will stay on the job, maybe doing some homework while waiting. Yearbook deadlines, especially, can come right after or even during Thanksgiving and Christmas vacations and students often have to give up a holiday to beat the clock. And so with all staffers who take their jobs seriously.

☆ Staff members will be scholastically superior but they will not become involved with conflicting outside activities.

While working on a school publication can be exciting and fun, it takes considerable time even under favorable circumstances. If you are an important staff member and near the danger line scholastically, then any extra work demanded for the paper or yearbook may plunge you into trouble. You may have to drop off the staff. Then there will be a frantic search for your replacement. Much the same situation occurs when even an outstanding scholar becomes involved in too many activities.

At some schools, appointment to a senior publication staff job carries the explicit condition that the student will not be involved in any other major school activity. This may seem a harsh prerequisite. Often, the good student journalist is a fine actor, debater, athlete, musician, or highly interested in student government. But in the long run, it is wise to concentrate on the publication job. Not only will the periodical be better for it, but staff morale will build and a tradition of excellence will be established.

☆ Staff members should present a neat appearance when they represent their publication and practice tidy work habits when they are in the office.

Every time a staff member goes after a story or an advertisement, that person represents the publication and the school. Some of the people you meet may be making up their minds about what kind of paper and type of school you serve. Dress neatly. Be prompt. Be polite. Act with the good manners you would display on your first Saturday night dance with an especially attractive date.

To a large degree, the efficient operation of any periodical depends on the good work habits of all its staff. A few messy souls can clutter up an office for all the workers. Motion-picture portrayals of news rooms often have paper scattered over much of the floor and depict journalists as uncouth

boors. This dramatic license bears little more resemblance to actuality than a television series on high school life resembles your school and your classmates.

In a talk to school journalists, Paul Swensson, then executive director of The Newspaper Fund, Inc., identified the five parts of what he called "the face of a newsman" and then issued this invitation:

If you think you have a nose for news, if you have an eye for detail and distance, if your ears can hear the things unsaid, if you have a voice that carries, and if you have a chin for courage, come and join us.

Dedicate your talents to the voice of democracy, the world of the printed word, the world of free people and free press.

Journalism wants and needs your kind.

The Staff in Action

Now let's look at how students in key positions might swing into action on a school paper. The procedures are not too different for a broadcasting station.

☆ The editor-in-chief has ultimate responsibility for the paper.

But, all along the way, this student has to work with subordinate editors and with the faculty advisor. Usually this cooperation begins with individual discussions or a conference with senior editors to discuss plans for the next issue or, a single project, yearbook. Among decisions to be made might be:

What'll be the more important news stories? (For a yearbook, what will be the theme?)

How much advertising will there be—or, put another way, what will the *news hole* be?

What are feature story possibilities?

What sports activities are going on?

What photographs are available or should be taken for the issue?

What should the editorials say this time?

Are there any superior ideas from exchange papers?

When should copy editors report for work?

What about the schedule for pasteups?

What day will the issue be ready for distribution?

If deadlines have not already been established by editor, advisor, and printer, this early session should decide what various ones will be. Once these things have been settled, they funnel down to reporters, photographers, copy editors, and pasteup experts.

Meetings of the whole staff should be held regularly. Although the decisions outlined earlier must be made by a smaller group of executives, the staff should have a chance to advance ideas, too, and to ask questions about decisions that have been made by the top editors.

Since good reporting is basic for any good paper, you should be familiar with the two kinds of reporters: Those assigned to *beats* and those on *general assignments*. Both are important and necessary. Each has a different kind of job.

A beat reporter collects news from an individual, office, or department. The job is to obtain all the news from that source regardless of whether the editor knows about it or not.

A beat reporter, for instance, might be assigned to cover the principal's office. The job would be to talk to the principal's secretary and ask for news. Of course, the reporter would want to talk with the principal, but don't forget that information may come from many sources and some of the best are assistants and associates. A beat reporter might learn about next semester's new courses as approved by the school superintendent and just forwarded to the principal. The news might concern a visit to the school of a professor from a nearby university who wanted some students to participate in a new way to teach social studies. Information could be about an alumnus who had been recently elected to Phi Beta Kappa and who had written about it to the principal or a teacher.

A general assignment reporter handles news about a special event or situation, such as a speech, club meeting, trip to a neighboring television station by a social studies class, or some other specific happening that the editor wants covered.

Such a general assignment reporter might be told to cover next Wednesday's assembly at which the student governing organization is going to announce plans for the senior-junior prom. Another general assignment reporter might interview a foreign student from India who arrived just a few days ago and who is making friends in classes.

When reporters, either beat or general assignment, have collected the facts, they write straight news or feature articles.

Copy is scanned by a senior editor to see that reporters carried out instructions and then is given to the copy editors who "process" it for publication. A proper-size headline is written.

While the news department is providing stories and pictures, the business staff solicits advertisements from local merchants, collects the copy, and marks it with appropriate instructions for composition.

The editor-in-chief or members of the editorial board write editorials or determine policy which is then expressed by an individual. Regardless of whether the editor or someone else does the writing, opinions should express the opinions of the publication, not just those of the writer.

Now the edited news copy, editorials, and advertisements are ready to go to the compositor. Back come the galley proofs, which are checked. When corrected, proofs are pasted up and pages approved for printing.

After the copies are printed, the business staff takes over distribution to subscribers and to advertisers who also want to see how their material looks in final printed form.

Mimeographed papers generally have more staff members because, unlike their colleagues who send copy to compositors, the staff of Mimeographed papers do the actual "production" of their papers themselves. The same trend is true for technical schools where printing is taught and classmates do the work for academic credits.

Whether they put out a newspaper, magazine, or yearbook, staff members should have a place to meet and work. The problem of finding space should not be a recurring responsibility for an editor-in-chief and business manager; they will have enough problems without that one. If space for typewriters, supplies, and files is not handed down from year to year, which is by far the best policy, then key staff members and faculty advisor should try to solve the situation immediately after the students are chosen for their positions of next year.

☆ Every publication staff should have its own home, a regular place to work.

Once the space is obtained, students should insure that it is kept as neat and tidy as possible.

If at all possible, the staff should have a regular time to meet—probably once a week after regular school hours for planning and much oftener when an issue's deadline is approaching. If your school is on two sessions each day, this may present a complicating situation. At the worst, it may be necessary to hold two sessions, one for the early students and another for those who attend classes later. In any case, several senior staff members should attend both meetings so that there is a continuity in what takes place at both. Few football teams have to practice for a big game in split shifts, and the same arguments should be made with school administrators when it comes to getting approval for concessions on a publication's staff meetings. In some schools, seniors may be exempt from required study hall attendance. In such cases, they have to arrange their schedules so that they do homework at other times and that their grades do not slip to make them ineligible to continue working in extracurricular activities.

The business manager, after discussion with the student editor-in-chief, should provide adequate supplies. These should include typewriters, desks, copy paper, copy pencils, typewriter ribbons, paste pots, scissors, rulers for the copy desk, pencil sharpeners, and all the essential forms for the business office, such as receipts for subscriptions and advertising as well as for accounting of expenditures. Larger and more expensive items such as desks and typewriters usually are provided by the school administration or student governing organization and are handed down from one graduating staff to the next. Late in the spring or early in the summer, this equipment should be checked; if, for instance, typewriters need to be repaired or cleaned, this should be done before classes start in the fall. Thus everything will be in good shape physically for the initial fall gathering of the staff.

☆ Staff members are responsible for all equipment they use—and they should be keenly aware of that fact.

The business manager may want to follow the practice of some professional publications and affix to each piece of permanent equipment its price and date of purchase. It may surprise staffers to see how much more respect is shown a typewriter, for instance, if a small, neat sign says:

Cost—$227.50
April 25, 1976

Also worked out in advance by top editors, business office representatives, and faculty advisor is the *free list*. Every publication has complimentary and exchange copies but, since each costs at least a few pennies to print, lists should be carefully and thoughtfully compiled.

Complimentary copies usually are sent to school board members, superintendent, local newspapers, libraries (both school and community), key city officials, and all advertisers. Some schools supply free copies to the principal and department chairmen.

Exchanges between high school publications are valuable tools for students. It sharpens the thinking of staff members to see what colleagues are doing under similar circumstances. Most exchanges will be with nearby districts where problems are generally alike. Information about athletic teams in neighboring communities will be especially useful if your school is to play them. But distant exchanges can be helpful, too. It can be interesting to find out differences between a school in Florida and one in Oregon. Most exchanges should be with schools of approximately the same size and in the same kind and size of community or, at least, with common interests. At least one exchange paper should be better than yours; it's good for the staff's soul to be reminded periodically that there is still room for improvement.

☆ Studying exchanges can produce many ideas for improved news coverage, features, layouts, and pictures.

While an alert staff benefits from exchanges, obviously the papers have to be read and inspected. All too often exchanges aren't even unwrapped and collect dust until a periodic housecleaning. To prevent this, the staff should decide at the start of each year with which papers it would like to exchange. Staffs of such papers should be asked if they wish to swap issues for one year. The list, when agreed upon, should be sent to the circulation department for inclusion in mailing lists. One staffer may be assigned to look through the issues as they arrive and bring ideas to the attention of the appropriate editor. One good idea is for each key editor to receive, with or without notes from the exchange editor, at least a half dozen outside issues each month. This assures that personnel get the feel of what is going on in other places.

Prize-winning papers often are bombarded with exchange requests from all over the country. Often this becomes too great a burden and the editors have to refuse. If a paper is worth studying, it probably is worthwhile to buy a year's subscription.

The business side has its responsibilities after the paper is out. Copies have to be delivered to all stores or organizations that purchased space. Some stores require this before they pay their bills and this is simply good business practice to confirm that publication actually took place. If prompt payment is not made, an advertising representative should call in person to collect the money or check. If papers are sold at campus stores, copies should be promptly delivered—otherwise potential buyers may borrow a friend's copy and a sale is lost.

News Beats

An efficient editor wants to make sure that the staff is organized to gather news as thoroughly as a vacuum cleaner sweeps up dust and lint. Here is an efficient setup of high school beats:

1. Administration. Principal's office, dean of students, vocation guidance, counseling advisor's office, and probably the office of the superintendent.

2. Athletics. Director of athletics, all coaches, and assistants in the athletics department. This coverage is the major responsibility of the sports desk.

3. Academic departments. Supervisors for all the subjects taught. If yours is an exceptionally large high school, this beat could be so large that several reporters would be needed for adequate coverage.

4. Advisors of all honorary societies.

5. Officers and advisors of all other clubs. Again, in a large school this beat would have to be split among several reporters.

6. Officers and advisors of all classes. Because junior and senior classes usually have more activities, persons assigned to these two might write more news. But don't forget freshmen and sophomores; they do newsworthy things, too.

7. Activities such as drama, band, glee club, orchestra, debating, and publications. Never forget that your own periodicals should be reported just as any other activity.

8. Your local and nearby dailies. A student should be assigned to check and clip newspapers for tips on happenings that will interest readers. If this job is done properly, the student responsible can have great responsibility for a successful school paper. The job is to fill the *assignment book* and *future book* with ideas that will blossom later as fully developed news stories and feature articles.

Some beats, especially busy ones such as a principal's office, should be checked every other day for a weekly student paper and at least weekly, regardless of how infrequently the publication is issued. These repeated checkings will (a) allow more time for gathering background and writing up the news; (b) prevent an administrator from forgetting or overlooking an event because it happened so long ago; and (c) avoid a traffic jam in news copy that could occur if every staffer only checked his beat a couple of days before the final deadline.

Other beats having little news need not be checked more than several times between issues. This will give time for writing news that breaks early and will prevent scoops if news develops just before deadline.

☆ A beat should be covered at least twice for each issue, once shortly before deadline.

Most of the people you will be checking for information and interviewing for facts and comments are busy folk. Many demands are made on their time. The courteous and efficient way is to set up an appointment to visit them—unless there is an emergency to get the facts for an approaching deadline.

Professional journalists have obtained smash stories from such unlikely sources as telephone operators and elevator men. As mentioned earlier, a secretary to an important school administrator may, if you establish confidence, tip you off to something that will yield a front-page story. Never print such tips without checking, because sometimes there is confusion on just what took place.

☆ Good tips on news sometimes come from people who are not in high positions.

If a staffer learns about an event which would make an interesting, important, or useful story, a responsibility is to let the editor-in-chief know. This is especially true if the event is not on a regularly assigned beat. If a story seems to overlap several beats, the reporter should inform the editor who picks the person to write it.

For instance, suppose a student reporter assigned to the principal's office learns about a new athletics program. The staffer should not assume that the sports editor and sports beat reporter already know about it; just maybe they don't. The editor will decide whether the administration or sports reporter will gather more material for a full-length story. Possibly both reporters will get all the information they can and then pool the news. The result thus may be more inclusive and more informational than if one had gathered the facts from just one beat and written them up.

Some happenings occur that are not included in the general division of beats. Here a staff general assignment reporter is sent to cover that specific event, such as a career-day assembly.

To stoke the files with tips on future coverage, an editor keeps a future book of all forthcoming events. One student clips each issue of the student newspaper and files the advance stories under the date on which they will take place. These are added to other clippings from the local daily paper that might lead to future stories on the same date. If the Latin Club is going to re-create a Roman banquet with no English spoken on December 18, that item will be clipped and filed under that date in the future book. Then, early in December, the assignment editor will pick a staffer to attend the banquet and write it up.

The business of giving out assignments may be done at a specific time to as many students as can meet then. More frequently, however, a list of assignments (sometimes including beat coverage, too, just to make sure all staffers are functioning as assumed) is posted on a bulletin board in the publication's office. Staffers check regularly and frequently—daily if theirs is a weekly paper. Each individual initials an assignment so the editor knows that it will be covered.

☆ Even when sick, a good reporter follows through and notifies the proper person of inability to cover the story.

If something prevents completion of the assignment, a reporter has responsibility to inform the editor or faculty advisor. This is particularly true if the staff member becomes sick. If the editor is absent, then word of the disability should be passed on to the faculty advisor—by the individual's parent, if need be.

☆ A reporter is on duty at all times.

Few lapses in performance can cause as much trouble for an editor and a publication as failure to carry out an assignment. Professional journalists have been honored for their devotion in getting the news—no matter what. Let students perform as any other reporters would.

A plaque honoring a newsman at the late *New York World* illustrated the respect which such faithful service may generate. Conspicuously displayed in the city room, this memento told how a newsman had sent his story on a big train wreck to the paper before he allowed his own serious injuries to be treated. Few high school students will be asked to make such a sacrifice, but it is a goal to keep constantly in mind.

☆ Deadlines are sacred.

Recruiting Staffers

Recruiting new staff members and picking the right individuals for senior positions later resembles, in many ways, the working out of a jigsaw puzzle. In both instances, one has to get the right pieces into the right places. In both cases, various methods have been tried and none is guaranteed to be fully adaptable for all situations.

Interesting beginners to try out for the paper is one of the initial jobs of key editors and business manager when they take over for the coming year. Announcements inviting candidates to apply may be made at an all-school assembly, over a public address system, through bulletin-board posters, or by Mimeographed notices sent to each home room. Word of mouth may be an effective approach if the paper has a record to be proud of.

When a meeting for the job candidates is held, the editor and business manager should outline opportunities for and advantages of working on the publication. They should be fair and candid. Since the editor and manager will want to know the background and previous journalistic experiences of candidates, a simple application blank should be passed out, requesting these facts plus name, home room, home address and telephone, and other extracurricular activities for which the candidate is applying.

A screening test should eliminate students who are only status seekers and are trying out for far too many activities. The test should not be too exacting, however. Those who pass should then be invited back for a training program consisting of a series of talks by key personnel on the barest essentials about the publication and on basic journalistic techniques. Then the group splits into those interested in writing and editing and those wanting to join the business staff. At a second session, simple exercises in arranging and writing news are given. The business manager provides comparable facts and exercises concerning subscriptions, distribution, advertising, and office management. At a third meeting,

candidates are actually given minor assignments to complete for publication or go along with experienced correspondents in a sort of "buddy system." Homework assignments to learn copyreading and proofreading symbols or subscription and advertising rates and procedures are handed out. Finally, those who have done well are considered for formal staff appointments and, if their progress continues for some months, listing on the *masthead*.

Many schools today have journalism in the regular curriculum, as part of an accelerated English course or as a special honors class. This is a boon for any editor-in-chief or business manager who wants new staff members with some idea of what to do. Thus part of the training job may be done in the classroom instead of being handled exclusively by the publication staff. In some schools, the class has charge of the paper with editors being selected from among the students. Such a publication, while reporting on events of interest to students, has become a teaching tool that caters to learning experiences.

Selecting Leaders

Picking the top editors and business executives has become a tug-of-war between supporters of selection by balloting—sometimes by the entire student body just like head of the governing organization—and those who favor promotion from within based entirely on merit from previous performances.

For those who favor school balloting for top editorships, the chief argument is that it conforms with the American ideal of democracy in action. True, but does it always work? No! Too often balloting becomes a popularity contest to determine which individual has the most friends and has little to do with a potential to produce a superior paper. A winner may not know enough about putting out the publication or be a poor organizer. As representative of cliques or groups of students, the newly elected editor may be under obligation to award lesser staff positions as political plums. In addition to being a poor way to run any publication, this method is almost sure to drive out most of the opposing groups, including some who might have been exceptionally able staff members.

For those who support a strictly promotion-from-within procedure, the argument is that tested ability is rewarded. However, authoritarian aspects arise if only the publication advisor and other teachers pick the student they think is best qualified. With all due respect to teachers, it may not reflect the most accurate evaluation of how a potential editor actually will get along with other staffers. There are some things that students may not always tell teachers. These important characteristics could make the difference between respect for the new editor and unwillingness to accept him as boss.

As frequently happens in life, solutions may lie in compromise.

One way that has worked in many high schools is to have senior editors of this year's staff plus the publication and class advisors pick the editor-in-chief and business manager for next year. This combines the students' assessments with teachers' evaluations. Thus it becomes more than a popularity contest and more than awarding the job to the hardest worker. After two or three years' work with the upcoming staff members, seniors have an accurate idea of their capabilities and personality traits. Teachers can bring a mature assessment and should be able to view scholastic records plus other teachers' personality ratings, if need be, in confidence. They can guard against any slips in case the seniors fall short in this exacting decision.

Other schools have established boards of publications which include students, faculty, administrators and, in some cases, even parents. Student members may be elected or top editors may hold ex officio appointments. Such a setup overcomes the popularity-contest hazard but does not always insure true insight into work habits and personality traits.

Never, though, should any student-faculty selection group instinctively split along those lines. After all, a common interest should be the welfare of the school and

continued excellence of its publications. Should irresponsible individuals fail to recognize this common goal and make the publications board a battlefield of campus politics, student representation should be curtailed or the plan revised. But any student who is mature and responsible enough to produce a good periodical hardly needs such admonition.

Many schools have found it helpful to have applicants for key staff jobs file formal applications, stating their experience on the publication, other work in allied areas, scholastic record, list of other activities, and names of several students and teachers who might be checked as references. Such applications might well include a statement of purpose in which the applicant outlines plans for the publication and lists prospective subeditors. This procedure is especially good if senior editors and business manager serve on the selection group because they are familiar with qualifications of people who'll be in the chain of command.

☆ Qualifications should be established and well publicized.

Some selection boards interview each applicant—but they keep in mind that at a tense time like this an able student may not be as glib and articulate as one who has far fewer qualifications.

There is no reason why a junior can't handle the top job if truly qualified. Selectors ought to use the same yardstick that a football coach does: Send in the best person without regard to class affiliation.

☆ Picking a new staff for next school year should be done and should be announced while senior editors are still around school.

Such early selection during the spring permits new editors to put out the last issue of the school year under the watchful eyes of retiring editors and allows them the summer to prepare for the coming year. On a yearbook, the designated editors receive extensive briefings instead of actually performing in their new jobs. In either case, the experienced predecessors can caution against possible booby traps. Spring appointments also permit the newly appointed

Broad range of high school journalism is depicted in recruiting poster for Empire State Scholastic Press Assn., headquartered at Syracuse University, typical of strong state journalism organizations.

editors and business manager to attend special summer courses that many colleges offer.

Should there be extra inducements beyond the prestige and glory for key publication personnel? While that is enough for a vast majority of student editors and business managers, some administrations allow academic credit for work on a paper, yearbook, magazine, or broadcast station. This is slight repayment for the time spent but it certifies the importance of communications activities as meaningful academic experience. Some sticky questions have to be worked out by a school that allows this:

Who should be permitted to receive credit? Just a couple of senior persons—or everyone who puts in time equivalent to a single course?

What limit should there be on the number of semesters for which credits are allowed?

Should some letter grade be assigned for the work?

Who is to determine that letter grade, if it is granted?

Regardless of whether connected with a newspaper, news magazine, yearbook, or broadcasting station, a staff organization that is effective and efficient will insure the final result is a better performance. As Shakespeare said, that desired result "must follow as the night the day." Building the staff is not something to be done hurriedly, thoughtlessly, or with favoritism.

4 The Language of the Press

People engaged in secret occupations—legal as well as illicit—speak a special language to protect that secrecy from outsiders. When printing from movable type was invented around 1450 A.D., the discovery was shrouded in the deepest secrecy. To protect monopolies, printers were even forbidden to leave their cities except with official approval and under stern governmental restrictions.

So printers developed their own jargon. The *printer's devil,* for instance, was just an apprentice boy who did the odd jobs around a print shop but his diabolic nickname impressed the outsider into believing there was some black magic involved in this awesome new craft.

During the centuries since Johann Genzfleisch zum Gutenberg invented movable type in medieval Mainz in Germany, printers developed a rich and complex language about the wondrous art of *letterpress* printing. Early newspaper editors spoke this language well, for they were printers themselves; in most instances they became editors and publishers simply to create work for their printing presses. It is still useful for the editor—scholastic or professional— to "speak printer." For the editor must work closely with the people in the *back shop,* the *mechanical departments* of a newspaper.

In 1899, another great inventor, Aloys Senefelder, discovered *lithographic printing.* With it came great enlargement and enrichment of the printer's vocabulary.

In recent years, Senefelder's printing method has usurped that of Herr Gutenberg; practically all high school newspapers and many, many professional papers are printed by a variation called *offset lithography.*

But we ought to know the basics of letterpress if for no other reason than that the largest newspapers in the country are still printed by that method.

The simplest example of letterpress is a rubber stamp. Characters in relief capture ink and then deposit it on paper.

For regular letterpress or *relief printing,* metal type is used. This may be set by hand, individual pieces being taken out of a container, a *California job case,* and arranged into words and sentences in a metal receptacle called a printer's *stick.* Or it may be set mechanically on a machine called a *Linotype,* in which case a whole line of type is created as a single piece of *type metal.*

In the simplest letterpress, the *platen press,* the paper is placed on a metal shelf and is pressed against the inked type. Such presses are common in high school printing classrooms.

Commonly used for smaller newspapers was the *cylinder press.* Here the type lies on a metal bed. The paper is wrapped around a cylinder which is rolled across the type to transfer the ink to it.

Metropolitan papers use a *rotary press.* Now the type is on a cylinder and the paper is pressed against it by another *impression* cylinder. The paper feeds off a roll in a

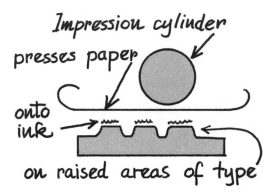

Schematic of letterpress printing. This version is cylinder or flatbed press.

continuous *web*. Only after the entire newspaper has been printed is it cut into separate pages and folded into the familiar unfastened "book" which is delivered to our home every day.

The *stereotyping* process is used to create the curved type surface. A flat newspaper page is made up conventionally. A *flong*, a thick piece of material much like papier-mâché, is forced down upon the type under tremendous hydraulic pressure. It becomes a faithful mold—a *matrix* or just *mat*—that carries even the finest detail of all the relief elements. This mat is placed in a semicylindrical container into which molten type metal is poured. The result is a half-cylinder of metal, about an inch thick, from which protrudes the relief characters that were in the original page. This *half-round* is affixed to the cylinder of a rotary press.

(Because the *stereo* plate is a duplicate of the original, we use its name, stereotype,

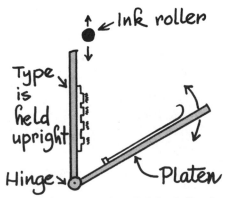

Schematic of platen press, also called clamshell or clapper.

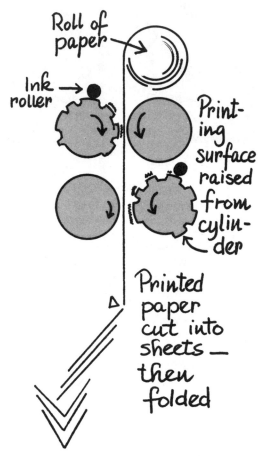

Schematic of rotary letterpress. Note curved printing surfaces and paper feeding from roll.

today to refer to literary clichés and unimaginative and repetitive mental concepts.)

But while letterpress is still used for the big dailies, the greater number of smaller newspapers and most high school ones are printed by offset. So scholastic editors should know this process well.

It is based on the simple principle that oil and water will not mix. Even more, they repel each other.

In his original invention, Senefelder drew an image—letters or pictures—on a slab of smooth limestone. Then he sloshed water across the stone. The stone wetted by the oily image repelled the water.

Then he passed an ink roller, a *brayer*, across the stone. The water on the stone repulsed the oily ink; but the greasy crayon image accepted the ink. So there was a layer of ink precisely and only on the original image. When paper was pressed onto the stone, this layer was transferred onto the paper and a lithographed image was thus printed.

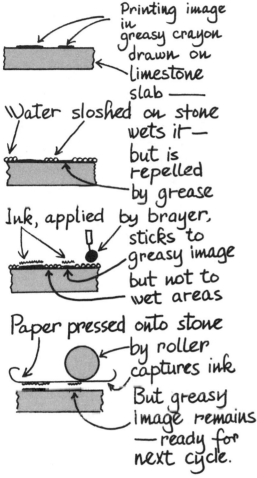

Printing image in greasy crayon drawn on limestone slab —

Water sloshed on stone wets it — but is repelled by grease

Ink, applied by brayer, sticks to greasy image but not to wet areas

Paper pressed onto stone by roller captures ink But greasy image remains — ready for next cycle.

Schematic of lithographic printing.

The application of water and then ink was repeated for each successive piece of printing.

The familiar Currier & Ives pictures are lithographs. The colors may be printed or may be applied by hand to black-and-white pictures. This direct lithography, still using limestone, is a popular medium for fine art today.

Today *offset* lithography is used for commercial printing. It widens the usefulness of original lithography. The principle remains the same. Instead of the heavy and awkward limestone slab, we now use a thin aluminum plate. The printing images—type and pictures—are placed on the plate photographically instead of by hand, obviously speeding up the whole process.

The familiar progression of wetting, then inking the plate remains. But the image is printed, not onto a piece of paper, but onto a rubber *blanket*. Then, when the paper is pressed against the blanket, the image is set off—or offset, of course—onto the paper.

The reason for this intermediate element, the rubber blanket, is to print very fine detail onto rough paper. *Newsprint*, the paper used for newspapers, seems smooth to our eye and fingers. But microscopically it is rough. When relief elements are printed on such rough paper, they may not reach down into the "valleys," they may punch into the "hills" or print only partially on the "slopes." But the flexible rubber blanket readily bends to conform to the irregular surface and the printed image is uniform over its entire area.

Speed of offset presses can be much higher than comparable letterpresses because the aluminum plate is so much lighter in weight than stereotype plates or other relief printing forms. There is also the advantage of using cold type as we shall discuss later.

There is a third major printing method, *intaglio* (pronounced in-*tahl*-yo or in-*tag*-leo) or *gravure*. This is used by newspapers primarily for printing Sunday magazines and similar supplements. *Parade* and *Family Weekly* as well as *The New York Times Magazine* are familiar examples. But the method is never used for high school newspapers or magazines so we need not concern ourselves too much with it.

All printing methods use type; if it is in relief, it's called *hot metal*, if it has been set photographically or produced on a typewriterlike machine, it's *cold type*. So this part of the printer's lexicon goes all the way back to Gutenberg, always growing but never becoming obsolete. This is the glossary that is absolutely essential to the editor.

For the writing and printing of English—and many other languages, of course—we

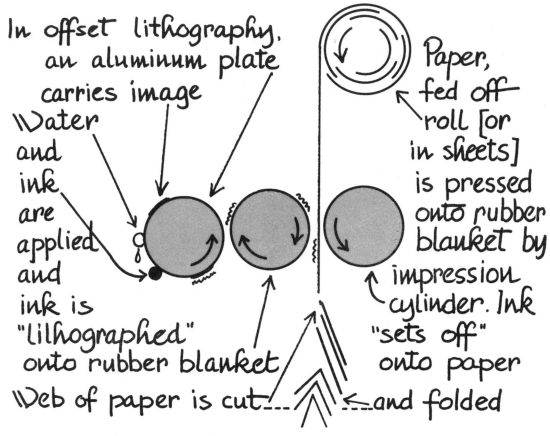

In offset lithography,
an aluminum plate
carries image

Water
and
ink
are
applied
and
ink is
"lithographed"
onto rubber blanket

Web of paper is cut

Paper,
fed off
roll [or
in sheets]
is pressed
onto rubber
blanket by
impression
cylinder. Ink
"sets off"
onto paper
and folded

Schematic of offset lithography.

use the *Latin alphabet,* this most wondrous of tools for thinking, learning, and communicating.

The Latin alphabet began as a set of pictures of objects. The head of an ox, an "aleph," for instance, was simplified into stylized drawing that looked enough like the original to be readily identified. Eventually this design was turned onto its side and finally upside-down into a shape we use today.

In children's books today we say: "A is for apple, B is for ball," and so on. The ancient Phoenicians, who developed this system, did just the reverse. Instead of "A is for aleph," they said, "Aleph is for A"; the drawn character was not a picture of an object, but of a sound. The second sound was that of B, represented in Phoenician by the simplified sketch of a house, a "beth." Even today we retain those two words in our term, "alphabet."

All characters of Latin alphabet derive from pictures of objects. These are typical.

This   became
picture.. this symbol...
                              then

This picture.. ∀ ⊲ A

Ψ ⊁ K

Φ ϙ Q

Even the most cursory glance through a newspaper or magazine shows the innumerable variations in design of the Latin letters. They are almost countless. (Haber Typographers, Inc., whose courtesy provided those interesting type specimens on the end papers of this book, has more than 1,050 different typefaces, many of them in as many as a dozen different sizes.) So journalists, typographers, and printers must have a quick and easy way to distinguish one face from another. This is done much as we distinguish individuals among the millions of human beings on our globe.

We might think of this vast number of typefaces as the whole of humanity. Just as we do with human beings, we first divide them into races.

There are six *type races*. Then—again as with humans—races are subdivided into *ethnic groups* and, further, into *families*.

From Phoenicia the alphabet moved to Greece and then to Rome. The ancient Romans, around the time of Christ, developed the *Roman* race of the alphabet. It is distinguished by thick and thin strokes, swelling and diminishing of curves and tiny finishing strokes—called *serifs*—at the end of main strokes.

Memory device for Roman type. Note how curved lines swell and thin. Laurel wreath and sandals made famous by Caesar's legions remind us of serifs at end of strokes.

The two ethnic groups of Roman are *Old Style* and *Modern*. Note that these names have absolutely nothing to do with the time the design was first made. The first Modern, Bodoni, was designed around the time of the American Revolution; a gorgeous Old Style, Palatino, was done just a few years ago.

In Old Style, the difference between thick and thin strokes is slight; its serifs are rather heavy, often curved, and are *bracketed*, connected to the main stroke by a curve. Modern Romans have marked differences between thicks and thins and their

serifs are thin, straight, and unbracketed. (You might like to look at the many specimens on the end papers of this book and note the difference described here.)

The second type race is *Text* or *Black Letter*. It was modified from the original Roman by scribes of the Rhineland. It has the honor of being the first type race to be printed from movable type. For Gutenberg was a German and naturally sought to make his printed books look like the handwritten ones of his native land.

Memory device for Black Letter type. Sharp peaks of medieval roofs remind of angles of letterform. And church reminds that this letter is called Text because of its use for texts of religious documents.

Text is an angular face with few, if any, curves. There is a great difference between thick and thin strokes and the letters are relatively narrow—the space between strokes is thinner than the strokes themselves.

Text is the only race without ethnic groups. We should note that this race is often—and incorrectly—referred to as *Old English*. That name refers only to a type family. To use it for a whole race is like referring to the Caucasian or Oriental race as "Smith" or "Chu."

The third race is *Monotonal*. As you might guess, all strokes are of apparently identical weight. There are no serifs. Its ethnics are *Gothic* and *Sans Serifs*. Note that the term "Gothic" is often misused; it has absolutely no connection with Gothic architecture. Rather, it refers to the ugly Goths who used to harass the Roman legions. Gothic letterforms are based on an oval, those of the Sans on a circle. It is difficult to tell these two ethnics apart. Sometimes curved strokes of the Gothics are made thinner, *pinched*, as they meet a

Sans Serifs' mnenomic perpetrates another pun: "Footsteps on the Sans of time."

straight stroke, the *stem*. If there is any variation of the stroke, even almost imperceptible, we know it's a Gothic.

Gothic type was named for ugly marauders who terrorized Europe, not for handsome architecture of Gothic churches.

Then comes the *Square Serifs* race. Basically a monotonal letter, it has serifs—heavy ones. If the serifs are as thick as the main strokes, the letters are in the *Egyptian* ethnic group. If the serifs are heavier than the main stroke, the ethnic is *American*. (Note that the name "Serifs" always has an *s* on the end.)

Remember Square Serifs by a forgiveable pun: Square Sheriff.

If you want to try a little experiment, you'll discover the origin of the next race. Start out by lettering your name in Monotonal capitals; little kids would call it "printing." Do this over and over, trying for the highest speed you can achieve. In a little while you will find that connecting letters is faster than lifting your pencil. You'll also find the letters are tilting to the right (if you are right-handed) and that you unthinkingly are simplifying many of the letterforms. This is *writing* as opposed

Script letters are joined together—even if not by wedlock.

to *lettering* or "printing." Handwriting was used since the earlier days of the alphabet as the common, informal channel of communication. When metal type was invented this form became the *Written* race. Its ethnics are *Cursive*—which means "running"—and *Script*—which means "written."

Both ethnic letterforms are identical. Script letters are joined; Cursives are separate, often so slightly it's hard to see the divisions.

BROADWAY

Shading affects face—of persons or of type. So Shaded letters are those which have something done to face of letters.

The last race is *Ornamented*. (Note: It's Ornamen-*ted*; not -*tal*.)

There are three ethnics in this race: *Shaded, Shadowed,* and *Novelty*. If you will look at examples from the first two, you will find that they are almost always recognizable as members of one of the other races. If anything is done to the face of the letterform, it's a Shaded letter. If anything is added to the letter, it's Shadowed. Remember, though, that just as soon as this ornamenting is done, the type is no longer in its original race, it is now an Ornamented.

When the letterform is radically changed, the result is a Novelty. You often see letters made of ribbon, or rope, or planks—all

OLD BOWERY

Shadows are cast away from object. So Shadowed type has additions away from body of letters.

Novelties. Those that resemble the calligraphy of Japanese or Chinese ideograms or of Hebrew are also in this ethnic.

Letters may be both Shaded—with something done to their face—and Shadowed—by adding something outside the face—as was highly popular in the Victorian era. These are not considered as a separate

Exaggerated forms create Novelties—in type faces as in dogs.

ethnic but are identified by the most conspicuous ornamentation or, if the design is highly ornate, as a Novelty.

Each type family, like its human counterparts, has a family name. This may be, like "Swensson" or "McLeod," the name of the father or, in the case of type, the designer: Bodoni, Cooper, Goudy. Or, like our "Scot" or "English," family names designated national origins; in type we have Helvetica, Ionic, and Caledonia, for instance.

"Black," "Strong," and "Little" were descriptions converted into family names; in type we have Hobo, Casual, and Wild West. And, of course, there are type names

that are just names: Stymie, Metro, and Corona, among many others.

All members of a human family share a "family look" and so do types. Among humans we have tall and short, heavy and skinny, blonde and brunette, all variations among individuals who still share a "family look." In type we have variations of the basic family design.

A typeface may vary in *weight, width,* or *angle.* If the letterform remains the same but the thickness of its strokes is increased, the new form is called *Bold, Heavy, Black,* or a similar term. If the strokes are narrower, the form is *Light* or *Book.*

If the height of the letter remains constant and its width is increased, we have an *Extended* or *Wide* series. If the letterform is squeezed horizontally only, it is *Condensed* or even *Extra Condensed.*

If a Roman letter slants to the right it is an *Italic.* If a series in any other race slants to the right it is an *Oblique.* In common usage, though, any letter that tilts to the right, be it Roman or not, is called Italic. A rarity—thank heavens! for this is an ugly form—is the letter that slants to the left, a *Backslant.*

Each such version is a *series* of typed and is identified by the family name plus one or more of these adjectives. So we have Spartan Bold, Bodoni Book, Venus Extended, Trade Gothic Condensed, Caslon Bold Italic or, almost the ultimate in variations, Cheltenham Bold Condensed Italic.

A series breaks down into a *font,* a division denoting size, and its name tells the size and the series: 8-point Fairfield Medium, for instance.

When just the family name is used, it refers to the normal or regular letter design. Those adjectives are never used in a title.

A font consists of the *capitals* or *majuscules,* the original form of our Latin alpha-

Italic type slants to right, just like famed Tower of Pisa—which is Italic structure.

Category	Example	Subcategory
Roman	Medicine	OLD STYLE
	Ludgate Hill	MODERN
	ministrant	ITALIC
Text	𝕬𝕭𝕮 bcdefgh	
Mono-tonal	riddance	SANS SERIFS
	Blue River	GOTHIC
Square Serifs	**Display**	EGYPTIAN
	Magnetic	AMERICAN
Written	*Modern Print*	SCRIPT
	Beautiful	CURSIVE
Orna-mented	ABCDEFG	SHADED
	BCDEFGHI	SHADOWED
	COUNTRY	NOVELTY

Races and ethnic groups of type.

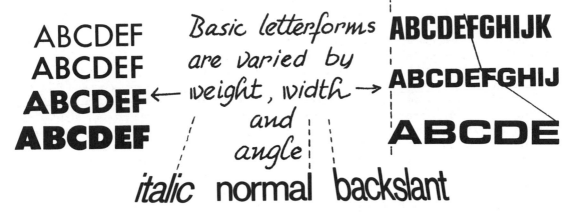

Variations of letterform effected by weight, width and angle.

bet; the *small letters* or *minuscules; Arabic numerals* and *special characters* such as $ ¢ & * % #, etc. For book work—but rarely for magazines and newspapers—we might have *small capitals*, in the same form as the majuscules but of the approximate size of the minuscules. A font of metal type also has spacing material, *quads*.

The minuscules are further broken down. Letters that are defined by an imaginary *baseline* at the bottom and *meanline* at top—such as a, c, e, m, n, etc.—are *primary letters*. Those with projections above the meanline—b, h, d, for instance—are called *ascenders*. The neck itself, as well as the letter it protrudes from, is called an ascender. If the projection is below the baseline—as p, q, g, etc.—both the letter and the tail are called *descenders*.

Type sizes are designated in *points*, the basic unit of printing measurements. Although there is so much talk these days of metric measurements replacing inches, pounds, gallons, and miles, it is safe to assume that the printer's point will remain in use for at least the lifetime of any reader of this book.

A point is $\frac{1}{72}$ of an inch. Twelve points make a *pica* and there are, of course, 6 picas in an inch.

Vertical type size is expressed in points; line lengths, in picas.

Paper sizes are usually in inches although sometimes picas are used as well.

An "8-point" type face, for instance, means that the distance from the top of a b to the bottom of a p, plus tiny *shoulders* above the ascenders, is 8 points. This size has little to do with the size of the primary letters, the dimensions that really affect readership.

From 5- through 12-point type is usually called *body type* and larger sizes are *display type*. But it is the use, rather than the size, of type that puts it into one of these categories. Sometimes headlines are as small as 12-point and are thus display type. Sometimes very big news stories are set in 14-, 18-point, or even larger type which, by its use, is then body type.

All type used to be called by names but only one retains its old label today. That's *agate*, 5½ point. This is the size normally used for classified ads and tabular material such as box scores. Any type, even 6-point, when used for such purposes, is referred to as agate.

◀ **Melior**

Semi Bold

ABCDEFGHIJKLM
NOPQRSTUVWXYZ
1234567890 & $ ff fi fl
abcdefghijklmnop
qrstuvwxyz.,-:;!?'

Typical font of Roman type. Note ligatures with lowercase f in third row.

Extra spacing between lines of type—in addition to the shoulder—is called *ledding*. Hot metal type is spaced by placing thin strips of metal between the lines. This strip, 2 points thick, is called a *ledd*. Properly this should be "lead," as in the name of the metal of which it is made. But the phonetic spelling is used by most journalists, especially to avoid confusion with the similarly spelled journalistic term which is pronounced *leed*, and often spelled phonetically, too.

Ledding may be added in increments of half-points. Type so spaced out is designated as *8-on-9* or *8/9*, for instance. That means that the type itself is 8 points in size and that 1 point of ledding has been added so that the thickness or depth of the line plus that spacing is 9 points. Eight-on-9 is common for newspapers; for classifieds we might use 5½-on-6, ledding it just a half point, or we may not use any extra interlineal spacing at all, thus making it *set solid*.

When metal type has been *composed* into lines and *grafs* (paragraphs, of course) it is stored in a shallow metal tray, a *galley*, until it is *locked up* in a chase. While it's in the galley, a rough printing impression is made, the *galley proof*. This is carefully read to detect errors and give instructions for their correction. The technical aspects of this are discussed in Chapter 9.

Cold type is produced in two basic ways. *Strikeon composition* is that made by striking a relief letter through an inked or carbon ribbon onto paper. The simplest strike-on machine is an ordinary typewriter and some excellent publications, both professional and scholastic, are "typeset" on an old Smith-Corona. Other machines are far more sophisticated; some even have in-built computers to set *justified* lines, those with even right as well as left margins.

Photocomposition is done by relatively simple machines to very complex ones that cost scores of thousands of dollars. They have one thing in common: They produce photographs of letters. All start out with a photo negative of a series of type. By projecting light through these clear images on a black film, a photo of that character is placed on photopaper in exactly the same way as a snapshot you take with your Pocket Instamatic. Various sizes of that type are produced by using lenses in the machine to enlarge or reduce the original negative image.

Cold type in body sizes is produced in long strips, the equivalent of a galley of hot metal type. A *Xerox, Thermofax*, or similar machine makes a photocopy of the original type, the equivalent of the galley proof and still called by that name. This copy is used for proofreading.

The printing of type is a relatively simple process by whichever method used. But the printing of photographs is considerably more complicated. In fact, it requires a magician's sleight of hand. This fascinating process is described in Chapter 12.

The person who sets the type is a *compositor, typesetter*, or *operator*, short for *keyboard operator*. The one who assembles typographic elements into pages is a *makeup man, lockup man* in hot metal, or *pasteup man*. The *platemaker* has an obvious job as does the *pressman*.

Directing the work of these craftsmen is the *typographer*, in journalism, the editor or the *makeup editor*. *Typography* is the basic philosophy regarding the art and skill of using typographic elements as tools of communication. *Layout* is the application of such broad and unchanging principles to the specific problems of arranging a single advertisement, page, section, edition, or issue.

The principles of typography apply to all scholastic publications, newspapers, newsletters, magazines, or yearbooks. They first determine the *format* of a publication, those basic specifications of page size, margins, number of columns, etc.

By using the specialized jargon of printing, the editor can transact typographic business more quickly and more accurately. So, without making a federal project of it, it will be useful for you to learn the rudiments of that language as suggested here; the complete dictionary of the graphic arts is far, far greater.

Then you may share in the whimsical boast of an editor who once said, "The foreign languages I speak are French, German, and printer's."

Law and Student Journalists

Few other phrases in the U.S. Constitution are bandied about as much—and misunderstood as much—as freedom of the press.

It inspires and sustains professional journalists—and often perplexes them. It's no wonder that student journalists are confused about the whole concept. This is especially true right now when the courts are defining these liberties in the specific context of scholastic journalism and in the process have often issued contradictory and obfuscating opinions.

During the past decade, the nation's judiciary affirmed for scholastic journalists those press freedoms earlier guaranteed the commercial and professional media. By the mid-1970s, high school freedoms were more sharply defined than ever before but they still were not crystal clear. What remained to be distinctly outlined were the accompanying obligations that always go along with rights and opportunities. Also there was apparent discrepancy between rights of college staffs and those of secondary school publications.

Like American news professionals for two centuries, school journalists rest their claims for press freedom on the First Amendment to the U.S. Constitution. Upon this single sentence stands the entire structure of what we call the American free press:

Congress shall make no law respecting the establishment of religion, or prohib-

iting the free exercise thereof; or abridging the freedom of speech, or of the press; or the right of the people peaceably to assemble, and to petition the government for redress of grievances.

The Founding Fathers debated whether to put guarantees into the original document itself but opted not to. However, early in the ratification process, supporters of the Constitution found that they had to add a catalog of do's and don't's in ten amendments, the Bill of Rights. Otherwise, the states would not accept the document.

In trying to define what press freedom means, some jurists—a minority but influential—succinctly argue: No laws whatsoever! Others claim that there must be a few curtailments for the so-called public good and that the courts will decide whether these embargoes truly "abridge" the media's liberties.

Freedom from *prior restraint* is a key principle. You can print the peccadilloes of a shifty mayor or the gaffes of an inept principal. You can tell your readers of mischief by the president, either of the United States or of the senior class. You can expose misfeasance, malfeasance, or nonfeasance of anyone from your basketball coach to the state governor. No one can prevent you from printing and distributing such statements.

But (there always seems to be a "but") once you have done so, you are responsible for those statements. If you have violated laws and regulations against libel, obscenity, or invasion of privacy, you can be called into court for accounting and possibly for punishment. You can even be sent to jail or prison. But that is *after* you have printed something, not before.

☆ Journalists have a right to publish but they must take the consequences for what they do.

The key reason for press freedom in the First Amendment is to enable the media to perform their function as "watchdog" of American liberties and of the government. To emphasize that, professional journalists favor the phrase "the right to know" instead of "the right to report." A basic right of the whole citizenry—not just of journalists—is involved here. In a democracy, the government is the servant, not the master, of the people. And the people have the right and need to know what elected officials are doing and how well they are serving.

The media thus become the public's surrogates. When a reporter is denied access to news, it really is the public that is being denied. While the doctor, the grocer, the homemaker, or the student have rights—as part of the general public—to watch a state legislature or Congress in action or to examine long lists of county assessments, most citizens can't take the time to do this. So typical Americans turn to the mass media and when those are hindered or curtailed, the citizens suffer. The public also is hurt when journalists put out less than their best efforts.

The Tinker Decision

High school students' rights of free expression were established for the first time in a landmark case: *Tinker* v. *Des Moines Independent Community School District* (1969).

In that decision, the U.S. Supreme Court held that high school students had rights of free expression. The case did not involve a school publication but, rather, whether two students could wear armbands protesting the Vietnam War despite school administration requests to remove them. The Tinkers, then aged 13 and 15, refused the requests, were suspended from school,

Key to unlocking chains of censorship is labelled AB 207, title of controversial California legislation, in prizewinning cartoon by Matt Wuerker of Palos Verdes, California.

brought legal action, and eventually won on appeal to the U.S. Supreme Court. Justice Abe Fortas, writing for the majority, said:

> School officials do not possess absolute authority over their students. Students in school as well as out of school are persons under our Constitution. They are possessed of fundamental rights which the state must respect. . . . In the absence of a specific showing of constitutionally valid reasons to regulate their speech, students are entitled to freedom of expression of their views.

The justices said that wearing of armbands was akin to "pure speech" and thus the Tinkers' actions were associated with First Amendment guarantees of free speech and free press. The decision also pointed out that intercommunication among students was "an important part of the educational process" and that to ban wearing of the armbands could not be ordered on "a mere desire to avoid the discomfort and unpleasantness that always accompany an unpopular viewpoint."

The Tinkers' actions were "entirely divorced from actually or potentially disruptive conduct," the majority decision said. But then the justices cautioned that "conduct by the student, in class or out of it, which for any reason . . . materially disrupts classwork or involves substantial disorder or invasion of the rights of others, is, of course, not immunized by the constitutional guarantee of freedom of speech."

The court decision did not offer real guidance on what circumstances would warrant voiding constitutional guarantees for students. Precedent has established that the rights of expression are not absolute. Justice Oliver Wendell Holmes in the unanimous decision in *Schenck* v. *United States* (1919) wrote, "The most stringent protection of free speech would not protect a man from falsely shouting fire in a theatre and causing a panic."

Debates on public issues should be wide open, robust, and uninhibited—and no outside agency can interfere. However, even this accepted principle is not absolute. For instance, a few restraints exist in time of war or when public order is endangered by incitements to violence and overthrow of the orderly government by force.

Since the U.S. Supreme Court, as the highest judicial body, sets precedents for future decisions, lower courts soon were using *Tinker* for cases involving student publications. They were making interpretations that did not always agree with each other although the judges all thought they were following the *Tinker* decision and its philosophy.

In 1968—before the *Tinker* decision—two student editors of an underground paper were expelled from Central High School in Joliet, Ill. Their publication, *Grass High,* called school regulations "asinine," claimed that a dean had a "sick mind," and asked fellow students not to accept "propaganda" from administrators. About 60 copies were distributed. The Joliet Board of Education expelled the two under regulations that allowed such action if pupils were "guilty of gross disobedience or misconduct." The two editors brought legal action, claiming violation of their free speech rights. A U.S. District Court supported the Board of Education on the grounds that the editors' actions amounted to "an immediate advocacy of, and incitement to, disregard of school administrative procedures."

In 1970—after *Tinker*—the Court of Appeals for the Seventh Circuit (*Scoville* v. *Board of Education,* 1970) reversed earlier

decisions, saying that no facts supported any belief that distributing 60 copies of *Grass High* would lead to disruption or to interference with enforcement of school policies and further, even if they had, the school officials had to justify the expulsions when school rules infringe on freedom of expression.

Another case in which judges tried to apply the *Tinker* decision involved the *Stamford Free Press,* an "independent" Mimeographed newspaper distributed at Rippowan High School in Stamford, Conn. The Court of Appeals for the Second Circuit (*Eisner* v. *Stamford Board of Education,* 1971) held that Stamford school officials could require written material to be submitted for approval prior to publication "only when there is to be a *substantial* distribution" and when it could reasonably be anticipated that such distribution "would disrupt school operations."

As the appeals court said, "it would be highly disruptive to the educational process if a secondary school principal were required to take a school newspaper editor to court every time the principal reasonably anticipated disruption and sought to restrain its cause."

A different judiciary, the Court of Appeals for the Seventh Circuit, heard a case involving three students at Lane Technical and Bowen High Schools in Chicago (*Fujishima* v. *Board of Education,* 1972). That appeals court held unconstitutional a rule of the Chicago Board of Education which said distribution of books, tracts, and other publications would be banned on school premises unless approved by Chicago's general superintendent of schools. The judges held prior restraint of publication was "long a constitutionally prohibited power" and that it applied to student editors, too. The court's decision said school administrators could promulgate "reasonable, specific regulations setting forth the time, manner and place in which the distribution of written materials may occur" and could punish any student who violated these rules. However, no blanket prohibitions in advance.

The court also said students who publish or distribute "obscene or libelous literature" on school grounds may be punished under established rules.

In 1973, U.S. District Court Judge George Beaver held that the prohibition on prior restraint by school officials applied to an official, in-school publication as well as to the underground papers that had previously been involved in legal actions. The case concerned the *Liberty Link,* of North Liberty, Ind., whose editor had written an article on planned parenthood which the principal banned for publication. Judge Beaver ruled that school officials "shall not prohibit publication of articles in official school newspapers on the basis of the subject matter or terminology used unless the article or terminology used is obscene, libelous or disrupts school activities."

Some courts have imposed dual standards: One for college publication editors and writers and another—more strict—for high school students.

In one case (*Schwartz* v. *Schuker,* 1969), a U.S. District Court upheld expulsion of a New York high school student when he distributed copies of an underground paper. The judge argued that "the activities of high school students do not always fall within the same category as the conduct of college students, the former being in a much more adolescent and immature stage of life and less able to screen facts from propaganda."

Also most legal authorities feel that private schools are not under the same restraints as public schools. These judicial opinions rest on the reasoning that public schools and their officials are agencies of the state and thus are required to uphold the constitutional "due process" rights. Until the courts rule otherwise, private school staffers appear to be denied the full thrust of freedoms already granted to their peers on public school papers.

The Journalism Education Association (JEA) summed up current attitudes about scholastic journalists' rights and obligations in an official position statement which began:

> The Journalism Education Association (JEA) upholds the right of students to exercise the freedom of expression of the

First Amendment to the Constitution of the United States. Student journalists have the right to report on and editorialize about controversies and crucial events in the school, community, nation, and world. However, they must observe the same legal responsibilities as those imposed upon all news media. Thus, student journalists must refrain from publication of material which
> (a) is obscene, according to current legal definitions;
> (b) is libelous, according to current legal definitions; or
> (c) creates a clear and present danger of the immediate material and substantial physical disruption of the school.

Student publications shall not be subjected to prior restraints or censorship by faculty advisers or school administrators.

How can staffers, advisors, and administrators live in a fair degree of harmony with the court-mandated scholastic freedoms?

1. By eliminating prior restraint or outright censorship by advisor, principal, or other school administrators.

2. By administrators and advisors talking problems over with student editors and writers and through involving them in all vital decisions concerning a publication.

3. By advisors and administrators, especially principals, learning about the changed situation of students' rights.

4. By all staff members developing a sense of responsibility. (Just because it is legally possible, doesn't mean you *always* have to do it.)

Professors George E. Stevens and John B. Webster of the journalism program at Purdue University offer this advice in their book *Law and the Student Press:*

> Students and faculty could avoid many conflicts if they could agree on guidelines for the student press and if students were involved in deciding important questions connected with the operation of student publications. Although the courts require only "reasonable" rules and not necessarily student participation in boards of

Freedom of press for student journalists is subject of prize-winning cartoon by Bob Staake of West Torrance, California.

publications, some problems might be solved without legal action if students were brought into the decision-making process.

Once the courts come in, they are unlikely to go away and disappear. Concerned with the legal aspects of the case rather than good journalistic practices, judges hand down decisions that may satisfy no one involved in the dispute. Justice is not concerned with decisions that make people happy. Thus rushing into court may not bring the best solution for students, principals, advisors, or other administrators. All parties to a dispute concerning scholastic journalism should try especially hard to work out their own solutions to differences.

Court decisions have already complicated the situation and created new perplexities. Observers of the scholastic press have called attention to two grave incongruities.

The same courts that have ruled that an advisor or principal may not keep anything out of a student publication have also ruled that the advisor or principal must pay monetary damages because of deleterious material that has been printed. This is like penalizing your parents because your neigh-

bor's children—who obviously are not under your family's control—are committing punishable acts.

In decisions covering professional press, the courts have limited liability to those who committed an illegal action or had the authority to prevent it.

A second area of major concern to many observers is the failure of the courts even to acknowledge the *gatekeeper principle*. Throughout the production of a publication, various gatekeepers keep out certain material. A reporter doesn't write all the facts of a story. The copyreader eliminates certain words and phrases, perhaps even whole paragraphs. The section editor may wastebasket a whole story. The editor-in-chief may close the gate against a whole variety of stories. The publisher may forbid any editorials in behalf of—or against—a certain political candidate. Indeed, the publisher ultimately can keep out anything at all from the publication, from the lead story to a picture to advertising for an X-rated movie—or even a G-rated one.

Most friction on scholastic publications arises from the assumption that the Board of Education or the principal is the "publisher" and the advisor is the publisher's deputy. Now the courts have negated that premise.

But judges have never designated anyone else as the final authority. By decisions to date, there are no acknowledged gatekeepers at all. Such functions of copyreaders and editors are extra-legal—if not illegal.

By this lack of recognition of a chain of command, a cub reporter might insist that anything and everything written must be published. For the courts have not distinguished between a story that a school superintendent tries to keep out of print because it might embarrass the administration or a story that the sports editor throws out because the writer has done a poor job, the story won't interest a broad readership, or there just isn't enough room for it.

This attitude—"You must print my copy!"—has already caused grief to young reporters on the commercial press. Coming from the artificial world of college journalism, with no publisher as gatekeeper, the undisciplined writer is shocked, dismayed, and angered to learn that in the real world there are publishers and their deputies who can—and constantly do—close gates on material.

☆ All press freedoms bring editorial responsibilities and opportunities.

☆ Student journalists should learn to live with both. So should faculty advisors and school administrators.

Libel, Obscenity, Copyright

Some journalistic indiscretions and mistakes are so serious that they are not protected under guarantees of the First Amendment. As indicated in some of the quotations earlier in this chapter, two principal ones are libel and obscenity. These topics have been in a state of flux for more than a decade and scholastic news writers and editors should be familiar with what has been happening and what the current situation is.

Let's look at definitions of these terms.

Libel is to hurt an individual's or institution's reputation or community standing by making false statements. In libel cases, truth provides an impressive defense; the person bringing legal action must establish that the information was disseminated deliberately when it was known the facts were false or when there was reckless disregard in ascertaining whether they were false or not. This is known to the courts as "malice." This seldom applies to an "honest" error or misunderstanding. Other defenses in libel cases are (a) accurate quotations (even when the facts are false) from courts of record and legislative proceedings, such as a state legislature or the U.S. Congress and (b) valid criticism and fair comment, even when they may devastate the person discussed.

Obscenity is distributing material that caters predominantly to prurient interests, offends community moral standards, and, taken as a whole, has no redeeming social values.

Some commentators on the school press believe that more cases of libel and obscenity may arise as students exercise—

possibly clumsily or even frivolously at first—their newly granted independence from restraints that previously were placed upon them. Thus junior journalists will encounter the bitter side of freedom because some things are not protected by the First Amendment or any other privileges. Many of the same barriers exist for professionals and students will be learning more about how journalism really works.

With the precedent-making decision in *New York Times Company* v. *Sullivan* (1964), the U.S. Supreme Court enlarged all media's protections in libel litigation. That case involved a suit by the Montgomery, Ala., commissioner of public affairs to recover $500,000 damages for errors in a *Times* advertisement soliciting funds to support civil rights activities by Southern blacks. The *Times* did not dispute that factual errors appeared in the ad which was signed by 64 individuals, some of them nationally known. A jury in Alabama found that Commissioner L. B. Sullivan had been libeled and awarded him the full amount he asked. The state's Supreme Court upheld the judgment.

Upon appeal to the U.S. Supreme Court, the Alabama court judgment was reversed. It was held that the possibility of a good-faith critic of government thus being penalized for his criticism "strikes at the very center of the constitutionally protected area of free expression." The justices held such restraint could dampen the vigor and limit the variety of public debate, which is a vital ingredient of the democratic process. Damages could be collected only if the complainant could show that "actual malice" existed. It soon became apparent that this was not easy to do.

The majority opinion said in part:

The present advertisement, as an expression of grievance and protest on one of the major public issues of our time, would seem clearly to qualify for the constitutional protection. The question is whether it forfeits that protection by the falsity of some of its factual statements and by its alleged defamation of respondent. . . .

A rule compelling the critic of official conduct to guarantee the truth of all his factual assertions—and to do so on pain of libel judgments virtually unlimited in amount—leads to a comparable "self-censorship." . . . The rule thus dampens the vigor and limits the variety of public debate. It is inconsistent with the First and Fourteenth Amendments.

The constitutional guarantees require, we think, a federal rule that prohibits a public official from recovering damages for a defamatory falsehood relating to his official conduct unless he proves that the statement was made with "actual malice" —that is, with knowledge that it was false or with reckless disregard of whether it was false or not.

Justice Hugo L. Black, with Justice William O. Douglas joining with him, wrote in a concurring opinion:

An unconditional right to say what one pleases about public affairs is what I consider to be the minimum guarantee of the First Amendment.

I regret that the Court has stopped short of this holding indispensable to preserve our free press from destruction.

During the years since the *New York Times-Sullivan* rule was stated in 1964, many judges have extended it from public officials to public figures associated with public controversies, and, in quite a few instances, to individuals featured in the news. However, where journalists are slovenly, sloppy, or careless, to the extent of professional malpractice, the courts have not hesitated to allow libel damages. Some of these set record highs in the amount of money paid.

Eventually the rule was invoked in defense of a school paper, this time on the University of Arizona campus. A member of the Arizona student senate sued the editor and advisor of the campus paper *Wildcat* for $30,000 libel damages and the *Times-Sullivan* decision was used successfully by defendants (*Klahr* v. *Winterble*, 1966). An editorial in the *Wildcat* attacked student senator Gary Peter Klahr as "the

campus demagogue" who might "so disgust real senators that student government would crash down around our ears." A controversy over campus funds in the student senate triggered the comments. The defendants claimed that Klahr was a "public official" and thus the *Times-Sullivan* rule applied. A state Superior Court judge agreed but Klahr went to the Arizona Court of Appeals. He lost again. The appeals court said it was inappropriate to have one libel law for officials off-campus and another applicable to student government officials upon campuses.

However, legal commentators argue that student journalists still have never clearly been granted the same rights as professional news writers. This caution applies particularly to high school staffers because the case just cited involved a university paper, and other courts have said that what applies to them does not automatically apply for high school students. Thus these younger journalists should be careful that their comments rest on a solid factual base and that the school's orderly operations will not be disrupted.

Areas with the most booby traps for writers and editors of the scholastic press include:

1. Sloppy writing, editing, and makeup,

Tom Little, Nashville Tennessean
Professional journalists such as award-winning cartoonist Tom Little of "Nashville Tennessean" uphold rights, responsibilities of student journalists. (Courtesy Mr. Little and "Tennessean")

including putting the wrong—and infrequently libelous—caption under a picture. Everything should be doublechecked.

2. Coverage of controversial issues where truth may be difficult to determine.

3. Attempts at cuteness for the sake of a wisecrack. The "victim" may not think it was so funny and could sue—if his reputation was damaged.

4. Letters to the Editor. Always confirm that they are authentic.

5. Quotation captions in yearbooks which have possible double meanings or inuendoes.

Two successful libel suits have even involved captions under yearbook photographs. In the one case, damages of a million dollars were asked by a 16-year-old and her family from the Merrick, N.Y., Board of Education, school principal, and yearbook printing concern; it was settled out of court. In the second instance, a ninth-grade junior high student sued the South Orange-Maplewood (N.J.) Board of Education, publication advisor, and yearbook printers in 1970 and was awarded $11,000 for damages to his reputation and $27,000 for mental suffering.

A long-held assumption has been that anyone who could have prevented the libel conceivably could be sued for damages. That includes students—both writer and editor—advisors, printers, principals, superintendents, and even school board members.

State practices vary widely on whether public schools and colleges are agencies of the state itself and can be sued. Some hold that they cannot be; others rule just the opposite way. Staff members and advisors should ascertain the specific legal details for their state and live with them.

One potential way to protect all those who might be sued for libel is for the school to purchase libel insurance. Many commercial publications buy such protection and the potentialities could well be explored by school board members and superintendents who make and approve budgets. Libel insurance protects much the same as property and automobile liability insurance policies.

What's obscene?

Even the U.S. Supreme Court, which is the last authority for answering legal questions, has had great trouble answering this question. It involves so many variables. Although some later decisions have shifted emphasis, the high court's decision in *Roth* v. *United States* (1957) provides the current legal test for obscenity:

Whether to the average person, applying contemporary community standards, the dominant theme of the material taken as a whole appeals to prurient interest.

From the court's point of view, sex and obscenity are not synonymous, a concept that survived long after the Victorian era. Changing mores in United States society have made it hard in contemporary times to define what is legally obscene and what is not. But despite this problem, a majority of the U.S. Supreme Court justices have held that obscene material is not entitled to First Amendment protection.

At least one college editor has been convicted and fined for distributing a "lewd, obscene, indecent, and filthy" article. James Wasserman wrote a piece of fiction for class and received an A. Since he was editor of the *Lanthorn* at Grand Valley State College, Allendale, Mich., he decided to publish it. He was arrested on high misdemeanor charges of distributing obscene material. Found guilty, he was fined $100 although the judge could have sent him to jail for up to a year. Wasserman appealed and the majority of the Michigan Court of Appeals upheld the judge's fine.

A rule of thumb for evaluating possible obscenity: Would you be willing to show the article to your favorite grandmother and tell her that you were the author or an editor who had approved it for publication?

Like professional journalists, student staff members can be held guilty of contempt of court. One college editor learned this in the 1960s. Annette Buchanan, editor of the *Daily Emerald* at the University of Oregon, was subpoenaed to tell a grand jury investigating the drug scene the names of seven unidentified drug users whom she had quoted in the paper. She refused and was fined $300 for contempt. Despite arguments that to force disclosure of confidential news sources was unethical and that the request breached First Amendment guarantees, Miss Buchanan's fine was upheld by the Oregon Supreme Court. During the early 1970s, several professional reporters went to jail for weeks—one almost two months—rather than disclose the identity of confidential news sources.

Copyright is another legal matter that may confront student staffers. Under copyright laws, authors (and that includes artists, photographers, and advertising copy writers, too) are entitled to the "exclusive use" of their creative works. Thus their proprietary rights and financial rewards are safeguarded much as inventors are protected by patents.

Copyright may be a restraint if staffers want material of others that bears proper copyright protection and it may safeguard their own work from pirating, as it were, by others.

☆ Copyright applies to literary style and phraseology, not to ideas or facts.

During the recent years of Xerox and other duplication processes, the whole concept of copyright protection has eroded, especially by academic faculties and students. Also the courts have upheld the "fair use" of otherwise totally protected materials. However, anyone writing for publication should remember that colleagues' efforts are protected for style and terminology if proper procedure has been followed.

Material is protected by copyright only after these specific procedures:

1. A copyright notice must be printed on the front page or the page immediately following. This includes the word, symbol, or abbreviation "Copyright," "©", or "Copr." plus the name of copyright holder and year of copyright: Thus it might read "Copyright 1976 by John Smith" "© 1977 by Central High School News."

2. Two copies of the publication, text, or script must be sent to the Register of Copyrights, Library of Congress, Washington.

3. Proper copyright forms (Form BB) must be filled out and submitted.

4. A $6 fee must be paid.

Regulations for copyright are enacted by Congress under a proviso in the U.S. Constitution. Revision to bring the basic copyright statute of 1909 into conformity with contemporary technology has been attempted in vain for far more than a decade.

☆ Student journalists who follow the prescribed procedures may protect their own writings by copyright.

A somewhat related (but legally different) journalistic sin is plagiarism or appropriating another's writing and passing it off as your own. Copyright is violated only if the necessary procedures have been followed. The "sin" in stealing—and that's what it is—is just as grave for uncopyrighted material. This violates morality and ethics and no responsible journalist would want to be guilty. Editors on literary magazines that print creative pieces are far more likely to encounter plagiarism than those working with news items.

Broadcast Law

Freedoms of the print media, as pointed out earlier, do not transfer directly to broadcasting because, for one thing, licenses are required to use the limited number of airwaves, which belong to the public. Before the initial governmental regulations under the Radio Act of 1927, the situation quite properly was described as "the cacophony of competing voices, none of which could be clearly and predictably heard." Thus federal licensing, barred by the First Amendment for print, was welcomed by broadcasters. Eventually the courts ruled that "a broadcasting license is a public trust subject to termination for breach of duty."

When applying for a license, or for an extension of it, a station must show that it will serve the public good or, according to broadcast law, will perform in "the public convenience, interest, or necessity."

The amount and quality of public service programming thus is an important factor in license applications. A station also must show that it will not abuse its monopolistic use of a channel owned by the public at large. It must demonstrate that its programming has appeal for and will serve at least a substantial portion of the community audience. For renewals, station performance as well as its plans are considered.

Because of the "public trust" aspects, the *Federal Communications Commission* (*FCC*), the government agency that issues licenses and renewals, provides guidelines for broadcasters. Among these, the more prominent are the *equal time provision* and the *fairness doctrine*.

The equal time provision insures that politicians running for the same office can air their views on an equal basis: Same amount of time and at times just as attractive to the audience.

The fairness doctrine requires that stations provide facilities and time for opposing spokesmen of any issue on which they have taken an editorial position. Even more, they must actively seek out such opponents for rebuttal statements.

A student broadcaster might editorialize in favor of year-round classes to economize on the use of existing buildings. Another student may think this an unworkable proposal and marshal arguments against it. In all fairness—and because starting broadcasting stations to air different opinions is impossible—this opponent must be allowed rebuttal on the same medium that carried the original viewpoint.

The in-school "station"—even though not compelled by law to give equal time—certainly is morally bound to do so in any student election campaign.

There is a recent trend to extend this doctrine beyond political personalities to all controversial issues. And often this poses acute problems for a broadcaster. If a station covers a Democratic rally, where strong political speeches are made, it seems reasonable and fair that the Republicans have equal time to present their views.

But suppose a news broadcast reports that a pipeline has burst and spewed an oil slick dangerous to wildlife. Does the oil company have a right to present its case in an attempt to mitigate a bad impression made upon the public? No one really knows in commercial broadcasting. Court and agency decisions have been unclear and confusing.

As a student broadcaster, however, you will want to apply yardsticks of fairness to everything you do.

You will not slight any organization in news coverage, even if you don't like one group.

You will not allow one participant to dominate debating time.

You will not place any person in an embarrassing position or phrase questions that will put an individual in an unfavorable light without a chance of explaining.

☆ Absolute fairness is required in the visual as well as the audio presentation of television.

Television has been a common medium for only about a quarter century, a very short time compared to the existence of newspapers. It is still a developing medium, almost daily finding new techniques to convey information better. So student journalists should spend time watching commercial television newscasts—and listening to those on radio, too. Watch and listen, not as the casual audience usually does, but with the view of seeing what's good and what's bad, why something works or doesn't, and how student broadcasters might emulate the best features of their professional counterparts.

Laws and regulations don't always tell the journalist, either professional or student, what should be done. Rules seek to insure that the more flagrant violations of fairness and propriety will not go unnoticed and unpunished. But really the statutes can never take the place of a built-in code of ethics, a sense of justice, and a feeling for decency.

Like their professional colleagues, student journalists should recognize that with every right goes a responsibility, with every freedom goes a duty, and with every liberty goes an obligation.

BOOK

THE SCHOOL NEWSPAPER

These faces are Black Letter

Gathering the News

As a reporter, you are sort of a juggler who has to keep two objects in the air at the same time. You have dual goals: (a) gathering facts about an event or an idea where you serve as eyes and ears of the news audience; and (b) presenting the information with accuracy and a flair to capture the interest of readers and listeners. Unless you both gather and write the news carefully and well, it's almost sure to be poor journalism.

You will go out to find facts, to dig out details—no matter how reluctant a news source may be to answer your questions or how difficult it may be to locate someone who knows what really happened. Then you will have to present the information, no matter how complicated, so that readers and listeners will be interested in what you saw and heard—and will understand it. When you succeed, that is good journalism.

Relman (Pat) Morin, Associated Press correspondent who won two Pulitzer Prizes, explained his preparation for a series:

How do you go about it? First, by saturating yourself in ABC information, reading yourself blind. Then, having acquired a small base, you begin interviewing, talking to as many technicians with as many different points of view as possible. But the Moment of Truth is still to come. This is when you feel ready to start writing. For now you confront a whole different problem, "How do I make this clear and interesting for the reader

who has little or no background knowledge?"

Not all journalists are highly proficient at both collecting and writing news. That is sad—but true. In fact, on some metropolitan dailies, a *leg man*—who can be either male or female—may be on the scene figuratively soaking up all the information and a *rewrite man* in the office may handle the assembly and writing of the facts. On a school paper, however, staff members should strive to do both functions—successfully, it is hoped—because that will better prepare them for careers later. And when both functions are done well, you are acting—as you should—as stand-in for the news audience. You are an eyewitness to history in the making and thus performing as a high-level professional journalist.

In this chapter, you will learn about gathering the facts; and in the next, you will read about news writing.

☆ A reporter obtains information from a wide range of sources.

A skillful reporter obtains facts and background from:

1. Direct observation or an "I Was There" approach;

2. Direct interviewing of individuals who were involved in the event or can supply background; and

3. Use of reference materials such as clippings in the morgue, school records available to the media, notes on a police

blotter, publicity news releases, or advance texts. Releases and advance texts also are known as *handouts*.

As a reporter, you might be on hand in person for a big news event. This undoubtedly would be true for most lectures, ball games, news conferences, and other scheduled happenings. Then you report what you saw, heard, and felt. But there are far more reportable things that are not planned in advance, such as accidents, fires, robberies, teen-age rumbles, and other unexpected surprises. For these, you have to depend on secondhand accounts from witnesses or participants. And that procedure could involve you with all the hazards of unreliability of subjective recall, special-interest prejudice, and personal bias.

To illustrate, as a reporter at a baseball game you note the play-by-play but also go to the dressing rooms and talk to players and coaches. You could interview the umpires and quote them on the reasons for a decision that brought boos from the home fans. And even before you enter the press box to cover the first inning, you would have obtained a copy of the team's previous victories and defeats, listing of players and their uniform numbers, and individuals' records to date.

If a local celebrity is talking at your school assembly, you should follow the pattern of the professional journalist in covering a story. Before you go to the auditorium, even long before the speaker ever reaches the school, you look up the speaker's background in clippings and reference books. During the talk, you note the chief points in the presentation, jotting down key quotations so that you have an accurate record of the actual words for later use. You may talk to the individual or to the principal to find out further details—if there are loose ends dangling at the end of the assembly.

During the interview with the speaker, you gather additional information that can be added to your main account or handled as a *sidebar* or *with story* that is printed alongside the main account. Major news events often rate this additional coverage so readers are adequately informed.

☆ Don't bother the speaker for information available from other sources.

Such background material is found in printed references such as *Who's Who in America*, news clippings, or from faculty members who may know the speaker.

If the assignment is to cover a fire, you would approach the job differently and could be on the scene when the flames swept high and then a wall collapsed with a great roar. But you would also talk with eyewitnesses who saw the first flames crackling out of a second-story window. You would have had no advance notice but you could interview experts on the scene, seeking information of a special sort that might not be readily available from just watching the blaze. For instance, you could ask the senior fire department official about the probable cause, the number of fire fighters and the kind of equipment on hand, and whether there were any injuries. Of the building owner, you would inquire about insurance and seek an estimate of the total damages. You would, in short, seek out anyone who had information about the blaze that your readers would like to know.

Let's cite a specific case history. You have been told to gather information for a news story on an explosion and small fire in your school's chemistry laboratory.

First, you would locate some students who were in the lab when the accident took place. You would interview the teacher, too. Since they were all at the scene, they might be expected to relate just what happened. However, individuals see, hear, smell, and feel things in different ways.

So you follow the plan of most experienced reporters and seek out various eyewitnesses and try to reconstruct the incident from what they tell. Obviously not perfection but the method is usually better than depending on a single observer.

In the case of the laboratory explosion and fire, you could question the student who shouted the first warning as follows:

"Just where did you see the flame start?"
"How big was it?"
"What color was it?"
"Was equipment knocked over?"
"What equipment?"

"What was the student at that desk doing?"

"What was the student's name?"

"Where was the teacher?"

"What did he do?"

"What did other students do? Sound a fire alarm?"

Then you interview the student at whose desk the explosion occurred. It turns out that his back was turned momentarily when the flame started so he hasn't the details of what first happened, but he tells you about the equipment that the previous student could not see.

You talk to the teacher. He was not looking at the desk where the accident started but was helping other students. But he does tell you about the damage and gives a tentative estimate of the cost of replacing equipment.

So from the accounts of three eyewitnesses of various phases of the explosion and fire, you have enough information to start reconstructing what happened at the first flash, the effects of the blast, and an estimate of the damage done. Possibly you might have obtained more details if you had been in the laboratory at the time of the blast but then you, too, might not have been looking at the desk when the first flame shot out and you would have difficulty making an accurate estimate of damage if you had never bought laboratory supplies.

Professional reporters try to prepare in advance for interviewing, providing there is lead time before it takes place. This can be done for talks at a convention, visiting celebrities, and retiring faculty members. High school journalists should do this in preparation:

1. Find out about the individual you will interview;

2. Find out about the topic you hope to have discussed; and

3. Draft a few sample questions that you hope will be discussed.

☆ The more background you know about the individual and topic, the better your story will be.

If you are adequately prepared, you will not make the classic error of a young (and obviously inferior) cub reporter who asked a visiting state governor, "By the way, sir, what line of work are you in?"

Predetermined questions will give you a roadmap for an interview. They may prove especially handy in case you get stage fright when you enter "the presence." However, never let your previous thinking stand in the way of an even better story if it unexpectedly develops. If a news angle that is entirely new comes up, pursue it and forget the carefully thought-out (but possibly stereotyped) questions.

Although the interview is described as "the most perilous and unreliable method" for gathering information, it remains the essential means by which reporters obtain information for print and broadcast. So you should turn to what social scientists and professional reporters have found. Students who want to probe the techniques in detail are referred to Eugene J. Webb and Jerry R. Salancik, *The Interview or The Only Wheel in Town*. (This may be obtained as Journalism Monograph No. 2, from the Association for Education In Journalism University of Minnesota, Minneapolis, Minn.)

Since interviewing is a one-on-one relationship, practically any individual characteristic may play some role, either helping or hindering the quest for facts. Appearance and manner can help determine whether a news source will provide a flood of superb quotations or a string of "no comments." Age, too, is a factor. Professional pollsters have found that young people are more inclined to express their antiestablishment attitudes to younger interviewers. Males generally are less able than females to obtain revealing answers. Also, Blacks may reply differently depending on whether the interviewer is black or white, especially if the questions involve race-related topics. The key, apparently, is to have both interviewer and interviewee relate to each other.

☆ Questions should be kept simple and clear.

Wording of questions influences replies. The phrasing of a question may subtly hint

Typical reporter's notes. Check marks are made later by reporter in organizing story, to indicate importance of item. Usually 8½ x 11 copy paper is folded into thirds for note-taking.

that one answer is "better"—more socially acceptable. Words with double meanings should be avoided. A long question may be so involved that many respondents will lose the train of thought and reply inaccurately to what the respondent thinks is the question. If the topic is unfamiliar, it may be desirable to preface the question with an explanatory paragraph; then both questioner and respondent are in the same ball park of attitudes and opinions.

Indications of the reporter's interest and responsiveness also tend to bring longer and more detailed answers. Devices that some experimenters use to obtain more detailed replies included nodding the head, leaning forward, and muttering appreciatively, "Mm-hmm." These feedbacks to the person being interviewed built a common bridge and that brought longer and more detailed responses.

Covering speeches or conventions, which are primarily just a whole series of speeches, is a fairly frequent news assignment for student and professional reporters. Covering high school assemblies is one easy way to prepare for what will be a common—and maybe even your first—assignment as a professional. Ascertain background on the individual and the probable topic, as outlined earlier. As the speech starts, you take notes, much as you would during an interview. You, in effect, note the highlights and jot down any pithy remarks so that you may write them out in full as *direct quotes*. Thus you will have—in your mind and reinforced by your notes—a bobtailed sound track of what the speaker said. From this, you construct a news story.

Other frequent assignments involve individuals being honored, elected to clubs, chosen as officers, starred in sports or dramas. To report on these folks, you interview them. Talk to their friends—and their enemies. Go to their teachers. Search out data in school records, either official papers that the principal allows you to see or previous school publications, such as newspapers and yearbooks.

☆ Different types of news demand different procedures for coverage.

Some news rests primarily on eyewitness accounts and a reporter tells what he or she sees. Others depend on information gathered from other persons and this is obtained by interviewing participants or experts who know what you want to find out.

If you are assigned to cover a track meet, you might sit in the press box and keep account of all the events, you might concentrate on a couple of stellar performances of potential record breakers by being close to those contest areas, or you might do a color story by sitting with the spectators and watching their reactions. If you are covering the school play, you might sit in the audience or, with permission, go backstage and tell what none of the spectators saw. If you are explaining new hair-style regulations of the Board of Education, you would interview the superintendent, principal, and student government officers.

Beat assignments are a regular part of news coverage. Beat news sources that provide material are checked frequently in person to see what has happened since the last issue. This promotes confidence by interviewing the individuals as they learn to respect your professional approach. Al-

though you should make a special effort to see the news sources in person, you could use the telephone in an exceptional emergency. So obtain the phone numbers of persons on your beat so that you may call for some point you forgot or something that needs clarifying.

No matter whether the assignment is to observe an event or to interview some individual, a good reporter has the tools of his trade: Pencil and paper. They are as much a part of successful performance as a properly loaded camera is for a staff photographer.

Professional reporters frequently use white or yellow copy paper folded into thirds along the shorter direction like a three-partition folding screen. They write on the one outside first, then the middle section, and next on the final third. They are careful to number each third so that there is no confusion as to the order of thirds or of whole sheets. Other reporters prefer a notebook because this permits more orderly preservation of notes as ready reference for a longer time.

During a lengthy interview, a professional may have many pages of notes and, to help organize them, may mark the more important points as some papers rate motion pictures—with stars. Thus a topic of key importance might rate three or four stars, while subordinate material would merit only one or two stars. Least important material is left unstarred.

Reporters on daily papers or press associations have to write their news items promptly, but those working on monthly or quarterly publications may not feel such deadline pressures. Even then, professional journalists transcribe their notes promptly before they forget some of the supplementary matter that was not written down. When such a reporter comes to write the final copy, the typed-out versions are organized into a completed story. School reporters should write up notes promptly, too, because their memories are no better than others.

Many beginners ask, "Should I learn shorthand?" There is no single, simple answer to the question. British professional journalists are required to know shorthand. This is not true in the United States. As a general rule, if a journalist is well skilled with shorthand, such expertise can be tremendously helpful; but if a reporter has to think about the shorthand symbols as much as about the questions to be asked, forget it. To bridge this difficulty, many American reporters devise their own shorthand with, for instance, "Gov" for governor, "myr" for mayor, and so forth.

☆ Any system of abbreviations that you can use effectively and efficiently is O.K.

Although you go on an assignment with scant physical supplies of a couple of sharpened pencils and a sheaf of scratch paper, always remember intangibles that are of the greatest importance:

Have an inquiring mind;

Do not accept statements without weighing and, if need be, challenging them;

Pry out details that others failed to note;

Cultivate capacity for observation to gather colorful details and without bias; and

Be a responsible citizen.

Meyer Berger, late Pulitzer Prize-winner whose color stories are included in many anthologies of good journalism, frequently spent hours reenacting the events of his assigned story. Once he climbed through a jail window to find additional colorful bits for an account of a prisoner's escape. He wanted to know what the man saw as he crawled into the open. He was a perfectionist for those details that create an aura of reality.

A reporter's intangibles are important to the public, too. Unless the people in a democracy are adequately informed and enlightened, they will not have the bases for making wise decisions. One newspaper editor explained it this way: "The reporter is as essential to the healthy working of our democratic society as the politician." And some in the post-Watergate period would argue that it was a gross understatement.

So it is with high school papers, too. A responsible staff presents the news which students need to keep a school operating as a productive democracy. For such an informed public the paper then provides editorial leadership to clarify student goals, values, and responsibilities.

For both high school and professional papers, the process begins with a reporter gathering facts, accurately, fully, and without any bias.

7

Writing the News

A journalist who has gathered all the facts and sits down to write a news story is like a chef in a kitchen who has all the ingredients for baking a cake. In both cases, a lot more remains to be done.

Information about an event must be put together skillfully to attract and keep readers and listeners, just as an expert cook whips eggs, sifts flour, melts butter, and folds them into the batter for a delicious pastry. It isn't just throwing things together in haphazard fashion. Both news writer and cook have to know what they are doing.

A classic newspaper organization of information is to put the most important—the most startling, interesting, or significant—in the first paragraph. Next comes the second most important, and so on down the ranking until the least significant is at the end. This arrangement is known as the *inverted pyramid*. Such a presentation is a far cry from the chronological treatment favored by fiction writers who may start at the beginning and go through in sequence to the final scene.

Both of these techniques have pluses and minuses. Among the advantages of the inverted pyramid are:

1. Readers get the guts of the news at a glance. Thus curiosity is satisfied early. If not especially interested in more details, a reader need not continue to the end of the article for fear of missing something important.

2. If the story needs to be compressed to fit available space, it is more conveniently *cut* during makeup or pasteup by chopping off the last few paragraphs. They contain the least essential facts. With a chronological arrangement, middle segments would have to be eliminated—or the whole story reconstructed.

However, chronological sequence may be favored when a writer wants to start in low pitch and build up to a climax toward the end. Here readers have to finish the item to get vital information. The popular news weeklies often utilize chronological presentations because their editors assume that readers will finish articles once they start.

Other arrangements have their advocates and advantages, too. Some stories start out with a wisecrack that gathers attention and readers have to go on to find out the resolution. Frequently this is used for short, often humorous, items known as *shorts* or *brights*. Other techniques may be tried and if they attract and hold an audience, the writer has succeeded.

☆ Ways to write news are limited only by reporters' lack of imagination or inventiveness.

☆ Don't overdo experimentation in news style—but don't avoid it entirely.

The first paragraph or *lead* (pronounced leed) of an inverted pyramid story, obviously, summarizes the essential facts of an event and so it is called a *summary lead*. It answers those questions that are always in readers' minds: Who? What? When?

Where? Why? And, sometimes, How? In the journalistic jargon, these are the 5 W's.

Any one of six answers to these questions could provide the initial point to start a lead paragraph. Here are illustrations of how the same facts could be organized to feature the answer to any one of them:

WHO?

Principal John McQuire announced at Wednesday's weekly assembly that students will have to attend school on the Thursday before Easter, previously listed as a holiday, because of time lost last month when the "big snow" caused cancellation of classes.

WHAT?

Classes will meet on the Thursday before Easter, previously listed as a holiday, so that students may make up time lost last month when school was closed because of the "big snow."

WHEN?

On Wednesday Principal John McQuire told students at the weekly assembly that they will have to attend classes on the Thursday before Easter to make up time lost during the "big snow."

WHERE?

At the weekly assembly, Principal John McQuire, told students that they will have to attend classes on the Thursday before Easter to make up class time lost during the "big snow."

WHY?

To make up time lost because Central High School was closed last month because of the "big snow," students will have to attend classes on the Thursday before Easter.

HOW?

By attending classes on the Thursday before Easter, previously listed as a holiday, students will make up time lost when Central High School was closed last month.

To keep lead paragraphs from becoming overly long, experienced reporters may drop several of the answers to the 5 W's into the second or third paragraphs. Leads that feature answers to "When?" and "Where?" need to have special appropriateness to be effective because time and place seldom merit such stress. "Who?" and "What?" are standard and conventional. You can seldom be far off target with either of these, but sometimes others are even better.

☆ Don't clutter your lead paragraph with verbiage.

How a professional journalist effectively organized the 5 W's for what some consider the greatest news story of our generation is this beginning on the main story in the *New York Times* during July 1969:

HOUSTON, Monday, July 21—Men have landed and walked on the moon.

Two Americans, astronauts of Apollo 11, steered their fragile four-legged module safely and smoothly to the historic landing yesterday at 4:17:40 P.M. Eastern Standard Time.

Neil A. Armstrong, the 38-year-old civilian commander, radioed to earth and the mission control room here:

"Houston. Tranquility Base here. The Eagle has landed."

The first men to reach the moon—Mr. Armstrong and his co-pilot, Col. Edwin E. Aldrin Jr. of the Air Force—brought their ship to rest on a level, rock-strewn plain near the southwestern shore of the arid Sea of Tranquility.

About six and a half hours later, Mr. Armstrong opened the landing craft's hatch, stepped slowly down the ladder and declared as he planted the first human footprint on the lunar crust:

"That's one small step for man, one giant leap for mankind." . . .

Since it is best to learn the traditions first and then experiment after the basics have been mastered, cub reporters should be sure they can write effective summary leads before they venture far into esoteric experimentations. A beginner has to practice fundamentals of news writing just as a candidate for varsity football blocks and tackles repeatedly during early training.

Let's look at an example of inverted pyramid organization in a well-written news item. This story from the Kirkwood, Mo., *Call,* was developed from the bare informa-

Summary lead paragraph

Details on scope of contest

Contest procedures

Details of what was submitted

Quote from teacher

Details of judging

Details on essay topics

tion that two students had won a national writing competition into an article that is not only informative but has "people interest" about how they had done the prize-winning work plus their opinions on when and how students should learn basic writing skills:

Alice Chupp and Mike Holley, seniors, have been honored by the National Council of Teachers of English (NCTE) as winners of the NCTE Achievement Award in Writing.

Over 6,200 juniors across the nation competed for the NCTE citations. Of that number, only 850 finalists were selected. Alice and Mike were two of the 16 finalists chosen from Missouri.

The NCTE writing contest is held annually beginning in January. KHS nominated five contestants last spring, who were chosen in a blind writing competition judged by seven teachers.

Each nominated student submitted samples of his or her best writing, including an autobiographical sketch. They also wrote a one-hour impromptu essay, which this year consisted of penning a letter to one character in literature, films, or television.

"The topic came from the National Council," stated Mrs. Thelma Larsen, English department chairman, "and no one saw it ahead of time."

These materials were evaluated by state judging teams of college and high school English teachers directed by state coordinators.

Alice's essay topic was a letter to "Gregor Samsa" from the book *Metamorphosis,* while Mike addressed his to Roy Campanella.

"I had no trouble with the essay," Mike related, "but finding my best pieces of work turned into a mess. I wanted to send them a paper I had done earlier, so I went to Mrs. Larsen the day before the deadline to pick it up.

Quotes from winner

More quotes

Another quote from winner

Quote from other winner

More quotes

Still more quotes

Combined indirect quotes

"I forgot, though, that the department throws all English work away," he lamented. "So I typed up a story that night, making it up as I went along.

"By 12:30 a.m. I had collapsed over my typewriter, still trying to end the story somehow. I really didn't know how it ended until I finished!"

Both Alice and Mike disagree with the recent criticism leveled at high school English programs. "Junior high is the place to learn the fundamentals of writing," Alice commented. "High school courses should reinforce the basic writing skills.

"The problem lies in picking the right courses at high school," she continued. "Several electives which I took—like 'American Dream' and 'Gothic Novel'—really helped me."

"Kids don't have as many bad habits or ideas formed at the junior high level," Mike agreed. "If they learn right early, they won't forget it.

"In fact, eighth grade creative writing helped me most. I picked up skills early that other students don't have now."

Natural talent and reading ability definitely determine whether a student will become a good writer, according to both Mike and Alice.

A dramatic or exciting news event does not require synthetic heightening by overwriting. In fact, such attempts ruin the built-in emotion for many readers.

☆ When you write a dramatic story, don't gild the lily.

Speaking of his first by-line as a young reporter, Pat Morin, whom we already met in the previous chapter, told a story admonitory to any reporter who wants to overwrite.

Before World War II, Morin worked as a cub for the *Shanghai Evening Post*. Because he was the only newsman in the office, the managing editor had to assign him to cover a mass murder. Ten Chinese had been chopped to death with a cleaver. Morin returned and sat at his typewriter striving for a "shattering, Grand Canyon lead" when his editor offered some advice. As Morin recalled it years later:

As though from a distance, I heard the boss saying, "—don't write this at all."

I came to with a shock. "What do you mean?"

"Don't write it," he said. "Let it tell

itself. Tell it as you told it to me, in plain words, the plainer the better. . . . Use the quote. Use details that add to the visual picture. Take the customers inside that house and let them see it and smell it. But play it low. This story tells itself. It doesn't need anything from you."

If news gathering has been done extensively and carefully, this advice applies to most straight news stories. The essential job is to provide the readers with information "in plain words." Feature articles, which we will discuss later, are not quite so rigid, but many, many straight news events can be covered best by letting the story "tell itself."

Types of News Stories

A school newspaper or news magazine eventually might print every type of news story, including crimes, demonstrations, and even violence, and certainly politics, social, and civic events. Chances are high that the news in high school publications will fall into certain major categories, much like those in any daily.

For both school and professional papers, meetings and speeches are a backbone of coverage. In your paper, you might cover speakers and announcements at general assemblies or talks before departmental clubs just as your hometown daily prints news on Rotary and Lions' club meetings and other civic groups.

A conventional formula for covering a speech follows, one side indicating topics in your notes and the other showing how the material was arranged in a news story:

Notes
1. Glad to be at school.
2. Recalls when daughter attended school.
3. Water safety important as summer approaches.
4. Funny thing that happened to me while teaching swim safety.
5. Key safety rule.
6. Ten rules for safe swimming.
7. Summary conclusion.
8. Hopes to see students in swim classes.

News story
1. Key safety rule.
2. Water safety important as summer is approaching. (Direct quotation.)
3. Ten rules in safe swimming. (Omit 1, 2, 4, 7, 8 from story.)

Since many readers like to know what a person said in a talk, you sprinkle your copy with direct quotes from careful notes you made of pithy, colorful, and interesting comments. Some quotations point up a viewpoint so well that they are incorporated into common usage. For instance, "stagflation" was first used to describe the United States economy during a public meeting of experts and almost immediately gained wide popular use to describe when both inflation and recession hit at the same time.

When you quote an individual, you actually hold a public image in your hands. If you misquote and injure a reputation, that person has every right to be angry and hold you responsible. When you paraphrase what a man or woman says, you should not use quotation marks. These are your words, not the speaker's. However, it is not necessary —practically always space wasting—to include every "you know" and every "uh, uh" that a person includes, unthinkingly, in comments.

When a daily paper once wanted to launch an editorial campaign against the mayor, the city editor instructed the City Hall reporter not to polish up the direct quotations from the city executive. After a couple of days, the mayor got the paper's message and decided to agree with its editorial policy rather than continue to have verbatim quotations in print. A slight touch of journalistic blackmail? Yes; but probably for a good cause. At least the incident shows the power of verbatim quotes.

Most individuals do not speak entirely grammatically. What is heard as satisfactory language looks poor indeed in print. Reporters must remember that and their consciences have to be their guides on just how verbatim direct quotations should be.

☆ Quotations should convey the essence of truth.

A good test would be: Could you go back to the speaker with the quotation—and have an overwhelming belief that there would be no objections on the grounds of inaccuracy?

Covering a session or convention where there are a number of speakers and some business actions, including election of officers and passage of resolutions, is much like reporting a single speaker. This time, again, you pick the most important point for your lead paragraph. In the third or fourth graf, you may follow a common practice of professional journalists and summarize other important items that happened. Then you conclude the coverage of the topic you put in the lead. If there is enough space, you expand on the items you summarized in the third or fourth paragraph. Obviously, the inverted pyramid applies to both speakers and comments. If the resolutions or assembly announcements are more important than what any speaker said, lead with them and put the quotations in secondary ranking.

To illustrate, suppose that senior class election results are announced at a student government organization meeting, which also discusses plans for a senior class picnic, hears a request for allocation of additional funds for the spring track season, and listens to an AFS exchange student. Obviously, each of these could be a separate news item, but if you had space for only one comprehensive story, you could handle it like this:

1. Lead paragraph on senior class election results;

2. Additional information on statistics and names of losers;

3. Names of lesser officers chosen;

4. Plans for senior class picnic;

5. Disposition of spring track allocation request;

6. AFS student's talk;

7. Expansion on new senior president with school career and possible quote in plans for future activities;

8. Additional information on other officers and what they hope to do; and

9. Necessary details on senior class picnic.

Students who do unusual things rate *personals* on their prize-winning stamp collection or an accident that hospitalizes a varsity athlete just as do their parents in the local daily. With personals, it usually is best to use a summary lead paragraph and then develop details. Exceptions may be when there is heavy *human interest* or emotional material that demands feature treatment.

Trend pieces and *backgrounders* are less conventional news that require a reporter to dig out information that is not obvious. For instance, what has been the trend in graduates going to college? What schools have they selected? How has this changed over the past 10 to 20 years? What are popular majors? Or what's behind the new order for split sessions? What happens to the annual school budgets with two required sessions each day? What explanation does the school superintendent have? What do school board members say? This information may help students understand what is happening.

Advance stories are a regular news category especially useful for school papers. They help editors who dread to write repeatedly about events that students already know about. You may tell about the cast of the senior play that will open in two weeks and give a summary of the plot of the drama. You might list some of the forthcoming assembly speakers and provide information on their careers and qualifications.

Sometimes you may want to gather reactions from a number of people. These are known as *roundups*. Roughly, these resemble surveys or public-opinion polling but they are highly informal. For instance, where did faculty members spend their spring vacations? You might report on a half dozen or dozen teachers who went to faraway or unusual places. Or you might ask the same questions of selected students. Or what do students think of the proposal to offer a Russian language course for the first time? Or how do teachers react to a suggestion that all students be allowed to take one course each semester on a pass-fail basis and receive no letter grade?

Both high school and commercial papers devote considerable space to sports. A sports writer follows the same basics as any other reporter but has to have a background in the sport being covered. A girl reporter who had never seen a soccer game would be a poor choice for covering such an event. But, if she knew the rules and regulations of that game—as some do—there is no valid reason why she should be passed over for that job.

Sports writers, on many publications, have more freedom to experiment in writing, but beginners should remember that, to borrow a hackneyed expression for the 1000th time—even the 99th—is a grave journalistic sin. Originality is fine but clichés are minuses. And sports writers tend to indulge in such usage more than most other reporters.

As a wise observer of media once said, too few players hit a ball anymore; on the sports pages, they wallop the horsehide, the spheroid, the pill, or the pellet. Few teams win a game; according to sports writers, they trounce, spank, annihilate, top, or tally a win. And athletes are labeled gridders, hoopsters, thinclads, or warriors. The clichés have worn to disintegration but many writers don't seem to know that, especially cub reporters.

Is it any journalistic sin to talk about just plain, old-fashioned players, a baseball, or a football victory?

Mechanics of News Writing

The formula for typing a news story is almost as standardized as the way you conduct a track meet. Here are some of the rules:

1. In the upper left corner of each page of copy, put the *slug,* a short identification, and the page number. On the second line, put your name and home room or phone number. The top of a page might look like this:

French Club—page 1
James (Room 11-B)
or
Honors assembly—3
Kline (698-2298)

2. Begin the body of the story about half-way down on the first sheet. Thus the *copy*

editor may write an identification slug or possibly the headline itself in the open space.

3. Leave about an inch of white space at the top of subsequent pages.

4. Always double-space copy. Some editors even have staff writers triple-space news copy.

5. Never write on both sides of a page.

6. Type the word "more" at the bottom of each page except the last one. On the final page indicate the end of the story with an appropriate symbol, such as "30," "###," "—0—" or your initials.

7. Avoid hyphenating a word at the end of a line. If you do, the typesetter doesn't know whether it should be "copy-reader" or "copyreader" in print.

8. Do not split paragraphs at the end of a page.

9. *Adds* and *inserts* should be marked and should include the slugline. Inserts should indicate plainly on what page and after what paragraph the new material is to be placed.

Always remember that before you hand in a story, you must check copy for errors, such as spelling, grammar, and typographical mistakes. Use copyreading symbols. Also be doubly careful of proper names, addresses, and dates, where errors might be especially difficult for copyreaders to catch.

An add or addition is further information that a reporter attaches to the original copy. For instance, it may be new facts obtained from another news source just before the deadline. If the new facts are of primary importance, the lead and top paragraphs should be rewritten to include them. Or such information may be handled as an insert near the top of the story and pasted between paragraphs already in typed copy or set into type.

A really effective writer is able to transfer facts and ideas with minimum distortion and little effort on the part of the reader. This is the goal whether of a writer of a best-selling novel or a reporter telling of an event that will shock readers around the globe. Most experienced reporters have developed their own guidelines for great writing. These rules have almost become second nature for them. If you asked them how they do it, they would agree on a set of axioms that would look something like this:

1. Organize your ideas and facts before you start to write. This takes time but it is a worthwhile investment because thus you will have a design to follow.

2. Write naturally with words that come readily to mind. These usually will be short and familiar ones and easily understood by readers.

3. Seek vivid nouns and verbs, cutting down on adjectives and adverbs that add little and clutter your prose with verbiage.

4. Use active verbs; avoid the passive.

5. Strive for shorter, rather than longer, sentences—but vary the length to prevent monotony. The same is true for paragraph lengths.

6. Use humanizing details, anecdotes, and examples to make your story come alive. Try to dramatize statistics.

7. Translate technical jargon but be scrupulously accurate.

8. Be clear. Avoid shortcuts, such as initials for organizations' names that may confuse readers.

9. Keep yourself and your opinions out of a news story. (This embargo does not apply if you witness a spectacular event such as a bank robbery or assassination attempt; in such cases, you are writing an eyewitness story, not straight news.)

10. Always remember that your goal is to get facts and ideas into the readers' minds with minimum effort on their part. This forces *you* to work harder.

A small book, available in hardcover or paperback, will be most helpful in developing your writing skills. It is *The Elements of Style* by William Strunk, Jr. and E. B. White.

News writing is a learnable skill which uses many techniques. It is also a talent which may be inherited but also can be strengthened. The successful journalist develops both.

Writing Commentary

An unrelated fact, it has been said, may be one of the most misleading things in the world. Raw facts, because they are hard, unyielding, and indisputable, require more than just straight news treatment if readers are to get the most rewards from their newspapers.

So a responsible editor needs material that puts the facts in their proper perspectives. That is why there is such a wide opportunity for feature articles, news analyses, personality sketches, and even humorous anecdotes that humanize the newsmakers. The problems of getting good background thus confront student editors and writers just as they do professionals.

In the previous chapter, reporters were warned to keep their emotions out of their reportage and write without bias, prejudice, or personal feeling to influence the reader. This chapter will tell how a publication influences and aids readers in understanding events and provides perspectives for making up their minds.

Feature Articles

Readers always are interested in the story behind the news. Journalists are asked repeatedly, "What's the real story?" or "What's behind it all?" It is as if what got into print were only the surface of what happened. That's partly true. If reporters wrote only as if they were inhuman tape recorders and movie cameras, the questions would be justified. But more and more of contemporary coverage includes just the material to answer these queries. Great journalistic efforts go into providing the perspective of the news. That is done through interpretation, background, analysis, and human interest. Readers also want to know about the personalities of persons in the news. In brief, what makes them tick? That information is supplied in personality sketches or *profiles*.

John F. Kennedy once put his finger directly on this aspect of reader interest. According to Benjamin C. Bradlee, executive editor of the *Washington Post*, the late president told him, "What makes journalism so fascinating and biography so interesting is the struggle to answer that single question: 'What's he like?'"

Unlike straight news writing, where much of success rests with effectively organizing information in an inverted pyramid format, feature-article writing may adapt some of the ingenuity of the fiction writer—while sticking solidly with the basic facts. The information must be scrupulously accurate but how one presents it is limited only by lack of imagination. Some of the effectiveness depends, of course, on how well facts are collected before the writing begins.

A feature may range from an oddity or bright of one or two paragraphs—just long enough to provide a chuckle or surprise—to many, many columns in a series of background and explanations on, say, a pending school bond issue and why it should be passed or all aspects of drug use by students.

To illustrate, here are some shorts:

As a project of his art classes, the wall in Mr. Pat Riley's room (S102) is getting a new coat of paint.

Advocate, John Marshall High,
Oklahoma City, Okla.

In his second period chemistry class, Mr. Zook accidentally stumbled over the trash can. He calmly remarked, "I kicked the bucket."

Star, Halifax County Senior High,
South Boston, Va.

A batch of individually dull school statistics can be turned into an attractive feature:

School sometimes seems long and dragged-out. What would you say if somebody asked you, "How much time have you been in school this year?" You would probably say about 66 days if you haven't been absent at all. But what would the questioner's reaction be if you said, "Well, we started school August 19, and today is November 27, so . . . I've been in school 243 hours or if you prefer, 14,580 minutes or better yet, 874,800 seconds!"

To continue your education at Humble High, did you know that . . .

. . . there are approximately 2,146 desks along with 245 light switches?

. . . there are 98 faculty members at HHS?

. . . on an average day, the cafeteria uses six gallons of ketchup?

. . . enrolled in Humble High as of today there are 1301 students?

Purple Pride, Humble High,
Humble, Texas.

Here's another oddity:

Why did senior Dave Emery join LUK, senior girls club?

"I did it for different reasons. I did it because of a dare, to see if it could be done, and to find out people's reactions," said Dave, who is the first boy to join a girls club at UAHS.

"Some people think I'm crazy, some don't believe it, and others think it is kind of neat," he added.

Dave decided to join LUK when club secretary Sally Schaffner asked if anyone in her class would like to join the senior girls' club. Dave said yes, just to see what Sally would do. She gave him an information sheet to fill out and he paid the $1 dues.

Officially, he is a member. However, he has not yet attended any meetings, although he might do some of the club's activities if they are interesting to him. . . .

Arlingtonian, Upper Arlington High,
Upper Arlington, Ohio.

The longer feature articles come in a wide assortment, like human beings. Chief categories include:

· 1. *Interpretative* or *news features.* These help readers make more sense out of the jumble of events in the news. They build on the essential information in straight news items by providing explanations, background, analyses, or—as their title says—interpretation. One technique used by both school and commercial papers is a question-and-answer approach.

2. *Human interest.* These may be full-length personality sketches with a special humanizing touch. Highlights relevant to the news context are included but not everything in the person's life that might be in the résumé of a job hunter. To get away from the obvious or the routine in a personality story, you might try such ingenious interviewing techniques as ascertaining traits and habits that can be linked to the news situation and asking about the person's secret longings and dreams—the Walter Mitty personality. In writing this feature, you avoid the obvious clichés such as "soft-spoken" or "pipe-puffing" unless they have special relevance. Avoid saying "doesn't look like a high school teacher" unless you can be sure that most of the faculty fit a rigid stereotype that all students recognize. *The New Yorker* weekly prints such outstanding personality sketches under the title of "Profile" that the word now is used as a name for this category.

3. *Surveys* or public opinion and attitude *polls.* People like to know what others are

Editorial page of "Shield" of McCallum High, Austin, Texas, gives letters from readers top billing. Staffers make great effort to encourage such opinions from student body.

thinking and one way to find out is to conduct a survey. To be truly scientific is a highly complicated procedure but any editor can get readable copy by sending reporters out to talk with students. However, when you try this, you should make efforts to balance your sample with the total characteristics of the entire student body. For instance, if you have two-thirds upperclassmen in your results when there are far more freshmen and sophomores in your school, then your findings will be unscientific, slanted, and probably plain skewed.

Also be sure your questions are not loaded to favor one particular viewpoint. Test the key ideas without tying them to personalities who are popular or unpopular. If you asked about a proposal and tied it to a highly controversial figure, your results could be measuring popularity of the individual, not attitudes toward the plan. Furthermore, it would be silly to find out that students opposed double sessions that would separate friends and possibly inconvenience

them when you should be asking them to evaluate possible alternatives that were realistic.

4. *Anniversary* or *historical*. When any school or club celebrates an anniversary— 10th, 25th, or 50th—it's worth a feature. Some papers publish full issues on such school anniversaries and these are kept through the years as are annual yearbooks. Most students are intrigued by the historical background of their school and the way generations move through rapidly from year to year. If your school is named for a prominent individual, you should consider at least one feature each year about that person's life. If a principal has been at the school for 10 years, an appropriate feature might be done on him or her and what happened at the school during the decade; this would blend anniversary and personality types into a single article.

5. *Seasonal* or holidays. Much the same as the previous group, these are geared to special occasions such as Thanksgiving, Christmas, Washington's Birthday, Easter, and graduation. Some holiday occurs every single day so you have a wide selection.

6. *Vacation* and travel. Good features can be developed on what students and teachers did during their summer or between-semester vacations. An enterprising staff will pry these out. When a large proportion of stu-

Investigative reporting need not cover only controversial topics. Here "Clearlight" of Clearwater (Florida) High provides service to student by survey on comparative costs of flowers for Spring Prom.

Extensive coverage of problem of teen-age drinking is provided by "Pageant" of Proviso East High in Maywood, Illinois. Unusually wide survey of 2,119 students is covered on page one, strongly illustrated with hand art. Center spread covers story on national level and by interviewing professionals of community. Survey is detailed in box, lower left.

dents go to the same place, you could do a series of features. *The Totem Talk* of Sammamish High School, Belleview, Wash., published a November "Special Ski Edition" of four pages of features and a double-page picture display.

Feature articles might tell of vandalism, absenteeism, increased crime in the nearby streets, or other problems when they become important to a school. Or they might concern some current vogues.

For instance, a California school paper cited the popularity of informal clothing on campuses and told about the original Mr. Levi. While the topic was discussed by almost everyone, *The Cass Technician* of Detroit's Cass Technical High School won

In-depth coverage of upcoming bond-issue election is given two full pages in "West Word", Wichita (Kansas) High School West. Story at left details proposition; pros and cons are given at right. At lower center is report on survey among students, teachers and residents. Pictures illustrate overcrowding that bond issue seeks to eliminate; another points out drain on school budget to clean graffiti and repair vandalism.

a Quill and Scroll International Honor Award with three full pages on women's rights. One page reported on an attitude survey of high school students, another provided a short history of the women's movement, and the third discussed women and the law.

One-Theme Spread

Combining several articles plus pictures on a common topic can be most powerful, either in full-page or double-page spread. This is a school paper's nearest approach to television documentaries, which also blend words and pictures. Such television is one of communication's more forceful tools.

West Word of Wichita High West, Wichita, Kan., produced blockbuster coverage just before a community vote on a $30,000,000 bond issue for school construction and other improvements. The publication devoted two inside pages of a 4-page issue to related stories and pictures. It included its own public opinion survey, along with "Pro" and "Con" statements and seven pictures.

The Midway of University High School, Chicago, used a team of staffers to probe the lives of six persons involved with local drug use or prevention. The six-part combination, with hand-drawn art work, was selected by American Newspaper Publishers Association—Columbia Scholastic Press Association judges as a prize feature. It was called "Viewpoints on Drugs" and an editor's note said in part:

. . . The purpose of these six articles

is not to warn U-Highers about the evils of drug use. Nor are they intended to be educationally informative, though they often are. Instead, the purpose of these articles is to glimpse into the lives of six people who are in some way involved in the prevention or use of drugs. The articles are meant to probe the personalities of these six people. Their hopes, fears and frustrations. Hopefully, U-High students, parents and teachers will gain a greater understanding of the roles they play in the drug picture. . . .

One of the six features, entitled "The Doctor," began:

The office of Dr. John Chappel is cramped and dimly lit, with dirty paint peeling from the wall. Behind a large desk sits a tall and proud man with a strained, tired look in his eyes.

Dr. Chappel's office is located at the Special Treatment Unit (STU), a free drug clinic at 14th and Indiana. He works at three other free drug clinics in the Chicago area, and at Billings Hospital at the University. For his work at Billings, the University pays him. The State of Illinois pays him for his work at the four drug clinics.

Dr. Chappel speaks slowly and calmly, as if being careful not to make a mistake, yet he is outspoken in his opinion of drug users. "I don't think that drug use can be prevented, however, I do not think that drug users are bad people," he commented.

"They aren't monsters. They are people who have certain problems. People start on drugs for different reasons. Some are healthy and some aren't. For example, peer pressure and curiosity are healthy reasons, however, rebellious and psychological reasons aren't healthy."

Dr. Chappel further expressed his feelings toward drug users by relating his feelings if one or more of his three daughters used drugs. "I wouldn't be concerned if my children experimented with drugs for healthy reasons because it is natural for children to be curious or to respond to peer pressure. However, I would be concerned if they continued to use drugs.

I feel that experimenting with drugs can be dangerous, but so can walking across the street without looking." . . .

The judges said of the articles:

Each took the reader into the life of one person involved in the drug culture of the school or in the cure. Scenes were drawn carefully and quotes from the interviewees were well chosen for their pertinence and impact. All in all, a superb production.

Most schools may not confront the dramatic potentialities of the University High staffers, but here's a month-by-month listing of ideas that may serve as starters for seasonal feature stories:

September

New faculty members.
Summer activities of students and faculty.
New elective courses.
New books in the library.
Freshman orientation.

October

Plans for scholarship examinations.
United Nations Assembly background.
Columbus Day.
Community election campaigns.

November

Senior jewelry orders due.
National Merit Scholarship semifinalists announced.
Annual book week.
Thanksgiving.

December

PTA bazaar.
Christmas holidays.
Students' vacation plans.

January

New electives to be offered.
Faculty vacation trips.
Student organizations' plans for new term.
Dr. Martin Luther King birthday.

Departmental plans and evaluations of achievements.

February

Faculty changes.
Lincoln and Washington birthdays.
Entering freshman class.

March

Class "celebrities" chosen.
St. Patrick's Day.

April

April Fools' Day.
Inductions into national honorary society.

May

Election of student government officers for next year.
Proms, past versus present.
Seniors measured for caps and gowns.
Spring fashion show.

June

Scholarships to graduates.
Graduations, past versus present.
Review of year's activities.
Graduating seniors' evaluation of their four years in school.

Ideas for features need not be confined to the school campus. In recent years, scholastic editors have paid much attention to students' rights, violence at school and out, and practically any topic that touched them in their roles as students. With this leeway, it would be hard to exclude any relevant ideas. About the only applicable test is: Does it involve our readers? One way to insure that result is to localize any ideas that grow from a clipping in another paper, either an exchange from another school or from a local daily.

Columns

Alert editors find that there is more to successful editorial policy than just transmitting and interpreting the news. So they turn to columnists who add a special flavor. Columns may round up some briefs that can't stand as individual shorts but still deserve mention. They also include reviews of records, moving pictures, books, dramas, and television shows, and these columns are done with an informal style of writing that allows a personal touch not permitted in straight news.

The gossip column which thrived earlier in the century is dead. Good riddance! In its place may be a collection of briefs that, while not strong enough to stand alone, provide illuminating and appealing bits of news. Here are a few ideas:

Mike Malone has been promoted in his after-school job.

Teacher Thompson has a special recipe for making candies.

Principal Peters spent part of his Christmas holidays beachcombing off the Carolina coast.

Billy Black got an old-time jazz-time record at a low price for his collection.

Andy Arno appeared on a TV quiz show and won a $50 prize.

A worthwhile aim for any editor is to print every student's name at least once a year and columns offer a way to that goal. It is easy to publicize the football captain, senior class president, and Homecoming Queen—but what about the other members of the student body that play less spectacular parts in activities? They are worthy school citizens and merit coverage for what they do—even if you have to make special reportorial efforts. Some school editors keep a list of everyone in the school and check off when a name has appeared in print. To find valid reasons to write about those unchecked names is a real test of journalistic creativity.

In handling a column, keep these points in mind:

☆ Never, never write a column just to fill space.

☆ Avoid embarrassing anyone. Delete an item rather than risk potential hurt.

☆ Don't grind a personal ax or tell a private joke.
The paper is not your private possession

and to use it for that purpose violates good journalistic practice.

☆ Avoid even a suggestion of off-color references, particularly double entendres.

☆ Good taste must prevail.

Some school publications have promoted expression of ideas by allowing students to air their attitudes and opinions at length. These are, in effect, sort of guest columns with writers shifting from issue to issue. Some of these may grow out of letters to the editor or they may be written specifically for a section frequently on the editorial page.

Serving the readers is one of the primary functions of any publication, as can't be pointed out too often. This function can be well performed by those columnists who write advice and comments on what records, books, or even clothes to buy and what motion pictures, television programs, and radio broadcasts to see or listen to. In the modern world, there is such a plethora of things to do that we can't possibly do them all. So anyone who helps us to make wise choices is performing a useful service. In many of these fields, a sophisticated and knowledgeable commentator or columnist of the school generation may be more on target than older people who write similar columns for local papers. But remember that it is imperative that these younger columnists and critics be informed and possess true depth of background. Otherwise, their writings may be little more than space fillers.

Since student performances in the arts—plays, concerts, and displays of paintings, photographs, and sculptures—require coverage, school editors and their staff members need to know the differences between *criticism* and *reviews*.

In true criticism, a writer is giving personal evaluation. When you are a critic, your writing is subjective. Thus your evaluations must rank as worthy of acceptance from an authority. If you can't do that, then it is far better to write a review. Here you maintain objectivity regarding value judgments and just tell what happened. You do not evaluate the performance as either good or bad.

For example, a review might report what the play was, names of performers, what roles they had, what the plot involved, how many acts there were, and so forth. But a reviewer would not tell whether the players were ready to go to Broadway next season or whether they should never consider the theater for a professional career. A reviewer, of course, might tell of audience reactions to the performance and thus relay some evaluation.

☆ Write reviews rather than criticism—unless you have a background well beyond your peers.

By writing reviews you avoid the temptations either to caustic, sarcastic comments that professional drama critics often shower on sloppy or incompetent performers or to Pollyanna praise.

Since students represent a multimillion dollar potential market for leisure products, many school publications, especially those at larger metropolitan schools, receive news releases and invitations to special press conferences. This attention comes especially from rock bands, starlets on the way up, and record manufacturers. No doubt, this is flattering; but there may be traps for the unsophisticated. If genuine news for your readers is given in the release, use it. If promotion of a play, movie, book, record, or TV program is the chief ingredient, forget it!

When a publisher sends a book which mentions your school or quotes a faculty member, this is potential copy. But if the book discusses general educational problems, you have the choice of localizing the material by obtaining comments from persons in the school community or forgetting the review.

When an actress at an interview arranged exclusively for student editors talks only about her new play or movie, the entire idea may be dropped as potential copy. If she talks about her own high school days or offers advice to newcomers in the theater, then a report on the session could well interest your readers—and be worth publication.

☆ No rules say you have to publish unwanted publicity materials.

Editorials

Writing an editorial provides an editor with a chance to become an articulate leader of community thought. Such is the case regardless of whether it is a metropolitan daily, country weekly, or school publication. The editorial page becomes the one place where a paper tries to tell readers what to do and what to think. A powerful instrument, it should be used with special care for accuracy and with unhesitating courage if you are positive your cause is right. It is a privilege to write editorials. But editorial writers also have responsibilities. Their logic must be impeccable; their motives above reproach; their style powerful and persuasive. They must possess an ability to find and serve the truth as they see it—and they should not be blinded by bias or prejudice.

☆ Editorial writers must display neither faulty logic nor phony style.

Purposes of an editorial are:

1. To add background information or explanation. These explanatory or informative editorials fill gaps in knowledge, such as explaining why split sessions are required or supplying historical information about an aging school building.

2. To influence readers. These argumentative editorials try to point student thinking in a certain direction, such as appealing for larger attendance at basketball games, picking better candidates in a school class election, pointing out that vandalism at the school building takes money away from worthwhile activities. This type of editorial may argue against some proposal as well as in support.

3. To solve a problem. The good editor wants to make a constructive contribution by advocating a possible answer to a difficulty. But too often an editor, especially a student editor, is more interested in displaying pyrotechnical editorializing, thus aggravating—rather than solving—the problem.

4. To amuse. These change-of-pace editorials include those dealing with mood and color—the essay type—as well as the humorous type. Editorial paragraphs or those puns, parodies, or wisecrack epigrams that appear on editorial pages are included in this category, too.

The structure of an editorial generally takes two formats. One states a conclusion and then assembles the supporting facts on which the conclusion is based. The other uses a current event as a springboard and then moves through to the conclusion generating from it. Subjects for discussion, like those for feature articles, are legion and may arise almost anywhere. One survey, however, showed that students' personal habits and philosophies such as sloppy clothing and cheating on exams were the most popular topic for editorials, followed, in descending order, by national and international affairs as they related to students, extracurricular activities, student-administrative problems, and student-parent-school relationships.

Topics for editorial comment have expanded tremendously during the past decade —as have many other aspects of scholastic journalism. For instance, 10 or 20 years ago student editors were writing about such "old faithful" ideas as school spirit, sportsmanship at games, good study habits, class loyalty, and interschool rivalry. Now the content of editorials may be as controversial as newly acquired student rights, student representation on the local Board of Education, teacher evaluation by students, administrators' possible conflict of interest, busing for integration, bilingual academic programs, class attendance policies, and sex roles of students. These new interests don't mean that an effective editorial still may not be written about loyalty to one's own school; they simply indicate that editorial-page comments are a lot more argumentative today.

Expansions of areas for editorial writing reinforce the long-standing requirements for most careful research before the composition starts and for an unswerving dedication to truth.

Because honey lures more flies than vinegar does, the editor may often perform this most important function by *not* writing an editorial. The professional editor often makes a personal or telephone call upon a person with authority, calls attention to the problem, and sees the problem solved without fuss or fanfare. The student editor might try the same.

☆ An editorial writer always should know what he's writing about.

How does an editorial writer work?

Suppose you're exploring the topic of absenteeism. You find out how many students were absent the day before a holiday, on Fridays, when important tests are scheduled, and so forth. You notice that there is a pattern: Absenteeism is highest the week before Christmas and when the period between holidays is long. That's information.

Trying to think through to a conclusion, the editorial writer realizes that many students get jobs to make money during the pre-holiday season and that they also get bored when there are no breaks in school for a long period. The editorialist checks this thinking with others—fellow staffers, teachers, business executives, and personnel managers. They concur. Now it is time to write the editorial thesis: To cut down school absenteeism, we ought to have a longer Christmas holiday and we ought to provide some break between the New Year and spring vacation. That's information helpful in future planning.

On the theory that two (or three or four) heads are better than one, editorial policy is worked out more effectively by an editorial board than by one individual who concentrates on personal opinions. Larger metropolitan dailies do this without exception and this procedure adapts well for school editors, too. The theory behind this thinking is that editorials represent the opinions of the newspaper and are not the private domain of an individual whose name happens to be at the top of the masthead. However, no writers should have to favor viewpoints they do not believe in. Someone else writes these.

Lee Hills, executive with the Knight-Ridder Newspapers, offered this comment which should be mulled over:

An editorial page editor should also remember that his page speaks for the newspaper as an institution and must not be used as a personal plaything or an outlet for his own prejudices.

When Mexican-American students at Upland High, Upland, Calif., demanded a voice in their education, student Dan Kalbach wrote this editorial which was considered the best in an American Newspaper Publishers Association—Columbia Scholastic Press Association competition:

After years of suppressive denial, the Chicano has risen decisively to demand his equal role in society, to ask for rights that he shouldn't—but does—have to ask for.

The Chicano asks only for a voice in his own education. His requests are not unreasonable. In fact, they are well-founded on a legitimate grievance, that is, years of educational neglect. He asks the right to know his cultural identity, to know himself, to be a functioning part of his own education process.

His demands include the hiring of Chicano teachers, counselors, and administrators, the formation of an actuation center staffed with tutors available to all students, mention of Chicano culture in required history courses, and the evaluation of all standardized testing for language, cultural, or economic bias. He also asks that our teachers spend in-service training acquainting themselves with the problems of the Chicano student. For such a significant minority, these demands do not seem to be out of proportion.

Though the Chicano may not realize it, he speaks not only for himself, but for other disenfranchised students as well. The Board stated that the recommendations submitted by the Chicano/Mexican-American committee, "were in the main consistent with the general goals and objectives developed by the staff and adopted by the board and also the recommendations of the minorities committee presented to the board in January of 1971." The realization of those demands by the Board will provide better educational opportunities for all the students in the district.

But these demands still make an un-

avoidable appeal to today's Anglo-oriented
school system to show some *concern* for
the Chicano student. The Chicano feels
that he is not receiving his "piece of the
pie." There is a strong need to allow him
to gain a personal sort of possession of
this process that affects his life so deeply,
the process of his own education. Without
the understanding of the school and its
staff, he is frustrated; thus, we sat on a
powder keg that might have momentarily
exploded. It almost did.

The Board's positive response to each
of the ten major recommendations submitted by the Chicano/Mexican-American
committee was a classic example of dis-
cretion being the better part of valor. The
Board was aware, in their own words,
that "a major walk-out" was to occur the
day following the special meeting if they
didn't take a more committed stand concerning the demands. Although the
Board's reasons for taking a stand were
not the best, the results are fact. Upland
High School once again has regular,
seven-period days, less uncertainty, and
normal attendance. What remains now is
to see if the Board will put its money
where its mouth is.

Plaid Press, Upland High,
Upland, Calif.

Judges had this comment:

This editorial supporting the school's
Mexican-American minority in its request
for a strong voice in its own education
speaks out with strong conviction. It is
neither overbearing nor emotional in its
appeal. Arguments are well supported by
facts. It discusses what apparently was a
highly-explosive issue in a language that
reflects deep thought. This is an outstanding example of excellence in editorial writing.

The language itself of an editorial may
contribute to problem-solving—or to aggravating the situation. If you imply that the
principal is a mean old ogre who keeps students off the lawn only for sadistic reasons,
chances of persuading that principal to per-

Sensitive issue of interracial relations in Monrovia (California) High is treated with competence and responsibility
by "Wildcat," with whole page of in-depth coverage.

mit frisbees over on one side are mighty
slim. But if you proceed on the assumption
—and articulate it—that the principal is an
intelligent friend of the student body, surely
the administrator will be more amenable to
your suggestion.

To be most readable, editorials should
range from 200 to 300 words unless they are
short change-of-pace type or editorial paragraphs. Overly long editorials tend to drive
readers away. It is far better to have two
shorter comments than one longish one.
Some commercial dailies use two on the
same general topic with headlines like this:

Mounting school budgets . . .

(Text of first editorial)

. . . and declining enrollments

(Text of second editorial)

When you sit down to write an editorial,
keep in mind what the National Conference
of Editorial Writers, a group of profes-

sionals, says in its "Basic Statement of Principles":

> Journalism in general, editorial writing in particular, is more than another way of making money. It is a profession devoted to the public welfare and to public service. The chief duty of its practitioners is to provide the information and guidance toward sound judgments which are essential to the healthy functioning of a democracy. . . .
>
> The editorial writer should present facts honestly and fully. It is dishonest and unworthy of him to base an editorial on half-truth. He should never consciously mislead a reader, distort a situation, or place any person in a false light. . . .
>
> The editorial writer should have the courage of well-founded conviction and a democratic philosophy of life. He should never write or publish anything that goes against his conscience. . . .

A courtroom witness swears to tell "the truth, the whole truth, and nothing but the truth." As a testifier on news events for the reading and listening public, the journalist might well subscribe to the same noble oath.

News stories are "the truth . . . and nothing but the truth" but sometimes they are less than "the whole truth."

To tell "the whole truth" is the assignment of the interpretative reporter, in-depth correspondent, columnist, and, probably most of all, editorial writer.

Serious subject of cheating is handled in light but compelling manner in "Lion" of Lyons Township High, LaGrange, Illinois.

Editing Copy

A good copy editor is an indispensable journalistic technician who guarantees that stories are easy for readers to understand and that writers are kept out of troubles and embarrassments.

In the middle of the news chain from fact-gatherer to proofreader, a copy editor is a vital link. This editor polishes copy that is sloppy, inaccurate, or dull until it attracts and keeps readers' attention. Another responsibility is to correct errors that could bring lawsuits the publication or could damage its credibility. On most papers, the job also includes writing headlines.

Many a world-famous correspondent owes much reputation to the quiet work of copy editors who combed out clichés, corrected mistakes, and made the language dance instead of clump.

Every reporter should do copyreading before handing in a story. The news gatherer has the first responsibility to insure that names, dates, addresses, and titles are correct; that spelling, typing, and grammar are in order; and that quotations are accurate and make sense. Copy is put in correct form by using copyreading symbols, which —note well!—are not the same as those used in proofreading.

☆ Every news staffer should know how to use copyreading symbols.

Copy editing includes all of these copyreading mechanics plus making sure that the lead is as attractive as possible, that the facts are arranged in proper order, and that the story is objective and fair. A copy editor may use a typewriter to revise a lead or scissors and paste to reorganize the entire order of the copy, and may even telephone for additional information—if the original reporter is not immediately available for such work.

Tools for Copy Editing

While a copy editor might struggle through with an inquisitive mind, a suspicious attitude, and some sharp, soft pencils, some other useful tools are scissors, stapler, and paste pot. Handy reference materials for checking facts are school and city directories, local telephone book, detailed map of community, back issues of school publications, the paper's style sheet, dictionary, and thesaurus. Some general reference books such as the *World Almanac and Book of Facts* and one or more standard encyclopedias would be convenient, too.

Because reporters and especially copy editors have to check and double-check on so many facts, every reputable professional publication and broadcast station has its own library or *morgue,* as staff members call it. One metropolitan paper has more than 2 million separate clippings, pictures, and charts about people, places, and things that already have appeared in the news. (The name of "morgue" grew logically from its collection of *obits* or obituaries, those biographies prepared ahead of time for publication when individuals die or when they achieve new distinctions.) Student staff members should build their own morgue or use school references.

A number of communication publications will help staffers do better and more professional jobs. All the national school journalism organizations publish their own magazines and so do some regional and state groups. Among professional journals are *Editor & Publisher, Printer's Ink, Columbia Journalism Review, The Quill,* and (*MORE*). To guarantee reading of articles marked for required reading in such publications, some advisors give staff members written tests regularly. Others use routing slips so that key personnel have a chance to benefit from useful information.

High school papers have relatively simple editing setups, possibly one or two copy editors at a regular desk. Professional papers use a semicircular or horseshoe-shaped desk with as many as a dozen persons sitting on the outside or the *rim* and one inside or in the *slot.* Locations supply obvious titles of *rim man* or *slot man.* (These terms, of course, apply to women as well as to men.) Some dailies have one huge or *universal copy desk* to handle all types of news, regardless of where it comes from or what it concerns. Other papers operate with a series of *specialized desks* for local, national, cable or foreign, sports, foods and fashions, and even, in a few cases, education and the sciences. Some sports editors may even work right in a press box at a ball park if there is heavy deadline pressure to get into print.

☆ Efficiency of the editing is what counts, not where it is done.

Copyreaders and editors may use either a soft lead pencil or a ball-point pen. Many commercial publications supply pencils and their school counterparts might do the same —unless staff members start making off with them for class use.

Since there is more time between issues, some school publications have found it good policy to use gray copy paper for "working versions" of news stories, captions, and yearbook texts. After polishing for style, grammar, and space-fitting, the article is copied on yellow paper and is edited for the final time before going to the compositor. This allows easy identification of just what stage the copy is in—and provides easy-to-read material for setting.

☆ Make carbon copies of all final copy.

Thus a carbon is on hand in those rare occasions when clean copy is lost on the way to or at the compositor's shop.

Some schools set up a pool of volunteers who type edited copy that goes to a composing room. This is especially valuable if the school has typing classes; the school paper provides an opportunity to put classroom knowledge into practice and a routine copying job is expertly done.

If important changes must be made in the version on yellow paper, the copy editor may use scissors and paste to incorporate revisions at the last minute. When copy is neatly assembled this way, the version sent is still readable to the compositor. If editing makes copy smudgy or heavily overwritten, it is best to retype it so the compositor will not be puzzled. Messy copy opens the way for possible typographical errors or for delays while the compositor figures out the words. In either case, the wasted time will be reflected in increased composition charges.

☆ Always be sure copy sent to the compositor is easy to read.

Copy Editor's Responsibilities

Copy editing has been called an art and a science. And it is both. Beyond that it combines many responsibilities.

The successful copy editor searches for a whole variety of things:

1. Errors in facts;
2. Typographical errors or garbles in transmission;
3. Mistakes in spelling, grammar, and punctuation;
4. Inconsistencies in style;
5. Excess wordage;
6. Hackneyed and trite words and phrases;
7. Libel or obscene statements;
8. Errors in interpretation, regardless of

whether they arise from ignorance, bias, partisanship, or faulty perspective;

9. Complicated and involved style, which —though correct in form—makes it difficult for readers to follow with ease; and

10. Faulty organizations of facts.

When you as a reporter copyread your article, you watch especially for typing errors; but you keep your eyes open constantly for any other mistakes.

As a copy editor, you usually divide the job into several parts. First, you go through fairly rapidly to get the sense of the whole article and correct the more obvious mistakes. Then you take more time and try to catch all the errors, even if you have to stop to use a dictionary, school class rolls, faculty listings, or other reference sources. You scan the copy for length and cut out phrases, sentences, or paragraphs to fit instructions from an editor. You check and make sure that the ideas flow logically throughout the story. Then you turn to *breaker heads,* if they are needed, and finally to writing the headline.

Regardless of whether a journalist works on a high school paper, a bimonthly magazine, or a metropolitan daily with three to five editions each day, sometimes there will be great pressure for copy to be turned in promptly. The copyreader stands by to protect the writer, as much as possible, from this pressure. The writer does not have time to stop typing and check. The copy editor does that. Did the school win the championship in 1971 or 1972? Is the street address correct? Is the Nobel prize-winning scientist still at Harvard or did he move to another college? An appropriate reference book or file will tell. Incidentally, this dilemma of deadline copy is another argument for getting stories in as early as possible.

A reporter may pass over a typing error because of that mental quirk which prevents spotting one's own mistakes. The copy editor, as the second reader, is less encumbered and should detect it.

Mistakes in spelling, grammar, and punctuation are the most common and most glaring. Professionals often bemoan the lack of competence of college graduates in these areas. In fact, some publications give pre-employment tests to prospective staff members, and much of the time is devoted to exercises that will expose such deficiencies. High school is none too soon—maybe even very late—to begin stressing proper usage.

Although rules of grammar are becoming increasingly less rigid, they are not yet so loose as to permit some of the mistakes that appear in high school and college papers. The more common errors concern:

1. Subject-verb agreement. Example: "The possibility of taking two foreign languages *were* a key point in the program." The subject "possibility" is singular so the verb must be "was."

2. Pronoun-antecedent agreement. Example: "All staff members must contribute his best efforts to produce a good publication." The phrase "all staff members" is plural so the pronoun should be "their."

3. Dangling participle. Example: "Winners of the state basketball championship, the student body gave them a standing ovation as the team marched on to the auditorium platform." Team members, not the school body, are the "winners." This might be rephrased, "The student body gave team members a standing ovation at an assembly when they were honored for winning the state basketball championship." Or it might read, "Winner of the state championship, the basketball team received a standing ovation from the student body."

Many of the more common mistakes in grammar and spelling are in this "letter" adopted from *College English:*

Dear Sir; you never past me in grammar because you was prejudice. but I got this here athaletic scholarship any way. Well, the other day I finely get to writing the rule's down so as I can always study it if they ever slip my mind.

1. Each pronoun agrees with their antecedent.

2. Just between you and I, case is important.

3. Verbs has to agree with their subjects.

4. Watch out for irregular verbs which has crope into our language.

5. Don't use no double negatives.

6. A writer mustn't shift your point of view.

7. When dangling, don't use participles.

8. Join clauses good like a conjunction should.

9. Don't write a run-on sentence you got to puctuate it.

10. About sentence fragments.

11. In letters themes reports articles and stuff like that we use commas to keep a string of items apart.

12. Don't use commas, which aren't necessary.

13. Its important to use apostrophe's right.

14. Don't abbrev.

15. Check to see if any words out.

Your's truly,

Omission or insertion of punctuation may make a world of difference in meaning. Maxwell Nurnberg, who taught English at New York University, used a series of parallel sentences to prove this point:

(a) Thirteen girls knew the secret, all told.

(b) Thirteen girls knew the secret; all told.

Which is a libel on the female sex?

(a) I left him convinced he was a fool.

(b) I left him, convinced he was a fool.

Which sentence shows extraordinary powers of persuasion?

(a) What's the latest dope?

(b) What's the latest, dope?

Both are slang greetings, but which is insulting?

(a) Go slow, children.

(b) Go slow—children.

Which is a warning to drivers?

(a) The play ended happily.

(b) The play ended, happily.

Which is unflattering to the actors?

Copyreaders also have to be on the alert for "sound-alikes," when writers, either in a hurry or just ignorant, are confused and incorrect. Some of the prominent include:

A lot—allot

Its—It's

There—their—they're

To—too—two

Who's—whose

Your—you're

Skillful copyreaders weed out malapropisms or those ridiculous misuses of words as done by Mrs. Malaprop in Sheridan's comedy *The Rivals*. For instance, new club officers may be chosen unanimously but hardly anonymously. A great speech could be immortal but rarely immoral. The weather might be inimical for a certain type of plants without being inimitable. Presidential nominees often are picked by acclamation but seldom by exaltation. And on and on the list could go.

In addition to the conventional spelling, typing, and grammar errors, superior copy editors keep a watch for mistakes in what might be called internal factual accuracy. Do the various parts of information in the news item add up to the stated whole? For instance, here are a few examples:

Is a proper name spelled the same way in each reference? Sometimes an odd first name may be inadvertently substituted for the last one; the "Patrick Henry" in paragraph one may become "Mr. Patrick" three grafs further. "Jon Smith" may become the more conventional "John Smith." A transposition of letters can turn "Jane" into "Jean." Unless the copy editor knows personally which is which, the mistake isn't obvious.

Are titles correct? For instance, be sure an individual has a doctorate before you call him "Dr." If you are not positive of any title, check it out again—even if you have the embarrassment of telephoning the person's office.

Do the figures add up? If you refer to three-quarters of the graduates going to college, 5% joining the military, and one in four looking for jobs, you have to note that the total is more than 100% and thus something is wrong and has to be corrected. If a five-member committee is appointed by the senior class president and you find only four names mentioned, find out whose name has been omitted. Or are there only four members?

Do quotations make sense? Are essential parts (or any other fact) dropped out in a writer's hurry to get copy together?

Jay Robinson
Homeroom W-27
BASKETBALL

2-36 BB | *youthful basketball team opens season Thursday*

~~Next week the~~ Central's varsity basketball team ~~squares off for~~ *opens* ~~the first game of~~ the season against Westfield on the home court, *Thursday night.*

~~The contest will be played Thursday night in the home gym.~~

With 12 juniors and only ④ senio̱rs, the cagers will be one of the most youthful squads in the school's history. Only one letterman is returning *— Kevin Murphy —* ~~— Kevin Murphy — and~~ he will be ~~the~~ floor leader. According to Coach Ryan Horne, m̲urphy is one of the *area's* top defensive guards ~~in the area~~ and an improved offensive player.

Height, which has been a̲ major problem at Central for the past couple of years, will again be lacking. The big men for the Wildcats will be seniors Davy Linden and Randy c̲onvery along with junior Todd Nostrand, who all go about 6 feet ⟨three⟩ inches.

Howᵉver, Coach ~~Ryan related that~~ *Horne said* the team will make up in speed what it lacks in height. The squad will shoot a̲ lot, especially in the early season which will ~~also~~ help ~~serve the purpose of~~ getti̶ng the team more physically ~~sound,~~ *fit.*

The Cats will play the same type of basketball as last year. On defense, they will play mostly man-to-man with some various pressing defenses. On offensive, the team will be flexible.

~~According to Coach~~ Horne, "Against taller teams we will tend to stay outside more and against other teams we will penetrate more. It all depends on the opponents," *he said.*

--30--

Edited copy. Note use of copyreader's symbols.

☆ Take nothing for granted when editing copy. Be skeptical of every fact.

When editing any copy, the editor makes sure that it conforms with the style agreed on for the publication's consistency. "Street," "street," "St.," and "st." are all correct but only one should be used. The copy editor ensures that. Since most daily newspapers get the bulk of their out-of-town news from the two major press associations —*Associated Press (AP)* and *United Press International (UPI)*—their common style rules now govern most of the newspapers of the country.

A good copy editor should always seek to make a story more readable and that concerns style more than factual accuracy. Here are a few ways to do this:

1. If one word will do the job of five or ten, substitute that one.

2. If a sentence is long or complicated, split it into two or more parts.

3. If there are sentence fragments, convert them into full sentences. However, let a fragment stand if that is the most effective way to state the thought.

4. If a phrase is potentially misleading, fix it.

5. If the general tone is lifeless and dull, strengthen it with vivid nouns and action verbs.

6. If there is needless wordage, cut it like a chef carving a turkey—with skill.

Maintain a sharp lookout for clichés, stereotypes, and other hackneyed language. Here are a few of the more extreme that should be deleted:

Acid test
Beat a hasty retreat
Bolt from the blue
Breakneck speed
Breathless silence
Complete stop
Fair sex
Fills a long felt need
Goes without saying
Jammed to capacity
Major breakthrough (medical or scientific)
Met his Waterloo
Mr. Average Citizen
Mother Nature
News leaked out
Nipped in the bud
Point with pride
Sadder but wiser
Tender mercies
Totally destroyed
White as a sheet
With one fell swoop
Worse for the wear

Libel and obscenity, two of the hazards copy editors must be aware of, were emphasized in Chapter 5.

Libel laws vary from state to state but in them all the guiding rule is:

☆ Truth is the best defense against libel.

A responsible editor will willingly print a *correction* or *retraction* of a potentially libelous statement or inaccuracy but by far the best course is for the copy editor to correct it before it gets into the paper.

Obscenity is linked with the moral standards of your community. So remember that just because you and your classmates think that some references are hysterically amusing, even if off-color, it does not mean that parents and administrators will react the same way. A school publication advisor could be invaluable if a reporter, copy editor, or editor-in-chief has doubts whether to print.

If the reporter on the scene fails to get the news behind the story, hasn't told all the truth, or lets bias and enthusiasm rule, the interpretation may be wrong and could mislead readers. A good copy editor will help "tell it like it is" by drawing on accurate background information gathered over the years.

When copy doesn't flow logically or when facts are misplaced from their proper sequence, a copy editor will use scissors and paste to rearrange. Sometimes the copy editor rewrites an entire article or, on larger dailies, turns that assignment over to a rewriteman.

In addition to all the correcting and polishing of news stories, the copy desk also must keep a *log* of all material that is processed. Otherwise, there may be insufficient material to fill the pages or, more frequently, too much *overset,* material which will have to be discarded unless it is *time copy* that can be used in the next issue.

The first step in keeping a copy log is to determine how much advertising has been sold and thus how much room is left for the *news hole.* Then, as each story, headline, or picture is edited, an entry is made in the log:

Class election	5½″
2/2 Honor roll	6″
Senior play	4″
PIX, Play 2×20 picas	6½″

Periodically, the copy editor strikes a subtotal and notes how many more column inches are left vacant. Accurate copy logging enables better planning and avoids wasted composition costs.

The chief copy editor, usually helped by the editor-in-chief, decides where stories, features, and pictures will be placed in the paper.

Proofreading

The final insurance against mistakes getting into print is proofreading. The official proofreader on a student publication should be a most conscientious person, knowledgeable in spelling and grammar, and with a keen mind that will accept nothing on faith. The job is to check—and correct, if need be—the *galley proofs,* strips of paper 15 to 20 inches long and 1 column wide. While watching mainly for typographical errors, a proofreader also corrects factual mistakes with approval of a senior editor. (There may be a special reason for printing the word or phrase the proofreader thinks is incorrect.)

The best way to make corrections is by the *book method.* This requires one mark where the error occurs and another in the margin to show how the correction should be done.

Although a proofreader should be familiar with all the proofreading marks, six will be used most frequently.

Word or letters to be removed are marked in the type, letters with a vertical line and words with a horizontal one. In the margin, lined up with the error line, you write a *delete sign,* a stylized version of a medieval "d."

When a letter or word must be replaced by another, the error is circled and, in the margin, the correct letter or word is written. An underscore beneath a, u, and w and an overscore above o, n, and m, prevent confusion.

When something must be added, a caret— an inverted v—shows where the addition is to be placed. The material to be inserted is written in the margin. If space is to be added, the margin notation is a little tick-tack-toe diagram.

If two or more letters are transposed (such as "piad" when it should be "paid"), the incorrect letters are marked with a sideways "s" and in the margin is written "tr" for transpose. Of course, this requires that you mark the letters in such a way that the compositor can read them when correcting the line.

If space is to be taken out—moving two letters side by side—a closeup mark is used both within the copy and in the margin. This looks like a pair of parentheses lying on their sides.

Occasionally a proofreader discovers that a "correction" is in error and wants to retain the original version. Then a dotted line is drawn under the copy erroneously marked and, in the margin, is written *stet* (let it stand). This tells the typesetter to ignore the whole thing.

Charts of proofreader's marks are available from your printer.

☆ Proofreading and copy editing marks are not identical.

Staff members should know the differences and use them correctly.

Errors made during composition are corrected at the compositor's expense but if staff members change their minds after the story is in type, then it is an *author's alteration* or *AA,* which is paid for out of the publication's budget. So author's alterations should not be made except for the most compelling reasons such as, for example, a monumental factual mistake that slipped past every staffer who worked on the copy.

☆ Never "edit" on galley proofs.

One final, final chance for checking comes on the page proofs or the pasteup. But corrections should not be made at this stage except for an error that would call for stopping the presses.

On student papers, more than one staffer usually reads proofs. The more proofreaders the better. Typos are slippery and have amazing agility in escaping watchful eyes.

The best advice for proofreading is: Read with extreme care. But a few specifics should be noted. Each word—even each single letter—is read and not skipped over. The easiest error to overlook is one that produces an actual word. A mistake like "pzst" will almost leap from the page but when the eye sees "post" instead of the correct "past," many people have a tendency to skim over acceptingly.

Errors in headline type are conspicuous to readers but easily overlooked by proofreaders. One staffer could well be assigned specifically to make sure that the proper headline runs with each story. Mixing the "Class Prom" head with a "Class Play" story is easy to do.

Some editors put page proofs or pasteup on the wall, step back a couple of feet, and then read all the headlines. They claim errors in display type are more obvious at a slight distance. It's a method worth trying.

The advisor should make a final check of galley and page proofs or pasteup. Having a slightly different perspective, the advisor may detect a mistake that escaped attention of all staff members.

In the chase for mistakes, everybody who might help should get into the act.

Electronic Editing

"Revolutionary" is an overworked word. We are supposedly experiencing revolutions in almost everything from foods and fashions to life styles and cultural changes. The word has become trite but it is conservatively true that the printing industry has a revolution going on. More drastic and exciting changes have taken place in the past decade than in all the other years of journalistic history.

Nowhere is this more evident than in *electronic editing.* No high schools yet have the magic new equipment to do this legerdemain and chances are that it will be a long time before any do. Prices are too high for any except a few universities.

Student journalists ought to know at least a bit of background on the processes since they may be working with this equipment almost as soon as they enter professional journalism.

It starts with the routine typing of a reporter's story. The typewritten *hard copy* is fed into a scanner, a machine that "reads" copy by *optical character recognition (OCR).*

The just-read message is either stored in a computer's *memory* for later use or converted into *perforated tape* which directs operations of a typesetting machine without human intervention.

A more sophisticated machine works directly from the typewriter putting a code onto magnetic tape which also directs a typesetting machine.

Either the perforated, punched, tape or the magnetic tape is fed into a *video display terminal (VDT).* For this machine two adjectives are absolutely appropriate—"amazing" and "delightful." No other machine is as much fun to watch or to operate.

As the tape is fed into the machine, the words of the copy are shown on a small video screen. When the copyreader wants to make a change, a small blip of light, the *cursor,* is moved into proper position. The editor punches a key on an overblown electric typewriter and signals for replacement of a letter or a phrase, deletion of a letter to as much as a whole paragraph, or rearrangement of words, phrases, or whole grafs.

The edited tape is stored in the computer's memory bank until it is sent, via wires, to a typesetting machine that proceeds to produce cold type exactly as the tape directs it.

Now the reporter is not only a typist but also the typesetter. And the editor is also a proofreader. For once the tape is perfect, there cannot be a typographical error in the finished type. Machines, it's said, can't make typographical errors. Only humans can do that.

As it has in countless other phases of

Copyreaders' Marks

To do this → **Use this mark** ___ and ___ **This is the result**

To do this	Use this mark	This is the result
Spell out	in (Mich.) school journalists	in Michigan school journalists
Abbreviate	from Lakeside, (Florida,) came	from Lakeside, Fla. came
Close up	our foot̯ ball team won two	our football team won two
Separate	the outstanding trackman	the outstanding track man
Space	missed the space between̯words #	missed the space between words
Insert	all chem stry classes meet	all chemistry classes meet
	Thou shalt ∧kill (not)	Thou shalt not kill
Lower case	the Ᵽrincipal announced	the principal announced
Capitalize	these United states	these United States
	chocolate mi(kl) prices	chocolate milk prices
Transpose	to (slowly run) toward	to run slowly toward
Delete	was ~~completely~~ destroyed	was destroyed
Delete & close up	leᶜtters to the editor	letters to the editor
Let it stand	Leave copy ~~just~~ as it was STET in original form	Leave copy just as it was in original form
Connect matter	this copy will connect~~ without any blank space~~ to these words	this copy will connect to these words
	sentence ends ⌐ But no new paragraph is desired here,	sentence ends. But no new
	⌐This mark calls attention of typesetter to start of new paragraph.	
Paragraph	When we need a new paragraph, this mark is used. ⌐Then the next sentence is indented in the usual graf indent.	When we need a new paragraph, this mark is used. Then the next sentence is indented in the usual graf indent.

No paragraph

no¶ sentence ends.
What is now a separate graf
just runs as part of the previous
one.

sentence ends. What is now a
a separate graf just runs as part
of the previous one.

Run in

Scholarship winners are:
Bob Jones,
Sally Smith,
Barbara Ann Collins,
Victor Mantell, and
Terry Gorshin.

run in

Scholarship winners are: Bob
Jones, Sally Smith, Barbara Ann
Collins, Victor Mantell, and

Follow unusual copy

FOLO COPY

The United Stakes of America

the United Stakes of America

The United Stakes (CQ) of America

The United Stakes of America

Emphasize punctuation

These ˅inverted carets˅ call attention
of the typesetter to the quote marks.

And the little circle keeps the
period from being overlooked⊙

Italicize

The typesetter will now set "will" in Italic letters.

Boldface

The typesetter will now set "will" in boldface.

More copy

This story continues onto a succeeding page. (more)

End marks

This is the end of this story. —30—

This is the end of this story. XXX

Copyreader's marks. Note similarity to, but differences from, marks used in proofreading and that only one mark is used to make change.

American activity, the computer has found a home in newspaper plants. We hear about computers "setting type" but in most instances that just isn't so. What they do is justify lines. (In case you've forgotten what that means, it's simply that type is set with even right and left margins like the column you are reading right now.)

The great weakness of the computer is hyphenation in that it operates according to rules of syllabizing. English, being such a hybrid language, has almost as many exceptions as it has rules. So we constantly see such disturbing breaks as "hor/se" or "thro/ugh." By logic, this is correct—except that each word is an exception. The only way that this can be corrected is to feed all exceptions into the memory bank so the computer can scan this list before it makes decisions.

In only one instance does a computer actually "set" type. This is in a *cathode ray tube (CRT)* operation. A CRT is simply a television tube. When tape calls for a cap A, let's say, the computer tells the tube to form that character exactly as a picture is formed on a home TV screen. It is then pictured on photo paper.

Wondrous as all this machinery may be, it still cannot operate without the most complicated of all computers: The human brain. Only humans can communicate with

Symbol	Meaning	Symbol	Meaning
℘	Delete	⊢⊣	Em dash
ℰ	Delete and close up	en	En dash
⌒	Turn inverted letter	;/	Insert semicolon
⌒	Close up	:/	Insert colon
#	Insert space	⊙	Insert period
⋁⋁⋁	Equalize spacing	?/	Insert interrogation point
less#	Reduce spacing	Qu/Au	Query to author QU AU
¶	Paragraph	⌒	Use ligature
☐	Indent one em	SP	Spell out
[	Move to left	Tr	Transpose
]	Move to right	Set 1, 2, 3	In this order
⌴	Lower	wf	Wrong font
⊓	Elevate	bf	Set in bold face type
∧	Insert marginal addition	rom	Set in roman type
X	Broken letter	ital	Set in italic type
⊥	Push down space	Caps	Set in capitals
═	Straighten	SC	Set in small capitals
‖	Align type	lc	Set in lower case
⋀	Insert comma	═	Hyphen
⋁	Insert apostrophe	stet	Let it stand
⋁"	Insert quotes	no ¶	Run in same paragraph
(/)	Insert parens	ld>	Insert lead between lines
[/]	Insert brackets	hr#	Hair space between letters
⋀3	Insert inferior figure	out sc	Out—see copy
⋁3	Insert superior figure	✳	End of copy

Proofreader's marks. Note that symbols shown here are those written in margin. Each must have accompanying sign, as explained in text, at point of error or change. (Courtesy Mead Papers)

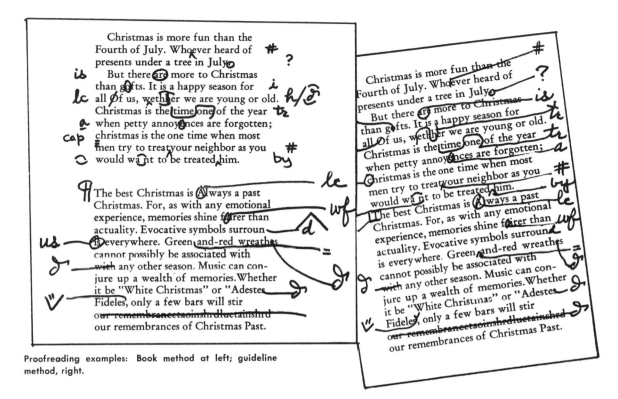

Proofreading examples: Book method at left; guideline method, right.

humans and consequently these electronic marvels will never render the human journalist obsolete. This miraculous hardware is merely another tool for better communication, just as the quill pen was replaced by a pencil which was replaced by a typewriter which was . . . , etc. And tools are only as good as the human who uses them.

So the student journalist need never fear replacement by a robot even before becoming a professional journalist. There is no replacement for the creativity, sensitivity, and judgment of the human mind in any field, but especially not in journalism.

Writing Headlines

"Headlinese" is a language just like English or French, with its own rules of grammar. The copyreader must master these rules just as the reporter must master those of English. Complications set in because of an additional rule. The headline must fit into a rigidly defined area. And just as rigid is the deadline which forces the headwriter to work under pressures of time.

Headline standards are exacting. Errors in a story may be overlooked by the reader, but flaws in heads are conspicuous.

The poor copyreader who wrote:

Police Add
Four Foot
Patrolmen

was kidded for years about the midgets he allegedly converted into policemen. This error, in 48-point type, just couldn't be overlooked.

After editing the story, the copyreader writes its headline according to specifications by the news editor or whoever is in the slot. The head serves three functions: (a) it grades the story by importance; (b) it lures the reader into the story; and (c) it is an element in the creating of page patterns.

Grammar of Headlines

☆ Headlines are written in the historical present tense.

This gives a sense of immediacy and excitement, a prime ingredient in a head.

Notice how a good storyteller drops into the present tense at the gripping part of the narrative: "Now Washington crosses the Delaware in the dead of night and catches the Hessians completely by surprise!"

The headwriter must beware, though, of a head that says: "Jones Dies Last Week." This in effect mixes tenses and confuses the reader.

The past tense is used in heads only as the equivalent of the English pluperfect tense, earlier in time than the regular past tense. When you say, "When I arrived in class, the lecture had already begun," you set two time frames, "I arrived" is in the past, "the lecture had begun" at an even earlier time.

In headlinese the usage is:

McMillan Played
On Broken Ankle,
X-Rays Reveal

Here "reveal" is past and "played," pluperfect. This usage is comparatively rare in newspapers just by the nature of their content.

Instead of the English future tense which uses some form of "will" with a verb, headlinese uses the infinitive form, "to do something". So an ordinary sentence that "a novelist is going to teach a course" becomes:

Novelist To Teach
Creative Writing
At Central High

☆ Drop articles such as "a," "the," "and," and most forms of "to be."

Eliminating articles speeds reading and gives an effect of great urgency. It also saves space. The same with "and," which is replaced by a comma:

Gavin, Andres Hit Homers

"Is" is omitted and understood.

The only other punctuation used in a head is the semicolon which takes the place of a period:

Gridders Win Trophy;
Gymnasts Take Second

A semicolon should be a warning signal to the headwriter. Often it indicates that the editor couldn't decide what is the most important facet of the story. But when two sentences are presented, the reader is slowed up. The best solution is to concentrate on the main aspect alone. If both topics must be headlines, it maintains urgency if a conjunction is used:

Gridders Win Trophy
As Gymnasts Place

In this case there probably should be two separate stories.

Sometimes the semicolon indicates a *shotgun head.*

A shotgun is a single head from which—like two barrels extending from a single gunstock—two or more stories read out. This confuses the reader who doesn't know which story to read first. Too often the dilemma is solved by reading neither. The reader never likes to make choices, even simple ones like this, and wants the editor to say, "Read this first; now read this."

If this specimen head were on a single story, perhaps the head should have said something like:

Central Athletes
Continue High
In Standings

☆ Build the headline on the lead of the story.

This applies, of course, to stories that are written with a summary lead. Features often take *teaser* heads, *connotative* ones rather than the *summary* or *definitive heads* on hard news.

Some critics complain about the repeti-tion of the head and lead, but experience has shown this form to have great merit. For the reader who skims only headlines—and in professional journalism these are far too many—there is, of course, no repetition. And it is essential to get the heart of the news no matter how abbreviated. If the head is built on a subordinate facet of the story, the reader has to read several paragraphs before the head makes sense and may get irritated therefore.

☆ Stress active verbs.

This axiom requires two grains of salt. Active verbs have more color and appeal than passive ones, it's true. But in some instances when the object of the verb is more important than the subject, the passive voice is not only acceptable but desirable:

Blyer Named All-State End

properly puts emphasis upon the local athlete while an active verb:

Coaches Name Blyer All-State

subordinates the name and local appeal.

☆ Give the news exactly the play it merits.

A head grades its story on its own importance but also in relation to other stories on the budget. On lean news days, certain stories will be played stronger than they would on a heavy day. But this must be done with great care.

You can't have an interesting, newsy page with only small heads; typographically you'd speak in a low monotone. You need to change the pitch of your voice in ordinary conversation; you need the change in your typographic voice, too. But you don't want to scream "Wolf!" too often, either, lest your reader fail to recognize a genuinely important story when it comes along.

☆ Set a regular procedure for handling headline copy.

Arrangements should be made with your typesetter. Some want heads written in the blank space above the start of the typewritten story. Some prefer heads on separate pieces of paper or sorted out by face and size. Some prefer heads on separate sheets of paper but pasted to the story. In all cases when head and body are separated, a system must be used to make sure they match up properly on the page; slug lines are the best device.

The vagaries of the English language complicate headwriting. There are two major strains in our language: Anglo-Saxon and Norman French. Anglo-Saxon has strong—and short—words; Norman words are more polite, elegant—and lengthy.

An accurate headwriter might want to say:

Student Government Officers Criticize Ticket Policy

but it just won't fit into the designated space. So the editor abbreviates to "SG". But it's still too long. So the editor replaces that long, polite "criticize" with a short Old English verb:

SG Raps Ticket Policy

or "flays" or "rips" or "hits" or does something equally violent—and inaccurate.

American newspaper readers often complain about distortion in headlines by too-strong verbs.

☆ Use only common abbreviations.

In the example just noted, 'SG' is probably the way the student body refers to the student government and is just as understandable as the full title. "US" and "UN" are used constantly and abbreviations such as "St." or "So." are commonplace.

But those made up on the spot are usually incomprehensible. The "Northern Washington County Association of English Teachers" certainly won't fit into a head; but "NWCAET" won't communicate even if we can squeeze it in. So you use abbreviations in heads only as they are used in regular writing. It's correct to write:

Victory Parade To Climax At Jefferson Blvd. Mall

but it is incorrect to say:

City To Repave Blvd. In Front Of School

☆ Avoid *label heads*.

Labels—also called *deadheads*—lack facts, action, or color.

Big Debate Today

fails to tell who will participate, what the topic is, why it deserves this space in our newspaper.

☆ Don't be afraid to use colorful words and phrases—but don't overdo them.

☆ Avoid clichés in heads.

Especially on sports pages, editors have problems finding words to announce victories. So teams rarely "win" or "defeat" the opponent; they "trounce," "wallop," "deluge," "swamp," "bury," "edge" or something else, ad nauseum. These are all good, strong verbs that have grown flaccid only by unthinking misuse and overuse.

☆ Avoid *mandatory heads*.

When the subject of a verb is eliminated to save space, the result is a stern order to the reader:

Grab Mugger In Park

In an old vaudeville act, the newsboy who was yelling that headline was rebuffed with:

Downstyle heads are used in all-Bodoni schedule of "Mortonian" of Jay Sterling Morton High East in Cicero, Illinois.

"Grab your own mugger; I already got one!"

☆ A headline should not require translation.

One of the most famous heads in American journalism comes from *Variety*, the show-biz newspaper, which announced:

Stix Nix Hix Pix

It was clever, of course, but it required an interpretor to tell most nontheatrical people that it meant "small towns don't like movies with a rural setting."

Other incomprehensible heads were not done on purpose. They come from violating the basic guides of headwriting:

Boy Scouts Find
Stolen School
Safe In Creek

Irate Motorist
Turns Into Car;
Student Injured

and one that conjures up an interesting mental picture:

New African
State Runs
Up Its Flag

Regular stories take *definitive* or *summary* heads that capsulize the story. Features often take *connotative* or *teaser* heads that lure by a provocative phrase that piques curiosity.

Anything goes in a teaser, even puns. When a midwest college decreed that sauna baths in the gym couldn't be used simultaneously by both sexes, the campus paper headed it:

Co-ed Per Sauna
Non Grata Here

The pun might be a visual one:

Gymnasts Do Best Work
While Upside-Down

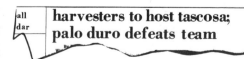

Misuse of downstyle. First word of head should be, and proper nouns must be, capitalized.

When a kitten wandered across the stage during a talk by a visiting celebrity, the story was headed:

Monolog
Becomes
Catalog

Style of Headlines

Not too long ago, journalism students had to learn many different forms of heads. But the trend toward streamlined typography resulted in the elimination of complex and nonfunctional heads.

☆ Headlines should be simple in form and large in size.

Most heads today consist of a single unit, a *deck*. Subordinate decks have been eliminated since it was discovered they didn't do anything useful in building readership.

☆ Flush-left heads are easiest to write, to set, and—most important—to read.

The headwriter needn't worry about a *ragged-right margin*. As long as each line of a 1-column head is more than half the column width, the head will be pleasing to the eye. It does not matter which line is the longer or longest.

In multicolumn heads, each line should extend into the last column of the story.

☆ One-column heads should be no deeper than four lines.

Three lines is a more desirable maximum.

☆ Multicolumn heads should be no more than two lines deep.

☆ There should be no more than 32 characters in one line of a head or 45 characters in a whole head, regardless of lines.

☆ All-capital heads should be avoided.

Their legibility is low. We recognize words by their top silhouette. In all-cap setting that outline is just a straight line without adequate distinguishing variables.

A little better is the most common head style, *upper-and-lower*. In this style each word is capped. Some papers do not cap prepositions, others cap them only when the preposition is the first word on a line.

The newest headline usage is *downstyle*. Capitalization follows that used in body type: The first word of a sentence and proper nouns are capped, all others are lowercase.

☆ Downstyle heads are the most efficient for the writer, typesetter, and reader.

☆ Heads should be written as they are read, line for line.

In body type the reading eye moves somewhat like a pendulum, swinging from line to line without even being aware of separate lines. But with a headline the eye reads just one line; there is a perceptible break; then the next line; then the third, if any. Therefore:

☆ Closely-linked phrases should not be broken from one line to another.

Such are, especially, prepositional phrases although other common phrases must be considered as really a single "word": United/States, George/Washington, Central/High, Football/Team, etc.

In applying this rule, make sure it is really a prepositional phrase under consideration. It's correct to say:

**Seniors Take Off
On Albuquerque Trip**

for in this case "off" is not a preposition but an integral part of the verb.

Bimos

Although contemporary heads are simplified to the utmost, there are some useful 2-element head styles called *bimos* (pronounced *buy*-mows), short for *bimodular*. The most common is the *kicker*.

The kicker is a short head, usually underscored, that rides above and just to the left of the main head.

Kickers should be half the point size of the main head. They may be in the regular headletter or in the *accent face*. The kicker should be no longer than one-third the width of the headline area. The main head must be indented approximately 10%. In the case of regular 11-pica columns, the indent is 1 pica per column. For wider

Kicker. Note size ratio between kicker and main head; underscore of kicker; indent of main head, approximately 10% of head area.

Dual kicker. Right one is non-functional because it is off normal path of reading eye and therefore only distracting.

columns, indenting is 1½ picas per column.

Customarily, Italic kickers are used over Roman main heads and vice versa but recent research indicates that this has no measurable effect on readership.

The accent face is a headletter in an exaggeratedly heavy version of the regular head type. Or it may be a strikingly different face. The accent is used in bimos, for catchlines with pictures and for heads on boxed stories.

To do its job properly, the kicker in regular headletters must be underscored to give it extra weight. The accent face usually will not require such weighting and thus eliminates the underscore.

The *reverse kicker* is also called a *hammer* because of its great impact. It's a "reverse" kicker because the size ratio is reversed; now the kicker is twice the size of the main head. It is underscored, not because it needs extra weight, but to be consistent with the regular kicker.

The hammer is kept short, no more than half the head width. The main head is in-

Hammer. Note ratio of hammer to main head; generous —20%—indent of latter.

| Vote results: | Classes elect officers for 1974-1975, Villano, Hoffman selected new presidents |

Tripod. Note use of colon, commonly used in this style head.

dented 20%, 2 picas per regular column, 3 picas per wide column.

☆ Main heads under kickers should be two lines deep.

The main head under a kicker may on occasion be only a 1-liner but under a hammer, two lines are always required. The kickers are not counted in determining the 32/45-character maximum discussed earlier.

The *wicket* consists of two short lines of smaller type followed by a single line of larger size, all on the same horizontal line. Wicket letters are half the size of the larger main head or perhaps one step smaller than that.

The wicket is the only head written flush-right. Then the longer of the two lines is placed flush-left in the column. There is a pica of space between the wicket and the main head.

The *tripod* reverses the wicket form. Now the head begins with a short line of large type followed by two lines of smaller type.

☆ The break between wicket and tripod and their main head should not come at, or near, the alley between columns.

If it does, it will look like two separate heads, side by side. To make sure that the reader sees these bimos as single units, the wicket or tripod should be written in ½- or 1½-column widths. The main head should always be at least twice as long as the bimo.

☆ Kickers should be written so that if they are lost or unread, the meaning of the main head will not be distorted.

It is easy for the reading eye to skip over the kicker and go right into the main head (which is the reason the main head is indented, taking it away from close competition with the kicker for the attention of the eye). And it is easy for the kicker to get lost in the composing room. So, take this head, for instance:

In Case of Rain

Graduation Scheduled In City Auditorium

If the kicker doesn't make it clear—for any reason whatsoever—that everything is conditional upon the weather, the main head surely gives misinformation; a contingency plan sounds as if it is the primary one.

Writing Headlines

Every newspaper should have a *headline schedule*. This is a collection of all the heads used by the paper. Each head should be shown just as it appears in the paper. It is not adequate simply to show a line of 24-point type and say, "This can be used in as many columns and as many lines as you like." Then copyreaders dream up their own headline forms. Usually such creations are abominations; at best they may destroy the typographic consistency which is essential for maximum readership.

☆ Only heads on the schedule may be used.

To make it easy for everyone to refer to specific heads, they are coded on the schedule. The *2-digit code* is the most efficient. The first digit designates the column-width of the head.

So, 1-4, 1-10 heads—or any heads designated by an initial 1—are all 1-column heads. A 3-1 head is 3 columns wide, etc.

The second digit shows the relative weight of heads in a column-width.

The 1-1 head is the heaviest of all 1-columners, the 2-1 is the heaviest in 2-column width, etc. There is no size relation among heads of various widths, though. The 1-1 may be in 24-point while the 5-1 could be in 48- or even 60-point. But always the code shows that the 3-4 head, for instance, is lighter than the 3-3 and heavier than the 3-5.

Advantages of this code are obvious. By means of only two numbers, let's say 3-4, the editor can tell the typesetter that this is a 3-column head consisting of two lines of 36-point Bodoni Roman, that it's indented 3 picas at the left, that there's an 18-point

1-3 Norton Calls
On City Hall
For New Aid

1-4 Fine Matron
For Monopoly
Of Party Line

1-5 School Bands
Give Concert

1-6 Blonde Victor
Dyes Tresses

1-9 Rain Forecast

1-10 Oil Sales Up

1-13 Neighborhood Skating
Opens With Ice Fete

1-14 St. Martin's Church
Calls New Pastor

1-17 Seven Hurt in Plane

1-18 Man(child) Bites Dog

2-5 Record Majority
Approves Bonds

2-6 St. James Conducts
Ordination Rites

Not Us!
2-9 City Denies Smell

Room for Industry?
2-10 Electronic Factory Area
Protests Zoning Order

In Orbit
2-11 Teacher Shuttles Between
Classes in Three Schools

2-H Lightning
Fire Razes Dairy Barns

2-W Neighbors
Protesting Factory Coming

2-T Snow Unpredicted Storm
Breaks Down Trees

Portion of headline schedule. Note that there are two larger 1-column heads (1-1 and 1-2) and four larger 2-columners, and that bimos are coded H, W, T with column-width.

Bodoni Bold Italic kicker and that there's a 3-point rule just as long as and under the kicker. Confusion is minimized: The editor actually sees the wanted head form and so does the printer. For each has a copy of the hed sked.

On the copyreader's sked are written the minimum and maximum *unit count* for each head. Each head has its own count.

The standard unit is the normal lowercase letters as a, b, c, etc. Each of these counts 1. The i and l count only ½ unit and in some

type styles, f, j, and t may be so narrow they only count a half.

The lowercase m and w count 1½ units.

One student worked out a memory aid: "All lowercase letters count 1 except the *flitjays* count only ½ and the *wammies* count 1½."

Capital letters count 1½ except the I which is only 1 and M and W which count 2.

Space between words counts ½.

(Remember that these are unit counts and have nothing to do with the 32/45 "character counts" for determining the bulk of a headline.)

Assume that the news editor has told the copyreader to write a 2-5 head. A line can take a maximum of 21 units. (The minimum is 14 units but rarely is this important. The problem usually is squeezing enough characters into the line.)

You might start out:

$$Central\ High\ Geologists\ Find$$

$$Central\ High\ Geologists\ Find = 26$$
$$1\tfrac{1}{2}\ 1\ 1\ 1\ 1\ 1\tfrac{1}{2}\ \big|\tfrac{1}{2}\big|\ 1\tfrac{1}{2}\ \tfrac{1}{2}\ 1\ 1\ \big|\tfrac{1}{2}\big|\ 1\tfrac{1}{2}\ 1\ 1\ \tfrac{1}{2}\ 1\ 1\ \tfrac{1}{2}\ 1\ 1\ \big|\tfrac{1}{2}\big|\ 1\tfrac{1}{2}\ \tfrac{1}{2}\ 1\ 1$$

$$Geology\ Students$$

$$Geology\ Students = 16$$
$$1\tfrac{1}{2}\ 1\ 1\ \tfrac{1}{2}\ 1\ 1\ 1\ \big|\tfrac{1}{2}\big|\ 1\tfrac{1}{2}\ 1\ 1\ 1\ 1\ 1\ 1\ 1$$

That's way too long. Finally, after several attempts, the headline is written:

Central Geology Class
Finds Diamonds on Trip

Some editors count characters as the first step to see if they are in the ball park. In this final head there are 21 characters in the first line and 22 in the second. That's close enough to make it worth counting units. The difference between the unit count and the character count comes from the flitjays, wammies, and caps.

The art of writing heads is an exacting one. The person who has mastered it will be a valuable member of a newspaper staff. The copy editor gets no by-lines. Sitting on the rim isn't a glamour job. But it is an essential one. The best news story in history is worthless unless and until it's read. A good headline is a major factor in assuring that reading.

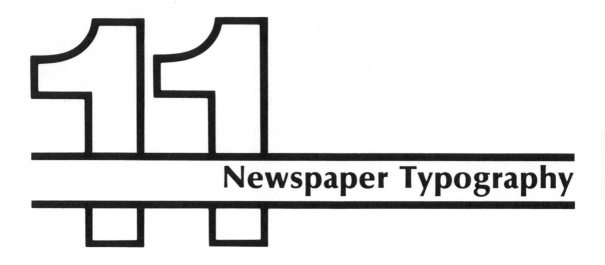

Newspaper Typography

To build a house, you need beams, boards, cement blocks, pipes, doorknobs, and countless other components. To build a good newspaper, you need body type, headletters, pictures, and constants.

The student editor must be as familiar with all these elements as an architect is with the materials he proposes to use. This chapter will discuss all the components except pictures; they're so important they get a chapter all to themselves.

Body Type

Body type is the most important single component of a newspaper. For it carries some 98% of all the information in a paper. In fact, the function of all of typography is to get readers to read body type. If people read only headlines and pictures, they will be poorly informed and the staff will have failed its job.

But body type is so unobtrusive that its importance is often—probably usually—overlooked. The wise editor, scholastic or professional, gives much attention to body type, though, in the original selection thereof and in its continued use.

The widespread use of cold type has been a great boon to the editor, for it has reduced the initial investment from thousands to only hundreds of dollars. With strikeon composition, a new face is available at even lower cost.

The student editor should ask the printer what body faces are available. Often the choice must be made from this limited group. The editor should also find out how feasible it is to obtain a new face for use of the student paper.

(There is a growing trend among larger high schools as well as colleges to have the staff do its own typesetting. In that case, of course, the staff has a wide selection of faces available for its initial choice.)

Choice of Face

In any circumstance, a good body type must meet several criteria. Newsprint, the paper on which most newspapers are printed, is of low quality. It was necessary to design metal typefaces specifically for such printing. The granddaddy of all news faces is Corona and its basic design is still followed by most both hot- and cold-type letterforms. Always ask to see "newspaper faces" when making selection.

Slick paper is often used for magazines; on it the *book faces* such as Baskerville, Caledonia and Caslon—among hundreds of others—work efficiently and pleasingly.

Body type should be Roman, for it is the only race that has satisfactory *readability*. This is not a matter of taste or judgment, it is a demonstrable fact, proven by much good and valid research.

This statement brings anguished protests from many student editors who want to use Sans Serifs for body type. They like the crisp, clean look of Sans and feel that it is more "modern" than Roman.

Unfortunately, Sans Serifs has low readability, far too low to be acceptable. "If that is so," says the editor, "it's because the reader just isn't used to Sans. I'll give him so much of it that he'll soon learn to read it as well as he does Roman."

That isn't the case, however. Readability does not come from familiarity; it comes from the design of the letters.

The difference between c, e, and o, for instance, is slight, only in a stroke of a few thousandths of an inch. Perhaps the varying thickness of the lines helps the eye make this minute distinction. But, however we attempt to explain it, the fact remains that Romans are high in readability and the Sans are low.

The next decision is the size. Eight-point is the most popular for daily newspapers and is probably the best for scholastic papers, too.

☆ Choice of body type should be made on its *x-height*.

This is the height of its primary letters, a far better indicator of readability than the point-size.

☆ You can see a pumpkin easier than a goose egg.

This old printer's saying stresses that letterforms based on the circle of a pumpkin rather than the oval of an egg are easier to read. A large *lowercase-alphabet length, lca,* indicates rounder letterforms.

So type should be selected by its apparent size rather than its numerically indicated size. The only good way is to compare masses of body type, at least 10 square inches of each specimen.

Once the type has been chosen, there are three things that the editor can do with it to affect its readability: (a) set the line length, (b) determine the ledding, and (c) use the *duplex.*

The most important typographic trend among American professional newspapers in the past decade has been to the adoption of *optimum format,* 6 columns—instead of 8 —on a *broadsheet* of about 15 x 21 inches or 4 columns—instead of 5—on a *tabloid* page, half of a broadsheet page.

It gets its name because it enables the use of body type set in its *optimum line length.* This is the mathematically deter-mined line length, the *measure,* which is easiest for the reader by all criteria including speed, ease, comfort and, most important, comprehension.

[Notice that we talk about the "length" of a line of type but the "width" of a column, an inconsistency of terminology that could be confusing.]

☆ The formula for determining optimum line lengths:

$$O = lca \times 1\tfrac{1}{2}$$

O is the optimum line length. The *lca* is the lowercase-alphabet length, the measure —in points—of a line containing the 26 minuscules. Each font of type has its own lca so you'll have to find out that of your own body type. This is shown in type specimen books or your printer can tell you.

☆ The formula for determining the readability range is:

$$Mn = O - 25\%$$
$$Mx = O + 50\%$$

Mn is the minimum length, and *Mx* the maximum, at which we can set body type. Setting it narrower than Mn or wider than Mx seriously handicaps the reading eye. So all settings should be within the readability range and as close as possible to the optimum.

The problem of reading efficiency obviously is not as great for a scholastic editor as it is for the editors of the *Los Angeles Times* or the *Kansas City Star.* For they must persuade their readers to consume thousands of times as many words as the high school editor's paper carries. But a major function of scholastic journalism is to prepare staffers for professional journalism. So it is valuable to learn principles that are vital in professional journalism even if they are less important in school publications.

A composing room is like a factory; it is most efficient when it is most standardized. For conventional setting, with columns about 11 picas wide, type can be set in 1-, 1½-, and 2-column measure. Any other widths are inelegantly termed *bastard measure* and should be avoided as inefficient for everyone involved—editor, compositor, and reader.

In op format, the editor needs only a 1-column setting of around 14 picas, a great economic boon. Some editors then use an 11-pica measure for an occasional accent. Increasing the op line 1½ times may be done, also, for accent. In either case, only occasional and short material should be so set. Two-column op matter is far too long for efficient reading.

Ledding

There is no formula for proper ledding. Solely by experience, printers suggest that for 7- through 9-point type it be ledded ½ point and for 8- through 12-point, it be 1 point. There is an overlap there; typical news faces can be ledded either a half or a full point.

The only way to determine the best way is to examine each kind of ledding after it has been printed in your own paper. If this is impossible, ask the printer to show you examples of variously ledded type in large masses.

Too little ledding makes the type look cramped; it is difficult to read and uninviting in appearance. Too much ledding makes it difficult for the eye to find the succeeding line after reading the first line. It also makes the type *fall apart,* look like too loosely woven cheesecloth instead of firm broadcloth.

Duplexing

The *duplex* of body type is normally its Italic or *boldface* version although it may be an altogether different face. Its function is to add *typographic color* to a mass of body type.

Typographers speak about two kinds of "color." That produced by printing in colored ink is called *ROP color.* ROP means "run of the paper"; no special printing is used.

Typographic color comes from changing tonal values of typographic elements. Type itself comes in various "colors."

Italic is too light for newspaper use. In masses it scares the reader away before he or she even begins reading a story. Boldface does the same thing although not until its

mass gets larger than that of Italic. Consequently the use of Italic dwindles constantly in American newspapers.

Boldface still has uses for cutlines and in sideless boxes.

A common use of bold was for *subheads, boldlines,* and *bold grafs.* Their common function is to break up large masses of body type. A dollar bill makes a good gauge; placed horizontally on a newspaper page, the bill should always touch at least one display element. If it doesn't, the mass of body type is too great. It looks as gray and foreboding as a dish of cold oatmeal. So the editor must drop some raisins in to make it more appetizing.

The subhead is a word or two, set in bf caps and centered, like this:

scampered to the goal line.
JOHNSON HURT
But he lay still as teammates, not knowing he was hurt, jumped up and down in joy.

The boldline serves the same function but eliminates the need to write, set, and print a separate line. The first line of the paragraph is set in boldface with the first word or words capped, something like this:

Tonal value of type is shown in varying "color" of jacket, pants and shoes of figure made entirely from typographic elements.

scampered to the goal line.

BUT HE LAY STILL, as teammates not knowing he was hurt, jumped up and down in joy.

Ideally about ten letters should be capped. But care should be taken that a complete name or phrase is capped lest the meaning be distorted. Do not cap bold lines this way:

JOHN H. Jones was elected to the new office of

or

BUT HE LAY still as teammates, not knowing he was hurt,

or

AS THE GRADUATES WALKED UP to the platform to shake hands

An entire paragraph may be set in boldface. A bold graf should be short. It is emphasized solely because of its position in a mass of type and not for verbal emphasis. Indeed, it is the fear that the bold type will give undue emphasis that makes many editors cool toward this technique.

☆ Don't mix boldface and lightface in the same line of type.

☆ Don't use boldface or Italics to emphasize a word or phrase in body type.

In newspaper style, emphasis comes from arrangement of words; in books we may use the duplex to stress words. In this book, Italic is used to designate a technical term.

To emphasize the deeper color of these devices, a blank line should be placed above the subhead and the boldline and both above and below the bold graf.

While all these devices are in use in professional papers, recent research indicates that they are ineffective, that the only "raisin" that will really make the reader salivate is the *breaker head*.

The breaker has the same content as a subhead, usually a label or a sentence fragment. But it is in a headline size, for school papers usually 12- or 14-point, in dailies 14- or 18- and sometimes as large as 24-point.

Use of breakers is arbitrarily set by the editors. Typically they will say, "Any story that runs longer than 10 inches will take breakers at intervals of approximately 4½ to 5½ inches." They choose their own numbers, of course.

Usually an appendix is added, "But if a story is arranged horizontally so it's no deeper than 3 inches in any column, breakers may be eliminated."

Breakers will have sparing use in a school paper because stories should studiedly be kept much shorter than 10 inches. But background and in-depth stories are growing in popularity and they usually run beyond the length where breakers become necessary.

Boxes

The best all-type color device is the box. Four-sided boxes, unfortunately, require bastard typesetting; the column must be narrowed to allow room for the side rules. This is expensive in time and money so the *sideless box* has been devised. Now rules are placed only at the top and bottom. Then body type can be set regular width and the pasteup man doesn't have to waste time making the sides and horizontal rules meet in neat corners.

Body type in a box should be set in boldface. The head, in the accent face—if there is one—should be very short, often just a label. In a sideless box, body type is full measure, the head is centered, the only time centered heads are used.

A pleasant variation is to indent the body type 1 or 1½ picas at the left only. In that case the head is set flush left for pleasant balance.

‖‖

Impact

Sideless boxes are so easy to make that they add no composing room expense. Yet they serve the same function as a four-sided box. Body type is set boldface, indented a full pica at the left only. Rules are used only top and bottom. An accent face makes an ideal head.

‖‖

Sideless box is mild but useful functional substitute for small picture to add color to page.

The box may be 1 or 2 columns wide. One-column boxes should be at least 3 inches and no more than 5 inches deep. Two-column boxes should be no more than 3 inches deep. In no instance should they be square.

Boxes become an acceptable—though obviously weaker—substitute for a picture of the same size. They must be treated like pictures, kept away from other boxes, from pictures, and from advertising.

Porkchops

Porkchops, a corruption of "portraits," are half-column pictures. They are useful as color devices but they aren't much good for showing what a person looks like. Their use is discussed in the next chapter.

the tea been able to raise $450 or e $700 that the fifteen uniforms cost. The complete outfit includes a

VICKI CAMPBELL

red warm-up suit, a practice warm-up, and the game uniform. Mr. Marshall has said that the amount will be pa ney gen

Porkchop—half-column portrait—is emphasized by white space at its side. Note handling of identification.

Headlines

The very word *headline* is synonymous with the excitement of news, and editors are greatly concerned with the *headletters* available and the form of the heads they create.

The choice of headletters contributes as much to the personality of a newspaper as the choice of sports jackets reflects the personality of a man.

For headlines the imperative is that they have high *legibility*—as opposed to the readability of body type. Legibility assures the instantaneous recognition of a few words. The highest legibility is that of the Sans Serifs but most Romans have legibility adequately high for headline use. Some Gothics, especially the more contemporary ones such as Helvetica and Univers, make attractive and functional headletters.

As with body type, the student editor may have to select headletters from the printer's available *type library*. Usually the typical print shop has enough faces on hand to allow a good *headline schedule*.

The schedule is a complete collection of all the heads that are used in a newspaper. It should be extensive enough to provide heads for every occasion that can be foreseen but have none that go unused despite the occasion for their use.

Five fonts—preferably all from the same family—will make a good head schedule for a student newspaper. This might be 14-point Roman, 18-point Italic, 24-point Roman, 36-point Italic, and 36-point Roman. Of course, if 18-, 24-, and 36-point were available in both Roman and Italics, the sked would be even better.

On occasion, a 48-point head is required. If that isn't available, a smaller size may be blown up photographically.

Addition of an accent face livens a hed sked in the way that a dash of chili powder illuminates Mexican cooking. The accent is a face markedly different from the regular headletter. It may be an exaggerated form of the regular letter; Ultra Bodoni and Spartan Extra Black are examples. Or it may be a Script or Cursive.

The accent face is also used for catchlines under pictures and for heads on boxed brights.

Heads are designated by codes. These can be as simple as starting with the biggest or smallest head and numbering them 1, 2, 3. Some codes are merely abbreviations for the specifications of the head; *2/2 36 BBX* would be "2 columns, 2 lines, 36-point Bodoni Bold Italics."

The highly functional 2-digit code is explained in Chapter 10.

Chapter 13 tells more about the use of

headlines. Heads are so important that they deserve to be in more than one chapter. But always remember that heads are subordinate to body type as conveyors of information; indeed, the major function of the head is to lure the reader into body type.

Newspaper Constants

A newspaper is like a store; most of its contents come in, are sold, and then replaced with fresher merchandise. This is the news content of a paper. But the store has permanent counters, shelves, and display cases which are always there. A newspaper has *constants*, elements which appear in every issue.

☆ The editor should personally check the constants in each issue of the paper to see that they are printing clean.

Printing elements for offset cannot wear out as relief printing elements do. But the same effect occurs when matter is clipped from a printed page and pasted up for platemaking. Always and only, *camera-fresh copy* should be used for pasteup.

Nameplates

The most conspicuous and most important constant is the *flag* or *nameplate*. This is the name of the paper as it appears in display form on page one. This is the trademark of the paper and must always be used in this established form. Note that the nameplate is not the *masthead*, even though too many people—even professionals who ought to know better—misuse the term.

More than any single element, the nameplate reflects the personality of the newspaper. It may be set in type—hot or cold, pasted up in *stickon type*, or handlettered.

Nameplates should not be changed every semester; like all good trademarks, they gain popular acceptance through constant and continued use. But they need not be as permanent as the inscriptions incised in the stone of the United States Supreme Court building. Flags can be changed; but they should be changed for good, considered purposes, not by whim or whimsy.

Faddish letterforms should be avoided.

Floating flags. These are all less than full-page wide and may run anywhere in top half of page. "Forge," with its strong eagle, is from Central Hower High in Akron, Ohio.

"Cathedral Chronicle" from Cathedral High in Springfield, Massachusetts, uses Ultra Bodoni, strong letter often used as accent face.

"Chieftain" of Pocatello (Idaho) High, appropriately ornaments conventional type, thus making distinctive nameplate.

"Evanstonian" of Evanston Township (Illinois) High, uses large initial to make distinctive otherwise common letters.

"Herald" of Harding High, Marion, Ohio, shows building, technique especially popular for schools that have new structures.

"Cass Technician" of Cass Technical High, Detroit, Michigan, uses Novelty letterform so eccentric it is almost non-verbal trademark.

Nameplates. "Line O'Type" of Moline (Illinois) Senior High uses conventional Roman type.

"News" of Arthur Hill High, Saginaw, Michigan, uses Ben Day to separate words of flag. Failure to capitalize proper nouns distresses purists.

"Catalyst" of Centennial High, Coquitlam, British Columbia, Canada, seasonally changes ornamentation at right of slash mark.

Faces that zoom to popularity usually fade just as quickly. It is an unhappy situation to have a flag that is badly outdated. Probably that's why the majority of professional newspapers use Black Letter for their flags. They figure that a style that's been around since Gutenberg's day will probably not go out of fashion in the next 50 years or so.

The name of the publication is obviously a factor in selecting the type and style for a nameplate. The "John Fitzgerald Kennedy Consolidated School Gazette" obviously has

to use a different style from the "Clay High News."

Decorated flags become more popular for newspapers of all kinds. For school papers many decorative elements come to mind. Maps are popular especially for consolidated schools whose district boundaries are like those of neither town nor county. Insignia of school, city, or county, drawings of the school building or local landmark, a mascot or symbol of athletic teams, or awards won by the school or by the newspaper are all appropriate and distinctive, and usually attractive as well, as a decoration obviously should be.

Flags should not be so overdecorated that they lose legibility. For the same reason too-ornate Novelty faces should be avoided.

Handlettering often lures the staff but should be approached warily. For lettering is an exacting art that few professional artists have mastered—and even fewer students. *Calligraphy*, literally "beautiful writing," grows in popularity because letters can be linked more attractively than they can in type.

"Senator" of Borah High, Boise, Idaho, runs conventional nameplate on compact-format page. On occasion, flag runs sideways. Picture of lion is extraneous and confusing and weakens nameplate. Note band at page bottom "selling" inside-page stories.

Fortunately, calligraphic letters and others that approximate handlettering are available in stickon letters. Photolettering shops abound in even smaller cities; they can produce a nameplate at a nominal cost. The staff's own printer probably can do the same.

The nameplate ought to be made in two or even three sizes. A tabloid should have a 4-column flag that can also run across the whole 5-column page. There ought to be another one that can run in 2- and 3-column areas and perhaps a third that is just 1 column wide. In the latter case the words

Mastheads. Name of paper appears in exact miniature of form on page one. "Sword and Shield" is from James Madison Memorial High, Madison, Wisconsin. "Campus Crier" is from Blue Springs (Missouri) High and "Triangle" from Columbus (Indiana) North Senior High.

of the name must be rearranged from one line into two or three. Such modification does not destroy the trademark value of the flag if the letterform remains the same.

☆ Do not separate page one folio lines from the nameplate with a rule.

The folios are an integral part of the flag and should not be divided from or set apart from the name itself.

Masthead

The masthead, as noted, is not the flag. The masthead is the formal statement that identifies the publication and usually runs on the editorial page. If a paper is distributed as second-class mail, a masthead is required by law. In any instance it is required by custom.

The name of the paper in the mast should appear in the same style as in the nameplate. Other elements are: The name, address, and perhaps the phone number of the school; frequency of publication; *volume* (the number of years the paper has been published) and *number* (during the current school year); names and/or insignia of press associations to which the paper belongs; emblems and/or list of awards won by the publication; and, most important, the names and titles of all editors and staffers.

In some instances, the law or school regulations require the name of the principal, superintendent, or school board members. Whether required or not, the faculty advisor's name should certainly be listed.

Because the listing of names is a major and well-deserved reward for the work that staffers contribute, every staff member's name should be listed whether editor-in-chief or re-typist or one who runs proofs back to the printer on a motor scooter.

Extraordinary care should be devoted to avoiding typographic errors in the masthead. It is hard to maintain your readers' respect when "they can't even spell their own names right."

But listing in the masthead should not be just a status symbol or another rung for a social climber. Only staffers who actually

CENTRAL OUTLOOK
"AN ALL AMERICAN PAPER"

PROMPT ⬥ PTG. CO.

Published Bi-Weekly by the Journalism Department, Central High School, 26th and Edmond, St. Joseph, Missouri 64501. Second Oldest High School West of the Mississippi.

Subscription Rate: $2.00 Per Year

Editor-in-Chief . . . . Judy Gibbs

Managing Editor . . . . Lynda Brown

Page Editors: Larry Glaze, Jennifer Cox, Ginny Vineyard, and John Stingley

Business Manager . . . . David Lewis

Cartoonists . . . . Mark Martin and D'Artagnan Stevens

Photographers . . . . Heidi Hinton, Mike Johnson

Reporters: Candy Burton, Diane Dickens, Ann Gilpin, Dean Guinn, Vicky Rothleitner, Amy Snyder, and Candy Widner.

Faculty Advisor . . . . . . Mrs. David Hornaday

Principal . . . . Mr. Frank Baker

"Outlook" of Central High, St. Joseph, Missouri, uses masthead to announce All-American contest rating as well as membership insignia of National Scholastic Press Assn. and Quill and Scroll.

work—and do good work—should be so recognized.

Qualifications for listing must be established and posted for all to know. A reporter should have a specified number of inches of published material. Copyreaders or circulation people should have a minimum number of hours of work. Ad staffers' efforts can be measured by the inches of ads they sell, prepare, or service.

If persons do not meet standards, especially of responsibility, their names should be removed until they have earned their way back. Beginners should undergo a probationary period of service before they become full-fledged staffers and are listed in the masthead.

But the laurel wreath of masthead listing should be neither given nor taken away arbitrarily. Standards should be in writing so that every staffer is assured of fair treat-

ment. Nor should listing be a mark of popularity; a lot of good newspaper people are crotchety curmudgeons who will never be "Miss Congeniality" in any contest.

Just as the masthead recognizes good staff work, so it can be a trophy case for awards that the paper has won. Never should false modesty decide that this is uncouth bragging; many great newspapers proudly announce their Pulitzer prizes in their mastheads.

Folios

Strictly speaking, a *folio* is a page number; but in common usage the term is expanded to include the name of the paper, the place of publication, and the date as well as the page number. On page one the folios are part of the nameplate and often include the volume and number as well as the newsstand price.

Running folios clear across the top of a page is considered old-fashioned and—there's no arguing this—they waste space. Modern usage is to set folios in 1- or 2-column measure, ideally so they can be run in either width in either one or two lines. Folios should run as close as possible to the top outside corner but this isn't necessary; they can run above any element of appropriate width in any column.

Logos

Page logotypes, logos, are used by professional newspapers to identify departments and sections, especially women's and sports pages. Often logos are used to please advertisers who aren't sure their ad ran on a society page unless it is plainly labeled.

Student newspapers don't need section logos. (Neither do professional papers!) The reader recognizes a sports page, for instance, by the heads and pictures on it. If the reader can't do this, you don't need a sports logo, you need a new sports editor.

Standing Heads

Standing heads also called *headings* are used on recurring features such as columnists, league standings, meeting notices, etc.

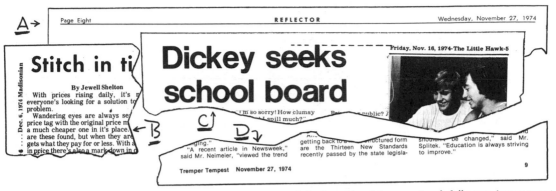

Most editors prefer straight headlines rather than these labels; but there are times when a simple label is adequate.

All headings in a newspaper should bear a strong family resemblance to the nameplate and to each other. There may be some slight variations to indicate the nature of the material under the standing head, but the common visual theme must always be maintained.

The name of the feature may be used as a kicker or wicket and combined with a news head. This, we hope, will attract the regular reader who recognizes the standing name and also the transient reader who is interested only in the newsy headline.

So, instead of just the label "Club Meetings," we might have that heading as a kicker, thus:

Club Meetings

Most Organizations Schedule Elections in April Sessions

Folio line style. *A* is conventional, full-page; improvement would be to change "Page Eight" to simple "8."

B shows lines running sideways, outside of page.

C is functional style. Narrow folios run within page.

D runs folios at foot of page, style more common to magazines than newspapers.

Art heads are those that contain pictorial matter—often the picture of the writer—as well as type. Art heads often degenerate into a "cartoonist's dream" and get so hokeyed up that they lose legibility as well as appeal.

The constants of a newspaper are much like the brass plate on a bank. They should be kept shiny, printed cleanly. It doesn't affect the assets of a bank by one penny if that brasswork is shiny or grundgy; but it sure has a major effect on the public's attitude toward the bank. So with a newspaper; unless the staff keeps its brass—the constants—neatly polished, the reader will feel that it doesn't have pride in its work. And lack of evident pride of a staff usually is reflected by a lack of student-body respect for the staff's work.

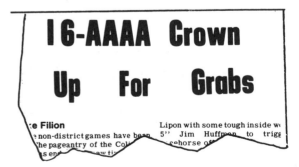

Excessive spacing causes head to fall apart, difficult to read quickly, easily. One en spacing should be maximum —and constant—within headlines.

12 Pictures in Journalism

Pictures were the first written communications; they continue to be a major tool of communications today, some 25,000 years later. Indeed, some cynics feel that we have come to such a complete circle that written words are being denigrated.

From the caves of Spain to the plains of America, primitive people "wrote" stories by means of stick figures. Realistic *pictograms* became *ideograms* of abstract words, then pictures of sounds, *phonograms,* to visualize words.

A combination of words and pictures is the most effective communication we know today. There is too much competition between word people and picture people; as a result too many editors believe they must choose between the two tools. This isn't true, of course. Sometimes a picture will carry the burden of communications with words as a supplement; in other instances, words will convey the gist with pictures as a corollary. Choosing the proper combination is a major display of editorial competence.

All pictorial material is called *art,* divided into photography and *hand art,* any pictures or decoration produced by an artist's hands instead of by a camera. Art may also be classified as *line art* or *halftone.*

Line Art

Line art consists of black-and-white areas only, in simple lines or dots or in larger masses. Wood or linoleum blocks made in art classes are good examples of line work; so are the pictures usually used on Mimeograph stencils.

But you can create an illusion of gray even though you use only black ink on white paper. You can *stipple* or *cross-hatch* an area with little dots or lines or apply a *shading sheet.* (Of the many trade names for the latter, *Zip-A-Tone* is probably the most widely known and commonly used.) These are thin plastic sheets on which are printed regular, mechanical patterns of lines or dots.

They are fun to use. Make a regular line drawing. Then choose, from literally hundreds of patterns, the one you want. Lay the shading sheet over the drawing and *tack it down* by rubbing a few spots with a smooth piece of wood or metal, a fingernail, or a knuckle. An invisible layer of wax on the back of the sheet adheres it to the drawing although the sheet is not sticky to handle. It can be lifted off and repositioned without leaving a smear.

With a stylus, a needle imbedded in a pencil-like wooden handle, cut around the area to be shaded and lift away the rest. The end of the stylus is cut at an angle; with this *burnish,* smooth down, the shading sheet so tightly it seems to be part of the original picture.

A variation is *transfer sheets.* The desired pattern is placed face down on the drawing; the sheet is transparent so you can see what you're doing. Using the same burnishing tool, rub on the back of the

Line reproduction. TV watcher is done in solid blacks. Hatching and stippling on clothing of center figure was done by artist. Tone on desk in right drawing is 30% gray Ben Day applied by platemaker.

sheet. The pattern is transferred onto the drawing and literally becomes part of it. A handicap, though, is that once it's down, the pattern cannot be changed.

In both styles of sheets, many, many patterns are available. As they can be used in combinations, the possible patterns are almost beyond number. They come in black or white, the latter used on black areas.

The platemaker has a similar process called *Ben Day*. In this case you indicate the areas to be shaded on the drawing. You use a pale blue crayon or paint which is invisible to the camera. From a catalog you select a pattern which the platemaker places right onto the printing plate.

Ben Day and shading sheets give exactly the same effect. The latter is usually much less expensive. Areas of light gray or color, *tint blocks,* over which type or pictures are *surprinted,* are produced by the same methods although here Ben Day is the most efficient.

Halftones

Halftones are optical illusions, carrying out the effect of Ben Day to a very sophisticated level.

Photographs—along with paintings of all kinds and pencil and pastel drawings—are *continuous* tone art. They consist not only of black and white but of many, many varying shades of gray.

Look at the picture of your friend in your wallet. Shadows are pure black; teeth and that tiny dot of light in the eye are pure white. The skin is light gray, shadows around the eyes, nose, and mouth are deeper gray. These areas blend into each other imperceptibly, unlike the clear divisions in line art.

The printer has no gray ink to work with,

only black ink and white paper and that's all. So here the magic, the illusion comes in.

The continuous tone is broken down, by use of a *halftone screen,* in an overall pattern of tiny dots. Where the dots are large with little of the white paper visible between them, the eye thinks it is seeing black or very deep gray. Where the dots are extremely small and surrounded by comparatively large areas of white, the eye is fooled into thinking it's seeing white or light gray.

Where the black dots cover exactly half the paper area, the effect is of 50% gray. By changing the size and concentration of dots, the eye can be deluded into "seeing" various tones of gray, the halftones.

The number of lines of dots in a linear inch designates the fineness of the printed picture. For newspapers, a 65-line screen is

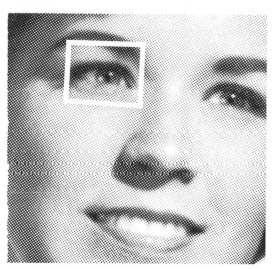

Halftone principle. Area outlined in white in large photo is enlarged in section below to show formation of dot pattern.

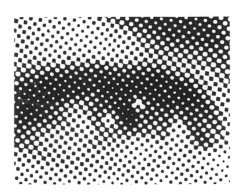

common. Sixty-five rows of dots vertically and horizontally make 4,225 in a square inch. For yearbooks and most magazines, screens as fine as 120-line are used and the dots are almost invisible to the naked eye.

Kinds of Cuts

Pictures in publications are still often called *cuts,* a carry-back to *photoengravings,* relief plates made by cutting away the background by acid. There are several variations of the basic *square halftone.* (This, incidentally, is rarely square; the name simply means a rectangular picture.)

The halftone may be circular or oval or even *free-form,* nongeometrical shapes, although these are not very compatible with rectangular printed pages and have limited use.

A *morticed* cut is one where an area has been removed, often for the inserting of the caption. A whole corner cut away is the *notch,* the simplest mortice. Less common is the *bay,* an open area bordered on three sides by the remaining halftone. The *interior mortice* is completely surrounded by the halftone.

Morticing can easily degenerate into gimmickry. Care must be taken that only nonessential elements are morticed from the photo, that the composition is not weakened or that the relationship between elements separated by a bay is not distorted.

Silhouetted halftones are those from which the entire background has been removed, leaving only the subject itself. This is usually used in feature material because in most instances the background of a news photo is necessary to tell the whole story.

A *modified silhouette* is one with two or more straight sides from which a portion of the outlined subject extends.

Halftones don't have pure black or white areas. In what appears black, there is a peppering of minute white *shadow dots* and in apparent white areas there is an equal sprinkling of tiny black *highlight dots.* So for pure black or white lines in conjunction with halftone, a *screened negative* is made for the photograph and a separate line neg for the other elements. The two negs are combined to make a single plate, hence its name, *combination plate.*

A fad that comes and goes—absolutely irrationally—is a black border around a halftone. This adds nothing—except labor and expense. The halftone pattern usually defines the shape without the need for a frame. If a corner of a photo is weak and the editor fears it may disappear during platemaking, the photographer is instructed to *burn* in the corners, darken them during photoprinting. Or the editor may darken the corner with a black grease pencil or with gray poster paint.

The halftone illusion may also be created with special screens. Coarse, irregular patterns give the effect of a crayon drawing; this is the *mezzotint* screen.

The halftone may be composed of parallel lines, straight or wavy, of differing widths or of concentric circles, also varying in thickness. These special screens cannot carry fine detail required for news pictures and so are mostly used for features. They are excellent for yearbooks.

A photograph made into a printing plate without the use of a screen is a *line conversion* or *linear definition.* All the tones of the photo that are darker than 50% gray will reproduce as black and those lighter than 50% will be white; there are no middle—half—tones. This technique loses almost all detail and must therefore be used with care. But the effect is striking.

This chapter will talk about the use of art of any kind and the writing of *caption material* that each requires—leaving its creation for Chapter 23. Although that chapter is ostensibly about yearbook art, it should be read in conjunction with this material because the same principles apply to all art, especially photography.

The basic axioms for using illustrations are:

☆ Pictures should be used functionally.

☆ Pictures should be cropped ruthlessly.

☆ Pictures should be enlarged generously.

☆ Pictures must be identified adequately.

A photograph normally is first produced as a *contact print,* a sheet containing all the photos on a strip of film and in the same size as the negative. A good editor can make choices from contacts, using a magnifying glass to see detail, perhaps even indicating preliminary cropping for the photographer to do as enlargements are made. Reading the film negatives themselves can save time and material by eliminating the need even for contacts.

Usually photos are then enlarged to 8 x 10-inch *glossies* with a very smooth surface that most platemakers prefer to work with. The *matte finish* common in studio portraits will look like an aerial map after platemaking lights intensify the shadows of the hills and valleys of the rough paper.

Only when a picture will be used in a larger size—a full page of a yearbook, for instance—are larger photoprints required. Then 8 x 12's or even 12 x 18's might be used. For the platemaker prefers to *shoot down*, make the plate smaller than the original art. In so doing any flaws in the photo are also reduced—to invisibility, we hope.

Occasionally a plate will be made *same size*, indicated to the platemaker by the symbol *S/S*. Only excellent photos should be used for this.

It is extremely rare to *blow up* a picture to make a larger plate. When that need arises—usually it's when the only portrait of a dead person is one of those wallet-sizes that comes from a coin machine—it is best to make a *copy negative,* just take a picture of the picture. The resulting photo is made larger than the plate will be and is *spotted,* bad flaws are painted out.

Cropping

☆ Find the picture in the photograph.

If from this axiom you get the feeling that *picture* and *photograph* are not quite synonymous, you're right. A photo is a chemical record of reflected light; a picture is a communication.

Cropper's L's. By moving two devices, editor can determine which rectangle contains essentials of "picture" in photo.

Crop marks in margins tell platemaker to use only area here marked by broken lines. Width of plate is indicated in lower margin.

Look for that portion of a photo that tells the story. Cut away all distracting and irrelevant portions. Just as unnecessary words fuzzy up verbal communications, so does excess photography. *Cropping,* cutting away unwanted portions, is the equivalent of blue-penciling too-wordy stories.

☆ Use *cropper's L's* to find the picture.

These are L-shaped pieces of cardboard, about an inch wide, which can be bought or, just as satisfactory, be homemade. By placing them over a photo in various positions, you can determine the rectangle that contains the "picture."

When the picture has been found, don't actually cut the photograph. Should you do that, you forfeit all chances to change your mind unless a new photoprint is made. That's too costly in time, effort, and material. So use *crop marks* or an *overlay* to indicate to the platemaker which portion of the whole photo to use.

☆ Crop marks are never placed on the photo itself.

They are marked on the margins of the photo with a grease pencil. Then, if you change your mind, or when the photo is filed for future use, it is simple to rub off the marks with a piece of tissue and start all over again. The caption for Example 1 shows how to make crop marks; read it carefully.

An overlay is a sheet of transparent paper fastened to the back of a photo and then flapped over the front. With a soft pencil, the desired portion of the photo is indicated. This method is especially useful

Platemaker's instructions may be written onto flap attached to and folded over photo. Width of plate and position in yearbook is specified. Crop marks are needed in only one side margin although both are used here. Where no marks are made, as bottom left, platemaker will go to edge of picture.

for nonrectangular pictures of any kind or for morticing.

Scaling

Because the plate is rarely the size of original art and because the platemaker is making screened negatives while the editor goes about other chores, the editor must know in advance exactly what size the reduced picture will be so he can make accurate page dummies.

☆ Scale all pictures before sending them to the platemaker.

When a photo is reduced, both height and width are changed in the same proportions. An 8 x 10 photo reduced to 4 inches wide becomes a 4 x 5, of course.

☆ Always give the width of a picture as its first dimension.

So the formula for scaling pictures is:

$$W : H = w : h$$

W is the width and H the height of the original art; w is the width and h the height of the plate.

In an equation like this all dimensions must be in the same unit. So convert the size of the photo into picas before you start scaling. And remember that only that portion which has been isolated by cropping is

the "original art"; don't use the whole photo you started out with.

Suppose you have a photo which has been cropped to $5\frac{1}{2} \times 8$ inches and you want to make a plate 22 picas wide. (You must always start with one known dimension for the plate, usually the width. In a newspaper or magazine, the editor usually decides that a picture will be one, two, or more columns wide. The height of the plate is then the unknown factor. But if the editor specifies the height of the plate, the unknown width can be determined by the same formula.)

Fill in the three known factors and designate the unknown, the new height, in this case, as x. So our formula is:

$$W : H = w : h$$
5.5 inches : 8 inches = 22 picas : h
33 picas : 48 picas = 22 picas : x
$$33x = 1056$$
$$x = 32 \ picas$$

Now, don't go running to your algebra teacher! You solve this equation by multiplying the "means," the inside numbers, which will then equal the product of the "extremes," the outside numbers. The means are 48 picas and 22 picas; the extremes, 33 picas and x.

A pocket computer simplifies the already simple arithmetic involved. So will a *slide rule* or a *scaling disk*.

While this method is simple, it sometimes involves fractions that are pesky to work with and so small we can't even measure

Expository art. "Torch" of Glenbrook (Illinois) North High clarifies new traffic plan with effective map.

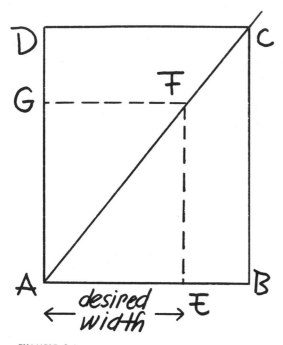

EXAMPLE 2-A

You want a plate 5 inches high; how wide will it be?

First draw the diagonal JL. Along JM measure 5 inches, the height of the plate, JN. From N send a perpendicular to the diagonal at O. NO is the width of the plate.

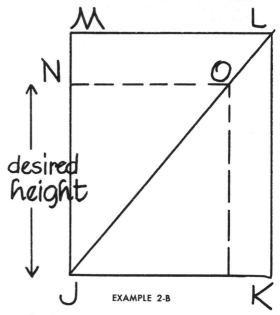

EXAMPLE 2-B

them with a *pica pole* or inch ruler. So a foolproof and faster system is used, the *common-diagonal method.*

This simple method can best be learned by working out a couple of problems with the aid of Example 2.

Assume in 2-A that the rectangle ABCD is the cropped area of a photo—its dimensions don't matter. You want to make a plate 36 picas wide; how tall will it be?

Draw the diagonal AC.

☆ Always draw the scaling diagonal from lower left to top right.

Along the bottom of the picture, on line AB, measure 36 picas, the new width, AE. At E raise a perpendicular until it hits the diagonal at F.

EF will be the height of the plate. And if you draw a line from F, parallel to AB to the left, the area AEFG will be exactly the size of the plate. There is no arithmetic to be done; just measure the unknown line and read the answer right from your ruler.

The same method finds an unknown width just as easily when the new height alone is known. Assume that in Example 2-B the area JKLM is the cropped original art.

On those rare occasions when you need to blow up the plate, the steps shown in 2-C will do the trick.

The small wallet-size photo STUV must be enlarged to make a plate 20 picas wide. First extend the sides of the original. Then draw the diagonal SU and extend it way

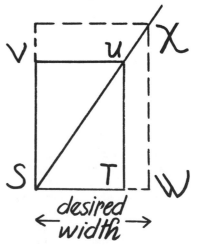

EXAMPLE 2-C

out into right field. Extend ST and along it measure 20 picas, SW. Raise the perpendicular WX and you have the new height. Draw XY to the extension of SV and you define the whole new area.

If an irregular silhouette, a circle or an oval are to be scaled, enclose them in a rectangle and use the same common-diagonal method as suggested in 2-D.

☆ Scaling should never be done on the photo itself.

It can be on an overlay. Or the exact rectangle of the photo can be drawn on another sheet of paper. The scaling may be made on the back of the photo as it's held against a window or a *light-table*, one with a translucent top and a light below it. If the work is done on the back, it must be done carefully, with a soft pencil, so the emulsion is not indented.

Captions

Words that accompany and explain a picture are called *caption material*. In newspapers they are referred to as *cutlines* or *idents*—for identifications. In magazines they are usually called just captions. (Because these names are not defined by law or dictionary, you may hear different terms used by your printers. Don't be disturbed; just add the new words to your own vocabulary.)

The writing of caption material is a refined art. Good captions increase not only the information carried by the picture but the pleasure of the viewer.

☆ Every picture must be identified.

An unidentified picture is not communication, it is "art." The objective of art is to stir emotion, any kind of emotion. If the same picture makes one viewer happy and another sad, the artist is satisfied. But a communication must convey precisely the same information to every viewer—and that cannot be done unless there are words to steer comprehension into the right channel.

Occasionally in newspapers or magazines and more often in yearbooks, *mood shots* or *salon shots* are used. These are merely

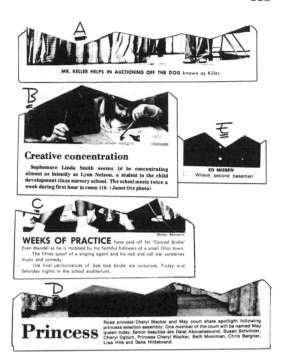

Caption treatment. *A* is singleton; it would be better in size larger type. All-cap setting should be avoided and, if used, not mixed with lowercase as here.

B is catchline set flush left. It may also be centered.

C is read-in catchline that, in content, is part of cutlines themselves.

D is sideline. It may be in one or two lines.

ornamentation; they please the eye but fail the intellect. These do not need captions. But even these are more satisfying with at least minimal caption matter.

Suppose, in any publication, there is a feature about "After Hours at Central High." A mood shot might be of a long empty hall with one solitary figure at the far end. This suggests the loneliness of an empty building. No caption is required. But the picture would be more satisfying if the reader knew who the figure was, a custodian or a late-practicing basketballer, if it were late at night or before classes in the morning, during summer vacation or fall semester, etc.

There are three kinds of caption material.

1. An *identification line* is just the name of the subject. It is usually set all-caps, boldface, centered. It may be expanded into *i & e lines* by the addition of an *expo* (expository) *line*, a descriptive phrase. Thus:

JOHN G. REYNOLDS
. . . elected senior president

The e-line is downstyle but also boldface and centered. This style is used for 1-column portraits although it may accompany rare larger portraits as well as pictures of inanimate subjects. Thus:

Old No. 23
. . . veteran bus starts final run.

The e-line is linked to the ident line with an ellipsis—those three periods. In newspapers, 1-column i&e lines are usually either the body type or a Sans Serifs of about the same point size. For larger pictures, the size is usually increased.

The second and the most common caption style is *cutlines*, just *lines* or captions. These may be the boldface of body type in newspapers or a Sans. In magazines they are usually in Sans or Italics. The Sans are always good in small portions and both they and the Italics are different enough from Roman body type that, in magazines or books, captions will not be confused with text material. The lines may be in one or more *legs*, columns.

2. Cutlines may be strengthened by a *catchline*, a line of display type that acts as an easy transition between picture and words. The catchline varies with the size of the picture, from 14-point to as much as 36-point, and is set in either the headletter or the accent face of the headline schedule.

The catchline may be centered or it may align with the left edge of the picture. In the latter style, cutlines may be full, lining up with each side of the picture, or they may be indented at the left only, still aligning at the right.

The display type may run under the left portion of the picture and thus become a *sideline*, one or two lines deep and aligned vertically on the depth of the cutlines.

Addition of the display lines increases readership of a picture and the area below it as much as 25%. They are widely used in newspapers, less frequently in magazines or yearbooks.

☆ Catchlines should be "catchy lines," not little headlines.

For a picture of a student who sings professionally, a little headline would say "Senior Cuts Discs" while catchlines might say "It's On The Record."

3. Cutlines ought to run at least four lines deep, no matter how many legs they're in. When there is neither opportunity nor need for lines this long, a *singleton* may be used. This single line of display type, again varying in size with that of the picture, combines the function of both catchline and cutlines.

☆ Cutlines should be succinct.

Cutlines should say only: Here's why this picture was shot; these are the people in it; here's something interesting or important that you wouldn't recognize by yourself.

With a *wild pic*, one that doesn't go with a story, cutlines may be much longer, *comprehensive* or *comprees*.

Cutlines are always written in the historical-present tense. While the event may be over, the action in the picture is immediate and continuing. The famous explosion that destroyed a Zeppelin was over and done in 1937; in the great photo that recorded it, "the Hindenburg burns fiercely" right now.

☆ Cutlines should start with action.

"Fans run onto the field as Jim Grant (far right) scores a touchdown . . ."

"Outstanding seniors are honored in traditional Awards Assembly ceremonies last Tuesday. Receiving major recognition are (left to right): Paul Fabius, Nancy Gilmore . . ."

Then identifications are made.

☆ Identifications are made from left to right and from top to bottom.

Although some people say that there is no need to say "left to right," that "everyone knows that," that is not so! True, that is the usual way of identification but everyone does not know that.

☆ Never take anything for granted!

And, if they do know that idents go L to R, your readers may not know that they run top to bottom. For even professional editors often fail to remember that we read

Kougar PRIDE

KANKAKEE VALLEY HIGH SCHOOL
WHEATFIELD INDIANA 46392
VOLUME IV
1974

Pattern shot makes strong title page for "Kougar Pride," yearbook of Kankakee Valley High in Wheatfield, Indiana.

a picture as we read type, moving downward. So, too often, idents for the front row are given first. Naturally this confuses the reader, for he must read the faces in the picture "backward," upward. And he is never quite sure which is the "first row." So labeling should always be in this order and in these terms: Top row, second row, third row (or middle row), and front row.

When one person is obviously the most important or most obvious, idents may begin with him or her:

"Sen. Mabel McGovern, wearing white dress, is greeted at the main entrance to Central High by Vincent Gray (left) and Terry O'Hearn."

If the greeters are a boy and a girl, Vincent wouldn't even have to be identified as at the left.

Page 6   ·   RED/BLUE   ·   December 4, 1973

New law ensures school bus safety

One junior high student was killed and 21 others were injured as a result of a school bus accident in Huntsville on Nov. 19, 1968.

The driver of the late model Blue Bird bus lost control while attempting to make a sharp curve on Bankhead Parkway. The bus hit a stone culvert and flipped over several times before stopping 90 yards away.

The bus had been inspected five days prior to the wreck and had been described as mechanically sound.

THAT ACCIDENT started a wave of action for bus safety in the city and the state. In 1969 Act 281, sponsored by Representative Charles Grainger, was made a state law.

Act 281 set aside safety regulations for all buses in Alabama. This includes an annual state inspection and an inspection by mechanics every month.

Inspectors ... steering, wheels, tires, brakes, lights, exhaust system ... If a bus fails to pass ... safety sta... of Edu...

"Waving her arms high in greeting, Alumna Victoria Mayhew comes back to Central just the day after winning an Oscar for her role as Pocahontas. . . ."

For all-essential consistency, cutlines style must be specified in detail and in writing. Typical specs might be:

The first line is not indented. After the action sentence(s), idents are introduced by a form of the verb "to be" and a colon. Then designate the row (if necessary) with a capped word. Then place, in parentheses, "(from left)" and another colon. Then the names. Names in each row make a separate paragraph that takes a normal indent. Thus:

> Colorful gifts sent from the student body of La Escuela de Tipografia in Guayaquil, Ecuador are accepted on behalf of Central High students by Sally McQueen, Student Government president.
>
> Taking part in the ceremony are: Top row (from left) Jean Crampton, George Peterson, Alice Demaron;
>
> Center row: Grant Manion, Dolores Reboza, Kathy Sallon, Bruce Roberts;
>
> Front row: Principal Robert Mantle, Sally, Gustavo Andrado, Carl Betts and James Dooley.
>
> Gustavo is a foreign exchange student here this semester and brought the gifts with him.

Note that the names in each row are followed by a semicolon and that the succeeding paragraph is really a sentence fragment, a grammatical form seldom acceptable in other usage.

Canopy head, across story and picture, is most effective way to link two such elements horizontally.

Only a simple title or explanation such as "Principal" is used with the names. When longer explanatory matter or titles must be used—as Gustavo's here—they follow in a separate graf. In the same last paragraph it could be noted, "Grant is SG vice-president, and Bruce's parents are hosts to Gustavo this semester."

The phrase "pictured here" or any variation on it should be tabooed. It is obvious that something is pictured; to point it out insults the reader's intelligence. For the same reason "above" is not required. Most captions are directly beneath a picture; this is a convention that is well understood by the reader.

Use of Pictures

Pictures serve two purposes. They expand and clarify written communications and they act as bait to lure the reader into body type.

☆ Pictures above type.

Because the reading eye travels downward from a strong element—and there are few stronger than a picture—its natural progression is from the picture down into type. Caption matter above a picture forces the eye to reverse its natural path from the strong element.

Of course, in a magazine or yearbook where a picture *bleeds*, runs right off the page, at the foot, the caption must be placed above or at the side. This may be done when necessary but such placement is less than ideal.

Photo is linked by reader to story immediately below it, not one in columns 2-4. If picture is not associated with story below, cutoff rule under cutlines should signal that to reader.

The axiom applies to the type of an accompanying story, too. The best way to harness the optical magnetism of a picture into drawing readers into a story is to make the accompanying headline the same width as, and directly below, the picture and its cutlines.

The eye will not normally proceed from a picture to a story at its side; for it doesn't link words and pictures horizontally. The only way such connection can be made obvious is to run a *canopy head* across both story and art.

☆ Pictures should not be separated from their stories.

Optical magnetism of photo is wasted by placement. In this position it does not lead reader into story, major function of all art.

If pix are the cheese and body type is the trap—and they most certainly are!—it is logical to keep them close together. To run a picture on page one, for instance, and say "Story on Page 5" is just as illogical as to put a piece of cheese in the basement with a card that says "The rat trap is out in the garage." It is, of course, just as malfunctional to run a story on the front page and note: "Picture on Page 5."

☆ Pictures should face into the page.

As an experiment, stand in the hallway

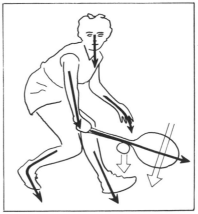

Lines of force. Arrows show force created by racket and shapes in body. Strong action of tennis stroke and ball, envisioned by reader, creates movement directly forward, into reader.

and look intently in one direction. Most passersby will also look that way. So with a picture. If the person in it is looking, pointing, or moving, the reading eye will be influenced to move that way, too. There is always danger that readers will be distracted away from the contents of a page; don't aggravate that hazard by urging them off with a picture that is "looking off the page."

By turning a photo negative over before printing the photograph, it is possible to make a *mirror image* of the original picture. So some editors, unable to place a picture so it won't point off the page, will ask the platemaker to *reverse the picture*. The term is inaccurate and confusing. A "reverse picture" is one in which all black elements become white and white ones become black. A film negative is a reverse image.

The best instruction is phrased: "Make this picture face to the right instead of left." But, although this is the correct phraseology, the actual practice is bad. In such a picture, people shake left hands, garments button the wrong way, hair is parted on the opposite side and any lettering becomes illegible. Even if such obvious discrepancies don't appear, the mirror image is subtly distressing to the viewer.

☆ Don't drop pictures into columns of type.

When the eye reads down a column of type and hits any barrier such as a picture, it instinctively caroms upward and to the right and continues into the adjacent column. It will come back to the type under the picture only reluctantly, if at all, because this entails a "backing-up" which the eye dislikes. The farther down a column at which this occurs and the shorter the leg of type under such a barrier, the greater the danger of it going unread.

☆ Minimize the use of *porkchops*.

☆ Don't use *runarounds*.

A porkchop is a half-column portrait; a runaround is the narrowing, then widening, of a column of type to make an opening into which the porkchop—or any other element—is inset. Runarounds are dangerous. They break reading rhythm. In a single column of type they produce lines that are far lower than the readability range.

Porkchops are tempting to editors who are always short of space because they take only a quarter of the space that the same pic would require if a full column wide. If a porkchop must be used, it should be pushed to one side of the column. The space adjacent to it should be left blank except for the identification. This will still save more than half the space needed for a full-column portrait.

The best solution is to use two porkchops side by side with their i-lines underneath.

Care of Photos

☆ Photos are fragile; treat them gently.

The surface of a photo is a thin and soft emulsion, easily dented by writing either on an overlay or on the back of the photo. Even though indentions are not conspicuous to the naked eye, under the intense lights used in platemaking they are exaggerated and become grave flaws in the printed reproduction.

☆ Never use paper clips on photos.

☆ Never roll a photo.

If one has been rolled and, almost inevitably, the emulsion is cracked, this can usually be remedied by washing in warm water and then sending it through the dryer again.

☆ Handle photos with clean hands and by the margins.

Fingerprints on a photo, although nearly invisible to the eye, will be glaring on the printed page.

Because pictures are such an important tool of the communicator, the student journalist should constantly study ways to use them more effectively. Examine professional publications for new ideas. But always test the logic of any usage and never do something only because it is a current fad.

Newspaper Page Layout

What's the most fun in newspapering? Everyone has an answer: Interviewing a celebrity, covering a championship contest, photographing a historic event, writing a 120-point headline. But the closest to unanimity is: Laying out the front page.

This job comes when deadlines are near and adrenalin flows freely. It is a welcome change after the many rather unexciting editing processes. It is the most conspicuous creativity of the editor, immediately apparent to even the most casual of viewers —as good writing and editing are not.

Laying out a page is an art; while it can't be taught, it can be learned. It is also a craft; and that can be taught. This chapter will try to set up some guidelines that will enable the student editor to combine inherited talents with taught skills.

On a professional paper, Page 1 is usually laid out by the news editor. Inside pages are done by the wire, state, metropolitan, sports, family, and other departmental editors.

When an editor says—as often happens "A good page lays itself out," the words mean that the page pattern develops so logically from the *news budget* that the pattern seems to evolve without any effort on the editor's part. That isn't quite true, of course, but it does emphasize that page design is largely determined by the *budget,* the collection of news and pictures on hand for a specific issue.

This is another way of saying that a good layout must be *organic.* It must grow from material available.

A good layout must also be *functional;* it must communicate. Every element on a page must do its own job and contribute to the collective job of the whole page. Elements that fail to do so are *nonfunctional.* Worse, in almost every instance, they are *malfunctional,* not only do they fail to do a good job, they do something bad. If they fail to serve and attract the reader, they distract. So all nonfunctional elements should be stripped from the page.

The function of page layout is:

1. To attract the reader by an appealing overall pattern;
2. To capture attention by pictures and headlines;
3. To lure the reader into body type; and
4. To guide the eye from one story to another in such a way that the reader gains maximum information with a minimum expenditure of time and effort.

Remember that the editor must do all this with the budget for the issue on hand, whether it's a heavy news day or a light one. We can't deepfreeze an overflow for the next issue and we can't report a robbery or fire that hasn't happened yet.

Suppose your budget for April 30 lists (among many others) these top stories:

1. New English courses announced for fall;
2. Foreign-exchange applications due.
3. Spanish Club has party; and

4. New lunchroom schedule pleases students.

For your next issue on May 14, you have a much heavier and exciting budget:

1. Track team wins conference championship;
2. Valedictorian announced;
3. Principal resigns unexpectedly; and
4. Chemistry lab explosion starts small fire.

The two front pages that will lay themselves out from these budgets will look a lot different, won't they? Much of that difference will come from the budgets themselves; but much will also be by design.

You might design your April front page something like this to make a light budget attractive through big art rather than the big headlines you just don't have:

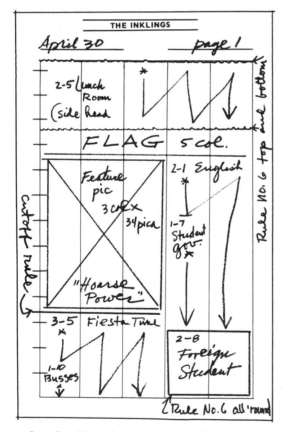

On the May front page, with so many big stories the problem is just the opposite: How can you present all the news without creating a distracting three-ring circus?

This is one way you might handle that:

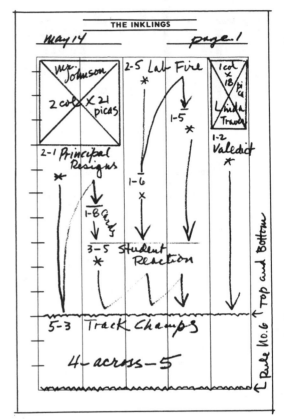

Note well that phrase "one way you might handle that." For this is only one way; there are many ways. But there is no "right way."

You notice, too, that these are both 5-column pages. This is the most common but—again—not the only possible format for a high school paper. The 4-column op format already discussed is a notable exception. The important thing to remember is that sound principles apply to any and all formats, from 2-columners to the 9-column pages rather common in Canada.

☆ Each front page should look as different as possible from all previous ones.

Each page should be so fresh and new that it attracts the readers the moment they see the page. You never want a reader to say, "Is this today's paper or last week's?" Readers should know immediately that they have never seen a page like this, that it must be brand new.

Those principles are based on the reader's procedure in consuming a page and charted in this diagram:

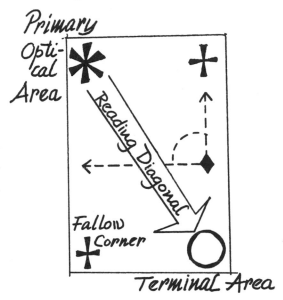

Reading-movement chart. Pull of reading diagonal is so strong, eye resists need to move against it, upward or to left as indicated by broken lines or anywhere in arc they define.

Whether you're reading a memo to the milkman, a page of history notes, or the page of a book or newspaper, you always start in the top left corner, the *primary optical area (POA)*. Always! Instinctively, the reading eye moves downward and to the right; for you know that when you get to the lower right corner you've finished the page and can turn it, flip it, or throw it in the wastebasket. The goal is always that *terminal area (TA)*.

The pull on the *reading diagonal* is strong enough to liken it to that of gravity. You can't turn it off or even turn it down. All you can do is place *optical magnets* in certain areas—especially the *fallow* corners top-right and lower-left—to lure the eye through the whole page.

Wherever the eye is on a page, it will resist attempts to make it "go backward"—upward or to the left. It will either refuse to backtrack or will do so only reluctantly, inefficiently, and with irritation.

All corners are anchored in "Hunters' Call" of Canoga Park (California) High. Lines of force to right would make more functional placement of picture in POA.

To serve the reader in the context of habits and needs, editors have articulated many "Ancient Axioms."

☆ Place a strong attention-compeller in the POA.

Your job is to convert a "looker" into a "reader." So you must, just as soon as possible, grab attention with a strong and/ or interesting element.

☆ *Anchor the corners.*

Strong elements are needed on all corners. In the fallow corners they attract the eye from the reading diagonal. In the TA an anchor defines the page and keeps it from just dissolving into an amorphous gray mass of body type.

☆ Pictures are the best anchors.

Sideless boxes will work. So will head-

Pictures of equal size create chimney in columns 3-4 of "Orange Peal" of Woodland (California) High.

lines; but a head should be no more than 1 inch from the bottom of the page for every column of its width. So a 2-column head can be only 2 inches from the foot of the page or it won't be a strong enough anchor.

☆ Decorate the basement.

The lower half of a page, the *basement*, needs strong display—at least one strong, multicolumn head and one strong picture. If the newspaper is folded, only the basement may be visible when the reader first sees the paper. So the basement must do as good a job as the top half does in luring the looker to picking up the paper and reading it.

☆ Isolate headlines.

Heads are like barkers at a circus; each one tries to lure the passer-by into a particular sideshow or news story. If half a dozen pitchmen share the same platform, the spectator will get a lot of noise but little persuasion. So, too, competing headlines, too close to each other, will distract rather than attract the reader.

☆ Avoid *tombstones*.

These are heads that run side by side. The only way to *break the stones* is to move one of the heads; *hooding* the head with a 3-sided box is not effective. Pictures are the best means of separating heads. But when a tombstone is absolutely unavoidable, the *bumping heads* should vary as much as possible in form and size. A 2-column 36 Bodoni, for instance, would be bumped by a 1-column 18 Bodoni Italic.

☆ Avoid *armpits*.

This inelegant term describes another form of *jammed heads*, when a narrow head runs right under a wider one. Not even a sidebar should be *pitted* like this. A minimum of eight lines of body type between

Three-column format is no handicap to sprightly page layout of "Press" of Tokay High in Lodi, California.

Marian Tomka here for Rotary stay

Laurant Levaux no longer has the foreign student market cornered on this campus.

Marian Tomka, a 19 year-old student from Austria arrived Tuesday and started school officially yesterday. He will reside with the Hill family, whose daughter Melissa is an exchange student from Lee studying in Austria.

The 19 year old Austrian is sponsored by the International Rotary Club, the same club which sponsored the trip to Austria for Melissa.

Students sponsored by the club must pay for the trip going and coming and such articles as clothing, said Principal Bill Evans.

Approximately $15 to $20 is allowed for each student for miscellaneous costs.

"The Hill family will provide him with a home and food," asserted Evans.

"We will help as far as defraying costs and fees are concerned," said Evans, noting that foreign students are never charged for lockers or other student fees.

"He'll probably need alot of help getting his feet on the ground," added Evans. Evans proposed tours around campus as one solution.

The Rotary program for foreign students differs from the American Field Service program, said Evans.

"The Rotary Club International is probably alot more stringent on rules and regulations than the AFS program," noted Evans.

One of the primary areas the two program differ is dating.

"To the best of my knowledge, Marion won't be able to date," said Evans.

'They go to school for 18 years in Austria...'

Upon arrival Tuesday, Tomka was initiated to a program of German, American Literature (junior english), French, Drama, Art and American History.

"He speaks English, so there was no problem scheduling him," said Ms. Betty Chandler, counselor.

"He seems very interested in trying out different things," added Ms. Chandler.

Tomka will attend the home until the end of school and will graduate with this years graduating class.

"He'll be a bonafide Lee graduate."

"We'll have to get him all sized up. He arrived just in time to be measured", said Evans.

Although he'll graduate with the class, his high school education will not necessarily end May 27.

"They go to school for 18 years in Austria," said Ms. Chandler, noting that the educational system in Austria is vastly different from America.

Rotary exchange student Marian Tomka from Austria, entertains Missy Heathman, his American parents' next door neighbor. Tomka is staying with the John Hill family.

Robert E. Lee

Bugle Call

Vol. 17, No. 9
Jan. 17, 1975
San Antonio, Texas

NEISD eyes AFT request

By Gabe Quintanilla
BUGLE CALL EDITOR

The question of whether North East teachers should unionize has recently been raised by a Churchill Social Studies instructor.

Promoter of the idea is Gerald Hastings.

"We want to try to improve the standards of teaching," said Hastings.

"Hastings refused to inform BUGLE CALL of how the proposed plan differs from the plan of the Texas State Teachers Association.

He mentioned that "many" teachers from this campus are followers of his group.

Hastings also refused to state who these members are or give an approximate number.

Most of the followers of the proposed union are Churchill teachers, stated Hastings.

The identities of the teachers who are supporting this group were withheld from BUGLE CALL. No explanation was given.

"You hear rumors floating around. Like that you'd be teaching all basic classes next year, or something like that," said one Lee teacher who said she has heard such talk.

See page 2

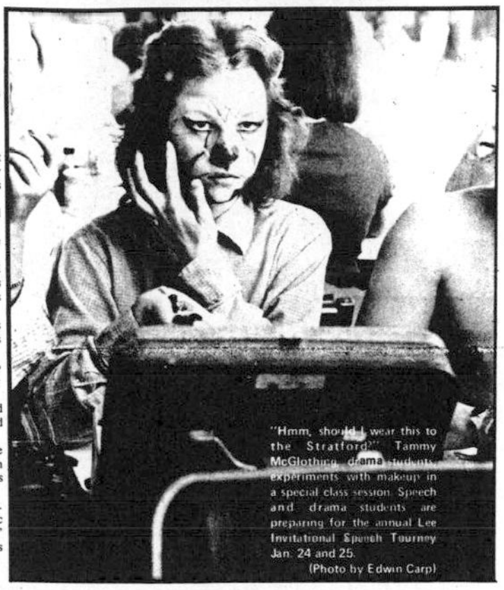

"Hmm, should I wear this to the Stratford?" Tammy McGlothing, drama students, experiments with makeup in a special class session. Speech and drama students are preparing for the annual Lee Invitational Speech Tourney Jan. 24 and 25.
(Photo by Edwin Carp)

Carnival coming

Food, fun and games will combine with education at the annual Vocational Career Carnival Jan. 21.

The purpose of the carnival is to acquaint students and parents with the opportunities found in vocational programs said Ms. Mary Lou Davis, vocational counselor.

Underclassmen will get the chance to see what type of opportunities are afforded in the respective vocational courses, said Dianne Nielsen, committee chairman.

Office Education Association students will present a display with office machines and posters.

Health Occupations Career Training will determine blood types and take blood pressure.

Nachos will be displayed by Homemaking students in microwave ovens.

Involvement in Your Future students will display cookbooks of teachers.

Radio-Television students will sell hot dogs and may also have tamales on hand. Displays about Radio-Television course will also be presented.

Baloons and cotton candy will be sold by Industrial Co-operative Training students. A large check written for $240,000 will be presented to show the amount ICT students will make this year.

Automotive students will display a Diagnostic Test which shows a test automobile electric system.

Furry characters and furry flowers will be offered by Food Services students. They will also sell homemade chocolate chip cookies.

Distributive Education students will have a display portraying an Old Fashioned General Store and a Modern Supermarket. D.E. students also plan to sell candy and distribute handouts on their vacation.

"The Carnival will probably be the best ever," said Dianne, adding that the school needs a system which orientates underclassmen of the advantages of the vocational department.

"How many people, when they bite into an apple, think of which store the apple was bought in?" quiered the carnival chairman, adding that perhaps the original purpose of the carnival is gone.

Students will be released from Physical Education, lunch, electives and study halls to attend the carnival.

Speech tourney to attract 600; judges needed

Six hundred poetic, humorous, serious and arguing will meet Jan. 24 and 25 at the Speech Department's Annual Forensic Meet.

Categories will number 18, including salesmanship speaking, which has not been offered at previous tournaments.

Judges are being sought because some 300 will be needed for the various events.

A booster organization formed by parents of speech students will also help with judging and concessions.

No Leeites will be eligible to compete in the meet, but many of them are running events.

Each category has a student chairman responsible for writing rules and guidelines, getting judges and time keepers and being available in the Gym during the contests to brief judges on their events.

George Grice of Trinity University author of debate books will be available to assist debate judges.

"Sometimes debate judges are not familiar with high school debating and techniques in judging are confusing to them," explained Ms. Gloria White, speech.

Inflation hits schools hard

By Lisa Ploch

Some school districts in this area are being affected by the increase in the utility bill.

In fact, the school districts may have to raise school taxes to pay their utility bills which have tripled over the last year, said Don Harris North East School Board member.

As stated in the San Antonio Express, North East District superintendent Ivan Fitzwater reported that the district's natural gas bill had increased 300 per cent in October.

In October, 1973, the bill was $1,521 and in October, 1974 the school district paid $4,590.

North East's electric bill in October 1973, was $37,151 and in October, 1974, it was $51,652.

The East Central School District will be staying the same at this point.

In the San Antonio Independent School District, they are being affected by the increase in the utility bills.

The rate in most school districts is set by the budget.

"The taxes may be raised because the cost of the living has gone up, the expenses to run the schools and the salary increase," said Velma Everitt, secretary in the tax office for SAISD.

At this point, Harris said that the Bexar County Federation of School Boards is still challenging the legality of the City Public service arrangement.

The federation is waiting for an Attorney General's ruling on the legality of the city taking 14 per cent of the City Public Service revenues in taxes.

Harris said the arrangments constitute a tax on the schools by the city.

Wolff young senior hits top spot

A 16-year-old student, often teased about being the youngest in his class because of his May birthday is the top student in the 1975 graduating class.

Jeff Wolff feels that being selected as the number one student in his class is not that important.

"I do not see the point in class rankings," said Wolff, adding that he was sure there were some valid reasons for ranking the students.

His friends often joke about his interest in computers.

Once during a trigonometry lecture the delayed program Wolff had fed into the computer before class began printing out.

Minutes after the first message clicked out another came.

This hilarious procedure continued throughout the class.

Chess is another interest of Wolffs. He dreams of programming a computer to play chess with him.

Among his numerous honors, Wolff has received the Bausch and Lomb award.

Other honors included achieving National Merit Semi-Finalist and being selected Who's Who two consecutive years.

Wolff plans to attend the University of Texas to pursue pre-law.

Jeff Wolff

Karyl Morton

Morton Star Trek fan highest girl

Karyl Morton was selected as the top girl student and follows Jeff as number two in the class rankings.

Karyl's main interest, according to friends, is Star Trek.

Karyl says band comes a close second.

She has been chosen to the district region and area bands for three years and also plays with the San Antonio Youth Symphony.

Biological sciences are also fascinating to Karyl.

"I participated in the summer Ecology Course this summer," said Karyl, explaining that the group is close knit and still gets together.

Karyl was recently notified that she was one of 20 high school students selected to attend a special college lecture seminar on government, foreign affairs and medicine.

"I am excited about the opportunity to go, but state band might conflict," said Karyl.

A long list of other honors follows Karyl.

Other than the many club offices she holds, she is also a National Merit Semi-Finalist, Montgomery Wards Award for outstanding teen-agers and selected to Who's Who two straight years.

Karyl and Wolff were both elected the Most Likely to Succeed in the Senior Class. (For additional superlatives see page six.)

Road opens to graduation

Seniors are already making preparations for graduation.

They are to bring $10 in cash to cover charges for the cap, gown and other graduation paraphernalia. The $10 must be cash.

Of that amount $5.75 will go toward the rental of the cap and gown.

The other $4.25 is channeled toward purchase of the announcements, calling cards and connected items.

Each individual announcement will cost 14 cents and personal calling cards, which come 100 to a box, will be $4.25 per box.

Also a leatherette souvenir, which contains an announcement and room for a calling card, is available for $1.40.

Cash outpour signals start

A mini-diploma, which is a plastic covered miniature of the student's actual diploma, is being sold for $1.40.

The representative from Southern Pabst Engraving called the diploma a practical investment, as it can be placed in a wallet to be shown to an employer as proof of graduation.

Another item which is available for $2 a box is Thank You notes. There are 25 per box.

An appreciation book which students can give to their parents, cost $2.75 and a memory book is available for $3, and has room for calling cards, pictures and school symbols.

Senior keys, which come in red or gray, and with either gold or silver plating, are being sold for $4 each and come on key chains, pins and necklaces.

Seniors are to figure the cost of the merchandise they are going to buy, add the tax then substract $4.25. A tax list will be made available before Jan. 21 and the balance due is to be paid when the merchandise is delivered about three weeks before graduation.

Seniors are also to know their exact height before Jan. 21.

SUPER NEW SOUNDS: Language Lab improvements hit East Wing scene. See page 3

ROCK ON ROCK: Inner workings of San Antonio's KEXL reveals heart. See page 4

CO-OP NO COP OUT: CVAE students save money on fruits, vegetables. See page 4

WHOA THERE: Girl basketballers maintain improvement at midway point. See page 5

Broadsheet format. One of rare high school broadsheets and possibly largest scholastic paper is "Bugle Call" of Robert E. Lee High in San Antonio, Texas. At 15½ x 22½ inches, it's larger than many metropolitan dailies. Page one is in 6-column op format; inside pages are in conventional eight columns. Note use of reverse for skyline banner and band of inside "appeals" at foot of front page.

Conventional compact makeup is used by "News" of Arthur Hill High in Saginaw, Michigan, but on occasion . . .

. . . staff will use standard tabloid layout of large picture, no body type, headlines announcing inside-page stories. Or, for greater variety . . .

heads in the same column is required to avoid a pit.

☆ Use horizontal makeup.

Body type arranged in wide, shallow areas seems to have much less bulk than the same copy run in a long single column. And the reader is always more ready to read a shorter—or apparently shorter—story than a long one. Body type in 1½- and 2-column setting may also be placed in horizontal elements.

☆ Use *flatout* material.

Also called *1-up*, the flatout technique uses one more column of space than columns

of type. (A few editors call it *1-down*, less type than space.) In the typical school paper this would be *3-across-4*, three legs of type in a 4-column space, or *4-across-5*.

Don't try *2-across-3*; the page then falls apart. And note that 4-across-5 may be four legs of 1-column matter or two legs of double-column setting.

The extra column of space is used to increase the *alleys* between columns with a lightening and brightening, not only of that area, but of the whole page. The head on flatout matter is set flush-left in the first column, which means that it's also to the left of the first leg of type.

Specifications for flatout should be drawn up well before this technique is used and given to the pasteup-man in writing. Here are two typical recipes, assuming 11-pica columns with 1-pica alleys:

. . . regular magazine cover will be used. This strong picture is in mezzotint screen. Note variations in nameplate treatment.

3-across-4	4-across-5
4 picas space	4 picas space
Leg of type	Type
4 picas space	3 picas space
Type	Type
4 picas space	3 picas space
Type	Type
3 picas space	3 picas space
	Type
	3 picas space

Notice the slight variation in the amount of extra spacing and how it is distributed. The editor, not the person who pastes up, must decide this.

☆ Don't *pile up rules*.

Do not place a box so it touches another box or an ad.

☆ Eliminate nonfunctional rules.

By applying the principles of functional-ism, we have already in most instances elimi-nated *column rules,* the thin vertical lines that separate columns in many daily news-papers, and *cutoff rules,* equally thin but horizontal rules that used to separate stories.

☆ The only place a cutoff is needed is under a wild picture.

This is one without a related story or one so placed that the story below it is not related.

Shorter rules called *30-dashes* that for-merly marked the end of a story are also obsolete—because they, too, are nonfunc-tional. When the reader gets to the end of a story, there is no choice and hence no signal needs to say "Stop!"

☆ Let the *fresh air* in.

Fresh air, in the jargon of the typog-rapher, is white space. As a breeze makes a crowded room more comfortable, so white space brightens a page. This air is added

Dominant head is that in POA, obviously outweighing any other on page. Trapped space above FERN PHILLIPS head weakens page pattern, is non-functional. From "Tiger Hi-Line" of Cedar Falls (Iowa) High.

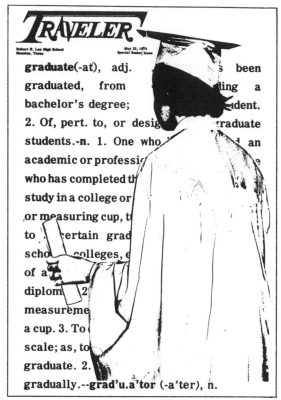

Compact makeup used by "Traveller" of Robert E. Lee High in Houston, Texas, is changed for special issues . . .

. . . to magazine style. Illustration is mezzotint. Note in compact page that picture may lure reading eye to it, jumping over story in column 1. Element in POA must be strong enough to preclude being overlooked.

by consistent spacing above and below heads, pictures, and boxes. The 1-up technique also adds air as did the substitution of alleys for column rules.

☆ Eliminate *jumps* off page one.

A story too long to run entirely on page one should be cut down to usable size or broken into two or three shorter stories. If a story must be jumped, at least one-third of it should be on Page 1 or in the continuation. It is unesthetic to run only a few lines and then jump the story; it is annoying to go to the trouble of following a jump and finding only a few lines there.

Headlines on jumped stories should be as large as if they were on a separate story. Don't use a single line of 14-point on a full column of continued type, for instance. The jump head must have the same *key word* as the page-one head. So if the front-page head said:

Movie-Star Alumnus Johnson To Speak at Commencement

the jump head must repeat a key word:

Movie Star To Speak

and not be written from that part of the story that was jumped, as, perhaps,

Smith Named Valedictorian

☆ Never should more than one story jump off a page.

Jumps from one inside page to another are especially annoying to the reader.

☆ Keep the page in *dynamic balance*.

Avoid attempting a perfectly symmetrical page. This is artificial and inaccurate because it presumes that each story or picture has a matching element of exactly the same length or weight. In real life this never happens. Worse, symmetrical pages are static and far less exciting than those that "lean" a little.

☆ Compromise gracefully between the ideal and the practical.

All of newspapering is such a compromise. Pressures of time, money, and equipment constantly keep daily editors from producing the ideal paper. They can't wait for a late development that would make a story more meaningful or complete. They can't send a reporter 150 miles to cover a story; so they must rely on a stringer. They can't run a 9-column picture, because the press prints only an 8-column page. Ad infinitum. So they compromise enough to meet the deadline. So the student editor, too, must compromise, but always reluctantly, even if philosophically. Always aim at the ideal; lower standards only because of inexorable pressures, never because you have compromised your own standards or, worse, because you either don't know better or are unwilling to work hard enough to attain the ideal.

Layout Procedures

Because of the infinite combinations possible from constantly varying news budgets, only the broadest of principles can be cited for laying out the front page. The following suggestions are workable and sound; many professional editors follow them. So they are useful guidelines for the student editor.

1. Place the flag.

If it's a *floating flag*, shorter than full-page width, it can go anywhere in the top half of a tab page, or in the top third of a broadsheet. Even if it's page-width, the flag may run under a *skyline story*, a story at the very top of the page.

2. Put a strong element in the POA.

Attention-compellers are pix, boxes, strong heads.

3. Place the lead story.

Historically American editors play their biggest story in the top-right corner. This is not a rigid requirement but it does give that strong head to anchor the top fallow corner.

4. Anchor the TA.
5. Anchor the lower fallow area.
6. Place an element under the attention-compeller in the POA.

7. Fill any blanks at the top of the page.
8. And blanks at the foot of the page.
9. Fill the rest of the page.

Always work in a clockwise, diminishing spiral as elements are placed in the center of the page. And always follow the principles discussed earlier in this chapter.

It may help the student editor to think of a page as a sheet of plywood, hanging freely on a pivot at the *optical center* of the page, 10% of the page-depth higher than the mathematical center.

Think of each element dummied in as a piece of wood being nailed to the plywood. The heavier the optical weight of the element, the thicker the piece of wood you envision.

As soon as you nail on the floating nameplate, the page tilts to one side. As you affix other elements, seek to bring the page almost, but not quite, into balance. "Not quite" because it is almost impossible to attain precise balance without distorting news to make exactly equal balancing elements. But also because you want a page a bit off balance. This gives a *dynamic thrust* which is interesting and even exciting. Notice how a friend with whom you are conversing, if the subject of conversation is interesting, will always lean a little, toward or away from the other person, or sideways. Only the bored—and usually boring—speaker sits or stands perfectly perpendicular.

Of course you don't want the page to totter so precariously that the reader fears it will fall over on its face. It should be dynamic, but it should be in dynamic balance.

Inside-Page Layout

Inside-page layout of a professional newspaper is complicated by the ads carried on most such pages. The editor has no control over the typography of advertising, yet must create pleasing page patterns of both news and ads. This is like an architect charged with designing a striking 40-story tower yet having no control over the appearance of the first 15 floors.

Student papers usually don't carry as

much ad linage as the pros do, but there is usually enough (at least the ad manager hopes there is) that its placement is an important factor in readership.

Placement of Ads

☆ Ads should *pyramid* upward to the right.

They should be so placed on all pages, right or left. Actually such placement of ads is not a pyramid but a half-pyramid.

☆ There should be ads at the foot of every column.

☆ There should either be a minimum of 3 inches of news space above the ad pyramid or the column should be filled completely with ads.

☆ Eliminate *wells*.

When a column of body type runs all or most of the full depth of the page alongside advertising, it's *in the well* and not very

interesting to the reader. This is aggravated when ads are placed in a double pyramid, creating a V-shaped area for news at the center of the page. The sharper and deeper such V, the worse readership suffers.

Inside-Page Makeup

Inside pages require as much care as does page one. They should be so attractive that the reader will consume them with pleasure and reward. Not only are readers entitled to quality on every page they have bought, the advertiser deserves assurance that the ad will be exposed to readers' eyes, no matter where it may run.

Conventionally, larger ads run at the bottom of the page with smaller ones built up from there. It is a convention that ads be placed *next to reading matter* (*NRM*). Many advertisers insist on such placement. So newspapers try to keep them happy even though current research indicates that placement of advertising has no measurable effect on its pulling power.

☆ Each page needs a *dominant head*.

To be dominant, the head must:
1. Have at least as many lines as the next strongest head;
2. Be at least one column wider than the No. 2 head; and
3. Be at least one step in point size larger.

If all three requirements can't be met, the others must be increased additionally.

The dominant head becomes the nucleus for a pleasant page pattern. A page without a dominant head doesn't look planned; it looks accumulated. Dominance comes only from optical weight, not position, although by sheer logic you may expect the dominant to be at or near the top of the page.

☆ Every page should have at least one strong picture.

☆ Pictures should be played at or near the top of inside pages.

Only those insiders which are *key pages*, without advertising, can effectively display pictures at the foot of or low on the page.

☆ Keep pictures away from the ad pyramid.

Ad pyramid is properly built up to right in "Bengal's Purr" of Lewiston (Idaho) High. This opens POA for strong display and encourages reader by breaking page into consecutively smaller column-portions.

☆ Avoid *naked columns*.

These are without a headline or picture at their top. They look raw and unfinished. Folio lines are usually adequate to dress the column head.

As on the front page, the POA of inside pages needs a strong element.

☆ All principles for Page 1 apply to inside pages.

The Editorial Page

Because young people usually hold strong views, and have the courage—or temerity— to express them and to expose themselves to opposing viewpoints, this page has always been popular in school papers. As in a professional newspaper, this page performs the important journalistic function of a free press: To give leadership in solving civic problems and to provide a forum for free discussion of them by editors, columnists, and readers.

☆ Typography must emphasize the difference between opinion and hard news.

To make the editorial page look different from other pages, you might use a different head schedule, if type for it is available. You can use different column widths, 4 columns instead of 5; 3 instead of the op-format 4.

Extra white space is attractive on the editorial page.

☆ Edit-page ads should be light and dignified.

Most editors prefer to keep all ads off the edit page but this is sometimes economically unfeasible, especially in a school paper with only a few pages. But it seems incongruous to have a serious editorial on a serious issue outshouted by a loud, brassy ad.

If ads must run on this page, the best placement is in a shallow rectangle across the bottom of the page. Next best: A tall vertical block of ads at the right side of the page. Advertisers like to be on this page and won't scream if their ad does not touch reading matter in such placement.

☆ Identify this page of opinion.

The nameplate is usually displayed prominently on this page to indicate that opinions expressed in editorials are those of the newspaper rather than a single individual. (This is the reason editorials are rarely by-lined in professional papers.) The addition of some label like "A PAGE OF OPINION," "COMMENTS," "VIEWPOINTS," etc., reinforces the difference between its contents and those of news pages.

☆ Don't run news on the edit page.

This blurs the distinction you try so hard to make. If news must run on this page, either the news or the opinion matter should be boxed to insulate the two contents from each other.

☆ The masthead should run at the bottom of the page.

The old way of running the mast at the top-left corner is nonfunctional. It doesn't

Editorials are prominently labelled in "Charger Account" of Dos Pueblos High of Goleta, California, to emphasize for reader difference between opinion of editorial page and hard news on others.

have enough popular appeal to warrant using the POA for it.

☆ Heads on editorials should be large.

If editorials are important—and few editors would deny that—they certainly deserve the same size heads as important news does.

☆ Avoid gaudy art headings.

Because this is the page where columnists usually appear, there is danger that too many illustrated headings will be concentrated here. Keep such headings simple and consistent.

☆ Editorial cartoons have great reader appeal.

It is a rare person who can translate a commentary on current events into pictorial form and then have the skill to produce a clear drawing of the idea. But cartoons have played such a vigorous role in the life of our democracy and have such strong reader appeal that it's worth all the effort of searching for a good cartoonist.

If you can't find one, you can get *canned cartoons* free from outside sources. You can usually obtain permission to reproduce cartoons from other school papers or from magazines serving student staffs. Finally, you can forgo the cartoon entirely or use photography to make an editorial point.

Actual pictures of vandalism in the lunch room, graffiti marring walls, or megalomaniacal initials carved into desks may make the point more emphatically than hand art or written commentary.

☆ Encourage letters to the editor; display them well.

The impact of a newspaper and especially its editorial page upon the readers can well be gauged by the number of letters to the editor that are received. Here's the place where opposing viewpoints can best help the individual reader take a position on controversial topics.

Establish and maintain consistent style of salutation and close. Usually letters begin with "To the Editor" or "Sir." Sometimes there is no salutation although this tends to take away the desirable feeling of an actual

letter. Formal closing, "Sincerely," or "Yours," etc. is usually dispensed with. The writer's name should be prominently displayed and often is set in boldface. Writers should also be identified by class year, office in a club, membership in a group such as an athletic team, the subject of a faculty member, etc.

Letters may run under a standing heading. They may be identified by a bimo head in which case the main head refers to the topic of the lead letter or to a group of letters, such as:

Letters:

Students Object To Shortening Pre-Thanksgiving Holidays

Letters that do not discuss the headlined topic carry small breaker heads.

The Sports Page

Sports pages are a mixed blessing to professional newspapers—and student ones, too. They are popular but they also occasion many criticisms. Unlike most reporters, sports writers are describing events that many of their readers have seen, in person or on TV. If the report does not coincide with what readers saw—or thought they saw—reaction may be bitter.

Sports page in "Red/Blue" of Huntsville (Alabama) High is anchored by good action picture. Note several stories rounded-up in SPORTS SHORTS. Lead story is set in 1½-column measure.

Sports page in magazine treatment is from "West Side Story" of West High in Iowa City, Iowa. LEAGUE head is teaser; BRIEFS carry all other sports news. Folio treatment is strong but perhaps wasteful of paper.

Magazine style recounts game story in interview with varsity player. This eliminates feeling of "stale news" for "Oracle" of West Springfield (Virginia) High.

Sports page from "Knight Crier" of North Penn High of Lansdale, Pennsylvania, is in magazine style. Strong play is given to girls' sports. Captions, set in large type, are weakened by excessive space between lines.

Sports page of "Tangent" of Wilson High of Portland, Oregon, gives strong coverage to girls' sports. Sidelines are used with caption material.

Sports page devoted entirely to girls' athletics is from "Echo" of St. Louis Park (Minnesota) High.

Editors worry because sports pages so often have a typographical style absolutely unrelated to that of news pages. Quite properly, the managing editor wants the paper to be an integrated whole, not a bunch of separate papers that happen to be printed and delivered as a single package.

Sports-page typography should follow all specifications of other pages.

☆ Sports heads may be larger than news heads on stories of the same length.

The world of sports is a noisy one. So sports headlines can appropriately be a little "louder," too. This is done, not by using a heavier headletter, but by using larger head sizes.

☆ Every sports page must have strong action pictures.

Box scores, team standings, and similar *tabular material* should be set in 5½-point type and ganged into a single area labeled "ON THE RECORD," "THE SCORE BOARD," or similar term.

This eliminates the spotty, measles look when such matter is appended to each story.

Departmentalization

School newspapers have been more definite, if not more successful, than professional ones in departmentalizing their content. Daily papers try hard to gang all local news on certain pages, international news on others, etc. Sports, social, and business news have long been in separate departments. But newspapers have never been as successful as *Time* and *Newsweek*, for instance, in doing so.

School papers often put hard news on Page 1, make Page 2 the editorial page, place only features on Page 3, and sports on 4. This is awkward and nonfunctional. Mixing news and features, for instance, maintains reader interest better than hermetically sealing them into separate areas.

Dummies

Dummy is a noun and a verb. It's the blueprint—very sketchy or minutely detailed—which guides the person who pastes up a page. To "dummy a page" is to prepare this blueprint.

Professional editors usually prepare only a *sketch dummy*. Even for student editors who make a *pasteup dummy,* the sketch dummy is a useful first step.

Dummy sheets are usually printed—or Mimeoed—on 8½×11 sheets although some papers use them in half this size or even smaller. The dummy is not in proportion; columns are much wider in relation to depth than in the actual paper. Inch gauges are noted on the sides.

Placement of a head is noted by writing the code and key word of the head in the proper area. The start of a story is indicated by an asterisk and a single line shows how the body type is placed.

Pictures are shown as a rectangle with crossing diagonals; a box as a plain rectangle or one containing a cross.

Flatout matter is indicated as "3-across-4" or "4-across-5."

The editor must show precisely how deep each head will be and how long each leg of type will be. The length of the material is known from the copy log talked about in Chapter 9.

Because a sketch dummy is in a kind of shorthand, the editor should practice this new form of writing. The best way is to take a printed newspaper page and draw a dummy from that.

These dummies are surprisingly exact when produced and followed by professionals. For student staffs, the pasteup dummy might be more precise. This dummy is made by pasting up duplicate proofs of all type material onto a piece of paper the same size as that of the finished page. (Sometimes columns are made a pica or two wider than in the actual paper just to simplify pasting on the elements.) Pictures are indicated by drawn rectangles, Photostats, or blueprints of the originals.

Each proof is identified by its *galley number* so the pasteup-man can readily find a given story. The editor marks this number in bright felt pens on each graf before cutting up the proofs. If, during the pasteing-up, a paragraph is cut in two, each

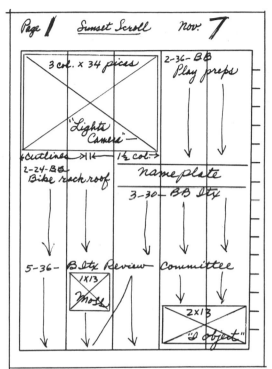

Sketch dummy is blueprint for . . .

. . . front page of "Scroll" of Sunset High, Beaverton, Oregon.

portion must be marked with the ident number.

Pasting is done with a light coating of rubber cement that allows the editor to change his mind, remove an element, and paste it into a new position.

Ad Dummies

The advertising department *lays the paper,* dummies in the ads. If the news staff has unusual editorial needs that cannot be met by conventional pyramiding, the ad department should be informed beforehand. Laying the paper should be done immediately after the advertising deadline. If any changes must be made to accommodate news matter, they can be done at once and with minimum trouble.

☆ The editorial department should have the right to shift ads.

☆ Every page must be dummied in great detail.

Some professional editors can dummy a page down to a single line of body type—and some—alas!—cannot. The better the editor can dummy, the better the paper. So this is an art the student editor should strive hard to master.

14 Selling Advertising

Americans are constantly surrounded by advertising. "Immersed" is the verb some would use.

A typical individual may average as many as 100 ad exposures every waking hour, according to one recent survey. To a considerable degree, advertising influences people's choices about what clothes they wear, food they eat, pills they swallow, automobiles they buy, and even their thinking about politicians, foreign policy, and legislation they favor. Yet one should never forget that advertising is not black magic. It can't make people buy or do something that they don't want to buy or do.

☆ Advertising is one way of persuading somebody to do something, usually to purchase a product or "buy" an idea.

This is as true for your high school paper or broadcast station as for commercial media.

Advertising has been—and still is—attacked. But it is not necessarily "well-phrased lies," as claimed by some. True, some ad writers tamper with truth but so do lawyers, politicians, business executives, and—as you know—students. In all these instances—including advertising—there are laws, regulations, or professional codes of ethics to enforce good conduct and to punish those who violate it. And advertisers are just as legal—maybe more so—as any of ing a prosperous year.

Many economists argue that the United States economic system arose, in part, due to advertisements that stimulated mass sales through showing people what products were available. Ads certainly have produced stimulus for the economy and its profits.

The mass circulation print and broadcast media obtain most of their financing from advertising revenues and so appeals to readers, listeners, and viewers are frequent, as much as 18 minutes every hour for broadcasting, even on "all-news" stations. Besides these channels, advertisers use direct mailings, billboards, matchbook covers, and loudspeakers in railroad stations, buses, and amusement parks—to mention only a few methods.

Broadcasters depend on commercials to pay for their operations and to earn a profit. Publications get approximately two-thirds or more of their total income from advertisers. Large ad revenues for both media make it possible, if owners and managers wish, to provide better news coverage by sending extra reporters and photographers to witness more events and to supply more background, analysis, and interpretation from extra specialists and commentators.

Although it does not pay all the bills as in broadcasting, advertising is an absolute necessity for a successful commercial newspaper. The cost of an issue to the reader pays for no more than the paper stock and ink. Expenses for gathering, processing, and printing the news have to be borne by revenues from ads.

Student publications do not depend this

Ad sales chart is staff incentive. Current linage is compared to last year's in large graph, accumulated sales by reps in bar graph at left.

much on ad income. A recent survey of the scholastic press found that at least one quarter carried no ads at all. For duplicated —Mimeoed—publications, the figure for those without ads exceeded two-thirds. The percentage of total revenues coming from school-press advertising varied widely, ranging from 90% to 15%.

But on those papers that do sell advertising, a student who gains this experience learns lessons that will prove valuable in later life, even in a career far removed from professional advertising.

Serving the Teen-Age Market

Why do merchants advertise in student media?

The teen-age market is an impressively large one. One study in the mid-1970s estimated it as at least a $20 billion market. That's certainly one that cannot be disregarded by any efficient merchant who wants to sell goods. Half of the teen-agers either have their own or use family charge accounts or credit cards. Approximately nine out of ten have their own bank accounts, either savings, checking, or both. More than a third go skiing during the winter, frequently during vacation times. And teen-age girls, it is estimated, spend $7.4 billion on clothing, accessories, and footwear during a prosperous year

Certainly you can assemble statistics on the attractiveness of the teen-age generation as a sales target when you go out to solicit ads for school media. Yet, unfortunately, many students ask local merchants "to give" them an ad. Too frequently, that is what merchants do. That is not a business transaction; it is charity.

☆ A self-respecting student ad representative will not accept a handout.

Advertising is a valuable commodity and can be sold on a strictly dollars-and-cents basis.

How is that done?

By practicing the very techniques of the ad the student is trying to sell: To persuade the merchant to buy an ad in your publication so that, in turn, readers can be persuaded to purchase products, whether they are a Coke, records, or a used car.

One way toward a more effective and successful presentation is to ascertain the actual numbers and potentiality of a school's pupils. A student ad manager should spend

Sales of advertising space in "Survey" of Marion (Indiana) High, are conducted as vigorously by student staff as by metropolitan daily. Extensive survey of school's 2,600 students showing their purchasing power of more than $1.3 million during school year, is summarized in promotional mailing piece.

some time and even a few dollars to obtain statistics about the purchasing power of the student body. Interviews with merchants often bring out facts about teen-age business volume. Local banks collect data on the size of this market. Polls and surveys of the student body could be even more accurate and they may be conducted in conjunction with classes in business, economics, journalism, or social studies.

A sample questionnaire could follow these lines:

I. *How much spending money do you have per week?*
   A. *Allowance* _____
   B. *Earnings* _____
II. *How much money have you spent in the past week on:*
   A. *Clothing* _____
   B. *Food* _____
   C. *Recreation* _____
      (include dates)
   D. *Records* _____
   E. *Books* _____
   F. *Transportation*
      1. *Bus and train* _____
      2. *Automobile* _____
      3. *Scooter, motorbike, etc.* __
   G. *Personal Items*
      1. *Haircuts* _____
      2. *Beauty parlors* _____
      3. *Shaving supplies* _____
      4. *Cosmetics* _____
      5. *Perfumes* _____
      6. *Gifts*
         a. *Christmas* _____
         b. *Birthdays* _____
         c. *Anniversaries* _____
         d. *Others* _____
      7. *Telephone* _____
   H. *Hobbies*
      1. *Record collecting* _____
      2. *Hi-fi, stereo* _____
      3. *Stamp collecting* _____
      4. *Model building* _____
      5. *Electronics* _____
      6. *Bicycle* _____
      7. *Others* _____
   I. *Any other* _____
              TOTAL _____

III. *How much do you estimate you have personally spent in:*
   A. *The past semester* _____
   B. *The past school year* _____
   C. *The past calendar year* _____
IV. *What major item has your family purchased in the past year in which you had a voice in selection?*
   A. *New home* _____
   B. *New car* _____
   C. *Television set* _____
   D. *Vacation trip* _____
   E. *Furniture* _____
   F. *Others* _____

This sample can be condensed or expanded to fit your needs. In any case, the answers will prove formidable ammunition for persuading any merchant that your paper reaches an important market.

☆ Whether a merchant eventually decides that it is good business to advertise with you will depend on your ad rate.

Advertising is sold by the column inch—a space 1 column wide and 1 inch deep—or by the *agate line*—1/14 of a column inch. National advertisers use the *milline rate*; they calculate how much it costs, per agate line, to reach a million readers at a given rate for a given circulation.

The milline rate for a student paper always is considerably higher than for a daily newspaper. But the student has a ready-made rebuttal to that: There is no waste in a student publication. Every copy —and presumably every ad—is read by every student whereas many a daily paper may be read only partially or possibly not beyond the headlines. Every student is a potential customer for an advertiser but some dailies circulate in areas so far away that a reader doesn't ever come close to the stores that advertise. Also, ads in student papers get higher attention because advertising has less competition than the same amount of space in a daily.

School papers offer a reader bonus, too. Many—if not most—students take their papers home where parents, brothers, sisters, and other relatives read them. These

Page 6   THE SHIP'S LOG, Freeport, Texas, Thursday, January 31, 1974

Feature Focus

	Seniors	Juniors	Sophomores	Freshmen
Money they have to spend per week	$14.00	$18.00	$10.00	$4.00
Money spent on Luxuries per week	$6.50	$10.00	$6.21	$5.00
Buy Clothes without Parent Supervision	Yes 84% No 16%	Yes 87% No 13%	Yes 70% No 30%	Yes 50% No 50%
Movies Per Week	About once a week	About once every other week	One every week and a half	About one every three weeks
Brands (Similarities)	3-Wiener's	3-Ultra-Sheen	No Brands in common	No Brands in Common
Bank Accounts	66%-Accounts 75% in FFNB	About 50% accounts 75% in FFNB	75% have acc. 50% in FFNB 25% in BBC	30% have acc. 50% in FFNB

Poll reveals power of student dollar

By JANIE HEATH

Money, money, money — most teen-agers constantly wrestle with the perplexing panorama of various tempting ways to invest their resources. With more students ... youth ...

section including all four classes. The results of this poll, shown in the table above, indicate that ... students spend a maj... of their inco... that catch th...

Individual responses were often unusual and offered food for ... polled said that ...ce of income or ...eir parents ...

Pizza parlors were favorite hang-outs. Interest... stores seem to le... to Hou...

money isn't any "younger" than adult money.

...erry's

...aurant

Vast spending power of students of Brazosport High in Freeport, Texas, is illustrated by graph summarizing extensive market survey. Reprinted, such data can be effective tool for persuading merchants to use ad space in student newspaper.

individuals represent a potential market for the advertiser, too.

Setting the ad rate for a student publication is difficult. Basically, the space is worth what a merchant is willing to pay for it. The publication that gets results for an advertiser is worth buying at any reasonable rate. But what is reasonable? Probably the best way is to determine the average rate used by school papers in your circulation and economic bracket.

Obviously a publication in a school of 2,000 should have higher rates than one with a 500 enrollment. But it should be noted that an urban school where students are close to stores probably will have more immediate pulling power than a consolidated rural school where the student body does business in many towns. A school in a wealthy section of a metropolitan suburb may have more purchasing power than one in the city's central core.

☆ The buyer is the final judge of equitable rates.

If the merchant does not protest, your rates are probably proper—if you have established a business relationship and the buyer does not look on the purchase as a charitable contribution toward good will.

State, regional, and national school press associations have data available that will allow you to compare your rates with those of similar publications.

In Seattle, a co-op all-city advertising sales program allowed merchants in that Washington city to buy space in all the high schools at a single rate, with each school paper receiving its share of the revenues

If a merchant did not wish all-city attention, it was possible to purchase ads in those papers that comprised a particular sales area. This program, according to those who directed it, eliminated "cut-throat advertising rates" and special financial inducements for firms to advertise in a few school papers.

☆ The student ad manager should have a well-laid selling plan.

First, draw up a list of prospects. Current and past advertisers are the core of such a listing. But a newly named manager should also travel around the school neighborhood and note those business places that are convenient to the student body and offer merchandise appealing to this group. The manager should check the yellow pages of the telephone directory for the same information.

To be a prospect, a business need not be across the street from school. A student may not go across town to buy a soft drink during a class "break" or after school, but he will travel many miles to purchase a hi-fi set, a bicycle, or ski accessories. And a favorite hamburger stand or coffee shop may attract students for miles after a game or dance.

As the list is being drawn up, a new ad manager, especially if the appointment is made in the late spring, will be drafting letters to the old reliable advertisers, thanking them for their purchases during the past year and soliciting their continued support for the coming terms. This sales promotion letter could cite:

1. Latest statistics on paper's circulation among students and faculty;

2. Estimates of total readership, being sure to include the bonus readers among students' families;

3. Summary of student body's purchasing power, probably from the most recent expenditures survey; and

4. Any special awards or citations that the publication won during the past 12 months.

While a merchant may have known this news previously, the letter will recall it again at the time for renewal of an advertising contract. Some schools follow up this letter with a visit before the semester closes, but others send ad representatives just before the start of classes in the fall. If an issue is distributed during the first week of classes, obviously, ad sales should be made in the spring, if at all possible, and by midsummer, at the latest.

After the list of prospects has been completed, ad staffers are assigned to specific potential buyers. For a fairly large community, this may comprise 20 prospects each. Each sales representative should have one or two accounts that are reasonably sure to buy space regularly. These successes provide encouragement to call on firms that are harder to sell. In some instances, a team of a boy and a girl work together in seeking ads.

In any case, sales personnel should practice the basic axioms of good salesmanship.

☆ To make sales, you must make calls.

☆ Each prospect should be called on regularly, at least once before each issue.

☆ A student solicitor should be neatly dressed, well groomed, and polite.

Each solicitor should remember that an ad sales representative represents not only an individual and a paper but the entire student body and owes it to classmates to make a good impression.

The individual gives the sales talk to the prospect, asks for an order, and departs.

☆ Do not act hurt if no sale is made.

If the answer is unfavorable, you should say a smiling, friendly farewell and take off—but return the next week, smiling. Any successful sales people can tell many examples of profitable sales and long-lasting business relationships that came only after countless fruitless calls.

It is difficult to sell an intangible, and few things are as intangible as the impact of space in a newspaper or time on a broadcast. So a smart solicitor always will have something tangible to show a prospect. This includes a copy of the latest issue of the paper and a dummy to show just how the ad might look when the prospect bought space.

If the merchant advertises in another paper, say the local daily, one effective device could be to clip that ad and paste it

MHS SURVEY
Publication of Marion High School
750 W. 26th Street, Marion, IN 46952
(317) 664-9051, ext. 49

Agreement

The undersigned firm hereby agrees to use 1/4 ~~column inches~~/page of advertising space in the SURVEY in each of the issues checked in the space below.

The undersigned agrees to pay any cost incurred by the SURVEY in preparing extra cost required advertising, according to the schedule below.

A copy of the SURVEY containing each insertion of the advertising will be furnished to the advertiser. All advertisers will be billed at the end of each month for the space used during the month. A tearsheet of each advertisement will be sent with the bill.

Desired copy may be attatched to this contract or specified clearly on the back. A salesman will check with the firm regularly for advertising copy--or at the request of the advertiser, ad copy wi ll be prepared or designed by the advertising staff of the SURVEY.

Firm name __THE PIZZA HUT__   signed _John Licavoli_

address __Main and Oak__   title _manager_

telephone __571-3133__   salesman _Susan Smith_

Rate Schedule

Rate A.......... per column inch...$ 1.75
Rate B.......... one-eighth page.....................($1.66/in.)....................................$15.00
Rate C.......... one-quarter page....................($1.61/in.)....................................$27.50
Rate D.......... one-half page.......................($1.57/in.)....................................$52.00
Rate E.......... full page...........................($1.38/in.)....................................$90.00

Extra Cost Schedule

spot color.................$10..	
spot color.................$10.00/color	
four-color................$100.00	
preprinted inserts..........$20.00/pg.	
stuffing charge.............$25.00	
b/w photos.................n/c	
reduction of art/photos......$2.00	
reverses..................$3.00	

Insertion Schedule

Check date for each insertion. You will be notified of any changes in the production schedule.

Jan. 24	(✓)	Apr. 25	(✓)
Jan. 31	( )	May 2	( )
Feb. 7	( )	May 9	( )
Feb. 14	( )	May 16	(✓)
Feb. 21	(✓)	May 23	( )
Feb. 28	( )	Sectional	
Mar. 7	( )	Issue	( )
Mar. 14	( )		( )
Mar. 21	(✓)		( )
Apr. 11	( )		( )

Advertising contract used by "Survey" of Marion (Indiana) High, includes rates, extra charges for color, etc., and publication dates. It is signed by advertiser and student sales rep.

right onto a page in your issue. Thus the prospect can see exactly how an ad would look in the student publication.

A whole series of special techniques exist for selling additional space beyond traditional advertisements. For instance, here are some ideas that have been highly profitable for student papers:

1. A professional directory of doctors, dentists, and lawyers who are barred by professional ethics and traditions from more conventional ads.

2. Ads built around special events with whole pages or even special sections. Among the events might be the big football home game, the regional basketball tournament—if your school is lucky enough to play in it, or graduation.

3. Shopper columns with ads (and which

Instead of selling copy, advertisement presents by-lined sports column. This serves dual purpose: Student readership is extremely high; news matter runs in revenue-producing space. Ads using real or apparent news matter must be plainly labelled as advertising.

legally must be labeled as such) which are written in the form of a chatty column. Not only do these tell what new merchandise is available in a conversational instead of a hard-sell tone but they are interlarded with general informative matter that aims at attracting readers.

4. Christmas or valentine greetings from students to other students or to faculty members. In these, caution should be used that nothing is printed that will seriously embarrass the individual to whom the greeting is addressed.

When a prospect buys space, the succeeding transaction should be conducted in a businesslike fashion. No sales should be considered complete until signed contracts are in the hands of both the merchant and the business staff. This way both sides know exactly what is expected. These contracts may be simple format, printed in bulk, with appropriate blanks to be filled in.

If a merchant has been promised a proof, it is the representative's responsibility to insure that it is delivered promptly—and returned just as promptly for pasteup or makeup.

☆ The ad manager should keep a looseleaf *ad log*.

After the contract has been signed and the copy for the ad received, the sales rep should make out a card with the following information:

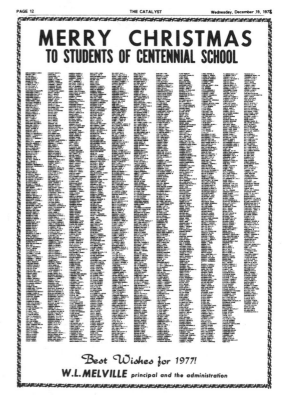

Unusual Christmas greeting ad lists name of every student in Centennial High of Coquitlam, British Columbia. Placed by school administration, it renders real service to readers who probably have no other source for names of all classmates.

Salesman: *Jim Brown*
Account: *Campus Clothing Shop*
Issue: *November 5*
Size of ad: *2 × 5*
Special Instruction: *On sports page if possible*
Illustrations: *Man's suit pix supplied.*

The ad manager transfers these data to the log. A separate sheet, or sheets, is kept for each issue. If the ad is to be run in two issues, the manager marks that down on the sheet for each issue. When the time comes for pasting up the paper, the manager checks off each ad as it is put into position. On the log is noted the page on which the ad has been pasted. As closely as possible, requests for special position are honored. Some schools allow that priority for advertisers who buy space in every issue of the year; positioning thus is a privilege for buying space throughout the year.

☆ Few things turn off an advertiser as rapidly as omitting an ad that has been contracted for.

A *no-run*—failure to get an ad into the paper—is an insult to the merchant and no one can complain at a refusal to do further business with a carelessly operated organization.

As soon as the paper comes off the press, the bookkeeping department should enter each ad, along with the amount of money to be paid, in the *journal*. Student publications usually send out statements immediately after each issue. Each statement should be accompanied with *proof of publication*. This is either the entire issue or the single page—tearsheet—containing the ad. Whichever is sent, it should be folded so the ad is on the outside, and usually the ad is circled in red crayon.

Payments should be acknowledged at once with a form something like this:

Window cards are supplied by staff so merchant's ad can be pasted on and displayed in window. This gives added recognition to merchant's support of newspaper.

After a specified time, charges are transferred from the journal to the *ledger*. Second statements should be sent out monthly on unpaid bills. If these reminders are not then paid, the student rep should call on the overdue customer and collect. This is nothing to be embarrassed about. Letting an account become overdue is neither good business nor kindness. If the call is made in a friendly, businesslike manner, the merchant should not take umbrage.

Student papers need an efficient bookkeeping system. One careful, responsible member of the business staff should be put in charge. A teacher of business procedures or accounting may be willing to help train staff members and to advise the student in charge of the bookkeeping system.

☆ The publication's books must be current and kept meticulously accurate.

One way to get a student advertising staff to maximum production is to keep a *performance sheet*. This technique exploits the competitive spirit. A chart shows the

The Central High School News acknowledges with thanks receipt of your check of $——— for payment of advertising in the issue of ———.

amount of ads sold, issue by issue, for the past several years. How this year's staff stacks up with its predecessors becomes graphically apparent. Perhaps a similar graph could be kept for individual ad staffers. However, this mandates that the list of prospects be equitably divided among all ad solicitors with no choice accounts to friends or the manager.

Managing a sales staff takes diplomacy as well as leadership. A student manager who gets the best performance from the ad staff has learned a lesson as valuable as many out of textbooks. And staff members, who work backstage when compared with writers who get their names on front-page stories, are gaining experiences that can help them long after they have finished their schooling and are selling ideas and products far more complicated than they did during their high school days.

When awards, listings on the masthead, and other recognitions are being passed around, advertising staff members deserve the credits of the valuable staffers they are.

Some advisors believe that the ability to obtain sufficient advertising revenues may be an essential key for a successful student publication since that money insures a certain amount of financial independence from both the school administration and the student governing organization. And independence, as all journalists know, is what makes for a free press.

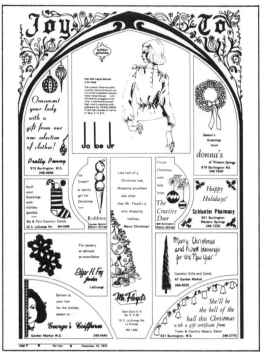

Unusual shapes enhance ads in pre-Christmas edition of "Lion" of Lyons Township (Illinois) High. This is half of 2-page spread, all hand drawn.

15 Creating Advertising

That part of a newspaper which is at the top of the page and which we call news and that at the foot which we call advertising are both information that a reader needs, wants, and enjoys. Advertising is really "what's new" about products and services. So it is essential that the same 5 W's of a news story be included in an ad.

Fortunately, these need not be spelled out as explicitly in advertising because readers contribute much of this material from their own backgrounds.

But, because advertising is "persuasive communication," the last W is the most important, "Why should I buy this merchandise or service? Why should I accept your idea or your political candidate? Why?"

Unlike a news story, written in the third person, an ad is a very personal message to an individual. So the most important advertising word is "you."

Again, unlike a news story, an ad—a good ad—begins communicating long before the reader actually reads it. Indeed, some ads, such as for the various cola drinks, have very few, if any, words; persuasion to buy the drink is often unspoken, conveyed by the picture alone.

Starting the Ad

The creative process may begin very early. As was noted in the chapter just before this, a *spec layout* is an excellent tool for an advertising sales rep. An ad is created in visual form and then presented and—we hope—sold to a merchant. Usually, though, and especially in the case of regular advertisers, the ad begins with a merchant telling the salesman, "I want to advertise a special on cardigan sweaters." The sales rep asks the merchant the 5 W's that the ad must answer:

Who? Who is interested in this merchandise? There's no point in trying to sell garden hose to a Bedouin; he has no use for it. There's no point in trying to sell these cardigans to a 40-year-old childless couple; they won't see an ad in the school paper. The potential buyer here is the student and the ad must be written and designed in a way to appeal to that reader.

What? What are you trying to sell? What is this sweater like in color, size, style (some readers may not be sure just what a cardigan is), material, fashionability?

Where? Where can the reader buy this if he or she decides that this is the ideal cardigan? The customer may need only the name of the store, although in some cases— if, for instance, the store is a new one—a street address may be necessary. Sometimes a map is needed if the store is in a suburban location. If the advertiser is a big department store, the department should be specified.

When? When does this special sale begin and end? When is the store open? When is this cardigan appropriate to wear?

Why? Why should the reader buy this sweater? Now you list the "features," those specific characteristics which make this garment different from—and perhaps better than—a similar one the reader might want or need or buy.

In "hard-sell" ads readers are deluged with reasons; in "soft-sell," readers are given enough information so they can persuade themselves to buy the merchandise.

☆ Keep the ad as simple as possible.

Simplicity begins with the advertiser. The merchant must decide how many items to run in an ad. The fewer the better; one is best!

Ads motivate readers to make decisions, a hard task for any human being. But it is easier to decide, "Do I, or don't I, buy this?" than it is to decide "Do I or don't I buy Item A? Do I or don't I buy Item B? Should I buy A or B or both?" The more options the reader has, the harder it is to come to a decision. So the advertiser must reduce decision-making to a minimum.

This doesn't mean that you can't use *tie-ins* of related merchandise. If you're advertising skis, let's say, you could—and perhaps should—mention that the store also has boots, poles, parkas, and other equipment. But skis should be the major item and the rest very definitely subordinate.

☆ Eliminate everything from an ad that doesn't contribute to the sales appeal.

When you are persuading your mother that you should go on a trip with a buddy, you are "selling." You know how hard it is to be persuasive when she is interrupted by the phone, the doorbell, or your kid brother. Advertising is called "salesmanship in print." It, too, has a hard selling job if the reader's attention is distracted by unnecessary elements within the ad.

☆ Write in your reader's idiom.

If you're offering nuclear equipment to a scientist, you have to use terms greatly different from those used to sell records to 11th-graders. Keep your copy in the same terms and style as if you were in friendly conversation with the reader.

☆ Keep ad copy honest.

There are laws against "false and mis-leading" advertising claims. But, more important, it is true that in business—as elsewhere in life!—honesty truly is the best policy. Accuracy is as necessary in ads as it is in news stories.

Hyperbole—obvious and intentional exaggeration—is beloved of Americans, in speaking and writing. People accept it for what it is. When you announce, "I'm starving," your friends don't expect you to expire immediately from acute malnutrition; they know it means just that you are hungry—maybe not even *very* hungry. In ads we expect to see movies described as "epics" or the "greatest ever made" when we know they wouldn't rate a B— if you gave them a report card.

But hyperbole in advertising loses its effectiveness just because the readers do accept it and depreciate it. "Telling it like it is" is a good formula.

☆ Keep ad copy brief.

Tell all that the reader must know to make a decision—then shut up. Remember that the reader doesn't need everything spelled out. If your mother were to read an ad, "Milk, 25¢ Quart," she would know without anyone telling her that milk is a good food, that it's pasteurized (because the law demands it), that a quart is enough for the whole family's breakfast cereal, and that two bits a quart is a great bargain (for she has just paid the regular—much higher—price at the market this afternoon). Only when there are features that are new or unfamiliar need they be spelled out.

☆ Keep the tone light. Use humor.

Teen-agers love humorous ads and will respond favorably to them. The greatest objection to humor is from the advertiser who fears that making fun of the store or its products will lose respect for them. This isn't so; humorous ads have proven their effectiveness. But don't press the reluctant advertiser on its use.

☆ The advisor should supervise all student-created advertising closely.

While this applies especially to humorous advertising, it is true for all ads. Immaturity, questionable judgment, and bad taste can be handicaps in all areas of student publications. But in advertising, repercussions are swifter and bad effects last longer because the advertisers' great investment in their business may be jeopardized—or they may think it is, which is just as bad, as you'll learn when you try to sell them another ad in your paper.

Advisors, being adults, know what is acceptable to the merchant, who is also an adult. The advisor will guard against alienating the advertiser even though the ad in question may be acceptable to a teen-age audience.

While the 5 W's may not be written out until later, they actually are the beginning of any ad. From the W's—written or just floating around in your mind—the headline emerges.

☆ The headline should address a specific person.

This may be either specifically or by implication.

☆ The headline should offer a benefit from the purchase of the merchandise.

So the *copywriter* begins doodling heads:

Scream for the Senators in this swell sweater. (Copywriters like alliteration.)

Warm for the football game, smart for the party afterward.

Without actually saying so, the ad addresses students; in the first example the students are specifically those of Capital High, for they're the ones who'd be rooting for the Senators.

The second head doesn't say what the merchandise is, but that's no major flaw; the picture can do that.

Thumbnail sketches are beginning of any ad. Starred one was refined for final use.

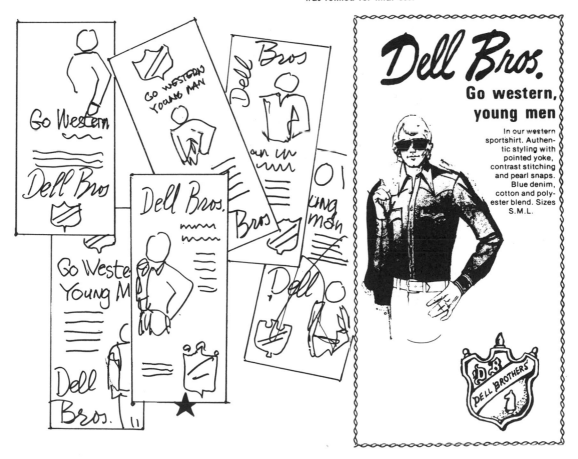

After the head has finally been written and polished—this may take seconds, minutes, or even hours—the *designer,* the *layout artist,* must "visualize the appeal." This is more than just "illustrating" the headline. The whole visual appearance of the ad—not only the pictures but the way in which pictures and type and logo, the store *signature,* blend together—will create an effect that subconsciously suggests to the reader that it's worth reading the copy block and—maybe even at that stage—that the sweater is "just what I've always wanted."

Dummies

The designer first draws *thumbnail* dummies, little and hasty sketches, about 1½ x 2½ inches. Size and shape depend, of course, on those of the finished ad. Thumbnails only suggest the type and art; they are the equivalent of a composer one-fingering on the piano while seeking a melody or a musical theme. Once a thumbnail captures the proper concept, it is converted to a *rough* dummy.

The rough is the same size as the finished ad. Pictures may be drawn in—without much detail but in exact size. Headlines are lettered same size. *Copy blocks* are *Greeked,*

Paste-up dummy of ad places all elements. Headlines are shown in exact height; width is not important on dummy. Numbers on illustration show where it can be found in clipbook. Copy blocks are exact size, keyed by letter to typewritten copy on separate sheet.

Centered · Symmetrical · Rectangular

Classical · Geometric

Ad patterns. These basic layouts must be adapted to meet specific material. Note that patterns are useful for yearbook and magazine pages as well.

indicated by parallel lines that create the approximate tone that the actual type later will.

A *comprehensive dummy,* the *comp,* is a detailed, same-size plan of the finished ad. It approximates as much as possible the actual appearance of the printed ad. Comps are those shown to the advertiser, especially when used as a spec ad.

The *mechanical dummy*—so called, but really not a dummy—is the exact replica of the final ad given to the platemaker.

Ad Patterns

Basic patterns for advertising are many. But you need not concern yourself too much about the terminology. Many ads—perhaps most of them—are modifications or combinations of patterns instead of textbook examples, anyway. And the names of the patterns are self-explanatory.

The *centered ad* is the oldest pattern. It is simple and attractive but it is also static, it has no movement. So it is fine for mes-

sages where dignity and authority must be suggested. For teen-age audiences it has limited appeal.

The *symmetrical* ad is a variation of centering. It pairs matching elements so either the vertical or horizontal half is a mirror image of the opposite half.

Classic and *geometric* patterns are similar. Classic layouts arrange elements in patterns made famous by great artists of the past. The *S* and *reverse S* are prime favorites for ads as well as for a Rembrandt painting because they lead the eye in graceful sweeps through the entire area. The *pyramid* is another favorite framework.

Geometric layouts are well defined by *frames* of display elements in the shape of *L*'s, *U*'s or other simple but strong forms.

Rectangular layouts are sometimes called *Mondrians* because they are inspired by that artist who arranged rectangles of various optical weights into striking paintings.

In a Mondrian layout, no area should be exactly the same size as any other; lines of division should never be at obvious fractions of the whole area, halves, quarters, thirds.

Jazz layout gets its name from music that

Jazz layouts. A, picture defines top and right margins; copy blocks establish both sides; signature marks bottom and right.

B, headline defines both sides; picture and signature, bottom margins. In both layouts elements are woven by no-orphan system.

This is excellent technique for yearbook and magazine pages, too.

requires audience participation. Musicians suggest, but don't actually play, a melody. They play only the harmonics. In a jazz layout, elements suggest a rectangle by touching each side with at least one element. More than one element may touch a single side or a single element may define two or three sides.

Ayers No. 1 is a pattern developed by the first advertising agency in the world, N. W. Ayers of Philadelphia. It has a picture at the top, then the head, the copy block and the logo or signature, the *sig cut*. There are many variations but always they follow the ancient axiom that "pictures must be above type."

Many contemporary ads do not fit neatly into any of these patterns. They are loosely defined as having *dynamic balance*. Of course, many ads that you see daily don't have balance of any kind; they are just plain bad.

☆ In laying out ads, the same principles apply as do to newspaper or yearbook pages.

So the ad staff should read Chapters 13, 18, and 24 closely, just another example of the interrelationship among all print messages.

☆ Build the pattern around a dominant element.

This may be a headline or a picture. Whichever, it must obviously be optically the heaviest element in the ad.

☆ Arrange elements so that the ad "hangs" almost straight.

Only a centered or symmetrical ad will be perfectly perpendicular. But the slight imbalance in other patterns is good, it gives life and excitement to the image.

☆ Place the strongest attention-compeller in the primary optical area.

☆ Use illustrations and *lines of force* within them to direct the eye to all parts of the ad.

Keep the ad so simple that the reader will concentrate on the message instead of on the layout. This is called "keeping the ad invisible."

☆ Orient the ad strongly.

An *oriented layout* is one in which each element shares a common alignment with at least one other. This technique is also called the *no-orphan* or *buddy system*. No element stands alone, an orphan; each one is buddied up on a vertical or horizontal axis with some other element. The more of such common alignments, the more tightly *woven* the ad is and the better it serves the reader and advertiser.

☆ Use only one family of type in an ad.

Just as a listener is confused when confronted with many spoken dialects, so too many type faces confuse the reader. Sticking to one family assures the harmony that keeps the reader happy and makes the ad sell.

An accent face—used very sparingly, for just a word, a phrase, or a line—will give interest.

☆ Use the largest body type that is appropriate and will fit.

Ten-point should be the smallest size used in an ad.

☆ Never set body type narrower than one column or wider than two.

☆ Avoid runarounds.

☆ Avoid all-cap heads.

Oriented layout. Diagram shows how each element shares
at least one axis with another. Broken lines show common
horizontal and vertical axes on which elements align.

The same principles apply to advertising
typography as to news typography. That's
why many of these ancient axioms are duplicated in different sections of this book.
But in advertising—usually at the instruction of the merchant—all-caps must be used
for what the advertiser thinks is emphasis
and appeal. 'Tain't so; but the customer is
always right. If you must use all-caps,
minimize the quantity of them. A few
words will not be dangerously illegible and
the more familiar the words, the easier they
are to comprehend: "Sale," "Free," "Off."

☆ Don't set headlines diagonally, vertically, sideways, or on a curved line.

☆ Never run the whole ad sideways or
upside-down.
Even if the advertiser wants this unor-
thodox placement, feeling that it will attract readers, most of those readers will
think it was a stupid mistake. This reflects
poorly on your newspaper and your staff.

☆ Avoid boxes and circles in an ad.
Ads gain impact from size. To subdivide

any area is to lower its total effectiveness.
Sunbursts are the worst; these are circles
with a jagged outer edge that actually distress the reading eye, the way the spikes of
a cactus hurt the hand.

If an advertiser insists on boxes, try sideless boxes, made just like those used for
editorial purposes.

☆ Avoid ragged-left typesetting.

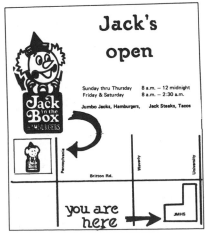

Map in ad effectively shows advertiser's location is convenient to John Marshall High in Oklahoma City, Oklahoma.

As with news heads, flush-left is the best style for ad heads.

Body type, ad or news, is best read when justified, even left and right columns. Such setting is *specified, specced,* as: *Bodoni Book, 10/11 === 15 picas.* First the name of the typeface is given. The next number, *10,* is the size of the type, 10-point. The *11* indicates that 1 point of ledding has been added and, after the long equals sign, is the line length. It is taken for granted that body type will be justified.

If we want type to appear in the same form as the typewritten copy—as poetry does, for instance—write on the copy *set line for line.* The result will be:

> This copy has been set
> so each line of type
> contains the same
> words and characters
> as a line of typewritten material.

This copy is not only set, it is written, line for line. You must write it so no phrases are broken from one line to another. You know how disconcerting broken phrases are in reading poetry, and in Chapter 10 we've noted the weird effect of such breaks in news heads.

If you want ragged-right setting, draw two parallel lines at the left of the copy concerned and write *set flush left.*

If you draw those parallel lines at the right of the copy and write *set flush-right,* the result will be like this:

> This block of type
> is set flush-right,
> a style that is
> not very effective
> for the reader.

Note in this example how confusion can set in because the phrase "is not very effective" has been broken and the first impression—which may never be corrected—puts the emphasis on "is," *is* effective. Proper division would be:

> is set flush-right,
> a style
> that is not very effective
> for the reader.

or

> a style that is not
> very effective
> for the reader.

Flush-right setting is hard to read because the reader always seeks a constant starting point for every successive line. With a ragged-left margin there is no familiar *axis of orientation—A/O—*to which the eye can return after the end of any line.

☆ Minimize, if you can't eliminate, flush-right setting.

Among the occasional exceptions to typographic rules is the one for *stepped type.* While this, too, fails to provide an A/O, it is effective in small doses and can be pleasing to the eye. It looks like this:

> Type set this way is
> often pleasing in certain
> layouts. This is stepped
> type. It creates a pleasant
> diagonal element on an ad
> while keeping the type it-
> self on a horizontal axis.

Such style is specced as:

> *Caledonia Bold, 11/12 === 9 picas*
> *Step down 1 pica per line.*

Two parallel diagonal lines are marked on each side of the copy involved.

When you use this style, remember that each line extends the amount of the step to the right of the previous line. In the example "Type set this way . . ." the last line is 7 picas to the right of the first line and so the block then isn't 8½ picas wide but 15½. Too often the block won't fit into the available area because the stepping effect was overlooked.

☆ Make sure that all type will fit into available space.

Ad heads are counted out just as news heads are, by the method described in Chapter 10. Body type is gaged by *copyfitting.* Suppose you want to fill a copyblock area 3½ inches wide by 4 inches deep, with 10-point Caledonia, ledded a point, 10/11.

Find some specimen of this face and size. Measure off 3½ inches and typewrite three or four lines of that length. You'll probably find that they'll vary a couple of characters, depending on how many narrow or wide letters such as l, i, m, w, or caps occur.

Determine the average and set your typewriter at that length. Then measure a block of Caledonia—or any other face—that is set 10-on-11. (Faces of the same point size will vary in number of characters per horizontal inch but not in vertical measurement.) See how many lines will fit into the 4-inch depth. Do not count fractions of lines. In this case you'll find that there would be 26 $\frac{2}{11}$ lines in a 4-inch depth. Ignore the fraction, make it 26 lines.

Set your typewriter the proper measure. Type 26 lines and you'll find that the copy you write will neatly fill the designated area. Then working backward, if you type previously written copy to these specifications, you'll quickly know whether it will fit into 26 lines or less or whether it will be too long and have to be set in a smaller type size.

If lines don't come out exactly in the typewriting, don't worry. A line two or three characters short will probably be balanced off by another one that goes beyond your average. As long as you don't vary by more than three characters in either way, your lines will even out. If in doubt, keep lines a bit short. You can always fill out an area by adding a little white space; but there comes a time when you just cannot squeeze in even one excess character.

☆ Use white space generously.

It is a highly effective selling tool. Every ad should have a generous frame of white space around its perimeter. This will not only frame and spotlight the message but will keep neighboring ads from encroaching upon the reader attention that your ad has attracted. Providing this "buffer zone" is always the first step in making a layout.

☆ Keep white space at the outside of the ad.

An irregular silhouette is pleasing to the eye. Trapped space weakens the layout and irritates the eye. White space is most effective in the fallow corners.

☆ Don't use pictures just to fill up space.

The function of ad illustrations is to expand upon and reinforce the written word, to attract attention, to direct the eye to important type blocks, and to create a pleasant atmosphere that will make the reader more receptive to the sales message.

Unless a picture does at least one, and preferably more, of these functions, don't use it. This applies to decorative borders, too.

☆ Pictures are the strongest selling tool.

Student ad staffers should learn to use effective art. When an ad sells merchandise for an advertiser, it also makes selling advertising space much, much easier.

There are three major sources for ad art. Students may take photographs or draw pictures. The advertiser may have pictures furnished by the wholesaler who handles the merchandise. The newspaper may have *clip books*. These are pictures, both photographic and hand art, printed on heavy, slick paper. The chosen ones are clipped and sent to the printer who will paste them, along with the just-set type, onto the mechanical from which the plate ultimately will be made.

Clip books are inexpensive. Those put out by *ad services* have a wide variety of pictures of all kinds of merchandise and in many different art styles, from photos to paintings to cartoons. Also included are the *attention-compellers*, decorative headlines such as "Halloween Sale" in wraithy lettering, ornamented with pumpkins and black cats, or borders made of holly or gift ribbons for Christmas, or bunnies and buttercups for Easter.

☆ Use attention-compellers sparingly.

Too often they distract, rather than attract, the reader. Make sure that there is an obvious connection between such compellers and the rest of the ad.

Other clip books contain art on only a single subject: Children, animals, athletics, autumn, furniture, women's wear, etc., etc. There is great variety.

Local photographs are the most effective art, however. Readers love to see models they know, or might know, in familiar settings. Students are the best models for ads in a student paper. A picture of Sally Smith and Jon Brown modeling spring clothes in front of City Hall, a public library, or your school, is infinitely more appealing than that of a TV star in front of Buckingham Palace.

Localizing should always be emphasized in the written copy. Models should be named and identified as students; the setting, no matter how obvious, should also be identified. This can be done as part of the selling copy block.

Some newspapers ask the advertiser to pay a small extra fee for the cost of materials involved in local photography. The demurring merchant, once such art proves its effectiveness, recognizes that its cost is a good investment. Some newspapers will not make this extra charge for the first time a merchant uses student models, a free sample as it were. Other papers never charge.

Professional models are paid, some of them astronomically. Students usually are more than willing to model for free. It's fun; it's a status symbol; it may be the start to a professional modeling career.

Often the model is paid a token fee of a dollar, though. Whether or not payment is made, the model must sign a *release,* like this:

> *I, we* ——————, *hereby consent and authorize Central Department Store, its successors or assigns, to reproduce the attached photograph of* —————— *in its advertising. Receipt of full consideration is hereby acknowledged and no further claim of any nature will be made.*
>
> *Date* ——————
> *Signature: (1)* ——————
> *   (2)* ——————
> *   (3)* ——————

"Full consideration" may be cash, a small gift, or just a spoken "Thank you."

If the model is a minor, the parents or guardians must sign the release.

A signed release is an absolute must. Without it the model might later sue the advertiser and/or the paper for invasion of privacy or for use of services for which proper payment hadn't been made.

As you've noticed again: Exactly the same principles that apply to ads also apply to news editorial makeup in newspaper, magazine, or book.

An important element in an ad is the signature. While the ad designer must place the logo harmoniously and effectively, the actual design of that signature has already been done—and probably quite long ago—by someone else. The ad designer's primary responsibility is to see that it is properly placed—indeed that it *is* placed. It is surprising how often even professionals forget this essential element.

All the material for an ad should go to the printer as a single package.

All copy—heads and body—is typed on a separate sheet of paper; it never goes on the dummy! The copy sheet is identified in the top left corner with the name of your publication (often rubber stamped), name of the advertiser, date it's to run, and size. This is given as 2 x 5, for instance, which means it's 2 columns wide and 5 inches deep.

At the center top is the page number of this typewritten material. In the top right corner is the "inventory" of copy for that ad: Typed verbal copy, dummy, illustrations and logo.

The typed pages may be noted as *1 of 1* for a single sheet. If there are, say, three sheets, they're numbered 1 of 3, 2 of 3, and 3 of 3. This numbering and the inventory are designed to signal immediately if there is anything missing. It's far better to start looking for a vanished picture at this stage than when you're on the deadline for platemaking or the press.

All verbal copy is specced as to type face, size, line length, ledding, and style for setting. Although the dummy is the same size as the ad will be, dimensions are written onto the dummy in numbers just to make sure the designer didn't slip on the measurements.

Proofreading Ads

Unlike daily newspaper ad people, the student ad staff doesn't see proofs on indi-

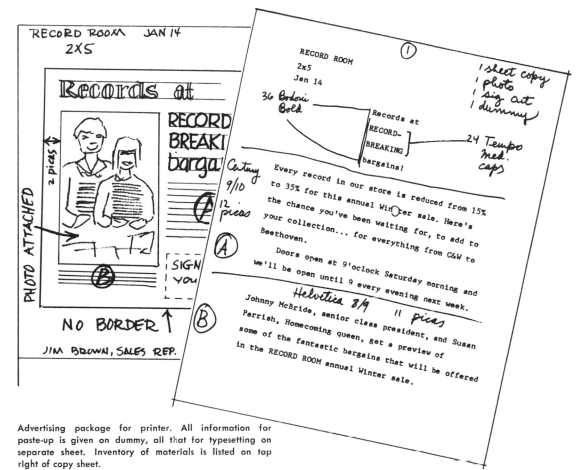

Advertising package for printer. All information for paste-up is given on dummy, all that for typesetting on separate sheet. Inventory of materials is listed on top right of copy sheet.

vidual ads; it must proof the ads on page proofs, the same ones used by the news staff. And ads must be proofread as conscientiously as the news is.

☆ Proofread ads always in a regular sequence. Use a checklist:

1. Is the size correct?

2. Have the proper pictures been used? It's easy—and greatly disconcerting—to have a picture of a blazer from Kampus Klothes appear in the ad for Mike's Men's Wear, its bitterest competitor.

3. Is the layout correct? Use a straight-edge to determine that oriented elements are truly on common axes.

4. Are headlines in the proper type and size and free of typos?

5. Is body type error-free?

6. Is the price correct? Despite widespread belief, neither the advertiser nor the newspaper is responsible for an incorrect price. The merchant does not have to sell merchandise at a wrong price; the newspaper need only correct the error in its next issue, and this can be done in a space just large enough to carry the item and correct price in the same size as that of the error. But many merchants, to maintain good will, do take a loss and sell merchandise at the incorrect price. In this case they blame the newspaper, which then seeks its own ways to make amends. All of which is costly and embarrassing.

7. Is the correct sig cut in the ad and properly placed? If there is corollary material with the sig—address, phone, shopping hours, etc.—check it with care.

Because elements in an ad are not arranged in neat rows, it is easy to overlook some of them. So it's a good technique to

Side heads. A uses coinedge rule to create sideless box, tie head and story together, and dress otherwise naked columns 2-4.

B uses full box and 2-column body type.

C is non-functional. Broken-box technique is not esthetically pleasing. Bimo heads—here a kicker—should not be used as side heads.

D is unusual. Head runs across first leg of body type. Large area of white under head creates trapped space that punches hole into page pattern.

tick off each element with a red pencil as you read its proof.

☆ A second staffer should determine that every element has been checked.

Although advertising revenues are essential to keeping a newspaper alive, ad staffers work backstage. So some schools give by-lines to the persons who have sold, created, and serviced the ad. The merchant is usually pleased to have these names appear in his ad because they intensify local interest and make the ad sell better.

But whether the staffer is publicly recognized or not, there are many satisfactions in working on a student ad staff. Producing revenue is always a pleasant exercise; creating an ad is as fulfilling as the creation of any other communication; contacts with local businessmen can help open doors later when the student is seeking a job; the professional advertising field offers interesting career opportunities.

Advertising is so much a part of American life that countless ad slogans have gone into everyday language. One of them is "It pays to advertise." It truly does. It pays in many ways—to the consumer, the advertiser and, of course, the person who creates that advertising.

Building and Servicing Circulation

"If you don't have good circulation, you have a dead body—and a dead newspaper."

People in the *circulation department* enjoy this analogy—and make it often. It's true that circulation provides the lifeblood to a newspaper just as it does to humans.

The most important job of the circulation department is to assure communication by providing readers for the newspaper's contents.

While circulation revenue, the money paid for subscriptions and single copies, is only a small part of a professional newspaper's income, circulation determines advertising rates and demonstrates public acceptance of the paper.

In both professional and student newspapering, there are four types of circulation:

1. *Free circulation* is just that. It provides newspapers to every home or every person in a given area. For many years free circulation was anathema to professional newspaper people. In many instances these papers were *shoppers,* completely filled with advertising or containing only such "news" as "came in over the transom," announcements and reports sent in voluntarily. The pros felt that such papers were unfair competition, were spared the heavy expense of operating a news department, and yet were riding on the reputation of regular newspapers.

Many established, conventional newspapers began as free *throwaways;* then, having gained public acceptance, converted into paid circulation. A trend today is to stay in free circulation but to furnish complete news coverage. Saturation of the market and high readership created by complete news coverage allows ad rates high enough to provide all necessary income.

2. *Controlled circulation* is free but is more selective. It is common among business publications. Only persons who are in specified positions in an industry or business receives a subscription. *The National Glockenspiel Journal* goes only to presidents, managers, and purchasing agents of glockenspiel companies; this assures advertisers that their message will reach all the people who buy from them and that waste circulation to people who are not potential customers is eliminated.

3. *Forced circulation* isn't as compulsory as it sounds. In this system subscriptions are automatically given to members of organizations and the cost is included in membership dues.

4. *Paid circulation* is the most highly desired. A person who pays for a publication truly wants it and will read it more avidly and thoroughly than something that came free and unsought. This makes advertising in paid publications more effective, too. So ad sales representatives stress their paid circulation. *ABC* certification is a major space-selling aid; the *Audit Bureau of Circulation* has examined the records and attests to the accuracy and numbers of the paid-subscription list. In order to send publications by second-class mail, circulation

must be paid and acceptance to this special class—which supposedly gives first-class service at lower postal rates—is considered the official cachet of "a real newspaper."

Paid circulation of professional papers is divided into: (a) home delivery—which accounts for most copies; (b) street sales, which are of greatest importance to the *metropolitans* in large cities; and (c) mail subscriptions. Dailies use the mails comparatively little. Weeklies, especially those in small towns and rural areas, distribute most of their copies through the postal system.

Let's see how the student staff can use these various methods.

"There ain't no free lunch" is a cynical observation that also applies to newspapers: "There ain't no free circulation." Someone has to pay for producing a paper. Advertising revenues pay most of the cost for professional papers. But student papers often can't sell sufficient ad space or at high enough rates; so usually they must be subsidized to some extent by their schools.

Constantly rising costs of operating schools and public resistance to higher taxes put such subsidies on the maybe list for most staffs. But they should prepare a formal request to the school board and substantiate it with good reasoning:

1. A school newspaper is usually the only way in which students and their parents can get news about their schools. It is especially valuable to the school administration to reach parents and other taxpayers. In many states school budgets must be approved by the electorate and in all states approval of special bond issues and assessments requires voter approval. To inform the public of the need for such financing, many school districts send out newsletters. It is more economical to send the school newspapers, and a broader look at the school is often a subtle, but real, factor in creating and maintaining good will of the community to its educational system.

2. A good school paper can create a wholesome school spirit. Many administrators credit school papers with helping to establish and maintain high standards of scholarship, citizenship, and service.

For the staff, free circulation has many advantages. It helps to sell advertising because the merchant knows that every single potential customer is being reached. It simplifies delivery. Papers are simply piled at strategic places in the school. More effective, but almost as simple, is to deliver proper quantities to each home room. This assures that absent students will get their copy when they return.

If a school is unable to subsidize the paper, help may be sought from the PTA, alumni or lettermen's associations, local service clubs, or similar civic-minded organizations. In many communities there are charitable foundations—not always well known—which might support activities whose benefits are as deep and obvious as those of student journalism.

In countless instances where tight school budgets curtailed or eliminated athletics or music programs, community groups have raised necessary subsidies. Student journalists must be just as adept and persuasive in presenting the case for subsidizing their publications.

☆ Free circulation is ideal for student publications and worth much effort to achieve.

Forced circulation of school papers is quite common. The price of the paper is included in the student activities ticket, which is sold under many names. Or membership in student-government association provides an automatic subscription. In many instances so many students belong to the SG, SO, SU, or whatever it's called, that forced circulation is virtually as wide as free circulation.

☆ Paid circulation is a challenge worthy of great staff effort.

For it proves that students want the paper and don't pick it up just because it's free. To get adequate coverage, the circulation department must plan and perform a major job.

A newspaper is a consumer commodity just like breakfast food, shoes, or records. It must be merchandised according to well-conceived and well-planned principles.

Circulation campaigns should be conducted at the beginning of each school year. Some staffs do it at the start of each semester but this is not efficient. It takes no more time or effort to sell a year's subscription than a half-year one. If your school has a midyear graduating class, arrangements can cover shorter subscription terms and also reach students entering as midwinter freshmen.

☆ Subscriptions are best handled through home rooms.

A 100% coverage should be the goal—one subscription for each student except those who have a brother or sister in the school. One subscription per family is all that's needed, although often siblings may want their own papers anyway.

If there are siblings, try to sell the youngest one. If students get into the habit of subscribing as freshmen, they'll probably continue throughout all the school years.

The home room pays a lump sum for all its subscriptions. The organization of such home rooms and methods of payment vary from school to school, but adaptations to your own setup are easy. If the group has a treasury, payment is simply made from it. Some ask students to pay for their own subscriptions. Some solicit contributions above this sum to furnish papers to those who can't afford their own.

To most students, the amount of the subscription is trifling, the cost of a hamburg or a theater ticket. But there are some students to whom this is a major sum. It is embarrassing to those students. They are too proud to explain that their father is sick and their mother's earnings are meager. Often they are pressured by classmates to make the 100% goal. If they don't, or if they deny themselves lunch one day to scrape up the money, they are hurt and resentful and their entire school days may be clouded by this unhappy experience. Any arrangement so such students will neither be left out nor made to feel like a charity case is worth seeking.

The reward for a 100% home room may be a reduction in price, usually 25%. Individuals may be offered a similar discount if they subscribe before a certain date.

Often it is possible to give added inducements to subscribers. In many communities merchants will offer a special deal to subscribers: Two movie tickets for the price of one, half off on hotdogs, discounts on records, sneakers, or sundry merchandise. In such cases special coupons for redemption are given to the subscriber along with the receipt, or the coupons may be part of the receipt which the merchant checks off when specials are given. For merchants this can be a valuable promotion. They are anxious to have students come into their stores and early to get in the habit of shopping there.

Lapel buttons that identify subscribers are a good sales gimmick. Some schools allow subscribers to vote for Homecoming King and Queen or in other popularity contests—even for the Ugliest Man on the Campus.

Rivalry between clubs or home rooms may be a wholesome incentive. The first one to turn in 100% subscriptions may be given a trophy to display the rest of the year, name one of its members king or queen of a major event or even skip classes some afternoon as the principal discreetly looks the other way.

A good subscription campaign is a combination circus, pep rally, and holiday party. Everyone can have fun. Plans should be made in the spring so things get off to a roaring start as soon as school resumes in fall.

Free samples are still an excellent way to sell any merchandise. Many staffs prepare their first issue early so it can be distributed free on the first day of school. This is helpful to the principal and faculty, too, because it gets information to students who otherwise may not yet be reached.

On the first day—or as soon as possible thereafter—when the students have had a chance to sample the contents of the paper, each home room is visited by a sales rep. As it's most effective if every room is covered at the same period, the circulation department must enlist the help of editorial and advertising staffers and probably other student leaders as well.

At a preliminary meeting, these solicitors should be told their duties and procedures. And they should be given a Mimeoed list of sales points to persuade their classmates to subscribe. These should list solid benefits. Never urge students to subscribe as a matter of obligation, to "show their school spirit."

Each solicitor is given a receipt book. The original receipt goes to the subscriber, the carbon copy to the circulation manager.

☆ Keep the campaign short and exciting.

A week is just about right. Fill corridors, classrooms, cafeteria, and gym with banners and posters. These can be prepared as an art-class project during the previous spring. Even this can be a contest, with the best artists receiving prizes—maybe subscriptions—or at least generous public recognition.

If your school has assemblies, ask to have a special one during this week. Invite a local newspaperman or woman to speak; no one can sell a student publication with as much enthusiasm or authority as a professional. An alumnus will probably be willing to come even a considerable distance for the occasion.

If possible enlist your school band or more informal musical groups to play at school entrances at the start of each day or in the cafeteria during lunch hour to maintain the carnival atmosphere.

Even if most soliciting is done in home rooms, there should be convenient places and times where students can subscribe. A table in the lunch room or at main entrances will attract many subscribers.

Competition should be encouraged among solicitors. The best ones may be rewarded with a free student-activities ticket or a season pass to all basketball games. Or they may receive extra points in meeting requirements for Quill and Scroll Society or toward earning a school sweater or key.

☆ Have solicitors report daily.

This minimizes errors. If something is wrong, it's easier to correct while details are still fresh in the solicitor's mind. It also removes the danger of getting subscription funds mixed up with the student's own money. Then it's too easy to spend it inadvertently and when the time comes for settlement, the solicitor may not have the cash to turn over to the newspaper.

Such a campaign obviously requires the approval and cooperation of the principal and faculty. The circulation manager should make a formal request in the previous spring. Perhaps the faculty can be addressed in a meeting just before school opens. If teachers are properly convinced of the value of the paper and the logic of the campaign they can be invaluable allies.

☆ Inform the student body of campaign results.

A common device is a thermometer, or similar scale, which is posted in the main hall and brought up to date just as soon as the solicitors have made their daily reports. There are many ways of varying this basic graph, ways that contribute to the ballyhoo of the campaign.

☆ Reach out for nonstudent subscribers.

Teachers and people who staff the office, lunch room, custodial services, busing, etc., are as interested as students in the school—and news about it. Some staffs offer free subscriptions to such adults. Sometimes the administration or the teachers' association pays for them.

Some teachers insist on buying their own subscriptions. These may be at regular rates or at special prices designated for such people whose cooperation the staff appreciates.

Alumni, especially recent ones, like to read the paper to keep track of friends. Graduates who go off to college often maintain ties with the school. It's a good tactic to sell such subscriptions for the following year to seniors—or their parents—in the spring.

Other alumni can be contacted in the fall by letters, phone calls, or personal visits to their home. Members of civic organizations, especially those with special interest in schools, are also good prospects.

The best prospect is always a satisfied customer. So those people already on your mailing list should be reminded by letter that their current subscription is due for renewal.

Subscription Prices

The circulation department either sets prices for subscriptions or single copies or plays an important role in such decisions with other departments of the paper. This is a difficult decision to make because you don't have the key guideline that most merchants have: What your competition is doing.

The price of any commodity depends on two factors: (a) cost of producing it and (b) the value that a potential buyer puts on it. So the staff must determine its costs for the coming year.

Costs should be determined on a per-page basis. And all costs must be considered, even those which are often overlooked.

Major costs are typesetting, pasteup, and printing. These are usually—along with the cost of printing paper—included in a single bill from the printer. This information is simple to obtain.

Photography costs are substantial. They include the depreciation on cameras and darkroom equipment as well as the price of film, photopaper, and chemicals.

Other costs are copy paper and supplies (if they're not furnished by the school); transportation of copy, proofs, and people to and from the printer; postage (which increases constantly and greatly) and telephone. Remember, too, that your free list is an expense although it doesn't at first glance seem so.

Now, how do you pay these bills? Most staffs try to obtain one-third of production costs from circulation and two-thirds from advertising. A subsidy may replace all or most of subscription revenues. Or it may be a separate revenue source used to lower either subscription or ad rates, or both.

It is difficult to determine the "average" rates for American scholastic publications. The sums vary as widely as the conditions under which the publications are produced. It's difficult to find a common denominator between a school of several thousands in an affluent suburb and one in a ghetto or one of a few hundred in an isolated prairie town. The lowest rate to come to the authors' attention is 75¢ a year; the highest is $4. The single-copy price is more standard, 10¢ or 15¢ for newspapers. (Magazines range from 25¢ to $1.)

Frequency of issue, of course, is a major factor in subscription rates although not of single-copy prices. A monthly can't charge as much as a bi-weekly unless it delivers the same number of pages during the year, and sometimes not even then. In most instances students prefer frequency to bulk. The size of the page is a minor consideration, usually only as it determines total bulk. The customer is always the final determinant. Does he value the product—be it newspaper, cola, or concert—enough to pay the asking price?

Then, of course, the staff must maintain such high editorial quality that the student body will be willing to pay the subscription rate and merchants the advertising rate.

Enlist experienced advice in determining rates. The advisor, printer, business teacher, and principal can help the staff set rates which will meet expenses, yet not price themselves out of the market.

Delivery

As soon as the paper comes off the press, it is the responsibility of the circulation department to get it into the hands of the subscribers or casual purchaser.

It all begins with good record-keeping and that begins during the subscription campaign—and even before. As soon as it's available, a list of every subscriber's name is compiled and grouped by home rooms. As solicitors report, they turn in their money and are given a receipt. The circulation manager keeps a ledger into which is entered each amount. From the carbons of individual receipts, names are checked off the master list. Some C.M.s keep two lists; they believe that with two people checking names, errors and omissions are minimized.

Circulation lists are invaluable and irreplaceable. So a safe place must be found to store them and there should be an inflexible rule that they are never taken from that room. Some papers keep a working list which does stay in the news room and file a duplicate in the principal's office where often there is fireproof storage.

On publication day, delivery is made to home rooms. If the room has 100% coverage, it's easy: Simply count out the number. Otherwise the circulator takes a list along and checks off as each student gets a copy. If a student is absent, the name is written on a paper which is kept by the teacher until the student's return to class.

Some schools have experimented with a central distribution system. Each subscriber has been given a card—or a portion of the student activity ticket is so designated. As the student picks up the paper, a hole is punched or an ink mark made to denote delivery of that issue. But because this method takes time and creates traffic jams, it isn't particularly popular.

Unless there is close to 100% coverage, there should be one or more places where single copies are sold in the school. The main entranceway or the cafeteria are good places.

In some instances copies are sold in nearby stores, especially those that cater to students. The circulation department delivers a specified number to the merchant, who signs a receipt for them. At the end of the week the unsold copies are picked up and the merchant pays for those sold minus commission, which is about a third of the price. Many merchants are pleased to waive this fee, however, because availability of the paper brings students into the store.

The circulation department should check such outlets daily, or even more frequently on the first day. If the supply is sold out early in the week, it should be replenished. Next time, the original number may be increased.

The circulation department is responsible for picking up the paper at the printer's. Often it expands its duties into those of a *traffic department* and delivers copy to the printer as well.

It's a truism that regularity of publication builds circulation. In New York City where much professional-papers circulation is from newsstand sales, it's estimated that for every minute that a newspaper is late in hitting the street, 10,000 sales are lost. Obviously losses aren't that great with a student paper, but it certainly is important that the paper come out not only on the designated day but at the same hour. Press day ought to be established in the minds of students as one to look forward to in pleasant anticipation—and assurance that the paper will come out when they expect it. So the circulation manager, *C.M.*, should keep in close touch with the editorial and advertising staffs and encourage them to meet the deadlines necessary to assure scheduled delivery.

The C.M. has not only the right but the responsibility of doing this—just as every staffer, no matter on what job, has a vested interest in maintaining quality performance in all departments. For on a newspaper—professional or scholastic—everyone's job depends on other people. You can't have several departments each working independently of the others. Each person and department must be part of a smoothly linked team.

The circulation department is the last link in this chain of so many disparate talents and skills. It is an indispensable link and as such demands and deserves the best people and their best performances.

BOOK

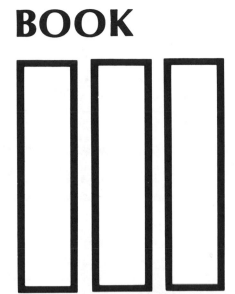

THE SCHOOL MAGAZINE

Franklin Gothic Triple (

Franklin Italic

Futura Semi-Cond

Bryant Expa

Futura Semi-Con(

Billboard Condensed

Madison Goth

Specimens of Monotonal faces

17

Creative Magazines

Scholastic magazine formats now range from the oldest to the newest trends in journalism. And their contents are as varied.

Classic examples of high school publications are literary magazines which display writing talents of students in essays and fiction with some infrequent references to events going on around the authors. The oldest known scholastic periodical dates from the Revolutionary period, as pointed out in Chapter 2.

Most recent of school publishing trends is the news magazine. These publications are patterned after *Time,* which was started in 1923 by Henry R. Luce and Briton Hadden as the first mass-circulation news weekly. Students have tried to duplicate it and its rivals at the high school level.

Regardless of whether editors and writers emulate the centuries-old traditions of a literary magazine or the contemporary news weeklies, they have ample opportunities to express ingenuity and imagination through innovations and creativity. The wide range of high school magazines allows for rampant individuality, which always is an intriguing journalistic challenge.

Literary Magazines

High school magazines come in many sizes and in even more varieties of styles and purposes. Each magazine grows out of its accumulated traditions and its special environment. That is as it should be.

In some schools, magazines grow almost exclusively from courses in creative writing and are showplaces for exceptionally good class work. Short stories, essays, opinion articles, and poems written as school assignments are screened for eventual publication. This is good as far as it goes, but it excludes nonliterary excellence as well as nonverbal, pictorial art forms.

In other places, drawings, photographs, and even good cartoons are published along with class assignments and superior writing that may be done specifically for the magazine.

In still other schools, a magazine serves as both a repository for good creative work, including art, and a channel for reporting news happenings. This hybrid, which combines magazine and tabloid format, is known as *magtab* and is taking a place in contemporary trends. It's discussed in the next chapter.

In other schools, the magazine serves as an installment of a yearbook and tells the unfolding story of the academic year as it takes place. If bound together at the year's end, magazines of this type replace an annual. In some localities, where this has been done, the yearbook has been discontinued.

Each of these variations of magazines requires a different staff organization and varied methods for handling copy. If the publication prints predominantly assignments from a creative writing class, editors and teachers of these sections must work closely together. Faculty may assign articles to fit the magazine's requirements for a wide range of content. For a publication that includes art, recruitment of the better students in these activities is a must. Some of this creative material, especially photographs and cartoons, would not regularly come from class assignments. For a magazine that tries to capture news events in words and pictures, a news editor functions almost identically with one on a newspaper.

A simplified operating schedule for a general literary magazine, might be:

1. After selection of key editorial and business personnel for the coming year, establish editorial and business policies. Most of these may be handed down from one year to another but it never hurts to take a close look to see if what was done last year is still best for the coming year. Some procedures may change from year to year:

How many issues should be produced? How many pages?

Is there sufficient money for a second color or even four colors?

Should there be any changes in type or page sizes?

What should be the target amount of ad space per issue?

2. Decide whether each issue will revolve around a central theme or will offer a wide range of appealing articles. This is a key editorial judgment for the entire year and it determines possible advertising sales, too.

3. Start work on the initial issue by contacting teachers of creative writing classes for manuscripts, getting student artists, photographers, and cartoonists alerted to your specific needs, and—if you plan much news coverage—recruiting and assigning students to write up items and features.

4. Choose articles for publication.

☆ Never base selections on personal friendships.

5. Edit manuscripts and check art. Review what was said in Chapter 9, because copyreading is copyreading regardless of where material is printed. As copy editor, you are responsible not only for style, correct spelling, and good grammar but for good taste and, very important, for the wordage fitting the allocated space.

6. Proofreading and pasting up or making up the pages.

While much of these activities is going on within the editorial staff, the business staffers—if advertising is used in the magazine—are soliciting contracts and obtaining copy. After the issue comes out, the magazine business staff has the same responsibilities for billing and collecting payments as their colleagues on the student newspaper.

The editor will find it useful to edit the magazine for two students, a boy and a girl who are good friends and who are interested in many things. An editor must make sure, always, that Sam is interested in things other than sports and Sue other than boys. They should be upper average—to coin a category.

The *progression* of a magazine, the way its contents are placed, contributes much to the pleasure of readers. What goes into a magazine depends largely on what is chosen and how it is edited, then how it is positioned.

☆ No editing can be done strictly by formula.

An editor must constantly make judgments on what to use and what to discard. Few editors, including those on school magazines, have to worry about filling space. Usually the problem is to sort out the best from an overload of material.

Selecting a good short story, feature article, or poem for publication always presents problems. For instance, how do you know it is good? The first thing is to ask: Do *you* like it? A "yes" answer is important but it is not the only criterion that an editor should use. This assumes, of course, that the editor is not too different from classmates. The editor visualizes the typical boy and girl and asks: Will *they* like it? In deciding both replies, an editor has to be as objective as a judge on a supreme court. If both answers are "yes," then the manuscript is well on its way to print.

Another test some editors use is: Does it do what it sets out to do? If it is a mood piece, does it arouse feelings of readers? If it is a sonnet, are the internal and external poetic patterns preserved—or is it just a sloppy jingle?

These same basic qualifying standards apply to visual work as well as written work.

If an editor is not sure, conferences with staff colleagues or faculty members may erase doubts and fortify the final decision. There is nothing wrong with cooperative effort unless an editor uses it to avoid responsibility.

Now let's look at some of the problems for each kind of manuscript submitted to a school literary magazine.

Essays and opinion articles have a long and honorable history and special appeal for many student writers. However, these authors must have something to say that will interest other students and must say it exceptionally well. Teen-agers are not usually experts in, say, nuclear energy and plasma physics and so a manuscript in these fields would be returned, almost without exception. Students are experts on their own adjustments to living in the last quarter of the 20th century. They face questions about such things as school conduct codes, hair styles, drug abuse, and a return to religious experiences. What they write on these topics can make exceptionally good reading, especially if personalized.

The late Heywood Broun, sports writer, columnist, and first president of the Newspaper Guild, was asked once why he wrote so many columns about himself and his feelings. He replied, "On these, I am the world's greatest living authority." Students might well follow his example.

☆ Write essays and comments about topics on which you have knowledge, background, and experience.

A successful essay has been called "conversation on a high plane." And it is.

A few English teachers may want students to pattern their initial essay assignments after the antiquated styles of writers centuries ago which are found in literature textbooks. (If they were alive, these classic essayists undoubtedly would adapt to the modern milieu.) Your publication need not use these old-fashioned styles. They are like finger exercises of a great musician, neces-

sary—but not great art. If class work is restricted to this style of composition during the initial weeks before the first issue comes out, an editor may (a) save some juniors' work from the spring; (b) get the teacher to allow a few exceptions from the general assignment for some gifted class members; or (c) obtain articles written outside of class.

Fiction is almost exclusively the province of literary magazines because of its absence from newspapers and yearbooks. Talented short-story writers may exist in your high school and they, too, are entitled to see their words in print. Since writers' numbers vary from year to year, editors have to shift the percentage of space for fiction, features, and essays to fit the supply of excellence available. This gears the publication to high-quality material.

What locale and what plot should school fiction writers select and their editors favor? Ones with which they are familiar! Little sense is made with a short story of a young gladiator in Rome. Even as a dream sequence it is pretty far out. A "gladiator" on today's basketball court, though, makes good material.

☆ A school audience is most interested in fiction that relates to its own experiences.

Successful short stories may help readers to discover things about themselves that they never before saw in quite such sharp focus. Ezra Pound, the poet, once described literature as "news that stays news." He meant that effective writing provides new insights for readers because it tells the truth with literary lighting effects just a bit different from those used previously. Tribute of a rare sort is reflected in the comment, "Gee, I wish I'd thought of that."

Feature articles and interviews certainly are entitled to considerable space in writing courses and school magazines. Increasingly in recent decades, mass-circulation magazines have turned more and more from fiction to fact reporting and most of these articles have been traditional feature articles.

Practically everything that was said in Chapter 8 about features in newspapers applies for magazine editors and writers. One difficulty is that some teachers and a few students feel that feature articles are not entitled to space in a "literary" magazine. This is unfortunate. It runs counter to the increasing attention for nonfiction in professional magazine journalism and thus is elitist and unrealistic.

Good poetry, always elusive, is hard to find and even harder to measure. Archibald MacLeish, who should know since he is one of the United States' widely respected poets, once wrote:

> *A poem should be wordless*
> *As the flight of birds*
> *. . .*
> *A poem should not mean*
> *But be.*

The young in heart (and that means, often, the young in age, too) are our best poets. William Cullen Bryant wrote his memorable and most famous poem, "Thanatopsis," when he was 17 and long before he became a famous newspaper editor.

Poems need not follow the rigid format of a Shakespearean sonnet but they should conform with the approved conventions of the literary form that they strive to achieve. Even free verse is difficult to write and it has a style of its own, although that may be far less exacting than, say, iambic pentameter.

Since people always are interested in what others are thinking, one increasingly popular feature for any periodical is the opinion and attitude poll. This has also established itself for scholastic papers and news magazines, which will be discussed shortly. But it's been used effectively in quite a few cases in literary magazines.

Other material used in literary publications includes reviews, especially of records; editorials; and humor.

In the face of the admitted difficulties in always finding superior material to publish, some editors have printed poor, inferior, and sloppy work because it was the best at hand. This is a matter of journalistic conscience as well as expediency. Compromises certainly should be kept to a minimum. Concessions are a vicious circle in

Hand art here excellent pen-and-ink drawing—gives proper tone, visual attraction to lightly-handled feature story. From "Chit-Chat" of Waggener High in Louisville, Kentucky. Artist's by-line is inadequate, just "Art by Carroll."

which weak published writings destroy much of the incentive for others to make superior efforts.

How does one edit creative work?

Editing a poem is sacrilege. An editor's choice lies in accepting the writing intact or rejecting it. Not even a word or two may be changed—though changes can be proposed to an author once in a long while.

Editing a short story can be done—sparingly. Here, again, magazine staffers are not permitted the same privileges of rewriting allowed to newspaper copy editors. Possible changes in emphasis or length may be passed on to the author for guidance, but only the writer does the actual revising and cutting. A brand-new literary magazine editor may find it helpful to have an English teacher or advisor join in conferences with a poet or fiction writer who has to be criticized—or guided.

In essays or opinion articles, copy editors and magazine editors have to be sure that they are really polishing an author's ideas and are not, even subconsciously, changing the meaning to fit their own bias. This is a matter of editorial integrity, especially if a by-line is used. In such an arrangement, a writer has a quite proper complaint if substantial changes are made without consent before publication.

Feature articles are close to straight news stories in regard to copyreading changes. Yet even here caution should be exercised to insure that polishing or tailoring to space is the real reason for extensive changes.

News items are edited the same for newspapers and magazines. Cutting to fit is done in both instances and reporters have no right to complain.

Since literary magazine staff members must visualize facing pages as a single *spread* or even whole sections as single units—rather than just concentrating on a single-page makeup—copy editors and senior editors have to be especially careful to keep track of how much space an article, poem, essay, or illustration will take. Thus they can complete the page with a filler complementary to the main piece.

Opening and closing sections of a magazine require unusual care. If an intriguing cover attracts a reader to open the pages, there ought to be an interesting introductory story to keep that attention.

A good magazine, it's said, should end like a good symphony—in a resounding chord. So get a strong feature on your last spread. As the reader lays down this issue, there should be a feeling of anticipation of the next one. Too many magazines today just fade away and readers miss the "upbeat" that they expect. This demands good content, well displayed, for the last spread, not just the jumps of items that have been continued from earlier pages.

Headings on material in a literary magazine serve a different function from those in a newspaper. For news copy, a headline summarizes highlights of the story. For features, an attempt is made to lure the reader into the article. A magazine audience, it is assumed, will read material if it is interesting.

An alluring magazine title will stop the readers' eyes, tempt them to dip into the piece, and, with a bit of luck, have them proceed to the end. But the title also has to be accurate and in keeping with both the

All-type design creates interesting cover. Although "Adelphian" is repeated many times, it is still difficult to discern. Occasional results of using type for ornamental purposes may be happy, as here, but it is generally better to use type only for verbal content. From literary magazine of Adelphi Academy, Brooklyn, New York.

article's content and the magazine's general style.

☆ Keep magazine titles attractive, accurate, and in harmony with the overall effect.

A whole array of headings may be used. Here is one breakdown that may be helpful to an editor who must substitute a better one for the author's own *working title:*

1. Label heads:

   Space Shock

   Campus Weather Station

2. Summary statements:

   Here's Why They Run Cross Country

   The Agonies of Being an Honor Student Frighten Me

3. Striking statements or phrases:

The Right to Talk Back

The Year I Found Out about Santa Claus

4. Descriptive phrases:

The Curse of a Brilliant Mind

Hitchhiking: A Game of Chance

5. Quotations:

I Would Like to Be on Television because . . . .

The Lord Helps Those Who Help Themselves

6. Parodies and literary allusions:

See No Evil

The Fine Art of Class-Cutting

7. Questions:

Why NOT a Student Member on the Board of Education?

What Makes a Good Student Good?

8. Direct address:

Your Due Process Rights Are Guaranteed

You Should Stay in High School, Principal and Teachers Agree

Headings on short stories and poems are designed to attract attention with a phrase or sentence, and about the only limitation is whether they are effective in explanation or in connotation.

Like the written portion of a school magazine, art work of all sorts should be determined chiefly by the available excellence. If your staff has good photographers and few, if any, good cartoonists, then use pictures. If you have good artists but no good photographers, then use drawings and sketches. If your school produces superior nonliterary accomplishments, then stress them rather than poor, ineffective prose.

☆ Art work should be geared to good ideas and to student capabilities.

If a school magazine totally performs its function, there will be a need for documentary photography of three-dimensional creativity. A clay sculpture is as worthy of recording as a short story. A skillfully designed stage set is as noteworthy as an essay.

Student cartoons have great appeal but they also have inherent booby traps that both students and advisors should be aware of. Student humor may be rather primitive; it constantly verges on poor taste and cruelty. More school magazines—and their staffs and advisors—have been immersed in hot water because of cartoons than for almost any other reason. Cartoonists often think it's uproariously funny to sneak some questionable gag into print, past editors and advisor. They must be taught to concentrate their humor in their work, not on practical jokes. An editor must always be alert to insure that all cartoons are legitimately funny and that ill-considered innuendoes have not escaped notice.

News Magazines

Facing shrinking budgets and ever longer time between publication dates, some scholastic editors sought a way out of their troubles by instituting news magazines. And for many of them it worked rather well indeed.

The school news magazines, which follow the pattern of the successful national weekly news magazines, shift emphasis from the event-oriented coverage of merely reporting and recording what is going on in and around the school. They turn to interpreting, backgrounding, explaining, personalizing people in the news—and entertaining. News magazines emphasize how and why rather than the other 4 W's.

It is the same approach that contemporary dailies use as television and radio provide the initial "flash" coverage of spot news. If you can't get the news to the audience first, then you can insure that it makes more sense by providing perspectives. That is where interpretative reporting enters.

When a school shifts from a traditional newspaper to a news magazine, editors have to make two adjustments:

Section logos. Pages 4 and 6 are from "Anvil" of Memorial High in Houston, Texas. Identification of publication itself is too light, 5-point type in lower right, no place or date given. Page 5 is from "Beak 'n Eye" of West High in Davenport, Iowa. Vertical placement makes it less readable and thus less functional.

1. Increasing in-depth content, sometimes digging far deeper than for summary lead-inverted pyramid reporting.

2. Imposing a new approach to writing up the news, sometimes almost adapting the techniques of fiction—but never, never faking.

☆ Staffers on a news magazine have no more right to play with truth than newspaper reporters.

If, let's say, rather drastic changes in graduation requirements are announced, the in-depth journalist will provide the basic facts in the official statement but will also try to answer these questions, among others:

Why was this change ordered at this time?

What effect will it have on seniors applying for admission to colleges next fall?

Will students have to spend more time in classes? In laboratories? In doing home work?

What changes will have to be made in faculty assignments?

In other words, an in-depth reporter will dig for the hidden facts, the information that isn't obvious.

Having completed the interviewing, the reporter will write it up in professional news-weekly style, possibly re-creating what will happen when a senior meets with a college admissions officer in the coming spring.

News magazine editors try to tell stories in terms of individuals. This appeals to people's interest in people. Such sketches or profiles are a far cry from the obituaries found in daily newspapers. For a news magazine, a writeup obviously supplies the essential facts of an individual's life but more space is given human interest, color, and anecdotes that show how the person ticks or typically behaves.

In sports, for instance, writeups in a school news magazine might be pushed primarily into the future rather than re-telling statistics and routine details of games already played—and previously reported in the daily press. For this you might discuss the strong points and weak points of the team that will be played in the next big game.

Another sports page idea could be a human-interest sketch of a star on your school football squad or a rival team, one that makes him come alive and appear as a person rather than just a yard-gainer. For instance, the reporter could ask:

What are your postgraduation aims?

What colleges are you considering?

Have you ever considered playing professional football after finishing schooling?

What is your favorite high school subject? Why?

What do you think of girls who are attracted to football stars?

Do you have an older brother, mother, or father who has been your ideal and inspiration?

Answers would make good reading, far better than warmed-over statistics on yardage gained in two games earlier in the month.

A scholastic news magazine could use letters to the editor, guest editorials, and opinion and attitude polls. Letters in *Time* and indeed most magazines are extremely popular and obviously readership is high. Mass-circulation periodicals frequently commission special polls so they may report on the trends in public thinking. Student editors also could adapt "best-seller" listings by ascertaining, from time to time, what records and books are most popular with local students.

Some administrators have reported that when students have real freedom to express what they think, the chances for a successful underground publication are considerably reduced. Another argument for reporting what students are thinking as well as what they are doing.

Standards of performance by the nationally circulated news weeklies are among the highest. If student editors want to utilize the format, they should ceaselessly study and restudy what the professionals are doing in content, writing style, and makeup.

News magazines are a sophisticated and complicated journalism. If your school is small or has only a limited number of talented students available for staff positions, this format may not be for you. But if you and your fellow students do opt to put out a news magazine, it will be a worthwhile learning experience—and it should be enjoyable.

"Labyrinth," literary magazine of Rippowam High of Stamford, Connecticut, is unusual not only for landscaped—horizontal—8½ x 11 pages but for plastic-comb binding. Name on cover is red, drawing in black. On SOLDIERS page, strong pen-and-ink drawing is rich brown, type in black. Page with several small poems is all black.

Magazine Page Layout

"Magazinish" is a vague adjective applied to a typographic style. It usually uses white space more lavishly than newspaper style does. It has to contend with longer stories and hence larger masses of body type. It uses more hand art and decoration and treats photographs more freely.

Magazinish style is used in newspapers as well as magazines, indeed more frequently in some newspapers than in news magazines.

Literary Magazines

Literary magazines use this free, open style almost exclusively. It begins with the cover, a typographic entity that only magazines possess.

☆ The function of a magazine cover is to coax the reader to pick it up.

Of course, persuading the reader goes back even further than this. Even as readers are finishing one issue of a magazine—the professional calls it *the book*—they should be so well pleased that they already look forward to the next issue. Thus an accumulative and continuing appeal builds up. This attitude comes into action as soon as the new issue of the magazine is identified. The identifier, the magazine nameplate, then is probably more important than the nameplate of a newspaper.

In the case of a magazine like *Time*, the nameplate is expanded into a frame that identifies that magazine even without the name itself. Like that of a newspaper, the magazine nameplate should be distinctive,

appropriate, and handsome. Legibility is less important than for a newspaper.

Three basic styles are divided about evenly among professional magazines. The *gallery cover* presents a picture almost for its own sake. It is not necessary—even if it is common—to tie the cover art to the season or an inside story. *Mad*, for instance, uses completely independent galleries.

The *mousetrap cover* uses the cover design most pointedly to lure the reader into the main story. While the story has the biggest sales appeal, the cover must be strong and attractive in itself. *Newsweek* and *Time* even label the accompanying copy as the *cover story*.

The *billboard cover* is used by magazines such as *Harper's* and *Atlantic*. It displays the titles of at least the major stories in that issue, depending on the common interests of the readers and the magazine to lure them inside.

Many books combine two styles. *Woman's Day* will use a gallery cover, and *McCall's* a mousetrap, and then both add a billboard element to that. *Time* often runs a diagonal strip across one top corner to billboard a story which may or may not be the cover story touted by the picture.

School magazines usually don't appear often enough to create a strong and memorable image. Pros believe that a month between issues is the maximum time for which a reader can maintain the habit of looking for and reading a periodical. So it is wise for the student staff to:

☆ Keep the cover design fairly constant.

☆ Keep the nameplate and its position unvaried.

By physical description, there are two kinds of magazine covers. A *stock cover* is a 4-page element of heavier and different paper that wraps around the "body" itself. (In this case Page 1 is not the cover but the first page of the magazine and the covers are designated as front, back, front inside, and back inside.)

When the same paper is used throughout the magazine and the cover is Page 1, it's called a *self-cover*. For magazines up to 32 pages, self-covers are functional and, of course, more economical than stock covers.

It is possible to buy preprinted covers in either two colors or 4-color process. The nameplate and billboard elements as well as the back and inside covers are printed locally. Such covers are not very expensive but they fail, of course, in a main function of a literary magazine: To be a showcase for student creativity.

In larger cities, Chambers of Commerce and tourist or convention bureaus often have such color covers available at very low prices or even for free.

Occasionally a staff will use gift wrappings or wallpaper for covers and the effect is far richer than the price tag.

In paper for the book itself, there is a wide choice. Newsprint is the most inexpensive; the most costly is *coated*, the "slick paper" so beloved of magazine staffs. Professional books using this paper are admiringly called "slicks." Ironically, though, if the paper is the shiny variety of slick, it can be a handicap because reflections annoy the reading eye. However, coated paper is available in dull finish.

There are many *textures* in offset paper; *pebble* and *rippletone* are most popular. These give richness to photography because each little "hill" reflects a highlight. If the texture is too marked, though, it may call so much attention to itself that the content of the book is depreciated.

Four yardsticks should be used in choosing paper:

Gallery cover of "Anvil" of Memorial High in Houston, Texas, used for its visual appeal, has no connection with inside material.

1. It must be suitable to the printing process used;

2. It must be available in economical sizes;

3. It must be pleasant and comfortable to the eye; and

4. It must feel nice in the reader's hands —give a pleasant tactile sensation.

The first requirement poses no problems if the printer is consulted before paper is chosen.

Texture influences both visual and tactile appeal. Color is a factor in eye ease; white paper is usually the best and most versatile. A recurring fad is the printing of a section of a magazine on paper of different color, texture, and perhaps weight. When color is used in any way, it should be a very light tint to afford maximum visibility, and thus readability, to type.

The economy factor is a major one in choosing paper. Avoid *cutting to waste*. Paper suitable to student magazines usually comes in standard-size sheets. If the magazine is of a nonstandard size, long useless strips of waste paper are left when the large sheet is trimmed down to proper page size. Though no one gets any use from this waste, the staff must pay for it anyway. Paper is sold by weight and—like lambchops—it is weighed before trimming.

Standard and popular sizes for student magazines are:

1. *Newsweek* size, $8\frac{1}{2} \times 11$.
2. *Readers' Digest* size, $5\frac{3}{8} \times 7\frac{1}{2}$, or a trifle larger, 6×9;
3. *Pocket* size, $5\frac{1}{2} \times 8\frac{1}{2}$; and
4. *Better Homes and Gardens* size, $9\frac{1}{2} \times 12\frac{1}{4}$.

These all cut without waste. But the first two are usually more desirable for a student magazine. They are large enough to display art work well; they allow more pages than in the other two sizes and thus provide a thicker package for the reader. A thicker magazine is more pleasant to hold while reading than a thin one, especially if it has larger pages flopping around.

You'll note that a square page cuts to great waste. Standard paper is always near a 3-to-5 ratio so a square of 3×3 will usually waste two-fifths of the basic sheet. While square pages come and go in momentary popularity, they are basically unsound. Squares are too static and stable to be exciting and appealing in themselves and they hamper the typographic design that can be achieved within those boundaries.

When page sizes are being determined, staffers must consider how many *bleeds* they plan to use. A bleed is an element, usually a picture, that runs off one or more sides of a page. When pictures are bled to any except the inside margin, it is impossible to print them so they come precisely to the edge. So, after printing, the page is cut smaller, slicing right through the printed picture. So, for bleed pages, the original sheet must be a quarter or an eighth inch wider than the trimmed page. The printer should be consulted before bleeds are planned.

The printer should also be consulted about the press on which the magazine will be printed. Often a press can print several $8\frac{1}{2} \times 11$ pages on a single sheet, a *signature*.

Linear conversion makes striking cover for "Klamath Krater" of Klamath Falls (Oregon) High. This is variation of basic magtab format.

But if pages are 9×12, fewer pages can be printed on a signature, thus requiring more press time and costing more production dollars.

Magazine Page Format

The $8\frac{1}{2} \times 11$ page is usually divided into two 20-pica columns with a 2-pica alley between columns or into three 13-pica columns with $1\frac{1}{2}$-pica alleys. The top and inside margins are then 4 picas each; outside and foot margins, 6 picas. Folio lines are then placed in the bottom margin. Or the top can be 5 picas with folios running there and the foot also 5.

Dimensions vary only slightly for the $9\frac{1}{2} \times 12\frac{1}{4}$ page. Usual ones are: Two columns of 22 picas with a 2-pica alley or three 15-pica columns with 1-pica alleys. Margins are: Top, 5; side, 6; foot, 6; gutter, 5.

For the digest size, 6×9, a good format is two 13-pica columns with a pica alley and margins of 4 picas at top and inside,

5 at the outside, and 6 at the foot. Three-column format is impractical for a 6×9 page unless very small type is used.

Staggered grafs is a useful technique on small-size pages, and for displaying short, 1-paragraph items.

On a page, say, 6×9 inches, the type page is usually 27 picas wide. For staggering, type is set 22 picas wide. The first story or paragraph is placed flush left, the second flush right, the third flush left again, and so on. The rectangles of white at the sides lighten the page attractively.

In the pocket size, the two columns are 12½ picas with a 1-pica alley and margins of 3 at the gutter, 4 at top and outside, and 5 at the foot.

In all these margins, assuming normal body type, you can use a single column and stay within the readability range. For variety you can set a very brief item at 6 to 10 picas narrower than double-column and center it.

And in all instances, of course, these dimensions can be changed a little to effect different column widths, alleys and/or margins.

Body Type

In literary magazines body type tends to be a bit larger than in other kinds of magazines and 9-point is the norm. Again, Roman is highly preferable for body type, Sans Serifs for captions. The Italic version of the body type is also good for captions. Magazine articles are typically lengthy; thus produce large areas of body type which must be relieved. As good as when it was devised in the period of *incunabula*—the cradle days of printing—is the *decorative initial*. The *rising* or *stickup* is the best. It's from three to six times larger than body type; it may be the body type, the headletter, or an entirely different face.

The stickup aligns at the bottom of the first line of body type and the white space at the right of the initial is a lightening element.

An *inset* or *sunken initial* is set into the top left corner of a block of body type. It aligns with the top of the first line of body

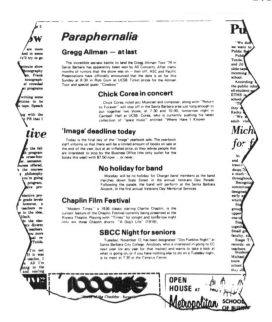

Staggered graf technique is useful to give interest to round-up of news items. Type is set quarter or third narrower than area width; alternated grafs are placed flush-left and flush-right.

type and the bottom of the lower line. This is difficult to achieve without painstaking and skillful manipulation and so the sunken initial is used more rarely—at least its proper use is very rare.

For both kinds of initials, the first word or phrase is set in small capitals or all-caps of the body type. At least half the line ought to be in caps but the capped element should be reasonably self-contained. It would be awkward to capitalize with results like these:

PRINCIPAL JOHN H. Jones was busy.
TUESDAY ABOUT noon is the best time.
ALICE SPOKE softly as she told . . .

Paragraph starters are *bullets*—large periods; stars; arrows; check marks; triangles; or the stylized *paragraph mark* which is standard in most body fonts. These are used at the start of a graf and are usually set flush left. In that case when there is no indent, at least one blank line must be placed between this paragraph and the one above it.

Special characters are many and often they may be appropriate to the subject

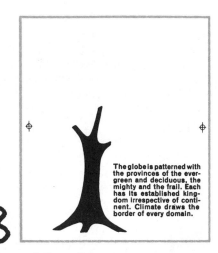

matter of the article. Every printer's type specimen sheets show them. Among the most popular are *florets,* stylized floral designs that run, in assortment, from azaleas to zinnias.

Any of these characters may be used as *gimcracks,* placed between paragraphs to break the type mass.

In magazine usage, Italics are used for titles of creative works such as books, plays, paintings, etc. and also to give phonetic emphasis to certain words.

Magazine Headletters

Magazines may use a single headletter in Roman and Italic and perhaps two weights, just as newspapers do. But it's certainly more fun—and possibly even more effective —to seek a *connotative face* for an article. Eccentric faces of momentary popularity help a staff achieve a "now look" for their book. These are best produced using stickon or transfer type.

If handlettering is used, it should be with the same caution as has been warned of earlier.

☆ Never sacrifice type legibility for the sake of novelty.

Magazine Art

Any art medium is suitable to the literary magazine. Much will be student work that is independent of articles. Much more background and mood art will accompany articles

or stories and these lend themselves nicely to the special screens and unusual cropping already discussed.

Often a second color is available for the staff and this can be used in several ways.

A *duotone* starts out with a single black-and-white photo. From it two plates are made. One is printed in black, one in a lighter color. The result is a new, third color that has a depth and clarity unlike that of a single halftone plate printed in one color. Duotones are inexpensive both to prepare and print.

Usually an added hue is used as *spot color.* A favorite use is as a *tint block,* an area of background color on which is *surprinted* type or line art. (Halftones over a tint block have a muddy appearance.) Unless the ink of the tint block is light in itself, it must be lightened by applying a Ben Day screen or its equivalent. Red, for instance, must be screened down to pink and navy blue to the value of a robin's egg.

Color may be added in irregular shapes to accentuate either hand or photographic art. In this case a *mechanical separation* is prepared using an *overlay,* a technique that's fun to master and to use.

Example 3 shows how this is done. It happens to be a section page for a yearbook but it's such a good example we'll look at it here rather than a couple chapters later.

The *key plate* will usually be printed in black or carry the most detail. In this case it's a combination of a photograph and a line drawing.

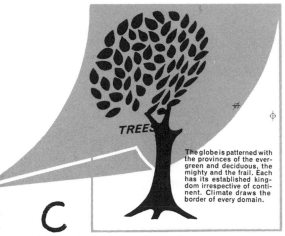

C

EXAMPLE 3

Mechanical separation prepares art for 2-color job. Dummy is in two colors; gray areas here are bright green in original.

Key plate, B, has all black elements, finished art and type.

Transparent overlay, C, is placed on key plate. Color elements drawn on it and headline pasted on . . .

D

. . . making this copy for platemaker. When both plates are printed in proper color . . .

E

. . . finished job is in perfect register. Tiny register marks which appeared on both black and green plates at about center in margin have been removed once they have performed their function. (Courtesy Howard Smith Papers division of Domtar, Ltd.)

Over the key, the overlay, a sheet of clear plastic, is hinged at the top by masking tape. On the overlay are drawn the elements that are to be printed in color. Note that this artwork is done in black India ink, or by self-adhering red plastic, no matter what color eventually it will be printed in.

To make sure that the two colors will match properly on the printed page, the artist draws a *register mark* on both the key plate and the overlay. When each plate is printed, its register mark must exactly print over the one of the other color. If it doesn't, the printing is *out of register* and the pressman must bring it back to proper position. Register marks are usually printed on margins that are later trimmed away, so the typical reader rarely if ever sees this device which is so familiar to journalists.

Color used as in this example may also be screened down to lighten its tone. Or it may be overprinted by a peppering of tiny black dots to make a darker shade than the original ink.

Much of the art in a magazine will be creative work, the product of art classes, hobby clubs, photographers, and the like.

It is best if hand art is done with a *monochromatic palette*. The artist uses only one color; black, blue, and brown are favorites. That color is darkened or lightened by adding black or white to it. The result will reproduce well in the black-white-gray "palette" of the printer.

If full-color work is to be reproduced in black and white, the original art can be sent to the platemaker. But it's a better idea to take a *b & w* photograph and send that. The photo will show whether the original colors will reproduce with enough tonal variation in black and white to give the effect of the painting.

If paintings are photographed, care must

Logos, in circular design, take place of headlines, identifying rounded-up stories in news magazine, "Profile" of Marshfield (Wisconsin) Senior High.

Evocative letterforms add interest to features in "Little Hawk" of City High in Iowa City, Iowa. Essential legibility is retained. Single word, Vandalism, ran in bright red.

be taken that glossy oils do not reflect a *hot spot,* a burst of light that hides detail. Never shoot pictures through framed glass.

Offset is ideally suited to watercolors and wash drawings, to original lithographs, etchings, woodblocks, linoleum prints, or, in fact, any medium used by any student artist.

Line drawings have many uses in a magazine. Student cartoons are always favorites of the reader. *Spots,* little decorative elements that may or may not be related to adjacent copy, add interest to the page. *The New Yorker* uses spots admirably; look at them.

Line work is done in India ink for any process.

If the school magazine properly performs its function, there will be constant need for documentary photography of creative work in three dimensions, as was pointed out in Chapter 17. Documentary pictures, which record in detail, need sacrifice no artistic quality. Indeed, the greatest documentaries combine a factual record with superlative esthetics. The student photographer assigned to this task will need complete mastery of lighting, focus, and composition.

Good idea that fails to jell because type is illegible in circle.

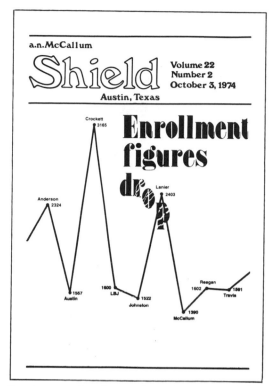

Expository art—here line graph—makes attractive, informative billboard cover for "Shield" of McCallum High of Austin, Texas.

Magazine Spreads

Unlike a newspaper, a magazine is always designed in *spreads*, two facing pages. The editor first prepares an *imposition chart* to show where each page will appear on a signature. If color is used anywhere on a form, it may be used on all the other pages, too, at slight if any extra cost.

☆ Always start a featured article with a 2-page spread.

The best time to convert a magazine scanner into a magazine reader is the first time a spread is seen. So it's better to capture attention quickly with two pages than to open with a 1-page layout and then, after the quarry you seek is off and running, attempt a second effort with a stronger display.

☆ Consider a spread as a single layout. *Jumping the gutter*, tying facing pages together, is difficult but necessary. A favorite device is to run a picture or a headline across these inner margins. The difficulty, though, is maintaining proper alignment. Because the pages of all spreads except the one at the very center are printed far apart on a signature or even on a different sheet of paper, any slight variation in folding, trimming, or stapling may create a disturbing misalignment. This is especially distracting in headlines. So, if a head must jump the gutter, it ought to be a wicket or tripod. Misalignment is not as apparent with these headline forms.

☆ Never break a word in a headline at the gutter.

Vertical misalignment of photos will put a white streak through a picture or place a streak of black on some other page. If pictures must be run across the gutter, be sure no important detail is on the break or within 2 picas of it in either direction.

Gutters are best jumped by maintaining exact margins and, on free pages, aligning

Parents' newsletter, two pages in each issue of "Krater" of Klamath (Oregon) Union High, serves influential, important constituency of school as well as students.

Misplaced headlines are malfunctional; they lead reading eye away from start of story instead of directly into it. Left, opening grafs are completely overshadowed by unusually strong head.

Center, head lures eye to far right of page, away from entire story, not only beginning. Pulled quotes break up masses of body type.

Right, diagram shows how eye enters page at POA, is drawn into head, then would have to go "against gravity" to get into story.

as many columns of body type as possible on the same horizontal axis.

☆ Don't bleed pictures to the gutter.

The effect is rarely good enough to warrant the investment required. Never, never bleed more than one picture to the gutter and never, never, never (that's three nevers!) bleed pictures so they meet at the gutter!

☆ Never place a headline to the right of or below the start of the article.

☆ Keep white space at the outside of the spread—especially in the fallow corners.

☆ Use the buddy system on all spreads. When an article must start with a 1-page display, it will be a right-hand page. Try to keep the facing left page as quiet, typographically, as possible.

Except that magazine pages usually carry more body type than those in yearbooks, designing pages of both these media is an identical problem. So the magazine *art director* should read carefully chapters 24 and 25 where these techniques are discussed in more detail.

News Magazines

Page layout for news magazines is a relatively simple job that can best be learned by studying the two leading professional examples, *Time* and *Newsweek*.

These use several styles of heads. One designates a section, such as sports, academics, entertainment, clubs, etc. Then there may be one or more sizes to head individual stories in a section. These are usually teaser rather than summary heads. A large section may use kickers on story heads to create subdivisions. A typical issue of *Newsweek*, for instance, broke the "National Affairs" section into "Congress," "The Cabinet," "Texas," and "Crime."

Student staffs should keep pictures in full-column measures. The national news magazines often have a picture sticking a pica or two into the adjacent column. This is too tricky and expensive for a student book.

The news magazines use the prepack technique of newspapers to give variety to what could basically be pretty dull pages.

Expository art is especially useful in news magazines.

Professional magazines devote considerable space to the masthead and table of contents. In student magazines, the table is a needless use of valuable space. A magazine of less than 32 pages doesn't require such indexing.

Magtabs

The *magtab* is a new breed of magazines; professional examples are almost all in the field of industrial journalism, those publications that used to be called "house organs."

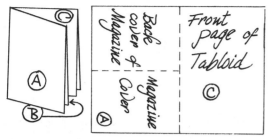

Magtab format uses single tabloid page to make two magazine covers when folded as in diagram. Apparent magazine unfolds to full tabloid pages front and inside.

"Warrior" of Wantagh (New York) High, is excellent example. This issue displays news story but more frequently cover art is teaser for investigative or lengthy feature inside.

Variation is full tabloid page as cover but treated as magazine rather than newspaper style.

The student editor using this format will be a trailblazer whose work will undoubtedly be watched by professional editors.

As you've guessed from the name, a magtab combines the format of tabloid newspaper and magazine. Envision a tab newspaper folded once. The front page then becomes two cover pages for a magazine. As readers "open the magazine," they find a full newspaper page. Pages further inside are made up either in conventional newspaper or literary-magazine formats.

Content is of two varieties, too. Conventional news is presented on newspaper pages; longer articles receive magazine makeup. Because a spread of two tab pages makes a pretty big area, facing pages are often treated as separate elements. The division may be accentuated by a fairly heavy border that runs around each page.

Each part of such publications—the mag and the tab—are designed according to the principles of the individual medium.

DRAMA dEPARTMENT bEGINS ACTIVE SEASON

by Bruce Johnson

The Drama department has embarked upon an unprecedented year of activity due to the driving, creative force of its new chairperson, Mr. James Iaquinta.

A graduate of the Carthage College theatre program, Mr. Iaquinta teaches all drama courses, and for the first time is in charge of all extra-curricular activities, taking the place of Mr. Terry Lawler who resigned last spring.

Though the department has presented a major theatre production, a 35 minute presentation in compet-

ition, and organized an active theatre club, Mr. Iaquinta feels the department has not yet reached its full potential. "As this is my first year as head of the extra-curricular theatre activities, my organization is still somewhat shaky," he said.

The nucleus behind the theatre program here is Drampers, the drama club. The name of this organization is derived from the Elizabethan theatre term for "the players." Dramatis Personae. After lying dormant for a number of years, Drampers re-emerged in the spring of last year as a small group of interested students. It has now grown to an active number of approximately 25.

"Like the rest of our program, Drampers is still in the formative stages," said Mr. Iaquinta. "We do have some concrete plans for the future, however, one of these being the children's play in the spring."

A play important for elementary school students in the area has been a tradition of the department for a number of years. Mr. Iaquinta plans on turning most of this year's show over to the students. "The production will be cast strictly out of Drampers," he said. "I plan to have one or two seniors do most of the directorial work, and my role will be primarily advisory."

Also expanding are the courses in drama, which have always been offered and are an integral part of the Language Arts Department.

The most popular drama course is Dramatics I, a semester course in the fundamentals of acting. Approximately 130 students are enrolled this year. "This is basically a self-discovery course in a lot of ways," said Mr. Iaquinta.

"Discovering vocal potential in the guise of pitch variance and control and applying these to characterization is the primary goal of the course."

According to Mr. Iaquinta, the final assignment of the course will be to produce a choral speech presentation. This includes preparing a script and developing vocal characterizations, facial expressions and hand gestures, but with no memorization of lines or any major stage movements.

"I took Dramatics I because I thought it would be fun," said Jody Neilson, junior. "The way Jim handles the class is great. He never cuts you down after you do a reading; he tries to help you to do better."

A different approach has been planned for the 24 students involved in Dramatics II, the advanced acting course. "I intend to take the students and cast them immediately into one-act plays," said Mr. Iaquinta. "We'll go through them, develop characterizations and get into the

Mr. Kobishop portrays a G-man who raids the Sycamore home.

cultural, historic and geographic research that goes into a believable character."

This procedure will then be carried on to a major, full-length production the second quarter.

Two sections of drama-play reading are also offered this year, due to increased interest. This course involves reading plays aloud in class, with an attempt to develop characterizations, but not to the extent of the acting classes.

"I try to let them see how the drama relates to them," said Mr. Iaquinta, "even though it was written 2,000 years ago and thousands of miles away."

The theatre classes have participated in a number of non-school events. A field trip to the Communication Arts theatre at U.W. Parkside was taken earlier in the year to show the students that there are places especially equipped for live theatre

performances.

The theatre department at UW-Whitewater was the site of a trip to view the school's production of Neil Simon's "Prisoner of Second Avenue."

"It's very important for the students to get out to see and experience live theatre," said Mr. Iaquinta.

This feeling was exemplified by Mr. Iaquinta in arranging for all of his students to see free of charge "The Promise" at Carthage College and "The Bald Saprano" and "The American Dream" at UW-Parkside.

"Working with Jim is like working with one of your friends," said Robin Davis, junior. "He doesn't take the establishment attitudes like most teachers."

The activity level of a theatre department is usually judged by its production schedule. The first presentation of the year was a 35-minute cutting from "The Madwoman of Chaillot," by Jean Giraudoux. It was presented at the sub-district one act play contest held here November 2.

The purpose of the contest was to gain performing experience, to be given a thorough critique by three experts in the theatre, and to move on to the next rung of competition if the show was presented well enough.

Since "The Madwoman of Chaillot" received all B (good) ratings from the judges, it will not move on to the district level.

"I'm sorry we're not going to the district competition, of course," said Mr. Iaquinta, "but in terms of what the kids put into it in the four rehearsals we had, and what they got out of it, it was definitely worth the effort."

Beginning with "The Man Who Came to Dinner" in 1973 and "The Torch-bearers" last year, the theatre department was proud of an innovative concept; the student-faculty play, "You Can't Take It With You," by Kaufman and Hart, which was presented November 14-16, had been planned as such.

"The faculty complains about the lack of school spirit on the part of students and how students are not willing to give a little time and effort," said Mr. Iaquinta. "When it came right down to it this year, I went around and asked a number of the faculty members whether or not they would participate in our production; none of them agreed to appear. I'm afraid that the student-faculty play is a thing of the past."

Mr. Iaquinta selected "You Can't Take It With You" primarily because it had a large cast since a number of people were interested. He feels it is important to give everyone possible the opportunity to perform. "I also felt it was an interesting show, because no one or two characters carry the

production," said Mr. Iaquinta. "It was a good experience for the students in ensemble acting."

Dee McDavid, senior, who played Penny in the production, commented on working with Mr. Iaquinta. "It's been a great experience; he's helped me a great deal with his constructive criticism and advice."

Besides school acting, Mr. Iaquinta is also active in Lakeside Players, Inc., a community theatre group. He has played Mortimer in "Arsenic and Old Lace," and most recently, Don Baker in "Butterflies Are Free." He also has plans for directing "Halfway Up the Tree" for Lakeside.

"When acting, I enjoy playing the unusual character," said Mr. Iaquinta, "not the lead role that everyone can relate with. It is these kind of roles that I think make a production interesting."

At Carthage, Mr. Iaquinta played such diverse roles as Hortensio in Shakespeare's "The Taming of the Shrew," for which he received their best supporting actor of the year award, to Sir Lancelot in the musical, "Camelot."

Active is the word for the department for the remainder of the year.

"Utopia Unlimited," a Gilbert and Sullivan operetta, is slated for production the second week in February and will be co-produced with Lakeside Players and Drampers.

"As the show is an operetta," said Mr. Iaquinta, "I don't know if there are too many students here who could handle leading roles. Tryouts will be

open to Tremper students and a place in the show will be found for just about everyone."

A bill of three one act plays will constitute the spring production, and any interested student will be given the opportunity to audition for the shows.

Mr. Iaquinta is very excited about the prospect of having the Wisconsin Mime Company here for an in-school field trip. "All theatre students and Dramper members would spend the day in a four to five hour mime workshop," said Mr. Iaquinta. "The day would be capped off by an hour long performance by the group."

As is the case with most department heads, Mr. Iaquinta has a number of goals he would like to see accomplished. He feels that the drama classes should be able to meet three times a week for two hours instead of the 55 minute "squirts," as he calls them, which are presently scheduled.

A group of students who are extremely interested in theatre and could form a hard core performing group by putting in three to four hours a day of rehearsal is another goal.

Mr. Iaquinta would like to see the student body realize that live theatre is an exciting form of entertainment that is not duplicated in any other media in existence.

"If I can begin to build an audience of students who realize that theatre can be fun and exciting, I think that that would be the best shot in the arm for drama here and for Kenosha theatre in general," he concluded.

Olga, a Russian countess, discusses her cousin, the czar, with members of the Sycamore family.

4   November 27, 1974   Tremper Tempest   5

Conventional magazine format is well done in "Tempest" of Tremper High in Kenosha, Wisconsin. In such "formal pages" each rectangle is completely filled.

Magazine Production

Magazines lend themselves admirably to student production, at least up to the plate-making step. This increases opportunities for more students to share in the operation.

Dummies have been prepared in the conventional manner previously discussed. Type has been set in some cold-type operation. Art is on hand. Now you're set to go.

Start with a sheet of Bristol board or heavy drawing paper. With a light blue pencil—which is invisible to the camera—draw the outside dimensions of the "paper page," the margins and column areas.

The nameplate is pasted into position.

☆ It is imperative always to use camera-fresh copy.

In the case of the nameplate, for instance, this would be a Photostat of the original artwork. Don't use the original art; it'll get dirty from handling.

☆ Never use clipped copy for pasteup.

Each time an element is reproduced, a little sharpness and clarity are lost. If the nameplate—or any other element—is clipped from the last issue of the magazine it will be less sharp than the Photostat. And when it is reproduced in the current issue it will start breaking down—becoming smudgy and fuzzy.

Cold type is protected by a thin coat of clear *fixative* which is applied by an aerosol can. Smudges on it can be removed with a soft art-gum eraser.

Next place the art. If it's line work and same size, you can put the original drawings onto the page. If the original must be reduced, you may make a reduced Photostat and paste it in. Or you can draw in a rectangle of the proper, reduced size and have the platemaker reduce the original and then strip it into the negative. If the art is halftone, same-size or not, it must be handled by the platemaker and you merely mark in the rectangle.

Next put in the type, first the heads, then body matter.

Headlines, in transfer or stickon type, should be first done on a sheet of good bond paper, then cut out and affixed to the pasteup sheet as a single unit. This makes it easier to avoid and correct mistakes of any kind.

☆ Use the T-square constantly.

No matter how eagle-eyed you are, you will need mechanical aids to make sure that everything is perfectly horizontal. Results of *eyeballing,* failing to use the T-square, may look all right in the pasteup but usually not in the printed page. A major reason is that we often align elements by the edges of the paper they're on rather than the type matter itself.

Many offset printers supply printed pasteup sheets covered by a grid of 1-pica squares in the invisible light blue. This makes it easier to align and place elements; but still the T-square can't be tossed out.

☆ Measure all spacing during pasteup.

If your style calls for a pica of space between a picture and its caption, don't just guess at it, measure it exactly. Guessing not only creates disconcerting inconsistencies, it will throw even the most carefully made dummy askew.

☆ Don't cut galleys of cold type until you're absolutely sure how you'll use it.

You may find that the dummy is a bit off and you are one line long. You don't want to carry that single line into the next column. So you consult with the editor. Perhaps he'll decide to shorten a picture enough to make room for that single line. But if you cut off that line before all the conferring is done, you'll have to paste down this tiny sliver all by itself, a difficult and messy job, indeed.

☆ Be sure all elements are pasted down tightly.

Curled edges will cast shadows that will be picked up in the negative. These must then be *opaqued,* painted out by hand, and production costs increase.

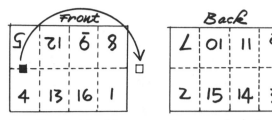

Imposition chart for 16-page magazine or yearbook signature. After eight pages are printed as in left diagram, paper is turned lengthwise (so point marked by black square lies on outline square). Then back of sheet is printed. Color available on any one page can be used on all pages on that side of sheet.

☆ Inspect all pasteups closely before sending them to the platemaker.

Magazine pages may be pasted up singly. But if they are done in pairs, platemaking costs are reduced. Use your imposition chart to make sure that Page 2, for instance, is paired with Page 15, not with 1 or 3.

It is comparatively easy to make corrections in the pasteup. But the only correction that can be made once the plate is produced is the deletion of elements; they cannot be

"Saddlebag" looks like conventional literary magazine but is unusual in that it serves whole community of Wickenburg, Arizona, rather than just students of high school that publishes it.

THE EDITORS, GEORGE WOODING, FRANK SNYDER AND SEAN MURPHY (From Left) PROTECT THE FOOTBALL OF STUDENT RIGHTS.

Dear Reader,

In publishing this edition of *Perspective*, the staff has concentrated its efforts on student rights. We hope that you will become aware that these rights are guaranteed to you by the United States Constitution, and, therefore, you are protected by the supreme law of the land.

But these rights are for protection only. Just as no school can force its policies on you, the same holds true for students. Remember that although student rights cannot be taken away, they can be abused, so use them wisely.

In addition to student rights, we have also published a wide array of news stories, features, sports, music, art and literature to enlighten you about Mavahi activities.

We hope you will enjoy the magazine, and in closing, the staff would like to wish you the best of luck in the New Year and to express its appreciation for your continued support.

Sean Murphy
Frank Snyder
George I. Wooding III

Table of contents of "Perspective" of Martinsville (Virginia) High, is enlivened by superlarge numbers and miniature illustrations from articles. Masthead runs at left and editors' personal column at right.

shifted in position or replaced by another.

There are two adhesives for pasting up. The old standby is rubber cement. If the cement is brushed only onto the cold-type material, it can be lifted off the pasteup sheet and replaced elsewhere. If cement is placed on both pieces of paper and allowed to dry before they are placed in contact, they will stick like a barnacle on the *USS Constitution*. Always apply very thin coats of rubber cement. If you use rubber cement, be very sure everything is lined up just so before you smack the two papers together. If you must separate them, once the cement has set, the only way is to slosh cement-thinner fluid—usually through a long-necked oil can—and dissolve the cement. This is awfully messy and inevitably the copy gets dirtied.

The best adhesive is melted wax. This is applied by a simple hand roller. Elements tacked down this way can be readily lifted and replaced. The wax isn't sticky to the touch and so tiny scraps of paper won't stick to the fingers of the pasteup man.

Wax doesn't adhere quite as tightly as cement does and so greater care must be exercised in delivering the pasteup—also called the *mechanical*—to the platemaker. It should always be covered by clean protective paper and handled gently.

Magazines have many advantages to the student staff. Many people can be involved in the many facets of producing a book. Where budgets are so tight that publication cannot be frequent, a magazine is not tainted as a newspaper would be by the staleness of news. Literary magazines are especially valuable in creating an audience for those creative activities that are as laudable as music, drama, and debate but are too often unheeded and unsung.

Even when a school has a good newspaper, there is room for a good magazine.

Mimeographed Publications

Little did the Crusaders dream some 900 years ago that they were contributing to the invention of that most ubiquitous machine, the Mimeograph. But they were—and a good thing, too. For the Mimeo is an excellent tool for scholastic journalism.

The Crusaders stenciled the Christian cross on everything they took with them into the Holy Land, from pennants to tents to animals. Out of a piece of thin leather they cut their distinctive cross. This stencil was placed on, let's say, a saddle blanket and red paint was daubed all over it. As it went through the opening, it painted the cross on whatever surface lay underneath.

If it's possible to cut a cross-shaped figure into a stencil, it's obviously possible to cut a T or t, for these are crosses as well as alphabetical characters. And you can cut an M or a J or an X (another cross). But when you come to an O or A or R the whole piece of the counter falls out and you get a black bullet, a solid circle. In order to stencil a proper O, you need to convert the counter, the white area at the center, from an island to a peninsula. You do this by making the O as two semicircles that don't quite meet, with the dividing white lines holding the counter in place.

The Mimeograph—a trademarked name that is almost a generic term; there are several other such machines, each with its own trade name—is a stencil printing device. Most of us are familiar with it but perhaps you've never thought of the principle involved.

A Mimeo stencil has a base of loose cellulose fibers covered with a waxy substance. Into the wax you make an opening, by means of a typewriter or a *stylus*. The fibers hold in place the counters on the letters, cap and lowercase, that have them. Yet the fibers are so loose that the ink, under pressure, can pass through freely and be deposited on the printing paper.

Ditto or *hectograph* machines excepted, the Mimeograph is the simplest and least expensive way of printing a school publication. Modern technology makes it a far more sophisticated tool than most people realize.

The major limitation is the sheet size, 8½ x 11 inches (letter size) or 8½ x 14 (legal size). In simplest use, the sheet may be used for a single page or backed up to print on both sides. The single page may have three 2-inch columns or two of 3½-inch width or a 4- and 2-inch-column format.

The sheets may be folded to create pages 5½ x 8½ or 7 x 8½. The larger of such pages may be folded again to 4½ x 7. The 5½-inch-wide page takes two 2-inch columns or one 4 inches wide. The 7-inch page uses two or three columns or a wide-and-narrow-column design.

There's a wide selection of colored Mimeo papers and inks. The paper should be of a clear, light color. A too-dark color makes reading difficult and a "muddy" color is esthetically unpleasant. Black ink has the highest visibility and looks nice on colored paper, too. Colored ink may be used on white paper or a lighter tint of the same color. Avoid ink of one color on paper of another. Especially avoid the perennial temptation of the Christmas season, red ink on green paper or vice versa.

Cutting a stencil may be done two ways. The simplest is to use a typewriter for body type and perhaps the heads, then to make illustrations and larger heads with a stylus. Or a pasteup may be made as for an offset plate as discussed earlier, and a stencil prepared electronically. The latter is the easiest and gives the best results, even reproducing halftones.

Such stencil-making machines are widely used. So even if there isn't one in your town, it may be practical to mail your copy to a shop in a nearby city that makes such stencils—at only a slight cost.

For either method, "typesetting" is done on a typewriter. An electric machine is the best because it assures uniformity of each stroke. But any manual typewriter can produce good "typesetting."

☆ The care that the typist exercises provides the ultimate quality.

Ordinary typewriters provide the same space for every character. So the chubby M and W must be squeezed to make them fit while the i and l look as lonely as a telephone pole in a 5-acre field. More expensive electrics have *proportional spacing,* which allocates more room for the wide letters and less for the skinny ones. Many ordinary machines now have half back-spacing so the typist can squeeze in an extra letter here and there.

Conventional typewriters have only one typeface, of course. But at least two machines offer variety. The *Varityper* and IBM *Selectric* offer several faces that can be readily interchanged. Neither has conventional arms that each carry a character and its duplex. Instead, the Varityper has all its relief characters on a curved strip of metal and Selectric characters are on a sphere about the size of a golf ball. When the typist hits a key, on either machine, the proper character is moved into position and then is smacked through an inked or carbon-paperlike ribbon onto the paper.

It takes only a few seconds to change the bar or the ball so that even a single word can readily be set in a different face.

Sophisticated typewriters have devices for justifying lines, creating a straight right-hand margin. But in most instances the typist must do so manually. Let's see how it's done:

After the story has been edited in conventional fashion, it is retyped by a *production typist.* Set the machine at the desired column width or else draw a line designating the right margin. Type each line carefully, as close as possible to the desired length. Hyphenation will be much more frequent than in ordinary typing and a small hyphenating dictionary will be a useful reference book.

When you come close to the end of a line but the next word or syllable is too long to fit in, fill the line exactly with ****** or //////.

If the line is too long, after you have typed it write the number of excess characters in the far right margin. It is better to type lines short because it is easier to add space between words than it is to tuck in extra characters. Two or three excess characters are all that can be manipulated successfully; lines may be as many as four characters short and still look reasonably well.

Now with a bright-color pencil you note where to put two spaces instead of one between words to fill up a short line. The closer such extra spacing comes to the center of the line, the less it disturbs the reader. Also note where you might tuck in an extra character into a too long line. Do this by pushing down the backspace key and holding it there while you strike the character key. Such tight spacing can be done within a word and should involve the narrow characters—i, f, t, j, and l or punctuation marks. Ordinarily you put a space after punctuation; eliminating this can tighten a line.

This manipulation requires skill and judgment that comes only from practice, and the production typist is a key link in making a good Mimeo or offset paper. You will learn tricks of the trade and will devise

Rare daily student newspaper is "Dixie Daily" of Robert E. Lee High in San Antonio, Texas. Although this paper —with 8½ x 11 pages—is printed on offset duplicator, composition is entirely strikeon; production closely parallels that of Mimeographed papers.

"Daily" is supplement of biweekly "Bugle Call," also unusual with already-noted broadsheet format.

your own techniques for justifying lines. All you need to remember is that the finished job should be pleasing to the reader and that the spacing-out or tucking-in isn't too conspicuous.

Finally the flagged version is either retyped once more or copied onto the stencil.

Before the stencil is actually cut, editors use the first *production draft* to make dummies. Instead of inches or picas, they use lines as increments and must be very precise in allowing exactly the right number of lines for the stories, headlines, and pictures. There is no opportunity to revise a cut stencil.

Typing stencils is such a familiar chore that it isn't necessary to detail separate steps. But a few admonitions are in order.

Typing is done first, then pictures are added. Drawings would tear as the stencil is pulled through the rollers of the machine.

☆ Clean the typewriter thoroughly before each stencil is typed.

☆ Maintain an even typing stroke so all characters are cut cleanly yet no bowls are completely cut out.

Typographical errors are corrected by covering the mistake with a thin coating of *correction fluid,* allowing it to dry—which it

does quite rapidly—then carefully striking the correct letter.

☆ Be sure to wait till the correction fluid is completely dry.

As it only takes seconds for the fluid to dry, time "saved" by impatient typists is negligible and haste often results in a fuzzy correction.

☆ The cut stencil is fragile; handle it with care.

If your magazine is folded, the stencil must be typed sideways in a machine with a wide carriage. Or the stencil must be cut in two, typed in two sections on an ordinary machine then pasted together again with *stencil cement.* An overlap of a quarter inch must be allowed for this pasting together.

Before you start pasting stencil halves together, it is wise to make a *pagination dummy.* Fold small pieces of paper together to make the proper number of pages for your magazine. Number them conspicuously. As you take the dummy apart, you'll see how stencil pages must be matched up. If you have a 16-page magazine, for instance, Page 2 will be on the same stencil as Page 15; the front cover pairs with 16, Page 3 with 14, 4 with 13, and so on. Only the center spread—in this case Pages 8 and 9—has consecutive, facing pages on the same stencil.

☆ Headlines are inserted after the typing.

Headlines may be produced on the typewriter, especially if the Varityper or Selectric is used. In that case the heads would be typed just as they occur in the page. But if a second machine must be used to obtain the headletters, all heads are typed in at one time. The fragile stencil would probably tear if it had to be shifted frequently from one machine to another to type the heads in order.

Pictures can be cut by hand into a stencil or art prepared by electronics or photography may be inserted.

Original drawings are first done conventionally, in India ink on bond or tracing paper, a very transparent but strong kind. This drawing is placed on a light-table, one made of strong frosted glass with a light under it. Peeling back the protective sheet of heavy paper from the stencil, place the waxy sheet into proper position over the drawing. Now cut the stencil of the picture.

The most useful tool is a *loop stylus*. This looks like one end of a tiny paper clip and goes around corners smoothly without tearing. To reduce that danger further, the artist may place a sheet of raw silk or cellophane over the stencil and work the stylus onto it. Silk sheets may be purchased from Mimeograph dealers. They last a long, long time and are a good investment. Any kind of thin cellophane may be used; take it off a box of cough drops or a hosiery package.

The stencil will reproduce only lines of course. But the artist may use the cross-hatching effect previously discussed. You can duplicate the effect of Ben Day or Zip-A-Tone, too. A plastic or metal sheet, on which a pattern has been placed in relief, is laid under the stencil. Then a smooth instrument—usually the blunt end of a stylus—is rubbed across the stencil.

This is the technique used for making the popular tombstone rubbings. A less glamorous demonstration is to lay a piece of paper on a well-textured surface like a fabric book cover or grained leather, then rub a pencil, held sideways and flat, across the paper to bring up the texture.

Many patterns are available and you can use your own textures. Window screen, sandpaper of various coarsenesses, leather or plastic simulations of it—all these are worth experimenting with.

There are also tiny wheels with tooled circumferences that will make shaded or dotted lines.

If you don't have a good staff artist, don't bewail your fate. There are excellent sources of pictures well suited for tracing by a good craftsman who is not a freehand artist. Clip books discussed in Chapter 15 are a good source. The A. B. Dick Company, manufacturers of Mimeographs, have booklets of art created especially for stencil-cutting. Clippings from magazines and newspapers, stored in a *swipe file*, may also be traced.

Photographically produced stencils are available at low costs from many suppliers of Mimeo materials and there are also free sources. For instance, the Christmas seals campaign furnishes seasonal art. Usually several small pictures are included on a single stencil of regular size. To use them, an opening is cut into the staff-produced stencil, just large enough for the insert. Then the photostencil is cut out of its sheet with a margin of about a quarter inch. The precut stencil is affixed from underneath to the regular one with stencil cement or, in case of near desperation, with correction fluid. Care must be taken that the edges of the inserted stencil don't hide any lines in the staff-cut stencil. The insert must be carefully fastened down so that gaps don't allow ink to ooze out. Now the actual "printing" takes place.

☆ Be sure the Mimeograph is clean and in good operating order before you start printing.

☆ If *slipsheeting* is necessary, be sure to have enough paper on hand.

Slipsheets of waste paper are placed between printed sheets to keep the ink on one from setting off onto the next one on the pile.

☆ Allow plenty of time for the ink to dry.

Usually at least a half hour is required before you can begin *backing up*, printing the reverse side of the sheet. Check the drying carefully before you begin the backup. High humidity sharply slows down drying.

After printing, *binding* begins, fastening separate sheets together.

If your publication is on separate, unfolded sheets, they are usually stapled together in the top-left corner. If pages are folded and number more than four pages, signatures must be *gathered*, the folded sheets slipped inside each other. Usually such magazines are *saddle stitched*, with staples driven through the fold from the outside. This usually requires a stapler with an arm longer than that of the conventional desk variety. Most school offices have such equipment; if not, the investment

Mimeographed "Scribe" of Madison Junior High in Eugene, Oregon, has printed nameplate, black letters on yellow panel. Lettering guides are used well for headlines.

is modest and the staff can buy its own.

Two staples are adequate to bind a magazine of up to 32 pages, the highest number that can be stapled by hand.

Or they may be *side stitched,* staples driven near and parallel to the left margin. Side stitching may also be used for folded sheets.

Stapling should be done with care even though it is hardly the most glamorous job in student journalism. If the staple doesn't penetrate at exactly the center of the fold or if it is not parallel to the edge in side stitching, the magazine will not open properly and the reader will be discomfited and annoyed.

So now you have a Mimeographed magazine. The process isn't too complicated, although it requires the dedicated skills of many people. Always the key to success is taking pains.

Stencil printing can be combined effectively with letterpress or offset. Some staffs have their covers printed for each issue and thus they can use a variety of pictures as well as of paper and ink.

Some staffs have only their nameplates

printed. If a whole year's supply of paper is printed at one time, the cost is slight. In this case the ink must be the same for every issue, but paper color can vary with slight— if any—additional cost.

Truly skilled staff members can produce color printing right on their own Mimeo using two or even more hues. Each color requires a separate stencil made through the mechanical-separation process described in the previous chapter.

The press run for the typical stenciled publication is comparatively short, under 300. In such cases changing colors is easy. A sheet of heavy oil-proof paper is placed over the ink drum to keep the black ink in the cylinder. Then a piece of absorbent cloth is fastened over the ink shield and is saturated with ink of the proper hue.

With this method the press operator must keep a close eye on the product. For fresh ink now is not fed automatically through the stencil. When inking becomes light, the stencil must be lifted and the cloth pad replenished.

Color work demands *loose* register; that is, the design must be such that if the various color elements shift in position as much as a full pica it will not destroy the effect.

Using such a pad also allows the printing of two colors at the same time. Here ink is daubed onto an appropriate area, rather than into the whole pad. This, of course, requires that the colors be rather widely separated.

A rainbow effect is achieved by placing dabs of various colors close to each other so that they will mix and create intermediate colors. One part of the stencil might be printed in blue, that on the opposite edge of the page in yellow, and where the two colors meet, in green. The effect of such printing is pleasant but entirely accidental. The lighter color should always be given a larger area to start with because the darker hue will ultimately take over the entire surface.

This technique should be used only with artwork; type printed in tutti-frutti is difficult to read.

Typography of Stencil Publications

The same basic typographic principles apply to Mimeographed publications as those printed by other methods. Modifications come only from limitations of the method.

Body type ought to be the Roman or Square Serifs of conventional "typewriter faces." Sans Serifs may be used because there is usually no great mass of body type where the Sans' low readability would distress the reader.

Script or Cursive should never be used for body type even though these faces are favorites of many typewriter users. Their readability is so low that even in the ultrashort stories of a stenciled publication the reader will find palpable difficulty.

There are several characters on the standard typewriter that can be used as paragraph starters or as gimcracks to separate items or grafs.

Favorites are * and # although you could use @ or +, or = and even &, depending on what's available on your machine. The first two, because they are totally abstract, are better than the others which denote specific meaning.

These same characters, alone or in combination, may be used to make borders for the sideless boxes.

Heads may also be cut by hand, either freehand or by means of a lettering guide. This is a heavy plastic sheet with grooves, corresponding to the strokes of the letterform, cut through. Letters are traced through the guide onto the stencil with a stylus.

Guides are available in many styles of letters. Because they are stencil forms, many letters must be separated into two for easier manipulation. For a capital R, for instance, you make a vertical stroke by using the guide for the I. Then bring the second guide, carrying the bowl and tail, into proper position and draw those two strokes.

Unlike other publications, Mimeographed magazines will use many all-cap heads. These have the same low legibility decried in Chapter 10, but they are necessary to provide the bulk needed for typographic color. This observation doesn't apply to electronically cut stencils where heavier headline type can be reproduced.

☆ Never use Script or Cursive letters in all-caps.

This warning has already been given for conventional type. It must be repeated here because these Written letterforms are popular with too many Mimeo users.

When heads must be set in the same face as body matter, several styles can add interest to a page. Samples shown here are self-explanatory.

The big advantage of *inset* and *hanging indent* heads are the white space that surrounds them. This is also a weakness, however. For with space always at a premium,

```
THIS HEAD    When the inset

IS INSET     head is used, there

             must be a generous

margin between the head and the

copy block. This means one more

short line than there are lines

in the head.
```

editors sometimes hate to leave this much paper blank and there is a tendency to *steal space* by reducing white areas below a functional minimum.

Although white space should never be considered wasted, there are some stories

HANGING INDENT. This head is actually
misnamed. For the head is neither
indented nor hung... the body type
is. The indent must be at least three
spaces and as the line gets longer
that indent must also be increased
to make it very conspicuous.

HANGING INDENT

IN TWO LINES. This style builds in a
strip of white space alongside the
top line of the head as well as that
created by the indenting. It is a
pleasant style.

HANGING INDENT;

NO RUN-IN

This style accentuates the white
area at the right of the headline.

which require minimum display. The *running head* is the simplest form and most conservative of space. The simple run-in looks like this:

RUNNING-IN THE HEAD is the way this
style is designated. The "head" is
actually only a capped portion of
the story itself.

A variation is the *read-in head* which is really part of the story. It looks like this:

A STATE SCIENCE AWARD came to Central
High this week when John Gray was
awarded second place for his entry in
the annual Science Fair at the state
capital. This style requires a strong
lead.

But notice that this style works only with a strong lead. If the lead is weak, the read-in loses much of its effectiveness, as here:

NOTIFICATION THAT HE HAD WON one of the
top 10 prizes in the state Science Fair
was received this week by John Gray.
Here a weak lead is exaggerated by its
use as a run-in head.

A common practice is to underscore headlines though this reduces their legibility. If underlining is used, it should be only with 1-line heads and never with all-caps.

Page patterns should follow, as much as possible, the principles outlined in Chapters 13 and 18. Small pages and comparatively large body type restrict opportunities for maneuvering the elements, but not fatally.

The major weakness of stenciled publications is one already noted: The great pressure of space that tempts the editor to jam elements too tightly into a page.

Another weakness is a psychological one. Too often the staff feels that it is so seriously handicapped by its printing method that it is hopeless to attempt a quality publication. This, fortunately, isn't so.

It is still the quality of a publication that determines its worth. If the content is good, the limitations on makeup will be cheerfully forgiven by the reader.

Another great asset is that a stenciled publication can be produced entirely by students. This not only brings the budget down to a realistic level for small schools but affords more students the pleasure of participation and the real satisfaction of seeing the fruits of labors entirely their own.

Because these papers are student produced, there is a greater variation in quality than in those printed by professional craftsmen. But anyone who examines such publications inevitably comes to the conclusion that most staffs aren't getting maximum quality from their machines.

Some of this is undoubtedly the fault of the machines themselves. Many schools have stencil machines that came over on the *Mayflower,* if not the *Nina* or the *Pinta.* But even a cantankerous and decrepit machine can do better work if coaxed by a conscientious, able operator.

Such operators can tap a strong backup force: Sales representatives for stencil machines. Most companies that sell the machines are eager to send people to instruct the student staff. They will not only demonstrate the processes discussed in this chapter but can pass along tricks of the trade to enhance the quality of the publication.

But even if, for any reason, the quality of a stencil publication is not as high as the staff would like, there is still good precedent to buoy the spirits. The American Revolution was sparked by the Colonial printing press. The printed word set souls afire and united the colonists in the creation of a new country. But the printing itself left much to be desired. Type was badly worn because import restrictions made replacement unbearably expensive. Paper, highly taxed, was so costly that refreshing white space was an unattainable luxury.

But the words counted! The words galvanized readers.

Stencil printing, no matter its limitations, can well be a 20th-century counterpart of Colonial broadside printing.

Over-design must be guarded against. Here boxing every story makes "busy" page. Boxes should be used only sparingly, then only in rectangular form, never in L shapes as LOTTERY story in columns 3-5.

20 Supportive Journalism

"Journalism" to most students—most Americans, in fact—means newspapers, magazines, radio, and television. Sometimes students broaden the definition a bit by including yearbooks.

But if we consider journalism as channels for disseminating information quickly to a mass audience, there are other media available—especially to school journalists. These are called *supportive journalism* because in most instances they are complementary to the more conventional media.

Bulletin Boards

As early as 60 B.C., scribes used to write out sheets of parchment or vellum, label them *Acta Diurna—Daily Events*—and post them on the walls of the Forum in ancient Rome. Now the bulletin board is again becoming a formal channel of communication.

Of course, bulletin boards have been around in some form or other, probably ever since man learned how to write. *Graffiti* were at first bulletins, not the wisecracks and obscenities of today. School bulletin boards are familiar to us all—an interesting hodgepodge of written communications, totally disorganized and often less than functional because long outdated matter detracts from fresh notices.

American business places fairly recently began systematizing the use of bulletin boards, and alert student staffers have found this to be an excellent supplement to the school newspaper.

One or more bulletin boards are required, depending on the arrangement and size of the school and the established traffic patterns. These should be glass-covered and locked; unlimited access to open boards negates the purpose of a bulletin system.

Bulletins should be changed regularly so the student body will expect fresh news and establish a habit of regular reading.

Colored paper identifies various kinds of news. Official statements from administrators might be on white paper. Blue may be used for sports; green for clubs, pink for features, and yellow for most important general stories.

In some instances the name of the "publication"—with perhaps a logo for each news category—is printed at the top like a letterhead.

Sheets are usually 3 x 8½ or 5½ x 8½—a third or a half of a regular letterhead sheet. This not only saves space on the board but saves paper and places a physical limit on the length of the story.

Stories must be short. You don't want to create congestion around the boards as students pause too long to read lengthy reports—if they ever would. Reading is more difficult when the "type" is a typewriter and when it is under glass that might send back an irritating reflection.

Stories are covered as they are for the newspaper. Indeed, in most instances the bulletin service is produced by the newspaper staff. Reporters tell the editor what stories they have covered. The editor decides whether to hold it for the next edition of the paper, whether to post it at once or—the case in many instances—to post the bulletin, the very brief 2- or 3-sentence news story and do a broader report in the next issue of the paper. The reporter then writes either or both reports. It is edited by a copyreader and then retyped, on the proper-colored paper, either by the reporter or by a staff typist.

The bulletin carries a headline. This is typewritten, too, in the manner or style used for Mimeographed papers and discussed in Chapter 19.

At a given time the circulation staff posts the bulletins. First they remove dead ones. Bulletins may run as long as a week or any number of days between one and seven. In the lower-left corner of each bulletin is the typewritten date that it should be removed.

The board may be divided, with actual colored-tape lines or just imaginary ones, something like the pages of a newspaper, and bulletins posted in the appropriate area. Sports news, for instance, might be in the lower-right corner. The most important ones should be in the top left; for the bulletin board, just like a newspaper page, has its POA, the top-left corner.

Bulletin editors like to have light items just like newspaper editors. These may be humorous remarks or situations in the classroom, interesting but not important occurrences, little-known facts about students or faculty. Typical *lights* are these:

> The reason that Bob Chatham, senior, was late for class this morning is that his 2-year-old brother swallowed the car keys.

> During a lecture in social science yesterday, a cat jumped in the open window and walked all around Miss Sally DuMaine's desk. Observed Joannie Eaton, junior, "I thought this was supposed to be a dialog but it has developed into a catalog."

> Principal Elwood Cather and Mrs. Cather are celebrating their 35th wedding anniversary tomorrow.

Pictures are welcome bulletin board material. These may be 8 x 10 glossies with typewritten cutlines. Hand art may be used as well as news sketches, expo art, or editorial cartoons. All must be properly identified. Do not use the bulletin board for an art gallery; "just pretty" pictures should go into other display areas.

Advertising space can be sold to defray the slight cost of materials involved.

A feasible method is to sell an $5\frac{1}{2}$ x $8\frac{1}{2}$-inch piece of paper on which the advertiser can place any message in any form. Often it is handlettered by the student ad staff. Sometimes it is an ad clipped from a daily paper or the student newspaper and pasted onto the sheet with or without additional information. The advertiser's letterhead might be used and this would give extra display. Bulletin ads may be sold as an extension of an ad placed in the school paper.

Ads usually run for a week although obviously they might run longer. Usually if an ad runs less than a week, the per-day rate is higher. Although it's rarely a problem, it is wise to limit the number of ads that appear on any given day lest they fight each other for attention and even detract from the news itself.

Lost-and-found notices—standard fare in classified-ad pages of daily papers—are usually run without charge for students and faculty. If outsiders want to reach the student body via bulletins, they are charged as they would be for want ads.

Newsletters

Even after printed newspapers began—and dating as far back as *Acta Diurna*—newsletters were circulated throughout Europe. These were letters—handwritten, of course—that told, not that Junior had cut his first tooth, that Kathy was going steady, and that Grandma's arthritis was worse—but of the same public events that make news in today's newspapers. Newsletters were a potent unifying force before and during the American Revolution.

Today newsletters are a flourishing segment of American journalism. Usually they are directed to a highly specialized audience. One of the early and still major ones is the *Kiplinger Letter,* carrying information for businessmen. Many—probably most —newsletters concentrate on information for a specific industry or professional group. Your teachers' association quite probably has a newsletter.

Newsletters often try to give the impression that they have true "inside news," although often it is material that is far less than exclusive. Newsletters also stress immediacy. Many are "set" in a typewriter face to suggest that the sender just got a hot tip, sat right down to bat out a hasty typewritten missive, and speeded it on its way.

The format of a newsletter is simple, often in typewritten style and with headlines like those of a Mimeographed paper. A true newsletter carries no art, especially not photos.

In scholastic circles a newsletter is really a Mimeoed paper, usually just one side of one sheet. Instead of being circulated among students, copies go into either each classroom or home room. So coverage can be done with a score of copies rather than hundreds. In some cases a student will read the letter aloud to the class, a variation of the PA-radio system we'll discuss in Chapter 21.

Newsletters may be daily, where immediacy is a strong asset; weekly; or come out only when a big story breaks. Production is just like that of a Mimeoed newspaper except that layout is much simpler and thus can be done on a daily basis.

News Bureaus

School news has appeal far beyond the student body. Not only do friends and relatives want to know about student doings, people with no direct connection to the school retain their interest as alumni, friends of education generally, or as taxpayers concerned that their dollars are being spent wisely.

Large and medium-size dailies usually have one or more education reporters; smaller papers that can't afford fulltime

education coverage will send general-assignment reporters to cover major school events. Scholastic sports are a staple of local sports pages, of course.

To serve those media, print and electronic, that don't have regular school reportage and to expand the coverage of those that do, a growing number of schools have established *news bureaus,* operated by students. This may be an extra endeavor of a paper or magazine staff or may well be the work of an entirely separate group.

The news bureau staff compiles a list of all media that might be interested in news of the school. This includes daily and weekly newspapers, not only in the city but perhaps in a much wider area. Radio and TV stations serving the area are listed, no matter where the stations are located. Statewide newspapers and the large metropolitans should be on the list.

Then the staff should look for smaller publications—those put out by churches, fraternal organizations, civic clubs, unions, etc.

All such outlets are grouped in categories so there is no wasted coverage. A big-city daily would be interested if your school were to go to a year-round schedule but would be unable to use news about the senior play. On the other hand, a weekly paper would give generous space to the play and, of course, give the new schedule even greater display. The city camera club's newsletter would be interested in a photo

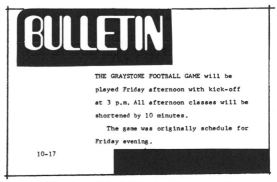

Standard form used in bulletin-board system. Items are identified not only by heading but by distinctive color— red for bulletin, blue for features, green for sports, etc. Date in lower left corner indicates when notice is to be removed.

exhibit in the school lobby while the League of Women Voters' bulletin would like to know that a senator is coming to talk to an assembly, class, or club.

Proper departmentalizing will assure that *news releases* go only to those outlets where there is a reasonable chance for their use. This eliminates waste production and postage costs.

State and regional publications of education associations usually welcome certain kinds of school news.

Staffers should read all these potential outlets regularly—and listen to the electronic ones with the same attention—to determine what kind of school news interests them. The more distant the media are, the more they want only important news, especially that about policy matters. But local outlets want more personalized news so that they can capitalize on the fact that "names make news," especially familiar names.

A serious criticism against professional news media is that they neglect true education news—what's happening in the classroom—and stress, instead, the doings of administrators and school boards. So often the school news bureau can help cover the classroom, a difficult job for the professional reporter.

Stories are produced mostly by the beat system. Most major breaking stories will be covered automatically by the daily press although there are still general-assignment pieces that the professionals haven't covered—or can't cover.

The same procedures of reporting, writing, and editing are followed as for the school paper. Then the editor or *bureau manager* decides to what list each story goes. Few stories should go to every outlet on the list; those major ones which might interest most of those outlets will probably be covered by their own reporters.

The story is typed—or perhaps Mimeographed, depending on the number—on a special letterhead.

This should be distinctive not only in form but especially in color so that the busy professional editor, who gets hundreds of such releases every day, may grow familiar with the general appearance of releases from your school and at least look at them before consigning them as unusable to the wastebasket.

The sheet is labeled "News Release." Also the name of the school, its address, and phone number are given. Sometimes the principal's name is given too. Then there should be a box, or its equivalent, where is printed: "For more information call ———— at ————." The name of a person who has additional information and the phone number, either at school or at home, are then typed into this printed indicia.

A headline is typed at the start of the story. The professional editor won't use it but will write one to fit the schedule. But the function is the same as that of a head in a newspaper; it tells the busy editor whether there is interest enough in the topic to read the release. To allow room for the written headline, the release should begin about a third of the way down a page.

While this must be taken with a grain or two of salt, we know that short stories are much more appealing than longer ones to professional editors. So if the release can be kept to one page, odds are much better that it will be used. But don't omit essential information just to avoid a second page.

The news bureau performs a public relations function. Not only public schools but private ones as well must be supported by the general public. In many states, voters must ratify school budgets; in all states, they must approve bond issues or extra taxation for school support. The more information the public has about the schools, the greater is its support of them.

So the news bureau must be especially alert for those stories that reflect favorably on the school.

That means that unpleasant news, too, must be covered—and just as accurately and promptly as the more favorable stories.

This is often difficult. School administrators don't like to have bad situations exposed to public views—and thus invite possible censure.

The staff must persuade—or at least try to persuade—administrators that bad news cannot be swept under the carpet. The more they try, the worse the situation gets. Unanswered questions or deliberate ignoring of touchy subjects will erode confidence in an administrator, a school system—and a news bureau.

Public relations experts are emphatic that prompt, honest announcement of bad news can erase much bad public reaction. Suppose that the statewide test results show that your school is averaged lower than comparable ones in the state. When the principal releases this news, mention could be made that a bad flu outbreak had caused widespread absences while classes were reviewing for the exams. This is a plausible explanation and will be accepted by most people.

But if the bad news is released by some other source or uncovered by a professional reporter—as inevitably it will be—the principal's follow-up explanation will look like a weak alibi.

So the news bureau must cover stories as fully and impartially as an independent newspaper. All pertinent facts must be given and all information must be impeccably accurate. If a bureau tries to gloss over bad news by giving incomplete—or, worse, distorted—information it will sacrifice all credibility and might as well go out of business.

The bureau may also furnish photos. Because of the cost of photo materials, this material should go only to the few outlets which offer reasonable odds for the use of the pictures.

With anytime material—for bureaus have excellent success with features—a notation may be added that pictures are available for only a phone call to the bureau.

Distribution is normally by mail. But to handle news that must make deadlines, student *runners* may hand-deliver releases to nearby outlets. If the mails must be used for more distant outlets, schedules should be available on the movement of mail. How late can letters be deposited in the school mailbox for pickup today? What is the latest pickup in vicinity of the school? How much time is saved by running the letters down to the post office? At what time do mail trains, buses, and planes leave? Does special delivery save time? Would a 10-mile drive to the next town speed a release to the state capital? The staff needs reliable answers to all these.

The quickest way to get the story to any outlet is by telephone. But long-distance calls cost money. If this method is to be used, there must be a budget to cover these fees.

All local outlets should be notified at the same time. A daily paper becomes mighty unhappy if a TV station was notified before it was. And vice versa! Station WOOF wants to get the release from you, not from a broadcast from WUGH. So copies should be given to several staffers who have access to separate phones in or out of the building. At a predetermined time, each should call one outlet, so there will be no favoritism or occasion for griping or hard feelings.

News bureaus, either independently or in a mutual exchange, can provide background material to other school newspapers, on news of general interest or in preparation for a contest between the two schools.

Radio stations will sometimes want to tape the release or even put the student on the air live, direct from phone to radio. So the students chosen to serve those stations should have poise and good speaking voices. They should—if this is a common practice —read the release aloud a couple times before making the call, just as if they were radio announcers.

All these supplementary media are journalism and all the criteria of good journalism apply to all of them. No matter how information is conveyed to a receiver, it must be accurate, clear, and interesting. But the greatest of these, as St. Paul might have said, is accuracy. This is the accuracy that delivers not only the truth and nothing but the truth, but the whole truth, the essence of honesty.

All these media, while named here as supplementary, are important facets of professional journalism. Familiarity with them by student journalists may open career opportunities. And they make students more aware of these media so they can use these channels most effectively when they are engaging in any kind of an adult career.

Just because they are supplemental for purpose of labeling and discussion doesn't at all mean that they are secondary in importance or significance.

Good staffs not only accept editorial responsibility but articulate it for readers. Here are policy statements of "Hunters' Call," Canoga Park (California) High . . .

. . . "Rebel Yell" of St. Joseph High, Jackson, Mississippi.

Here's Our Policy

Communication is the key to success in this everyday world. It unlocks the door of ignorance, the cage of mediocrity, and the gates of wisdom.

It is toward this goal of communication that the 1974-75 Rebel Yell is geared. To achieve it, the following policies will form the foundation of this publication.

1. All school & local events will be given coverage as deemed appropriate by the editorial staff. Due to the limit of the staff and time, all events will be covered to the best of our ability.

2. National & international news will be a part of the publication in their relations to the S.J.H.S. students.

3. Editorial topics will be determined by the editorial staff and the right to write specific editorials will be reserved for Rebel Yell Editors. Guest editorials from neighboring high school papers will be published.

4. Community service projects will be sought and undertaken by the newspaper.

5. Unsigned letters to the editor will not be published but the newspaper will withhold signatures upon individual request. The editorial staff withholds the right to publish letters.

6. The staff will be open to all members of the student body. Editorships will be limited to members of the Journalism class.

7. The Rebel Yell will be published 8 times during the school year.

Editorial policy defined
YOUR CP newspaper

Hunters' Call has three purposes: to help students learn advanced journalism techniques; to publicise school activities; and to serve as a forum for the opinions of students, school staff and members of the community.

A newspaper can best perform the last-named editorial function if it is uncensored. To that end, Hunters' Call has a signed contract with principal Hugh Hodgens which, among other things, allows us to express any opinion about any topic—even though that opinion may not be popular with school administrators. The only things we cannot print are articles which are obscene or libelous, which would disrupt the running of our school, which criticize religious or racial groups, or which advocate lawbreaking. There are many senior highs throughout the nation (including some in the Valley) where students do not have the above rights.

All unsigned, two-column editorials (such as this one) represent the opinion of the H.C. Editorial Board. They do not necessarily reflect the opinion of the student body as a whole, nor of the staff of CPHS. All signed articles are the opinion of the author only. Our editors recognize their responsibility to print a variety of views on controversial issues; we therefore encourage all students to submit letters to the editor, editorials or articles for possible publication.

All clubs who wish coverage of their events should contact us. It is often difficult to get to each and every activity and any information will be appreciated.

Hunters' Call is your newspaper. If you disagree with what we're doing or have any suggestions, it's your responsibility to tell us. We will listen.

BOOK

IV

BROADCAST JOURNALISM

Bulletin Bold
Stymie Medium
Girder Extra
Stymie Black It
Thompson Cabl
BOWLING GREE
CARNIVAL CONDENSED

Examples of Square Serifs race

21
Radio and Television News

There's good reason to call the news industry "the press." For centuries all the mass media were printed. The first newspaper began in the 500s in China and continued until 1935, printed from wood blocks most of that time. In Europe the oldest newspaper, *The Relation*, began in 1609. It was printed, of course, and in the city where the inventor of printing, Johann Gutenberg, once lived.

But while we still refer to "the press," the term has been expanded by the addition of radio and television news, so much so that today some 65% of all Americans find TV their major source for news, with 47% naming newspapers, and 21% radio. (Obviously, some named more than a single source.)

At least that's the finding of the latest of a 15-year series of studies by the Roper polling organization. These figures have been challenged by the print media who wage fierce competitive warfare with the broadcast media for the national advertisers' dollars.

Many neutral researchers also believe that that survey may be loaded somewhat in favor of the broadcasters who pay for the studies.

But the cumulative figures of many similar surveys indicate that the three media are publicly rated in that order—TV, newspapers, radio—for impact and dependence, and that the only difference is a relatively few percentage points.

Both electronic media, but especially radio, have become part of American school life. There are more than 700 educational *open air stations* actually broadcasting today, many of them operated by schools and using student talent. There are also some 300 *carrier-current stations* which "broadcast" along wires that lead to buildings, usually dormitories, without going out far, far "onto the air." These are almost all on college and university campuses.

Scholastic television is rarer, primarily because of the huge cost of equipment. There are a few school systems, in large cities, that have regular TV stations and some university operations. More schools have some form of *closed-circuit television* where student-produced programs can be carried by wire to individual classrooms.

The "closed-circuit radio" equivalent is the public address system which is quite common among even small schools. This system can readily be used for electronic scholastic journalism.

This chapter will concentrate only on the news service of the broadcast, leaving the entertainment aspect to show-biz books. Because scholastic radio, whether it is truly "wireless" or the ubiquitous PA system, is noncommercial, there is little opportunity for students to learn about airways advertising except for public service messages. So this phase of the business, also, will get only minimal attention here.

To use school facilities—the public address system or closed-circuit television—the proposed staff should have a detailed proposal to make to the principal. Usually this administrator must grant permission.

A typical script and a lineup for several days or a week should be submitted. Arguments should be listed in writing as well as presented orally:

1. It is necessary to make schoolwide announcements regularly. Amplifying these with news of student interest will assure an attentive audience for official announcements.

2. The 5- or 10-minute broadcasts—the shorter one will probably be most practical —will not take substantial time from classwork and if this occurs during home room, probably no working time at all will be required.

3. Expenses will be nonexistent or negligible.

4. The broadcasts will not compete against the school paper; they will be a complement.

5. Broadcast news is an important segment of American life. It should be studied just as print journalism is. For some people it will be the first steps in a career; for most people it will give those insights which will make them better users and evaluators of the electronic press.

About midmorning is the ideal time for such a broadcast although there may be another in the afternoon. Or the staff may have opportunity to present bulletins at unspecified times, as the news breaks.

A midmorning schedule allows the staff to cover very immediate news although much news will be coverable during the preceding afternoon. The time, of course, will depend upon the principal's decision, or the time that home rooms are in session.

The staff operates much like that of the school newspaper. The *news director*, the equivalent of the editor-in-chief, may have a *managing editor*, just as print publications do, or take on the duties of both jobs.

Reporters work just as their print counterparts do: They cover beats regularly and take general assignments. Some may concentrate on features; others may prepare the equivalent of newspaper columns, light or serious.

Student reporters usually write their own material but there may be people who, like those on newspaper rewrite, just write with others doing the actual legwork.

Then there are *announcers*.

In the other department are advertising people. Commercial stations have salespeople who sell time. Student "stations" would have *reps*, people who find public-service advertising needs. Then there are the writers who write and produce the commercials.

Many organizations that use public-service commercials have them prepared on tape cassettes or as *electrical transcriptions*, phonograph records. Their use simplifies procedure but denies student writers the chance to get experience and to feel the thrill of hearing their own creativity publicly aired.

Commercial stations have many other staff positions; but we are now looking at a simple system.

TV staffs would, of course, be augmented by artists, letterers, chartmakers, and property personnel who gather and arrange or make the visual adjuncts to the news program.

Reporting

☆ The basics of all journalism, print or electronic, are the same: Report the news accurately, interestingly, and briefly.

Newspapers are confined by the number of columns in their news hole; broadcast reporters are limited even more by strict time slots. Most stations either are served by networks or else use program material packaged in precise time periods. Network newscasts cannot run overtime or they will conflict with a Wild Western or a talk show; local broadcasters then have only the precise minutes scheduled between network programs. So, unlike newspapers that change the number of their pages as news and advertising volume fluctuates, radio and TV stations ration themselves to exactly the same time for every newscast except when a truly big story is breaking.

But that's the way it is in professional broadcasting, so the student radio reporter and writer must learn to work within that rigid framework. This is really no terrible handicap; brevity is usually a virtue in journalism.

The radio reporter works just about as one does for a newspaper. There are beat reporters and general assignment reporters. They cover the same kind of news, the predictable which comes from beats, spot news, and features. So techniques outlined in Chapter 6 apply to all reporters.

But the radio reporter has an extra tool—sound—using a tape recorder to make the scene more vivid to listeners. With the extra abilities come extra problems.

Of course, "pencil-and-paper" reporters use tape recorders, too, to replace or augment written notes. But that is only for their private use, unlike the public airing of radio tapes. Here we shall concentrate on that reporting which produces tape primarily for broadcast. Naturally all of the miles of tape recorded every day by a professional staff doesn't get onto the air; indeed, the fraction thus used is tiny. But the tape also serves as notes for that portion of the story which will be read by an announcer in the studio.

There are two kinds of broadcast news reports. The *live* one is spoken—usually ad lib—as the event occurs. Broadcasts of sporting events, of congressional hearings, or of presidential inaugurations are typical examples.

For a *delayed broadcast*, a tape made on the scene—or a portion of it—is incorporated into a later broadcast. In both these instances the interview is an exciting part of the broadcast. Eyewitness accounts, told by the witness, are far more gripping than an impersonal accounting by a third party. Listeners are interested not only in the event but in those often trivial details which brand themselves into the mind of the participant, and the unstudied but often colorful phraseology in which they are expressed.

Like the newspaper reporter, the radio reporter often arrives on the scene after the event. By interviewing someone who was there, the broadcaster can achieve the same immediacy as if the reporter had been on time and was describing an ongoing event.

The studio interview, too, may be live or delayed.

Generally, the same technique is used for a broadcast interview as for a printed one. Seek the complete and accurate story. You want it told—either by the reporter or by interviewed subjects—in an interesting and logical fashion. And, for broadcasting, you want to exploit the I-was-there feeling.

Here we shall look at those techniques which are unique to broadcast interviews, especially those for radio.

☆ Live radio interviews require more preparation beforehand than those for print reporting.

The interview must be kept moving along, there is no opportunity to edit out dull and uninteresting material, especially the "ums" and "ohs" and "ahs" and long periods of silence that punctuate ordinary conversation.

☆ For a studio interview, the reporter must do homework.

Learn as much as you can about the person to be interviewed and the topic of the discussion. Then write out—or at least think out—the questions that will get to the nub of the news quickly. The questions need not be asked in exactly the same order as you have listed them but should follow naturally from responses of the subject.

Suppose the coach says, "Yes, Johnson's ankle is well enough for him to start against Central. We're hoping that he and Crandall will team up to give us a quick lead."

You then would logically ask, "Does that mean that Crandall is back in the starting lineup again?" You had planned to ask that anyway although the question was farther down on your list. It is better to inject it at this point rather than to change the subject by the next listed question and then return to Crandall later.

☆ Never ask yes-or-no questions. Ask "Why?"

This will properly allow the subject to do most of the talking. Questions should be kept short for that reason, too. It is boring to have the reporter dominate a conversation by giving long speeches only thinly disguised as questions.

☆ Avoid inane questions.

Veteran broadcasters are still snickering at an interview with the wife of the first American to ride a rocket around the earth. "Mrs. Glenn," she was asked, "were you nervous while your husband was orbiting the earth?" The whole world knew she was nervous, for most of the world was nervous at the same time. To ask the question is like asking, "Did you get wet when your canoe capsized?"

Just because a reporter asks a simple question does not mean an omission of groundwork, however.

You're going to interview the assistant principal on vandalism in your school. Well before the interview, you'll go to the files and find out all you can about her. If her master's thesis was on adolescent violence, it will make her views on the current situation more pertinent. There may be other interests on her part that will make the views more significant to the listener.

"How long have you been assistant principal here, Mrs. Smith?" This question doesn't mean that the reporter is ignorant; it is merely a good lead-in to the next question.

As she answers, "This is the sixth year I've been in this job although I was here at Union High for three years before that," then the reporter can logically ask, "Have you noticed a significant difference in the amount of vandalism during that period?"

Usually there is a chance for conversation with the subject before a studio interview begins. This gives you a chance to revise your list of questions. Also by knowing how the interview will proceed, the subject can give advance thought to the answers.

A common technique is to say, "While we were talking before the broadcast, you told me about your experiences in the Far East. Could you share that with our listeners?" This brings that topic easily and naturally into the conversation.

☆ The reporter must be in charge of the conversation.

You must ask questions that go directly to the heart of the topic and then keep the guest from digressing. You must be so firm that at times you may seem less than polite. In a radio interview it is entirely permissible to say, "I'm sorry I must interrupt. But our time is going fast and I would like to have you tell us about . . ." That would be rude in ordinary conversation where you would endure conversational meanderings in polite silence.

If the subject uses highly technical phrases, the reporter should rephrase the answer into terms the listener will understand. "Is this 'information reference center' you mention just a 'library'?" Or you might ask, "Just what is an 'information reference center'?"

"Does 'lack of verbal facility' mean that a student doesn't write well enough?"

☆ Address the subject by name frequently.

Listeners may have tuned in late or may not have been paying attention at the beginning of the interview. Then, as their interest is grabbed, they would like to know who is talking. If several persons are taking part in the conversation, the different voices should frequently be identified.

Often people will become stilted in their conversation because they think that anything that goes on the air should be the stuff of Churchillian oratory. Police officers, for instance, tend to talk in the same artificial, pretentious—and faddish—phraseology in which their official reports are written. In an interview overheard even as this part of this book was written, a policeman said that "the investigating officers exited the premises." That means, of course, that the police left the house.

Certain phrases seem to be on everyone's tongue for a period, then are forgotten. We still remember during Senate investigations when nothing ever happened "now" or "then" but always—interminably always— "at that point in time"!

It is difficult to keep these clichés out of the subject's mouth. But the reporter should be scrupulous in avoiding such use and should counter the cliché with a better term as much as possible.

☆ Get background sounds onto the tape.
Sounds are highly evocative in putting the listener into the scene. It is sometimes a good technique to listen just to the background sounds. The crashing of surf and the cries of seagulls will conjure up a beach scene in those few seconds before the reporter begins, "On the beach at Sunset Bay, the senior class picnic is going on . . ."

If the sounds are not readily identifiable, the reporter may call attention to them. "That rumbling sound was a large earthmover pushing a huge mound of gravel into the area where the new gym is being built. Now, as you were saying, Mr. Brown . . ."

At the end the listener must again be told the name of the person interviewed and of the reporter and where the interview took place.

Weather Reporting

Most school newscasts end, as professional ones do, with the weather report. This has high listener interest. In northern sections of the country, winter weather may truncate a school day so buses can complete their runs before a snowstorm makes roads impassable. Athletic and social events—perhaps a whole school day—are often postponed. In other areas, rain may snarl schedules of outdoor events; in some places advisories about tornadoes or hurricanes are important information for everyone.

Weather data may be obtained from many sources. The United States government has thousands of reporting stations and their phones are listed under Commerce Department, then under National Weather Service. All airports have weather information. But many schools find it interesting to maintain their own weather stations and even to make forecasts of their own. A thermometer, barometer, rain gage, and wind-speed indicator will provide all the data most school broadcasters find necessary. Often all these are in some science labs already and often a science class will operate a weather station. In smaller communities the government uses volunteer recorders and so anyone involved in the project serves two useful purposes.

Only a daily medium—radio, TV, bulletin board, or newsletter—can give useful weather information. The school print media because of their less-frequent publication would report only such major weather stories as have caused school closings, postponement of school events, or, of course, calamities that have struck the whole community.

Because people who have lived through a weather disaster, or heard lurid accounts of the Great Tornado of '98, sometimes panic over warnings, be sure that you stick to Weather Bureau facts and that the listener knows *who's* giving the warning or *making* the prediction.

Reporters should be familiar with weather terminology. A tornado *watch*, for instance, means that conditions are such that a tornado could be created. A tornado *warning* means that the danger of such disturbance is real and imminent. The difference is substantial and ought to be pointed out for the listener.

Keep both the copy—and the tone of voice in which it is read—in normal tones. There are many instances when professional newscasters have panicked entire communities needlessly by cry-wolf weather reporting.

Not quite as elemental as weather predictions—but perhaps of greater interest—is the forecast of tomorrow's menu in the school cafeteria. The student who detests sloppy joes will welcome the warning to bring a peanut butter sandwich from home.

Writing Radio News

The radio newswriter is a combination of reporter, rewrite person, and editor. This staffer writes a story from facts gathered personally or by others, converts on-scene, first-person reports into third-person copy, arranges and blends together both kinds of reportage into a harmonious unit.

Regular 8½ x 11 copy paper is used, one side only. Typing is triple-space. Copy begins 2 inches from the top and margins are a full inch on each side. Individual stories are kept on separate pages except when they are part of a roundup. This is the same style as for newspaper copy. A difference

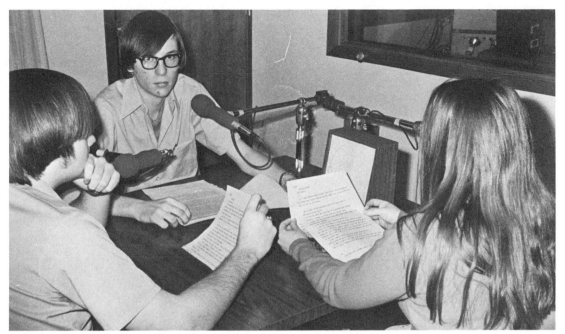

Students conduct radio interview for on-the-air station of Indianapolis school system.

is that the writer's initials and the date and time the story has been written are typed at the end of the copy instead of at the top.

Radio copy used to be typed in all-capitals. This is a carryover from the style of early news Teletypes which didn't have lowercase. But all-caps are hard to read and so most writers today use conventional capitalization and punctuation.

For benefit of the announcer, words, figures, and hyphenated phrases are never divided at the end of a line.

Although broadcast writers must include the 5 W's in a story, they think also of the *4 C's—correctness, clarity, conciseness, and color.*

It is even harder to correct an error in a later broadcast than it is in a later edition of a newspaper. Nine of ten corrections by a professional station reach an entirely different audience from that which received the erroneous report. In student broadcasts, because the audience is more specifically defined—almost a captive one—this discrepancy is not quite as great. But all facts, figures, and names must be assidu-

ously rechecked before air time to avoid irretrievable errors.

News sources must always be identified, especially in controversy. It must always be clear that it's the captain of the team, not the announcer, who predicts, "We'll win by two touchdowns!"

The main difference between broadcast and print news is the transience of the former. Radio news is presented once and briefly. The listener can't yell, "Just a minute, buddy. Go over that again and a little more slowly, will you?" Some broadcasters call this the "once-through-the-head" process.

For this reason, as well as because of time pressures, the story must be brief. Too many details may confuse the listener.

☆ Radio news must be written to be read aloud.

There is a great difference between the spoken and the written language. Even the most educated persons often speak in sentence fragments; ungrammatically—especially in the matching of plural noun with singular verb and vice versa; with vaguely defined pronouns; and with more slang and contractions than they would in writing.

So it is imperative that radio news writers read their work aloud, to see that the copy "reads well." Professionals can "hear" the spoken word merely by looking at the copy just as a musician can look at a musical score and "hear" the melody without actually playing it. But for the student writer, reading aloud is essential.

There are a few basics to remember:

☆ Avoid words with many "s" or "ch" sounds.

They twist the announcer's tongue and annoy many listeners. Microphones emphasize sibilants and often make them sound like a shrill whistle. Try to avoid converting a name that ends in "s" into a possessive. Don't say: "Mr. George Lewis's car was stolen." Phrase it: "Mr. Lewis discovered that his car had been stolen . . . etc."

☆ Be wary of alliteration.

"Peppers" is an easy word to pronounce; but when Peter Piper picks pecks of 'em, you have a real tongue-twister.

☆ Give phonetic spelling of unusual words, especially proper names.

Although the person who will read the news should look up the pronunciations of all unfamiliar words—even those of which there is the slightest doubt—you cannot do that with names of people. For those you must depend on the reporter.

The name of the late Soviet leader, Khrushchev, was as hard to pronounce as it was to spell and many professional journalists never mastered either. But the names of much less prominent people also come into the news. How do you pronounce "Przsnski"? Does Miss Herbert use the familiar English pronunciation or are the outside initials dropped as in the French form? Is "Smythe" the same as "Smith"? Which syllable is accented in "Mountalban"? These are embarrassingly difficult decisions to make while you are on the air.

The usual style is to spell the name properly, then give the phonics in parentheses: "High scorer on the invading team is a swift halfback, Clem Maida (Migh'-duh)." Note that the accent is also indicated. The wise announcer, incidentally, will say un-

usual words aloud many times before the broadcast so he can pronounce them correctly and effortlessly.

United Press International Broadcast Services uses an excellent phonetic spelling system:

AY as in mate; A as in cat; AI as in air; AH as in father; AW as in talk.

EE, meat; EH, get; UH, the; IH, pretty; EW, few;

IGH, time; EE, machine; IH, pity;

OH, note; AH, hot; AW, fought; OO, fool; UH, foot; OW, how;

EW, mule; OO, rule; U, put; UH, shut;

K, cat; S, cease; SH, machine; Z, disease; S, sun; G, gang; J, general and ZH, azure.

If phoneticizing still leaves doubts, rhyme the word: Roger Blough (rhymes with now).

☆ Simplify numbers.

Even in a textbook or something you read silently and at leisure, it's hard to put into words just what "279,000,000" is. And every time you hang a couple more zeroes on the end it gets harder. Reading them aloud at newscast pace is much worse, of course. So style for numbers must aim for accurate reading.

In copy, write numbers one through nine and numerals from 10 through 999. But write out hundred, thousand, million, and billion. (If a number is bigger than that, it's too huge for mere mortals to comprehend anyway.) So you'd have: 14-hundred, five-thousand; 13-thousand-500, etc.

Never say "a thousand"; it sounds like "eight thousand." Write "one thousand."

Round off numbers; make "$1,749" into "17-hundred dollars," or "more than 17-hundred dollars."

Spell out "dollars," too.

Dates are given as "March 1st, 9th, 31st."

Ages aren't used unless they are significant. Then make it "Ten-year-old Barbie Jones started high school today." Not: "Barbie Jones, 10, started . . . etc."

☆ Use only familiar abbreviations.

In addition to the common abbreviation of titles—Mr., Mrs., Dr.—only those which the listener himself would use are given in broadcasts. They are written with hyphens instead of periods: P-T-A, U-S-A, etc. Some abbreviations are spoken as ordinary words; in copy they are written in the same way: NATO, VISTA, etc.

Never abbreviate state names, especially by the cryptic labels used by the post office. If you write "Michigan" instead of "MI" the announcer won't have to figure out whether it's Missouri, Mississippi, Michigan, or Minnesota.

☆ Make punctuation obvious.

It's hard to tell the difference between "." and "," and ";" when you're on the air. So dashes are used to replace colons and semicolons, especially when an abrupt change of thought occurs within a sentence. "The first Central exchange student from Bulgaria— Ladizlaw Dobrynski—arrived last night." "Leading lady Susan Dorn—who practiced her role with her arm in a cast—had the cast removed just hours before the play began."

☆ Never start a lead sentence with a name.

The listener's ear must be warmed up so it actually "hears" what is being said. If you start out with "Mr. Ralph McGraw said he would flunk all students in his chemistry classes . . . ," the listener will come alive at about the seventh word and frantically ask, "Who said that? Who said that?"

So it's better to begin with "A veteran science teacher, Mr. Ralph McGraw, said . . ."

But don't use long or artificial titles. "Board of Education Subcommittee on Physical Resources Chairman Thomas Levin . . ." Make it "Mr. Thomas Levin, Chairman of the Board of Education's . . ."

☆ Minimize the use of pronouns.

Obviously pronouns are needed, they can't be eliminated. But the late-tuner-inner or the inattentive listener should know that it isn't an unknown "she" that the story is about but "Mrs. Brown, the guidance counsellor."

☆ Signal the listener that a quotation is coming up.

The listener can't see quotation marks as a newspaper reader can so we must use another signal to alert him. That used to be "quote" and "unquote," "this is a quote" or "and now we quote," and "end of quote." Instead we might say, "The coach praised *what he called* 'A real gutsy performance by Rod Wenz.' " or "The mayor then added *these words:* 'The library is essential to good education and it will be built.' " The Italicized phrases are those signals.

Quotes tend to slow a newscast and are used less frequently than in a newspaper story. But good quotes add color and authority to a story, so you don't want to eliminate them entirely.

☆ Don't be afraid to use "said."

"Says," "declares," "notes," and similar words come through objectively. There can be undesirable and even dangerous editorializing in stronger words such as "admits," "insists," "charges," "makes clear," etc.

☆ Signal listeners in advance that they're about to hear new voices. Then . . .

☆ Identify all voices—more than once if there are long excerpts or if the speaker is interrupted.

The listener can be oriented by an introduction, "Our reporter, Susan Gray, talked with Miss Sally Struthers, coach of the girls' volleyball team, at practice yesterday."

☆ Avoid statements that need qualification to be understandable or accurate.

☆ Qualify such statements before they are made.

Suppose your newscast says: "Seniors will be unable to get into the college of their choice if the new pass-fail grading system is adopted.

"That is the belief of John Hooper, president of the Honor Society."

The casual listener, in alarm, may fail to realize that he is not truly going to be denied college admission. For he may immediately begin worrying about the situation and thus fail to "hear" that this is only an opinion of a fellow student.

It is much better to report that "John Hooper, president of the Honor Society, expresses concern about the proposed new grading system." Then the reader is prepared for "John said 'Seniors will be unable, etc.'"

☆ Use signals to indicate that there are two sides to a statement.

It is better to say, "Although [that's the signal] the gym will not be available for commencement exercises, arrangements have been made to use the City Auditorium," than to report, "The gym will not be available, etc." and then to add, "But arrangements, etc."

☆ Use informal time references.

"Today" or "yesterday" are better than "Tuesday" or "Wednesday." "This morning" is sufficient; don't say "at 10:30." Above all, don't say "at 10:30 A.M. this morning"; 10:30 A.M. can hardly be in the afternoon.

Use precise time only when it is essential to the story. In talking about a game tonight, it will be useful to the listener to know that it begins at 8 o'clock. But in discussing the team's prospects, you need only say that "they'll meet the Vikings Friday evening."

☆ Use simple sentences.

Subject, verb, object is best understood by the listener. A reader can go back and untangle a convoluted sentence or match up an inverted set of subject and verb. The listener doesn't have this insurance for comprehension.

Professional writers rarely write a sentence longer than two lines; that's about 20 words. Some sentences, of course, are so punctuated that they are really two or more when read aloud. And that's the test of a proper sentence length: Does it read well out loud?

Short, punchy sentences in series give a staccato feeling of urgency and action. But there must be variation in sentence length or your newscast will become sing-songy.

☆ Use normal tenses.

Some fire-enginey announcers, by using only the present tense, try to give the effect that every event is occurring right now. The effect is irritating and self-defeating.

So use the same tense you would in recounting a story to your parents at dinner.

Don't be afraid of mixing tenses. "Principal Virgil Brockton *said* that grades *are* higher this marking period . . ." The act of speaking is over; the quality of the grades continues.

☆ Background the listener.

Never take it for granted that the listener knows all about a story, even if it's been Topic A for the past two weeks. Each broadcast story must be complete in itself. Even if it means deleting some new but nonessential detail, the listener must be filled in on past developments. "Fire Chief Albert A. Nelson said the fires in the library last week are definitely arson." Now a few details of this new development. Then: "Fires broke out in the book stacks on three consecutive days last week and on Thursday there were three separate blazes. None did much damage except the first one, Tuesday, which destroyed about two dozen books."

☆ Don't start a story with a question.

Because commercials use this technique so much, the reader may turn off that mental hearing aid when a question is posed because it isn't recognized as a news item.

☆ Tie paragraphs together with smooth transitions.

It should be good organization of facts that ties the parts of a story into a neat whole. Labeled as "the most overworked words in radio copy" are "meanwhile," "meantime," and "incidentally." Unless the first two are exactly the words to convey specific meaning, it is wise to avoid them. And if you're working for UPI Broadcast Services, you'd better not use the third taboo. "If something is only 'incidental' it has no place in a tight newscast," says its writers' stylebook.

☆ Use colloquialisms but don't do it self-consciously.

If in your area roads are "slick" when wet, say so. You don't have to use "slippery," a term which would be used in another part of the country.

But if the phrase doesn't come "trippingly off the tongue" as Shakespeare liked his dialog, if the listener can "see" quotation marks around those words as they are spoken, the effect is irritating.

While the experienced newscaster may sound casual, as if speaking informally to a friend, newscasts are always completely written—with the exception of on-the-scene reporting, of course. The Federal Communications Commission, which regulates broadcasting activities in the United States, demands that everything that goes out over the air as news or public-affairs programs be recorded, in writing or in tapes, for future reference. This is a good practice for school broadcasters, too.

The script is written on only the right-hand two-thirds of the page. The left-hand column is used for instructions. As in newswriting, each story is slugged, given a label by which it is identified. A typical student report might look like this:

(BUS WRECK)   3 minutes, 7 seconds
Three Central students were slightly injured this morning when their bus slid off McCoy Road, tipped over and rolled down a 20-foot embankment.

Henry Davis, a senior and leading miler on the track team, and two sophomores, Jeannie Golden and Mark Gagnon (Gan-yoh), were taken to Memorial Hospital. They were released after minor treatment. The other 27 students were checked by Mrs. Mabel Graham, the school nurse, after they were brought to school on another bus.

Sally McArthur, a junior, who was sitting behind the driver, described the accident:

TAPE: *40 seconds*
IN CUE: *"We were just coming around the bend . . .*
OUT CUE: *"Everyone stayed cool, real cool."*

(A helpful device here is to underline what is *not* to be read to avoid confusing announcer.)

City police said that an earlier drizzle of rain was turning into sleet or snow at just about the time of the accident and that roads quickly became slippery. At least a dozen traffic mishaps were reported throughout the city in a 20-minute period.

Mr. Alex Krapohl was the driver. He has been driving buses, both for Central High and Meadowbrook Elementary, for more than 15 years. He said that the bus was traveling at only 20 miles an hour at the time of the accident. Police say that several witnesses corroborated this.

Principal Horace McGee said:

TAPE: *32 seconds*
IN CUE: *"We have investigated . . .*
OUT CUE: *"There was no negligence involved."*

Our reporter, Billy Martin, phoned in from the scene just minutes ago and said that the bus probably will not be removed until late this afternoon because of the extreme angle of the embankment and the bad weather.

Mr. McGee said that announcements will be made during last period today about arrangements for a substitute bus to take students home this afternoon and also to pick them up tomorrow. Schedules will be revised only slightly, the principal said.

The "IN" and "OUT" cues are the opening and closing words of the taped portion of the broadcast. They show the person—in professional radio it is the *engineer*—where to begin and end the playback.

The approximate time is noted to the right of the story slug. For after the story has been written, it may have to be edited for time just as a newspaper story is edited for space.

Experienced writers know almost instinctively how long a story will take. Although no two announcers read at exactly the same speed, professional writers calculate that an average 6½-inch typewritten line will have about ten words and that the typical newscaster reads about 15 lines per minute. For copy written like the example here, it takes about five seconds per line to read. The best timing, though, is for the writer to read it out loud; this is particularly valuable to the student writer who then can check both the time and the reading rhythm at the same time.

Timing of stories is also necessary to prepare a *rundown sheet,* a second-by-second schedule for the whole broadcast. Such a schedule is most important for network and television broadcasts but it is a good tool for student broadcasters, too. The rundown might look something like this:

00:00	Headlines
00:10	Bus Wreck
03:17	Basketball
03:47	Honor Society
04:22	Tomorrow's Meetings
04:30	Menu
04:40	Weather

An alternative is to *back-time.* Here you start out with the total time of the broadcast and at the end of each portion indicate the time that is left. Thus the rundown above would look like this:

05:00	Headlines
04:50	Bus Wreck
01:43	Basketball

And so on.

The running time on the rundown is checked—by stopwatch—by the program director. If the announcer isn't on schedule at any point in the broadcast, the director uses hand signals to direct speeding up or slowing down by the announcer.

Announcing

The final factor in the quality of broadcast news is the human voice that transmits it. The speaker is the *announcer.* He or she may simply be a *news reader* (as they are called in England). They may write all or part of their material; they may be the reporter for part of it. The announcer who gives the major portion of a broadcast and who furnishes the continuity among taped or live reports from on-scene reporters is called the *anchorman,* a term especially loved among television people, and one that points out a changing condition. The announcer for many years had to be a man; it was believed that only a deep masculine voice could lend the proper credibility to the spoken word. But that fallacy has been dispelled and today women announcers are evaluated by their performance, not by their gender. Network anchormen still are usually men but certainly this should have no bearing in scholastic broadcasting.

The first requisite of the announcer is a good speaking voice. It doesn't matter whether it be high or low as long as the tone is "round," full-bodied, and not breathy or adenoidal. Practice will enable a person to develop a fine speaking voice even if it once had an unpleasant timbre.

The announcer also must have good enunciation. Each syllable, each word, must be articulated clearly. Poor enunciation is caused by laziness; people drop final "g's", swallow syllables, and slur sounds because it takes less energy than to speak plainly. "Laiz 'n' gemmun" is a typical sloppily spoken phrase.

When radio first became a major news source, announcers sought to speak in a "mid-American English." This is one that had no glaring regional accents, neither the dropped "r" of the New Englander nor the differently dropped "r" of the Deep South, neither the Bostonian "a" nor the flat "a" of Texas. People have argued over the basis for mid-American but probably that brand of American English as spoken in Michigan, Ohio, and Wisconsin comes closest to an "unaccented" pronunciation.

More important than *accent* is *accenting,* the stressing of words and syllables.

Accenting stresses the important, key word, or points out—as the previous sentence—a contrast between two words or phrases. Improper stress can drastically distort the meaning of the spoken word.

"The *real* reason for the change" means something much different from "the real *reason* for the change" or "the real reason for the *change.*"

We say that classes will be normal *Monday* morning but class periods will be shortened five minutes *Tuesday* morning, thus stressing the difference between the two days. It would be confusing to say "Classes will be normal Monday *morning* but will be changed *Tuesday* afternoon."

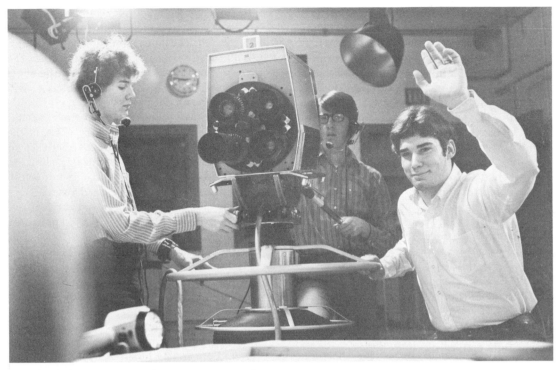

Student television crew at work on program sent by closed circuit to schools in metropolitan Indianapolis.

A disturbing, but unfortunately growing, trend is for unthinking announcers to stress the last syllable of a word or the last word of a sentence. So we hear about Washing*ton* and Tues*day* or that the President will "leave tomorrow on his *trip*."

Just as a writer has a responsibility to preserve the integrity of the written language, so the announcer must preserve that of the spoken language. Part of that integrity is the rhythm and even the melody of English. Even if you can't understand the words, you know if a person is speaking English or Spanish. There is a difference between German and Italian that is discerned even by the person who speaks or understands neither. "Melody" is created by the stress of words and by their pronunciation. To mispronounce a word in a broadcast is as unprofessional as to misspell it in a written report.

The announcer should read the script through silently once for the sense; then read it again, this time aloud, for rhythm and prounciation. You may mark the script to show which words are to be accented and how much; underscoring with one to three lines is a good device to show stress.

Vertical lines can be used to show natural breaks in the sentence—and a place to take a breath. If a phrase runs from one line to another it should be placed in parentheses as the signal that the announcer shouldn't drop his voice at the end of the line.

The announcer should keep a moderate voice level. Don't let excitement color your voice—unless you are reporting live from the scene of an event that naturally would increase the adrenalin content of your blood.

For a time it was fashionable to read news in a very excited voice, high-pitched, and breathless. But listeners soon grew impatient with announcers who made a report of a fender-bender collision sound like the sinking of the *Titanic*. Today's reporters prefer to let the import of the news, rather than the pitch of their voices, give immediacy and excitement.

Television News

Television has obvious advantages in covering live news, especially that which is scheduled in advance so audio and visual coverage can be planned. Athletic events are naturals; so are space shots, inaugurations, and similar events that take place within a well-defined dimension of space and time. Many observers believe that the funeral of President John Kennedy was TV's finest performance, although others argue for man's first landing on the moon. Both were plannable coverage.

But when the announcer must speak in a studio, lack of pictorial interest creates an obvious "news reader." This is called, by critics, "radio with lights." An understandable reaction is for announcers to make their own personalities attractive enough to keep the audience looking at handsome features. Then the announcer becomes a "personality" or, simply, an actor, certainly not a newsperson.

There are many devices, of course, to add interest to such news reading. In professional television many technical tricks can add excitement to a broadcast. A major benefit is motion, of course. Headlines and labels become kinetic delights when set to motion. Split screens that show two or more scenes, tricks with colors, rear projection, and similar stunts are commonplace. If nothing else, changing cameras gives a new angle for viewing.

Authorities on school broadcasting assume that typically a closed-circuit distributing system includes two cameras. They say the most common first purchase of TV equipment for a school is a camera-video monitor-tape recorder combination. They recommend a $\frac{1}{2}$-inch helical-scan recorder and suggest that this would not be out of the price range of most schools.

We assume this basic equipment for this discussion.

First consideration should be given to the *set*, the design of the "stage" on which performers work. In professional TV, these sets are lavish and expensive—also copycattish and inconsequential. For student broadcasts, a simple desk or table and a plain background are not only adequate but probably even desirable. If there is a class or a club in theatrical set designing and build-

ing, it can be tapped to provide the broadcast set. But student set designers and builders should be cautioned to keep it simple. Too garish a set will detract from the newscaster and the news. And, as the same set is used daily, too obtrusive settings will quickly pall on the viewer.

As much as possible, actual taped scenes of news events should be used. This is the strength of television. But, as analyses of even national TV news broadcasts show, in many instances such coverage is not available and still pictures are used instead.

These are the same news photos that are taken for use in newspapers and magazines. Polaroid pictures are ideal for TV use as the camera can move in for the equivalent of a bigger closeup. Conventional photos are just as good; the problem becomes one of developing and printing within available time.

For broadcast purposes the conventional glossy print can cause troublesome reflections. So a matte finish or the common Resisto print should be used. A *dulling spray*, available at any art-supply store, can be applied to glossies to remove unwanted shininess.

If new pictures are not available, filed art can be used. In all instances, the photos must conform to the basic needs of news pictures. The announcer must always provide adequate identification; TV pictures require this as strongly as printed ones do.

Expository art—maps, charts, diagrams, and graphs—is as useful for broadcast as for printed news.

If 2-dimensional art is not available, 3-dimensional *props* may be used. Because these are difficult to change during shooting, usually only the first story is thus illustrated. The props then remain for the whole program although they can be removed while the camera is taking a closeup.

Interest is added to a broadcast by continual—but highly controlled—changes of camera angle. While one camera shoots straight-on, the second is in position for a semiprofile, for instance.

Usually one camera is kept in position for the straight shot and, while it is on, the second is shifted to a new position. Or the second can be kept in a stationary supplementary position.

When a *zoom lens* is available, its use brings both variety and motion into an otherwise static scene. Without changing camera position, the image changes just as if the camera were moving swiftly toward or from the announcer, increasing or eliminating the surrounding scene.

In those rarer instances when only one camera is available, the director must keep it moving for the sake of visual interest. Stories should be planned so that the background art can be changed outside the camera's vision. This can be done by *dollying* the camera way over to one side or by holding art up for a closeup while the background is shifted.

Brief comments by participants or onlookers of news events may be added by video tape just as they are by voice tape for radio. Those who have longer contributions can be brought into the studio, their live appearance blended with a tape report and the announcer's report.

If possible, people should wear or carry something which helps identify them or the story. The coach, for instance, might wear a windbreaker and a whistle around his neck; drama club members might wear costumes or parts of them; the Spanish Club president could wear a serape and the head of the German Club an Alpine hat. While this may sound a bit theatrical, if care is taken the audience will not find it offensive; for it has been conditioned to stage effects on the video tube.

Editorials

Editorializing by broadcast media is still not intensive. When an editorial is presented, it is often by the chief executive of a station. The substance of the editorial, of course, is exactly like that of a printed editorial.

In many instances the station will offer a printed copy of the editorial on the listeners' requests. This is because, even more than in the case of news, the listener requires more than the on-the-air time to assimilate and evaluate an editorial.

You will notice that after every such editorial, people with opposing viewpoints are invited to state those positions during time offered free by the station. This is to conform in both letter and spirit with the fairness policy of federal regulatory agencies.

Advertising

It is doubtful whether student broadcasts will include advertising. A school that has an open-air station has a noncommercial venture, prohibited by law from selling advertising time. Closed-circuit TV or the school PA system would probably have little advertising appeal to local merchants although a strong case could be made for their advantages.

But there are enough public service ads so that the student broadcaster can get valuable experience in their preparation and delivery. Class plays, cultural programs in the community as well as in the school itself, blood collections, United Way campaigns, and similar activities come to mind.

As in a print ad, a broadcast commercial is "persuasive communication." The advertiser gives facts that bolster the proposition that it will be advantageous for the listener to do the suggested action, be it to buy merchandise or to donate blood. Commercials are 10, 30, or 60 seconds in professional broadcasting and the student might as well start immediately working within those time frames. So only the most important or most appealing reasons can be presented.

There are two kinds of commercials: One is a simple statement of sales pitches, sometimes in musical form; the other is a dramatization that makes the point more obliquely. In most instances the minuscule drama is reinforced by a concluding statement.

In the simple statement the audience must quickly be defined, usually by just addressing it: "Seniors! Yearbook pictures will be taken tomorrow . . ." Or, better "Seniors! When the 'Legenda' comes out in May, you'll certainly want your portrait in it. So . . ."

A rule of thumb for radio commercials is that the name of the product or of the store that is advertising should be given three times. This insures that the listener knows

the salient information even though listening with only half an ear. Whether three
is a magic number, the point remains that
repetition is a necessary assurance of comprehension. This is especially true when a
telephone number is given. Often the listener is told to get a pencil and be prepared
to write down the number. You ought to be
able to assume that a student audience will
have pencil and paper at their fingers but
even then it's a good technique to alert them
that writing will be required.

In dramatized commercials, you may
stress the negative or positive just as in
print ads. It is probable that negative approaches are used a bit more in electronic
advertising, because the bad effects of not
using a product are more dramatic than the
good results that come from its use.

A typical public service radio commercial
might go something like this:

	(BLOOD BANK) 60 seconds
SOUND OF AUTO CRASH	
VOICE 1 (Policeman, gruff male)	A bad one, Chief, looks like three Central High kids and one is bleeding bad.
VOICE 2 (Doctor, deep)	This one will need massive blood transfusions to pull through.
VOICE 3 (Nurse, woman)	Our blood bank is awfully low, Doctor. I do hope there's enough to . . . (fade out)
AN- NOUNCER	That person who needs blood so badly might be your best friend. It may even be you.
	Here's your chance to make sure the blood bank will not be empty when it is needed. The Union County Red Cross Blood- mobile will be in the boys gym Tuesday from 9 to 3. Give the gift that only you can give.
	Students 16 years and older may give blood. Please register before Monday noon with Mrs. Richards, the school nurse, in Room 213. She will give you

forms to fill out and further information.

VOICE 4 (Young girl)	I just gave blood so Paul can live. (Pause) And do you know what . . . it didn't even hurt!

Insertion of such commercials will make
a news broadcast sound more like the one
your audience hears on commercial airwaves and thus may enhance the stature of
a student program.

Nonelectronic Broadcasting

Even if your school doesn't have any facilities for electronic newscasting, it is possible to have a lot of fun and serve your
school community well by putting on such
programs in the cafeteria, study halls, or
library at regular times. All the processes
are the same except that in the last step
you rely on air waves without augmenting
electrical impulses to vibrate your listeners'
eardrums.

A few adventuresome staffs have even
presented documentaries in this live fashion, complete with props, slides, and even
home movies. Such a presentation is essentially the same as a revue on the stage or
tube. Split-second timing is required or
the show will drag. So it will be necessary
to rehearse both the "actors" and the "stage
crew" many times before the slick, smooth
pace is obtained.

Television has been a common medium for
only about a quarter of a century, a very
short time compared with the life of newspapers. It is still a new medium, almost
daily finding new techniques to convey information better. So a good textbook is to
watch commercial TV newscasts—and listen
to those on radio, too, of course. Watch and
listen, not as the casual audience usually
does, but with the view of seeing what's
good and what's bad, why something works
or doesn't, and how student broadcasting
might emulate the best features of its professional counterpart.

Just as a good newspaper is a superior
textbook for print journalism, so good station and network broadcasts are excellent
learning tools for electronic journalism.

BOOK

V

THE SCHOOL YEARBOOK

These are Written letterforms

Planning and Producing the Yearbook

Writing and publishing for the 21st century is a great thrill.

That is exactly what you are doing when you are on the staff of a school yearbook.

Yearbooks are read here and now, just as are scholastic papers and magazines. Students want to see their pictures—and those of their friends and of outstanding school events—and they want to read the text as much as in any other publication. Yet the annual is the only printed medium normally cherished and kept throughout the years. When you and your classmates gather for a 25th reunion, the yearbook undoubtedly will be consulted by all who attend. You will look at the pictures and joke about the contrast with your appearances in the 21st century. It will revive memories and induce "Do you remember when . . ." stories.

As a yearbook staffer, you are really serving two audiences: The graduating class (and to a lesser degree all other classes) now and those same folk in the future. The responsibility of helping to preserve memories through pictures and text in an annual should not be taken lightly.

☆ A yearbook is written both for the present and for the future.

The fact that the book endures influences the work of the staff in several ways.

☆ Accuracy must be impeccable.

The book will be used as a record as well as a preserver of memories. Errors and mistakes are preserved for all time—with no chance for a correction.

☆ Information must be specific.

On the day when an annual is delivered, readers easily recognize schoolmates and faculty. You'll identify your favorite teacher from a group picture, even without mention in a caption. You'll recognize the photograph of the winning point-after-touchdown over your bitter rival in the closing minute of the Homecoming game. But memories fade and years from now most yearbook pictures become meaningless without comprehensive and accurate captions and complete explanations.

Verbal allusions, too, require identifications A reference, for instance, to "the case of Tom's missing basketball shoes" will be meaningless in a couple of decades although everyone knows what it means when the yearbook is distributed.

☆ Quality must be beyond fads and foibles.

A yearbook with a "modern" look, in the style of the moment, probably will look artificial and dated by the time your readers have their own children in high school.

Producing a yearbook is one of the biggest jobs any student can perform. It means long hours, hard work, and usually sacrifice of other school activities. But the rewards are great and they grow with the years.

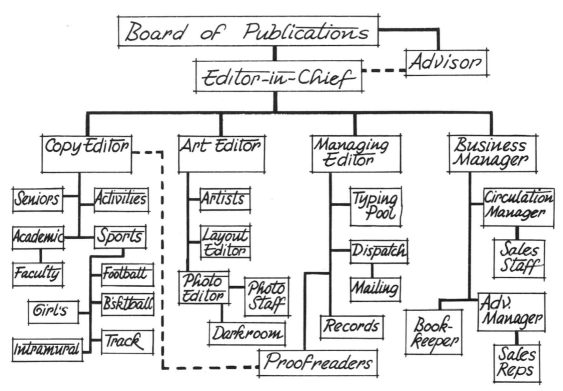

EXAMPLE 4
Yearbook staff organization based on production functions. Duties are assigned, positions designated according to sections of book.

Organizing Staff and Workload

Proper planning can eliminate much of the tribulations and some of the sweat.

☆ Staff organization is the first key to success.

The yearbook staff should be organized early in the spring of the year preceding publication. The editor-in-chief is a key individual and the selection for that job should be made only with deliberation. A candidate must be familiar with all aspects of yearbook production. For that reason, most schools insist that an editor have previous experience and almost all reserve this important slot for a senior. If selection becomes a popularity contest through all-school election, results may well turn into a disaster.

The essential thing is that the senior editors, especially the editor-in-chief, know about production and about handling people who will be working on the staff. An editor

also should have a sense of responsibility and not view the assignment as an opportunity for an ego trip or a frivolous job that permits some practical jokes on students. A new editor may be chosen by the retiring senior editors or by a publication board composed of both students and teachers.

The business manager is responsible for the yearbook's financial well-being and for keeping accounts. Thus that assignment is second only to that of the editor-in-chief. The business manager may be appointed by the editor-in-chief, retiring senior editors, or the publication board. Usually, when an editor-in-chief makes top appointments, they are submitted to the publication board for ratification.

Organizing a staff may follow any one of several plans. Filling every job must be assured to provide a clearcut channel from writer or photographer to copy editor to editor-in-chief to printer.

Example 4 shows one logical arrangement. It breaks the job of producing the book into the major components: Copy, art, production, and business. Note that the chart is

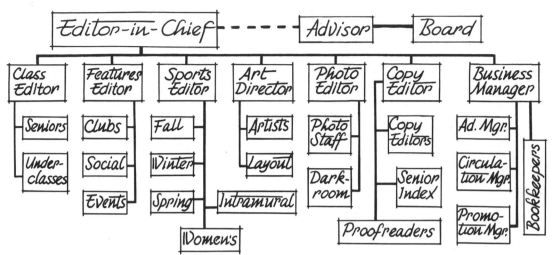

EXAMPLE 5

Yearbook staff organization based on general contents of book. In any such table of organization every necessary job must be assigned and lines of responsibility clearly indicated.

concerned with jobs, not people. One individual may do more than one assignment and in some cases several persons may be needed to cope with all the duties shown by a single square in the chart.

Example 5 shows another logical division of duties. The editorial board includes the editor-in-chief and key editors who make up the second row in the table of organization. The faculty advisor should be an important board member.

Several all-staff meetings should be held in the spring to develop a team spirit, to familiarize each member with assignments, and to determine some of the important matters that may vary in yearbook policy from year to year. In some schools the key decisions are made by the board of editors and if that is the case, they should meet frequently in the spring, possibly almost every day, for decision-making.

Just like those on school newspapers and magazines, yearbook staffers need an adequate workshop. There they can hold meetings, prepare copy for the printer, and, equally important, store equipment, copy, and art. Quarters need not be elaborate but must be secured by lock and key and be used exclusively by a yearbook staff. Most school administrators provide such office space.

The workshop needs as many large tables as can be squeezed into the area. A drawer file cabinet is a necessity. One drawer goes to the editor, another to the business manager, the third to the copy editors, and the other for general staff use. Storage cabinets —or at least shelves—are required for bulky art material.

☆ Working papers should be properly filed at the end of each day.

Papers and pictures otherwise may get worn or lost. A photograph dog-eared beyond use or the final page missing from an index comes as a shock—especially if the deadline for sending it to the printer is at hand.

A paper cutter is a valuable tool. This can be dangerous and can nip off a finger if used carelessly so it must be treated with respect. Don't practice false economy by buying a cheap cutter which will soon get out of square and its blade bow so it cuts arcs instead of straight lines.

If the artists, who frequently like to work elsewhere, want to be in the workshop, provide them with a drawing board.

When a school does not provide the senior editors with space during the summer, they should find some place to work, possibly in the home of the editor-in-chief. There, the top editor, busy on the yearbook assignment, can discuss developments with colleagues, if they too are around.

Did you ever go into the football coach's

office and see all the charts on the wall? They are the result of much planning and they are the gages for measuring the results of such planning.

If planning and controls are vital for a football team with only 11 players, they are far more important for a yearbook team of many more people and with a much wider range of talents and responsibilities.

☆ Make a list.

These three little words are basic for any organized effort. The more things that are committed to paper, the more your brain cells are kept free for creative work. And the fewer tricks faulty human memory can play on you.

Your lists ought to be in big letters and hung conspicuously in the yearbook office. They become incentives to meeting goals and deadlines; they are fine morale builders as they chart the progress of the staff.

☆ Don't let charts become just a stage setting.

Charts are important as aids to planning. But it is the planning itself that is the essential.

If you're going to a basketball game and then out for burgers and fries on a budget of a couple dollars, you'll make plans. When you're about to spend the substantial amounts of a typical yearbook budget and create something that will be cherished for decades, you ought to devote commensurately more planning.

The first list is the long-range timetable. One of its important functions is to remind that any yearbook is just one in a set of books; that what you do this year must be built on all the previous books published by your school; that your yearbook will be part of the foundation for next year's book and the following year and year and year.

Here is a typical timetable. To meet your needs it will, of course, be modified a bit. But the broad framework is accurate:

April (year before publication)

Editor-in-chief, business manager, and editorial board chosen.
Budget prepared.

Staff meetings held.
Theme selected.
Contract with printer signed.

May

Budget approved.
Rough pagination done.
Type selected.
Senior editors paginate their sections.
Art editor begins layout of introductory pages and section dividers.
Business staff begins plans for advertising and circulation campaigns.
Outside photographer contracted.
Photo editor works with school administration in scheduling group pictures.
Evergreen pictures—those with no time element—are shot. Early spring is an ideal time for campus shots; foliage is enough to lend charm, not so heavy it hides details.
Sports editor covers spring athletics. (Photo editor assigns camera coverage.)
Activities editor covers spring social events.

June

Many staffs prefer to have senior photographs taken in the spring. This creates a few problems but solves many more.
Business staff prepares and addresses letters to prospective advertisers, perhaps subscribers also.
Schedules completed for outside photographer and cleared with him.
Spring pictures developed and contact-printed.
Copy editor writes introductory matter.
Introductory and divider pages laid out, ready for printer.
Pages on spring activities completed, ready for printer.
First advertising sales calls made.

July and August

No formal schedule. Editors use this time to finish incomplete spring duties; wise ones allow plenty of time for just plain thinking.

September (start of academic year of publication)

Staff meeting first week of school. Staffers who haven't been involved during the summer are brought up to date on progress, and schedule for the months ahead is presented and explained. This is the meeting for a rousing pep talk; ask your printer to suggest a good speaker, one who is brief and inspiring.

Fill vacancies caused by staffers moving or becoming involved in jobs or other activities.

Review duties of each staffer.

Announce schedule of meetings and working hours.

Circulation campaign starts at once.

Material for senior section compiled.

Copy and photo assignments made for the rest of the year.

Advertising sales representatives resume making calls.

October

Class, faculty, and group photographs taken.

Cover material, style, and design chosen.

Layouts on fall activities, most of football pages and academics finished.

Senior layouts well under way.

Business manager reviews finances. If there is need for outside fund-raising affairs, now is the time to stage them.

Review budget. Must size of book be cut down? Or can you afford extra pages or extra color?

Before the leaves fall, get any necessary outdoor shots.

November

First shipment to printer. (Only complete 2-page spreads should be sent. Hold single pages.)

Choose paper for end leaves. Prepare necessary art work for them.

Prepare all advertising copy, art, and layouts.

Lay out all pages for which material is complete.

Work to fill vacant spots in signatures.

December

Order covers.

Second shipment to printer. (By this time, only senior section, clubs and organizations, activities, and sports are left to cover.)

January

Third shipment to printer.

Complete layouts of all other pages. (Again fill the holes in signatures; the printer wants to get forms on the press.)

Give final print quantities to printer and cover-maker.

February

The b-i-g month!

All copy to printer! (If there are activities which you can't cover yet, now is the time to arrange an extension on one or two signatures, if that is possible. Perhaps you will need to prepare some "emergency pages" that can be used in case it becomes impossible to get late material in on time.)

March

Proofs starting coming in. Read them carefully and return them promptly. (A whole crew at the printer's is waiting for you now.)

Stage your final subscription campaign.

Collect all outstanding money.

April

Have a postmortem. Jot down ideas for next year's staff.

Start on insert if you have one.

Tidy up the workshop. Get files in shape for next year's staff. Check all records to make sure they're accurate and up to date.

May

Help the new staff organize.

June

Here it is!

Distribute books to subscribers.

Arrange sale of individual copies if you have any to sell.

Distribute books to advertisers if this is part of the contract.

Collect all advertising accounts.

Pay all bills.

Use a fine-tooth comb on the yearbook. Again jot down ideas for new staff and point out pitfalls that you avoided—or didn't avoid.

Senior editors should meet with their successors and pass along paternal wisdom about their jobs.

Check for errors. If any have crept past your vigilant eyes, correct them now and place marked copy in school archives. Yearbooks are often used for reference; inaccuracies can be costly.

Relax and enjoy your well-deserved plaudits.

July

If you have a supplement, you've been working on it since April. Finish the job and send it off to the printer.

Before the top editors and business staffers get far into the above chart of operations, however, they need to answer a series of questions that will influence all their future plans. The earlier that key decisions are made, the better for the book's eventual success. Here are some key questions:

What will be the theme and structural approach?

Who will do the printing? The same firm as last year?

What—if any—will be the use of color? Full-color pages?

What will be the approximate percentage of advertising?

What is the budget for expenses? (This, obviously, depends on some factors that have not been settled yet: The printing contract and the amount of ad revenue.)

What would be a realistic schedule of deadlines? (Again, the details have to be worked out with the printer although a generalized pattern was given earlier in this chapter.)

The Theme

An early decision—possibly the key editorial decision—is picking the theme, that single thread that ties together all the sections in the book. Occasionally a student editor dismisses the use of a theme as trite and unnecessary. What is overlooked is that any creative work has a central theme whether it's obvious or not. Without a theme, the yearbook becomes a collection of several individualized parts, like an anthology of best sellers that have nothing else in common.

Every yearbook has an inescapable theme: Coverage of the events of this year at your school and their influence on students. The more obvious theme is merely a device to show that basic material in a pleasant and logical manner. Within the range of being appropriate and logical, the range of themes is almost infinite.

Successful themes recently included "Putting It Together," "The Year Nothing Stood Still," "Top Secret: To the Parents of . . .," "Happiness Is . . . ," "A World of Its Own, but the Outside World Seeps In," "Rules of the Road: High School's a Busy Intersection on the Highway of Life," "Annual Report to the Stockholders," "The Individual," and "Our Enchanting Island" (Staten Island high school).

The theme should be lasting. A minor craze, such as, for instance, streaking, does not fit as a theme although it could well be among the minutia covered.

☆ The theme should be one that can be pleasingly developed in words and art.

Background of a school—historical, economic, social, or cultural—may figure in picking a theme. The Bicentennial period is here and it will provide thematic inspiration during the 1970s and 1980s as the nation—and yearbook editors—commemorate the Revolutionary period and the early years of the United States. Local celebrations, too, are possible theme topics.

☆ An effective theme should be evocative.

Among ways to do this are to suggest popular music or to reproduce newspaper headlines. Both can easily send a reader

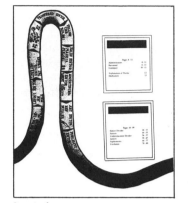

Theme of "Panorama" is games. Pathway of typical game board is visual device that ties yearbook of Spencerport (New York) High into integral unit.

back into memories.

Whatever the theme, it must represent the school in a favorable manner. It cannot glorify a small elite or poke ridicule at any individual or group. Yearbook copy should show the many diverse elements in a student body and how they rally to common goals.

☆ The theme must be handled in a fresh, imaginative manner.

With the theme chosen, senior editors have to develop it in the book's sections. This should be logical and must be unobtrusive. The theme should always be subordinate. It is like a few gold threads in an expensive scarf. They enhance the design but never hide it.

Progression

The next this-year decision is *progression* and *pagination* of the space for each section and subsection, and the order in which they will appear.

☆ Allot space in keeping with the importance of the subject.

There is a tendency to stress the picturesque aspects of school life, action on the athletic field, color on the social scene. But the less glamorous activities in the classroom should not be slighted.

While there are no hard-and-fast rules for allocating space to yearbook sections, a recent Columbia Scholastic Press Association survey showed the following division of editorial coverage in typical yearbooks:

Student Life	15% to 18%
Academics	15% to 18%
Clubs	15% to 18%
Sports	15% to 18%
Students and Faculty	25%
Theme, Opening, Division Pages, and Closing	8%

Advertising and index were not included in compiling the percentage totals.

It's probably easier to determine the order of sections first, then the number of pages for each. This is a typical progression:

Introduction
    Title pages
    Dedication
    Theme explanation
Administration
    School heads
    Faculty
    School superintendent
    School board
Activities
    Clubs
    Traditional events
        Homecoming
        Class proms
        Class plays, etc.
Academics
    Scholastic honors
        Honor societies
        Scholarship winners
        Competition winners
        National Merit Scholarships
        Science Talent Search
    Classroom activities

Sports
> Girls' sports
> Football
> Basketball
> Baseball
> Track
> Swimming
> "Minor" sports

Classes
> Freshman
> Sophomore
> Junior

Seniors
> Commencement
> Honors
> Officers
> Directory

Advertising

There is no "right way" to put together any book. As long as all the important aspects of the school year are included, they may be presented in a number of progressions.

In the one just listed, the introduction comes logically at the beginning and the seniors wind up the book even as they conclude their scholastic careers.

Successful books can be arranged by the calendar. All the events of autumn are given in the first section, then winter activities, and finally those of spring. Football, then, is not in the same section as track nor a Hallowe'en party with a spring prom.

Pagination

Now *rough pagination* is done. From the total pages in the book is subtracted the space for advertising. (This must be an estimate, of course, as the ad staff is just beginning its duties.) Then tentative numbers of pages are allocated to each section.

Yearbooks are printed in signatures of from 4 to 32—and even more—pages on a single sheet of paper. All the pages of a signature must be completed before platemaking and printing can be done. Too often an editor will purr with pride because "over a hundred pages have already gone to the printer!" But if these represent three signatures, each one missing a page or two, it is a far less noble achievement than if only 64 pages, but two complete signatures, had been completed. Plan pagination so you needn't keep a whole signature waiting for a page or two that you know will be one of the last that can be finished.

Now comes the most important "list" of all, the *production chart*. This shows deadlines—and how the staff is meeting them—for the complete book.

All deadlines are based on the date the book is to be distributed. May 15? Ok, allow seven days for shipping from the printer; you're at May 8. Allow four weeks for printing, you're back to April 10. Platemaking, pasteup, typesetting, each sets your starting date back earlier. By working backward like this, you establish a practical set of deadlines.

Production Charts

Because the key factor is the actual printing of the book, the printer should be consulted in the making of the deadline chart.

Such charts vary in slickness. A simple one might be like that in Example 6. The first column gives the initials of the editor. The second shows page numbers and contents. Then come the actual deadlines for each phase of editorial work. Each has 2 columns for the initials of the assigned staffer and the due date. Finally there's the deadline for the complete page and the notation when it was sent to the printer.

When a deadline for one part of the job has been met, the deadline square is filled in. If the deadline was met, the square is colored blue; if it was late, the square is red.

Just like a flashing red light, a red square or an open one yells "Beware!" to the editor who then prods someone to regain lost time by working under forced draft.

The chart may be expanded to indicate (a) receipt of proofs; (b) completion of proofreading; and (c) return to the printer.

A more elaborate chart is shown in Example 7. It shows 16-page signatures and alerts the editor to those that need only a page or two for completion.

☆ Signatures need not be sent to the printer in order.

But each must be complete.

The form of a production chart is not

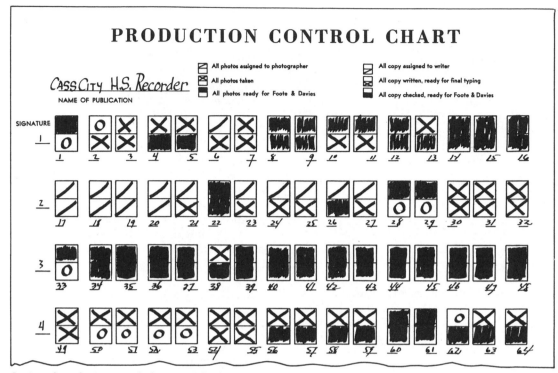

PRODUCTION CONTROL CHART

Cass City H.S. Recorder
NAME OF PUBLICATION

◤ All photos assigned to photographer   ◲ All copy assigned to writer
⊠ All photos taken   ⊠ All copy written, ready for final typing
■ All photos ready for Foote & Davies   ▤ All copy checked, ready for Foote & Davies

Portion of production control chart. (Whole sheet shows 10 signatures, 160 pages.) Top square indicates photos and art; lower portion, copy. Diagonal stroke shows assignment made; cross, assignment completed; black squares, material ready for printer. Zeros show that no material is needed on that page.

Note that first signature still requires art work for Page 6, final check for nine pages. Second signature has just been started; but third signature is ready for printer as soon as art for Page 38 is checked. Signatures need not be sent to printer in order, but each must be complete.

important as long as it gives the necessary information, preferably in a way that clearly shows progress—and especially missed deadlines—at the hastiest of glances.

☆ Yearbook work should be well planned, well controlled, and well recorded.

As the editor does the pagination and sets deadlines, a sticky problem is immediately apparent: The important events at the end of a school year and a school career happen after the deadline for the book.

Whether they recognize it at the time or not, commencement is a milestone for all students. A book purporting to be a record of a school year but not presenting graduation records is like the story of Robinson Crusoe without the last chapter. Do he and Friday live happily ever after?

The simplest solution—although far from perfect—is to record commencement plans. Name the valedictorian and other students who are to be honored; often this information is available before the last deadline. As this is usually confidential information, as few staffers as possible—preferably only the editor—should be involved. Photography from last year's school-close is used for illustrations.

Commencement exercises don't change much from one year to the next. In many instances not even the participants know whether this is a shot from the 1980 exercises or of those in 1981. But many seniors are still dissatisfied; they want a record of their own last days at the school, a period that becomes more poignant and cherished as the years advance.

Fall Publication

This is one of the reasons why some schools are publishing their books in the

Work Progress Chart *ACADEMICS*

Publisher's Deadlines 1st... *Nov. 15* ....
2nd...... *DEC. 13* ....
3rd............ *JAN. 10* ....
4th.................... *FEB. 10* ....

	Ed.	DESCRIPTION OF PAGE	Layout	Due	Art	Due	Photo	Due	Copy	Due	Deadline	Sent
35	FD	Divider	FD	9/17	BB	9/15			FD	9/20	9/30	
36	NM	Classroom Pix	BB	9/24			KT	9/17	KA	9/20		
37	"	" "	"	"			"		"	"		
38	"	" "	"	"			"	"	"	"		
39	"	Honor Roll	"	"			"		"	"		
40	"	Natl Honor Society	"	"			JO		"	9/16		
41	"	" " "	"	"			"		"	"		
42	"	NSF Winners	"	"			"		JB	9/22		
43	"	Science Fair	"	"			"		"	"		
44	"	Key Winners	"	9/25			KT		"	"		
45	"	" "	"	"			"		"	"		
46	"	" "	"	"			"		"	"		
47	EL	Awards Assembly	"	"			"		"	"		
48	EF	Crucible Club	"	9/22			JO		KA	9/16		
49	SJ	Athena Soc.	"	"			KT		"	"	9/30	
50	NM	Best Teacher Award	-	10/7	BB	10/1	S		"	10/1	10/12	
51	"	" " Pix	"	"		"	S		"	"	"	
52	"	Lantern Night	AS	9/22			KT	9/15	NM	9/18	9/30	
53	FD	Students' Creed	AS	"	AS	9/18		"			"	

EXAMPLE 6

Work progress chart. Note that pages are always paired, except first page of the book or section, which, because it is on a righthand page, does not have facing one.

fall. The complete school year can then be recorded. Another attraction is the lower cost. Many yearbook printers are swamped in the spring and then have little work during the summer. To keep their employees and machines gainfully employed during the dog days, they often offer alluring discounts. This might make it financially possible for some schools even to have a yearbook; for others it may provide desirable extras while staying within the original budget.

The main part of an autumn book is prepared on the same schedule as is one for spring delivery. Only those sections covering end-of-school events must be done in the summer. But the staff—unless the editor shows strong leadership—may not be quite as motivated to meet deadlines. To get the book out before classes end is a real incentive; it just isn't matched by a fall date that has no obvious urgency.

There is resistance against fall publication at the start. But many schools report that once the initial shock wears off, students accept and even prefer the later but complete book.

There are a few psychological handicaps, though. Usually the staff scatters—to vacations, jobs, school—during the summer and the final signatures must be done by a handful of workers. Fortunately this is not too heavy a load; an editor and a photographer probably can handle it without breaking their backs.

Delivery is a problem, too. By September or October, graduates are involved in many activities and in many places that make it inconvenient or even impossible to pick up books at the school.

Books may be mailed to the individual directly from the printer's. The staff merely sends the list of names or it may prepare actual mailing labels. Books are mailed only to graduates or underclassmen who have

FORM NUMBER FIFTEEN — THESE 8 PAGES PRINT AT THE SAME TIME		
FORM NUMBER SIXTEEN — THESE 8 PAGES PRINT AT THE SAME TIME		

PAGE NUMBER	PAGE DESCRIPTION	FORM

FORM	PAGE DESCRIPTION	PAGE NUMBER
	Softball Tournament *full-page pic*	113
114	SUB-DIVIDER Page *whole* *in Reverse* GIRLS INTRAMURAL GREEN	
	NO COLOR *Basketball* *½ page of Timmons*	115
116	*Bowling – 2 pix copy*	
	Field Hockey group pic candid of Sally	117
118	ACTIVITIES DIVIDER *hand art in* GREEN	
	Running copy 3 Initials in color	119
120	*Archery 1 pic copy*	
	CHESS *1 pic in line definition 3 pix / copy*	121
122	*Cheerleaders* HEAD IN COLOR *1 pic copy*	
	CHEERLEADER CONTEST *2-color process* FULL PAGE PIC	123
124	*Commerce Club 1 pic – copy*	
	Curtain Call Club 1 group pic; copy	125
126	*"Once Upon A Mattress" 3 pix / Tint block under cover of program*	
	1 pic – DUOTONE copy	127
128	*Film Club – 1 pic French Club – 1 pic / copy*	

PAGES SENT TO KELLER	113 118 122 127 — 114 119 123 128 — 116 120 124 — 117 121 125	ALL 12-5-78
PAGES NEEDED TO COMPLETE SIGNATURE	115 *Sent 12/5* 126	

REMEMBER: THESE SIXTEEN PAGES MUST BE COMPLETE IN ORDER TO PRINT.

EXAMPLE 7

Production chart divided into signatures. On these pages, that fit into looseleaf binder, numbers shown here in black are red in original, those shown here in gray are actually tan. Spot color available on any single page can be used on any other of same designation. Chart stresses importance of completing signatures rather than doing random pages.

moved out of the community. Other students pick up their books at school just as they would on springtime delivery.

Supplements

A possible solution to the dilemma is an *insert,* or *supplement,* a 16-page signature printed after the book itself has already been delivered. Covering spring sports, social events, baccalaureate, and commencement, the supplement completes the record of the school year.

The cover on the regular book is made so that there is room for exactly 16 pages. (You can't make a larger one work; a smaller one is too expensive on a per-page basis.) On the insert is adhesive material. A protective sheet of paper is peeled away, the insert is placed into the book and pressed so it is firmly pasted into place. If this simple operation is done with care, the

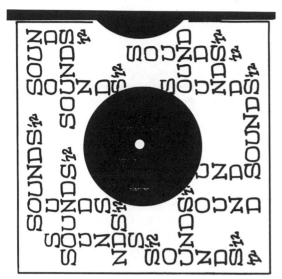

"Sounds of '72" is 33⅓ RPM record issued as supplement to "Maroon" of Kingston (New York) High. It evokes memories with band music, announcements on school PA system, exercise cadence counted in gym, even fire-drill siren.

insert is bound into the cover almost as securely as pages which have been sewn.

Usually the insert is mailed to yearbook buyers during the summer. In this case—as with autumn books that must be mailed—the budget must cover postage and mailing envelopes. The insert may be mailed only to graduates, with other students picking them up after classes begin after Labor Day.

☆ If inserts are to be mailed in the summer, arrangements must be made before school closes for vacation.

Some responsible person who will be around all summer must accept delivery of the inserts and then notify the students who will do the mailing.

As so many staffers are away during vacation, the business manager must be sure that there are enough responsible workers available at the proper time.

The mailers must have an adequate place to work and have access to it. This may not be as simple as it sounds; if you've ever tried to get into almost any school during the summer, you'll know that entry to Fort Knox is not much more difficult.

The mailers must have an adequate sup-

ply of stamps. Before school closes, ask the printer for a 16-page signature of the same paper on which your supplement will be printed. Put it into the same envelope in which it will be mailed. (This will probably be a manila one with a piece of stiff protective cardboard. Or it may be a padded envelope such as is used for mailing books. It's a good idea to send a blank signature from the school—or, preferably, the printer—to the editor's home, using each type of container, and determining which best protects the contents and what postage will be for each method.)

Have the post office weigh the package and determine what the cost will be. Inserts go at "book rate" or as "educational material," which have favorable postal rates.

Perhaps your school has a postage meter and will let your mailers use it. This saves loss, damage, or pilferage of stamps, and provides an accurate record of postage expenditures.

The insert should be a major sales point when orders are taken and should be stressed throughout the year. A Mimeographed sheet of paper placed in the yearbook—and all other communications media in your school—should inform students of the approximate time they can expect the insert in the mail.

The package should be conspicuously identified by imprinting or affixed labels, another job to do before school-year end.

A covering letter gives instructions for pasting in the insert tightly and permanently.

The danger, of course, is that the envelope may be overlooked and misplaced before the student is aware of its arrival. Even worse, it may be discarded as "junk mail" without even being opened.

Some inserts will be lost, in the mails or in the student's home. So it's wise to have the printer run off some extras. For a book with large circulation, 2% or 3% is an adequate overrun. With smaller numbers, extras may be as many as 10% to 20%.

Then, in the fall, you can give these extras—or sell them for a minimal price—to those students who haven't received theirs. Any left over can be used for display during the sales campaign. Or they can be given or sold to people who are pictured in the insert. Many a student would like to send this record of graduation to relatives or friends and in a few schools the overrun is made quite high just to met this demand.

If you consider an insert even vaguely, discuss it as soon as possible with your printer to get budget and deadline data that will enable you to make a sound decision. The printer doesn't have to know until late in the winter whether you will have a supplement. But the cover manufacturer must know before beginning work so as to leave room for the insert.

Inserts—with all the extra work they require—do make a better book. This should be all the incentive a staff needs to take on the additional chores and deadlines involved.

The sums of money involved in a yearbook are substantial, probably the greatest expenditures a student will control until his vocational career begins. This job of producing a yearbook is a big one; it demands savvy, reliability—and firm production control.

Make your lists. Then enforce the deadlines they set.

☆ Deadlines are sacred.

Writing and Editing

With the theme selected and the production charts ready to show the flow of copy to the printer, staffers swing to gathering text and pictures. Contemporary yearbooks should be far more than picture books with name identifications, academic statistics, and records of sports and other competitive standings. But these are always included, too.

Although concentrating coverage on their schools, editors should not rule out the local community and the whole wide world. Schools are not ivory towers today—if they ever were. Students live in a larger world in which the smaller academic sphere is a part. Events far removed from classrooms, laboratories, and athletic fields may change a school's activities, even aspects of student life style. For instance, back during the winter of 1973–1974, the oil embargo and

gasoline shortage were a vital part of school life. Some yearbook editors included pictures of "No Gas" signs and other such material among their coverage of that school year. A good book's editor tells not only how it was at the high school that year but also how the world around Central High was that year.

But off-campus events should be recorded only if they had direct effects on the student's life as a student.

Basic techniques of writing and editing for a yearbook are essentially those of a newspaper or magazine which were discussed in Chapters 6, 7, 9, and 17. There are some noteworthy differences, however.

While all periodicals should strive for good writing, the longer life span of yearbook writing and the lack of intense deadline pressure found on papers and magazines should spur the staff to its highest possible efforts for quality and accuracy. Yearbook writers and editors should use that extra time until deadline to polish their copy. That includes eliminating clichés and too much slang. Colloquialisms of the moment fade rapidly and will appear somewhat funny or even unintelligible several decades in the future. "Purple prose" may be even worse in the yearbook than in newspaper or magazine because it's reread for years and decades. A yearbook's schedule allows time to write, to rewrite, and then to polish still further.

☆ Don't hesitate to rewrite your copy— or anyone else's.

Like other journalists, yearbook staff members should avoid dull lead-ins such as those beginning with "This year . . . ," "Coached by . . . ," or "Under the direction of. . . ." A first line of type should grab a reader's attention as much as a headline.

Some editors have used a literary essay to introduce each section with a high degree of success. Thus the yearbook has its own brand of in-depth reporting that sets mood and tone for the more traditional pages of text and pictures.

Since each conventional yearbook section presents its own peculiar problems, let's look at each in a bit of detail.

Good on-the-scene action photographs are especially vital in a student-life section. Pictures must record a cross-section of the entire student body, not just class officers and other students who gain attention repeatedly in the school newspaper or magazine.

In the academic section, tell the story from students' point of view, not the faculty's. Field trips to the state capital or neighboring scientific laboratory are highly attractive topics. Use class displays or lively classroom discussions instead of picturing a teacher standing at the front of a room.

Athletics include more than the traditional football, basketball, baseball, and track squads. An estimated two-thirds of any student body participate in no organized sports at all. They deserve coverage of their own sports action—skiing, bowling, horseback riding, and motorcycling as well as the interscholastic competitions that attract cheering crowds.

The clubs and organization section should capture the behind-the-scenes action showing some of the excitement that nonclub members never see. For instance, record and picture the stage crew building sets or an electrician maneuvering lights as well as showing the stars of the Dramatic Club production.

☆ There should be continuity in yearbook copy.

Differences in style between copy blocks in the academics section and sports pages, for example, should never be so great that readers are aware of a change. Ideally, the whole yearbook should read as if it were written by one person.

☆ Copy should be read by several people. Proofs by just as many.

The section editor and then the editor-in-chief are responsible for the highest standards of quality and accuracy. But human errors are reduced if several more people check.

☆ The editor-in-chief should read every word of copy before it goes to the printer.

Preferably, copy should be read in continuity, as it will appear in the yearbook.

Because copy goes to the printer piecemeal, the editor should keep carbons. After reading edited manuscript for—let's say—pages 80 to 96, an editor should check copy for preceding and following pages 78, 79, 97, 98, etc. If any has already been set in type, necessary changes are made in the live copy, not in type already set, to blend it into the others.

☆ Editing text in type costs money.

Copy Control

Yearbook copy editors have a much more rigid copy-control job than their opposite numbers on periodicals; space allotted for copy in a yearbook spread is inflexible. Many printers supply copy sheets on which finished copy is typed. These have vertical rules to show how wide to type copy to produce desired line lengths in various type sizes and faces.

If your printer doesn't have such sheets, you can make your own easily. A printer will furnish you with sample blocks of the body type. If you have, say, a block on a sports page that measures 18 picas wide by 4 inches deep, measure 18 picas on the type specimen. Count out several lines to determine the average number of characters per line. Then set your typewriter to that count. Type each line as close to full as possible without breaking words unduly.

Measure 4 inches on the specimen block to determine how many lines will fit into the available area on the spread. Remember that only full lines should be counted; if a fraction of a line extends beyond the specified area, it may bump into a picture or some other page element.

Some yearbook staffs like to have every copy block written so the last line is full. Short lines are called *widows* and a generation ago typographers labored mightily to "kill the widow." Today the tendency is to ignore widows if the lines are longer than one-third of the whole. If copy has been properly written, it is not wise to change it just so the type comes out in a neat square. The addition or elimination of words may well destroy the rhythm of well-written copy. If widows do bother you a lot, you may instruct the printer to center the last line.

☆ The function of type is to carry a message, not to create neat rectangles.

Editors should use common sense in handling widows. They wouldn't let only "es" stand alone in the last line or even a whole word as short as "I" or "all." Eliminating extremely short widows doesn't require massive surgery on the proof. But remember that killing widows becomes those author's alterations which are billed as extra composition costs against your budget.

Some yearbook staffs abuse "downstyle," the practice of minimizing use of capital letters. A few go to such extremes as using "june" and "san francisco" instead of "June" and "San Francisco." Worse yet, they even use downstyle for proper names. It should never be "principal joseph smith" or "quarterback jerry cline." They are individuals and their names are proper nouns. To lower case proper names is insulting, stupid—and incorrect.

☆ Proper nouns are capped.

Yearbooks started out, like the literary reviews, to display student work in creativity. But as more and more pictures were added, the text shrank. Contemporary yearbooks, however, are turning back to more logical balance of reporting of what happened in the school this year with both words and illustrations.

Some of those added words have provided in-depth reporting that preserves feelings, emotions, and reactions of the student body. Sometimes this is done more effectively in words than in pictures. Some things can't be captured by photographs despite the tremendous impressiveness of this art form. So the yearbook's written words must always be an integral part, not just something to fill up space around pictures.

If the job of combining words and pictures is done well by a yearbook staff, their classmates will enjoy their achievements both now and years from now. That is the student body's tribute to good yearbook planning and production.

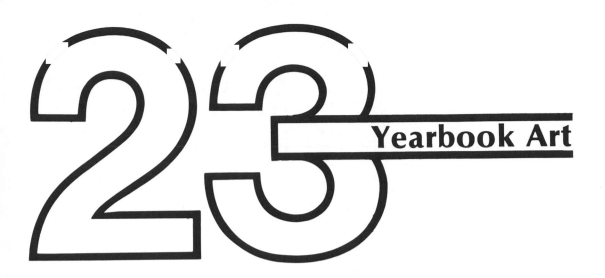

Yearbook Art

Simple arithmetic shows that pictures occupy a major portion of the space in a yearbook and even a quick look at the budget shows that photographic costs are equally high.

The subject of yearbook pictures must then be approached from two angles. Most important is the function of capturing memories; but also important is the economics, the costs involved. Both angles are further complicated because this is the only creative area in a typical book that combines work by student and professional photographers.

Yearbook art consists of photography and hand art. Principles previously discussed apply to all forms of student journalism and the yearbook staff is urged to reread Chapter 12, maybe even before continuing on this page.

Photography Planning

We'll look at photography first because it represents most of the pictures in a typical book.

☆ Good photo reportage demands good planning.

The first decision is: Do we use professional or student photographers? The logical answer is: Yes.

Professionals are best equipped to do individual and group portraits. Their experience and skill assures high quality of these important photos. The student photographer is more involved with the school and yearbook, tells the story from the student's viewpoint, and is right on the scene for those unplanned, unforeseen shots that delight the reader. The professional knows that taking portraits of an entire graduating class produces substantial extra business and so will usually furnish the portrait for the senior section at no cost to the staff and often will cover major news events without extra charge.

Choice of the professional photographer is an important one. The staff should discuss this in detail with the printer, advisor, and principal. Yearbook photography places burdens on people, facilities, and timetables that many good studios are just not equipped to meet. There must be assurances that the studio will meet all deadlines; otherwise the staff will be in parlous straits.

☆ Choose student photographers with great care.

First look at the applicant's work; is its quality high enough to meet the staff's standards? Then check on the student's reliability. Many an editor started on the road to ulcers because a student photographer forgot to cover an important assignment or thought it was more important to go on a date than to soup up the negatives.

Does the student photog have adequate camera and darkroom facilities? If the staff owns its own equipment and has a darkroom in the school, the problem is almost solved. But in many instances the student must furnish both and even under the best of circumstances will have to or want to do some work at home, late at night, or over weekends when the school is tightly locked.

A satisfactory arrangement is to have professionals do all the developing and printing for student photography. This usually effects substantial savings. (Note that it's necessary to keep a very close tab on all photo paper and chemicals used by staffers. Costs run high, wastage is easy, temptation is constant to make an extra print and give it to Debbie or Ray.) Sometimes students will do their own developing with the pro doing the printing. In many instances the professional will allow the student to use studio darkrooms or even cameras and many a young person has gone directly from this informal "apprenticeship" into a paying job at the studio.

When you were working out your set of deadlines, as discussed in Chapter 22, photo deadlines were set also. These, too, work backward from the time the platemaker requires copy. Be sure to discuss these with the professional photographer. To make just individual portraits for a typical senior class is a big job. Yet the pro has other work to do and can't devote full time to your assignments nor interrupt other jobs to get to yours immediately.

But just one late or overlooked picture can hold up a whole signature and throw the staff's timetable miserably awry.

A detailed list of formal pictures should be made the previous spring. Then the editor already knows that there will be approximately X number of graduating seniors, umpteen clubs, and umpty-ump athletic teams that must be pictured. The list is checked and, if necessary, revised as soon as autumn work begins.

☆ Photo assignments must be planned well in advance.

All photo assignments—except those obvious spur-of-the-moment ones that can't be anticipated—should be made in writing. The *photo order card* should tell the subject of the photo, approximate size in which it will be used (if that's known at this time), horizontal or vertical composition, light or dark tone, and right or left lines of force.

Photo assignment slip gives time, place, and subject, indicates approximate shape of picture desired to fit layout and approximate size of picture in print. If picture is to be very small, cameraman will avoid minute details that might be lost in extreme reduction. (Courtesy Jahn & Ollier Engraving Co.)

☆ All photo assignments should clear through the picture editor.

This will avoid duplication and will increase efficiency when a photographer can make several assignments in one trip. If there are any special instructions, the photo editor or the section editor should discuss them with the photog and amplify written instructions with oral ones if necessary.

Order cards are made out in duplicate. The photog takes the original (and uses the back of it for identifications). The editor keeps the carbon to guard against missed assignments.

A simple but good system is to place nine hooks on the wall near the picture editor's desk. These are labeled with the days of the week, "Future" and "Next Week." As soon as an order card is received, it is entered on the master photo schedule and the card goes on the "Future" or "Next Week" hook. Each evening, before going home, the editor moves cards from the "Next Week" hook to the proper day of the week. Thus on Tuesday night, the daily hooks will contain cards for the four remaining days of that week plus Sunday through next-week Tuesday.

When the assignment is made, many editors send a confirming notice to the president, secretary, or teacher of the involved group. This is a reminder of time and place, if the group should wear special clothing or bring props, and what phone number to call if the appointment must be changed.

☆ Establish—then stick to—a policy regarding postponed group shots.

Many staffs require a 48-hour notice to reschedule a group shot and 24 hours for an individual. It's important to police this rigidly. If the photographer must come back two or three times to get a shot of the Spanish Club, the Future Teachers have a right to demand the same.

☆ Instruct the photographer exactly how long to wait for latecomers.

Every group has at least one prima donna who has to dash into the washroom to apply more lipstick or just forgets about the date or who knows—and enjoys the fact—that everyone will wait for the grand arrival.

But if you shoot the Spanish Club despite Secretary Suzie's absence, the word will quickly get around and other groups will be on time and in full strength for their appointments.

Ten minutes ought to be the maximum that a photographer will wait for latecomers.

☆ Photographers must follow instructions.

Often, on arrival at the scene, a better way of shooting or posing may suggest itself. But the photog should first get what the assignment calls for and then do the "better" shot as an addition.

☆ Candid shots should be scheduled, not left to chance.

Continuing events need no extra *insurance shots*. If a shot in the parking lot turns out unusable, it can be repeated tomorrow

Caricatures of professional quality by R. B. Lokody enhance "Perannos" of New Canaan (Connecticut) High.

or next week. But be sure your schedule allows for such repeat work.

☆ Avoid photographic clichés.

If you can't avoid them, at least minimize them. The staff ought to draw up a list of the common clichés and insist that these will not be used in the book.

The list is long and the titles of these trite and timeworn poses are self-explanatory:

The handshaker; the check-passer; the pointer; execution at dawn—the stiff and pained subjects lined up awaiting a burst of rifle fire; three-people-and-a-piece-of-paper; the smile-with-approval; the fig leaf.

☆ Senior editors should meet weekly to review and revise photo assignments.

Postponed assignments and those that need reshooting may pile up so much that it will become most difficult to meet deadlines.

Yearbook Photography

The basic photographs in a yearbook are: Portraits, group pictures, news shots, atmosphere and mood, targets of opportunity, candids of various kinds, picture stories and picture essays.

Senior Portraits

Senior portraits are the most important single section of a yearbook. If other student portraits are used, they run a close second. While individuals ought to have final decision on the quality of their own portraits, the staff still has a responsibility for overall quality of the portrait section.

Students sitting for individual portraits should be advised to wear simple and appropriate clothes. Some communities interpret this as jacket and necktie for boys. Because some boys may not own such encumbrances, the staff provides this apparel for the occasion.

Girls will be happier in the long run with simple blouses or sweaters. Hollywoodish clothing (and makeup) tend to look cheap and gaudy. Sorority drapes, fashioned from fabric in a deep V from off the shouders, are resented by many students as status symbols.

A look at a 1950 yearbook will convince you that people with simple hair styling still look good while those who were in high style at that time look rather ridiculous.

Go easy on jewelry, too, in interests of simplicity.

While students have the right to wear anything they want, the staff also has the right to reject pictures that don't meet its standards—if those standards have been spelled out in advance and proper notice given.

The professional photographer should be instructed to avoid theatrical poses, to use the same basic background and lighting for each subject, to shoot in sharp focus; to retouch all pictures and to make all head sizes the same size.

Faculty Portraits

Senior portraits must be standardized; no one would argue that very much. But faculty portraits, because they are fewer, can be individualized enough so they will truly perform the function of a portrait. That is not to say, "This is the way Miss Jones looks." Rather, it should be, "This is the way Miss Jones *is*." A good candid shot is undoubtedly the best way to accomplish this.

A candid is not a fortunate accident. The photographer studies the subject, trying to find a stance, expression, or gesture that is uniquely characteristic. Only after long studying is the actual shot made. By chang-

Faculty pictures are all informal or candid in "Archive" of Northeast High, Philadelphia, Pennsylvania. Top-right photo is dominant, nucleus for pleasing page pattern. White space is all at outside.

ing the angle of the shot, the lighting or the exposure, the photographer produces a *manipulated candid* that many believe is the highest form of photographic art.

Of course, regular studio portraits of the faculty may be used, although much pleasant flavor is lost thereby.

Group Pictures

Making a good group picture is probably the most difficult job of the yearbook photographer. The first problem is that of composition; subjects must be arranged so that the grouping is pleasant yet so each individual's face is unobstructed and unmarred by heavy shadows. The photographer must always make a final check, just before snap-

Long sheet of print-out paper is appropriate prop for group picture of Computer Club in "Accolade" of McQuaid Jesuit High in Rochester, New York.

ping the shot, that all faces are on proper display.

The photographer must pose the group. Don't let the subjects pose themselves; only a person looking through the view-finder of a camera knows whether a pose is good.

Space between heads is always waste space. Subjects must be grouped much more tightly than they would normally arrange themselves. Keep both horizontal and vertical space between heads at a minimum.

A common flaw of composition is to have more than one group in a group picture. Don't have more than one "point of interest" toward which the subjects are looking. In fact, the camera itself is the best object upon which all of the group should gaze. If part of a committee is looking at a poster for Homecoming Week and the rest examine the crown the queen will wear, you have two "pictures" even though they are both on the same piece of photo paper.

Posing groups is a problem that weighs heavily upon yearbook photographers, though, and you might look at a few guidelines.

Beware of backgrounds. Drapery and wallpaper that are pleasant to the human eye often become accentuated by the camera. It is disconcerting to have a lighting fixture become antlers on a human or to have the foliage of drapery seem to grow out of the subject's ears.

Be especially wary of highly glossy walls or, especially, framed pictures or oil paintings in the background. They reflect light in flaring and unpleasant "hot spots."

☆ Group pictures are best shot against a plain background.

Ordinary, plain bed sheets—in pastel colors rather than white—make inexpensive but excellent backdrops. Rings sewn to one edge are hung on hooks in the molding or walls of the shooting room.

A fun thing is to take group shots in unusual sites and often unusual costumes. But this can be dangerous. If the background is too exotic, it may overshadow the human subjects. And if the group decides to pose in costume—unless it's a play cast, of course, or a Spanish Club in fiesta—the picture will fail to show how the subjects really looked in the year being recorded.

If the group is fairly small, outdoor settings can be most pleasant. Posing the group on a stairway, for instance, gives opportunity for the tall, narrow shot that adds so much to a page but is difficult to achieve in group photos. The setting, though, must always be—if not appropriate —at least not obtrusive or distracting.

Most group shots will be made indoors. It is necessary to have a room large enough

Poor posing fragments this photo into two distinct portions as indicated by broken lines.

Poor cropping wastes one third area of this photo. Cropping along broken lines would eliminate extraneous, dull areas.

so that people may change places during the posing process with ease and speed. The room must, obviously, be long enough for the camera to take in the whole group. Ceilings ought to be high enough to avoid erratic bouncing of light.

Spectators should be barred. The bystanders' inevitable wisecracking and heckling of the subjects make them self-conscious and the resulting photos will not be good.

In scheduling, be sure not to create bad traffic jams by having large groups follow each other too closely. If possible, alternate large and small groups. If the room has two doors, use one for entrance, the other for exit, again to avoid jams. School administrators are valuable allies in helping to plan a shooting schedule for groups and finding adequate space for the posing.

Lighting must be well balanced in group shots. There must be at least two light sources from the front of the group in order that every face will have the same tonal value. The background should be lighted with a subordinate source. Even in outdoor

shots, there is need for a "fill-in flash" to balance sunshine. Groups should be posed in "open shade," away from strong and direct sunlight that causes subjects to squint and produces ugly, heavy shadows.

Never shoot with the flash on the camera; it causes those dark menacing shadows that loom behind the subject. If a single flash is used, it should be taken off the camera and held as high and as far to one side as possible. Or the flash may be bounced off the ceiling in a familiar technique.

The darker the subject's complexion the more light is required. The photographer should experiment until he finds the proper exposure for dark people, not only Blacks but Orientals and Caucasians as well.

News Pictures

News pictures are records of noteworthy events. Even before taking off the lens cover, the photographer asks, "Just what is this picture supposed to say?" Suppose it should say, "Sam DeLauri is our exchange student to Argentina." The clichés—Sam shaking hands with the AFS chairman; Sam being handed an envelope by the principal; Sam, Mr. Brown, and Principal Smith

Mood shot is fitting last page. Familiar scene of closing of school day effectively closes book also. No captions are necessary on rare picture like this.

Atmosphere Pictures

Atmosphere shots are those that evoke strong emotion and memories. These are the "artiest" of all photographs. The photographer must do much planning to find the exact position and the exact time of day to capture the stately entrance to the school, the emptying parking lot on a winter's afternoon, the lunchroom line, or the group lounging around the burger shop across the street.

Targets of Opportunity

Targets of opportunity are, in a large sense, "lucky shots." These are unpredictable and unrepeatable occurrences. The dog that wanders on the stage during honors assembly, the principal washing an office window for a clear view of a lovely day, the football captain vainly trying to retrieve a bottle of milk that's sliding off his cafeteria tray. When these vignettes occur, the photographer must, of course, be lucky enough to be on the scene, but must also be perceptive and quick enough to record it on film.

Picture Stories and Essays

Picture stories tell a narrative in chronological order. It might be, say, about the student manager of the football team on game day. He comes in early to check uniforms and equipment, he hands out tape to the players, he dries the ball during the

lined up for the firing squad—do not report the story. So why not ask Sally Strong, who was in Argentina last year, whether she has some souvenir that says "South America." The picture might be of Sally—or Mr. AFS —putting a sombrero or serape on Sam. That tells the story more interestingly, to be sure, and probably more accurately.

Most sports shots are news shots. The casual reader may think the photog has just been lucky to get a shot of Stretch Jenkins putting in the winning basket. But it wasn't luck. The photographer has noticed that when the score is tight or tied in the last minute, the coach always has the team maneuver so that Stretch gets a chance at his famous hook shot just before the whistle. So the photog went up in the balcony and got in position to capture the decisive play from the most advantageous angle. No luck here, just good planning.

Unusual composition adds so much charm that it makes up for large areas of photograph that otherwise would be wasted.

TROUBADOUR STAFF MEMBERS

Ahrens, Paul (Layout Editor), 5
Aron, Neree (Assistant Editor), 13
Baga, Julie (Editor), 8
Dixon, Tim
Gebelein, Richard
Gerhard, Ed, 14
Grossman, Karen
Haas, Ruth, 3
Hushebeck, Sarah, 1

Kirsh, Louise, 2
Landis, Jane, 10
Lang, Cindy
Lucier, Bob, 12
McIntyre, Don
Miller, Bob
Mitchell, Joy
Sano, Jeanne, 7
Sarosky, Cheryl, 6

Smith, Laura, 4
Tourville, Pat
Trout, Sue
Von Zatorski, Sioux
Walsh, Deb, 11
Whittaker, Don, 9
Ms. Marina Hollenshead (Art Advisor)
Ms. Janet Martin (Literary Advisor)

Identification of irregularly posed subjects is made easy by numbering in outline diagram. This is staff of "Troubadour," literary magazine of North Penn High in Lansdale, Pennsylvania.

game, he fixes a broken strap on a helmet and, finally, he shares in the exultation of victory.

A picture essay, however, is more concerned with emotion and reaction of the photographer and the viewer. It starts out with a pictorial statement: "An after-school job is very satisfying." Various satisfactions are shown: Meeting interesting customers in a store, learning a skill in a garage, expanding on an academic education, getting background for future education or job plans, and, of course, getting that neat paycheck. Like mood shots, the picture essay offers a fine chance to show the photographer's creativity, sensitivity, and skill.

Needs of Layout Editor

The photographer must always remember that the picture must be part of a layout, reproduced by a printing press.

No printed image can be better than the original photo. So technical excellence is very important. But there are other factors that must also be fulfilled. These are the need for *harmony, contrast,* and *lines of force.*

Photographic Harmony

Harmony is a pleasant repetition of like or similar forms. The popular *pattern shot* is an example: Stacks of textbooks awaiting first-day distribution; reiterated patterns of louvers in a row of lockers; a neat pattern of tables in the chemistry lab taken from an unusual vantage point.

Harmony comes, too, from similar poses or expressions in pictures taken at very different times and places: A basketball referee holding a peremptory arm exactly as the traffic cop at the crossing does; a girl smiling over an ice cream cone; a teacher smiling over a good paper.

Harmony comes from common subject matter: How a dozen students attack a pizza or a giant submarine, hoagie, grinder, or whatever a Herculean sandwich is called in your school.

Harmony comes from the same subject captured in various moods: The statute of Lincoln in your school, all alone at dusk, surrounded by students at the start of the day, sharp in the summer sun, and hazy in the thin light of winter.

Harmony can be captured by the photographer and it can be found—even in disparate photos—by the editor.

Photographic Contrast

Contrast is achieved by many techniques, too.

Contrast may be tonal: The deep gloomy

picture against the delicate high-key shot. It can come from camera position. Notice how a television or movie photog constantly changes range; long shots will mix with closeups, floor-level scenes with those taken from a high vantage point.

Contrast comes from differing shapes. Most reproduced photos are at—or very near to—a 3 x 5 ratio. So any long and skinny shot or wide, shallow one will not only give pleasant contrast but will add great *dynamic thrust* to a page.

And, of course, contrast may be obvious: A towering basketball player and a tiny cheerleader; a section of the grandstand after your team has scored and after the opponents have; a bundled-up student entering school in January and one at the same door attired for summer heat.

Lines of Force

Proper lines of force are perhaps the most necessary for layout purposes. Pictures must "face into the page." And this is hard to do when all available shots for a spread face in the same direction.

This "facing" of a picture is produced by its lines of force. Any strong action carries the reader's eye along with it. So does a person or object pointing or even looking. There are many less obtrusive but just as strong "arrows" in most pictures. The human form has many arrows: Nose, arms, fingers, legs and feet, not to mention the V of a shirt collar or the folds in a dress. The editor must always look for such arrows and make sure they guide the reader into important elements on a page, not to unimportant or blank areas and certainly never off the page.

The photographer must provide lines of force in both directions, left or right. At a baseball game, for instance, you can't always stand on the first-base line; the runner will always be moving left to right. Sometimes you must shoot across, to the third-base line, where action will be right to left. It is important to change position often at an athletic event but the principle applies to all occasions where more than one picture will be taken. If the photographer always keeps this in mind, the layout editor will have a choice in direction, not only among pictures taken at a single event but those shot at many times and places.

Tonal Quality

☆ Photos must have good tonal value.

Because there is always tonal loss in a reproduced picture, you must start out with the highest possible technical quality. A good gage is the Kodak Gray Scale which you can buy for pennies at any camera shop.

Lay the scale on the picture and compare the tones. Ideally "white" areas should be no darker than 10% gray and "black" areas no lighter than 90%. Middle tones should have full gradation.

In portraits, examine the deep shadows along the cheekbones and under the nose and mouth. If they're too heavy they make the poor subject look like a fugitive from a horror movie. Make sure that teeth and the whites of eyes are bright; white clothing must be lighter than the lightest flesh tones.

Editors soon learn to make at least preliminary evaluation just by looking at a picture, using the gray scale only to check out their original quick judgment.

Make sure that there is visible detail in all shadow areas. And make sure that focus is crisp. Occasionally a photographer will shoot in *soft focus* to create a misty effect. But all too often such "soft focus" pictures are merely out-of-focus shots.

If a photo doesn't meet standards for platemaking, have the photographer do it over. Often this sets off a hassle; the student photographer may take this as an insult to ability and performance—a deadly personal insult. But the editor can't tolerate this; quality must be maintained even if temperament raises its ugly head. And if the photographer can't—or worse yet, won't —do an adequate job, get a new one.

Often student editors are reluctant to return a print to a professional photographer because they doubt their ability to judge professional work. However, if this is done courteously and reasonably, the pro will not take umbrage. A studio runs prints through in such great quantities that an occasional fluff does sneak through. And most studio work is for display of the original. There's a lot of difference between Junior's portrait in a frame on the mantelpiece and one that is printed in a yearbook. Two sets of standards apply and you must always use the proper yardstick.

In printed reproduction, many editors insist that heads be the size of a dime. This is a bit generous, a slightly smaller size will do. But make sure that all faces in print are big enough to be recognizable.

When two or more groups of the same size appear on the same printed page, head sizes in both shots should be equal.

Special Photo Treatment

Editors can enhance the photographer's work by using manipulative techniques. But they can just as easily depreciate the worth of a good picture by inept handling. So those techniques must be used with skill—and always sparingly.

Two terms consistently misused are *montage* and *collage*. A montage is a single photograph made by using two or more negatives. Its use is commonplace and usually the effect is pleasant. A collage is made by pasting together pieces of more than one photograph into a single visual unit. This rarely works out and there are veteran professional editors who insist that in their whole lifetime they've never seen a good collage. This is such a widespread feeling among the pros that the student editor is wise to throw this technique into the trash basket.

If two or more separate pictures are run as one element, there must be distinct and adequate separation, by white lines at least 1 pica wide.

Bas reliefs can be made photographically and are striking for simple, especially architectural, subjects. This method requires two negatives, the regular kind and a positive transparency made by exposing a normal negative to film instead of photopaper. The two films, slightly out of register, are taped together and used as a single negative to print a glossy.

An interesting effect is obtained by lay-

Special screens add interest to otherwise ordinary photos. This is parallel-line screen with dropout of white areas in face and hair.

This is blow-up so regular halftone dot pattern becomes conspicuous.

This is "steel engraving" screen. Note that some platemakers have their own names for special screens; be sure to use proper designation on your platemaker's copy.

ing a piece of loosely woven fabric over the photo paper before exposing it.

Reverses make striking effects, the image appearing in white on a black background. They are made by using a positive transparency for a photoprint, or the platemaker can reverse the tones.

Solarization is a controlled accident. After photo paper has been exposed in the normal way through a negative, the top lights in the darkroom are turned on for a brief instant. The result is striking but unpredictable. This technique is fun to experiment with but it may use up lots of expensive materials.

Sequence pictures require special care. These are a series of shots like frames clipped from a movie film, showing progression of a continuing action.

In sequences, each picture should be the same width, like those movie frames. This helps the reader orient the action in identical fields of view. An interesting technique is to blow up just one of these frames to show extra detail; but this should be in addition to that picture in the size of the other shots.

Hand Art

Photography carries the major burden of communicative art in a yearbook. But hand art comes into its own in developing the theme and creating mood. It is useful for ornamentation and as an accent in a page otherwise totally photographic. Divider pages are especially striking in hand art.

Varieties of hand art are legion. There is no need here to give how-to instructions; there are many good books on the subject and, of course, art students—who undoubtedly will be making up most of your staff of artists—are learning techniques in class or have good advice available from their art teachers.

Some of the more popular media are illustrated on these pages and should be sufficient to spur the interest of editor and artist.

Line work should be done only in black India ink and on white paper, preferably that with a slight blue tinge.

Ideally such art should be made 50% wider than the printed picture. If reduction is greater than that, fine lines may become crowded and clogged. But some reduction sharpens the drawing and certainly reduces flaws in the original art.

Watercolors and oil paintings can make good yearbook art. But if it is their color that is striking, a black-and-white reproduction may be disappointing. If the paintings are done especially for the yearbook, the artist might be urged to do them in monochrome—using only one color in its various tones.

The original paintings may be sent to the platemaker. But in a busy commercial camera room, it may be impossible to give them the tender loving care that their creators would prefer. So, as insurance, the originals may be photographed. This not only eliminates danger to them but enables the editor to see how well a color original will reproduce in b & w.

Pencil and pastel drawings are relatively costly to produce since the background must be removed by a special process.

The hand-art version of a collage creates a picture by pasting together pieces of paper of various textures or tonal treatment. If it is the texture of the paper alone that creates the desired effect, the original should be photographed with a strong light source placed so that the surface of the paper casts strong shadows.

Three-dimensional art not only provides pleasant variety but uses talents not usually associated with the print medium. Sculpture in clay, papier-mâché, and paper must be photographed to make platemaker's copy. So the photographer, by proper lighting, can greatly enhance the work of the sculptor.

The same clip books that were discussed in Chapter 15 may be used for yearbooks, of course. The slight chance of duplication by another yearbook is very slim and may be eliminated, to all practical purposes by modifying the original clip art by adding areas of black or Zip-A-Tone or by combining two or more clips into a collage.

Handling of Art Work

☆ Whatever the art, hand or photo, it's fragile and should be handled with care.

☆ 1. Avoid fingerprints on photographs.

☆ 2. Never write on the front of a photo,

Mosaic cropping not only adds variety to page but emphasizes vertical action of basketball. Such cropping captures spirit of game but loses accuracy of specific detail so should not be used for record pictures.

Line conversion can create pleasant portraits. Because much detail is eliminated by this method, editor must make sure that likeness of subject is not lost.

or on the back of any art, with anything harder than a grease pencil.

☆ 3. Don't try to smooth warped photos; the emulsion is sure to crack. (If a glossy is curled too tightly, rewash it and put it through the dryer again.)

☆ 4. Keep paperclips far away from art.

☆ 5. Be sure unwanted pencil lines are erased from hand art.

☆ 6. Continue your care when you ship art work to the printer. It must be packed flat, never rolled.

☆ 7. Use heavy corrugated board, *top and bottom,* and stout Manila envelopes.

☆ 8. Be sure to mark the package "PHO-
TOGRAPHS—DO NOT BEND."

Conspicuous red labels with this copy can
be bought at any stationery store; they're
a good investment.

In the field of yearbook art, especially
photography, the staff is competing with the
top professional talent of the world. Your
readers are exposed to such fine work in
every periodical they read and they expect
to find the same quality in their yearbook.

This is a little unrealistic; even the most
talented student photographer shouldn't be
expected to match David Douglas Duncan or
Richard Avedon's work. Yet your readers
expect just that. The familiar subject
matter of a yearbook is a tremendous asset,
of course. People will give higher marks to
a fair picture of someone or something they
know than they will to a technically perfect
photo of a distant or unknown subject.

So the editor and photographer must
concentrate on giving readers the kind of
photo coverage they want at the highest
possible level of photographic quality.

24 **Yearbook Layout**

What do a good yearbook editor and a champion figure skater have in common? Control.

A skater spins and whirls in what seems mad abandon; but always the body is under complete control, yet so effortlessly that the audience is unaware of the rigid self-discipline involved.

So with good yearbook layout. It is "creativity completely disciplined."

The weakest yearbook is the flamboyant one, one that indulges in spectacular leaps of fancy and gaudy typographic arabesques —but runs away from its designer.

Student editors often chafe under discipline from without and are too lazy or weak to impose self-discipline. They point to contemporary magazines, especially those appealing to younger audiences, and adopt those standards of typography. The editors forget, though, that the faddy magazine lasts only a month while their yearbooks last a lifetime. Things that are fun for a short-lived occasion get awfully boring and distasteful as a steady diet.

Yearbook layout is an art; it does demand creativity. This cannot be taught; but it can be learned. This book—just like a good teacher—can help a student learn creativity.

Good layout is also a skill and that skill can be guided by a set of precepts that printers have learned and developed since the days of Gutenberg.

☆ Layout must be functional.
This has been said before in this book

but it is so important that it must be said again. Every element in a layout—and the layout as a whole—must do a useful, necessary job. Three of them, in fact:

1. The layout must create a pattern pleasant to the eye so the looker is attracted and converted into a reader;

2. The layout must lead the reading eye through all the areas, and expose it to all the elements, of a spread; and

3. The layout must help communicate by linking words and pictures logically and obviously.

☆ Layout must be organic.
A good page pattern grows from the material the designer must work with. As that material, naturally, changes from one spread to another, so the layout must change, too.

Immediately you see the fallacy of doing layouts in advance of writing the copy and taking the pictures. To plan a layout and later make the material conform to the pattern is like planning a dinner before you know what kind of food will be available. Barbecued sardines and fried rice with whipped cream are an improvisation just a little less appetizing than many yearbook spreads. They are fine as abstract patterns but poor as the actual presentation of available food—or typographic elements.

In an organic layout the designer decides what element best expresses the most important idea of the spread. This element— art, head, or copy—is spotlighted; all other

Miniature dummies enable editor to study progression and assure both harmony and contrast. Gray areas indicate use of color. Note that all pages with circled numbers are printed on front side of press sheet; all others, on back. If color is available on either side of the sheet, all pages on that side can use color at no extra charge. (Courtesy Foote & Davies)

components focus reader attention on it.

☆ Layout must be invisible.

Never should a stage setting be so conspicuous that it detracts from the actors or the play. And never should the design of a yearbook distract the reader from the communication being conveyed.

Let's look at the application of each of these axioms.

Functional Layouts

The basic function of a yearbook—and therefore of its layout—is to communicate. Because typographers can measure how effectively messages are communicated, they can also establish positive, provable guidelines.

Several of these have already been noted in chapters 15 and 18. They apply to year-

books just as well as to magazines and advertisements and so you ought to go back and re-read them.

As with these other two media, preparation of a good dummy is a learnable skill and an excellent way to learn is to draw dummies for pages and spreads from previous yearbooks.

The designer first determines the function of the spread, then decides which element—art, head, or copy block—best expresses the message. Sizes of pictures are decided. Then, either with type proofs on hand or by copyfitting techniques discussed in Chapter 22, the designer knows what space the type will occupy.

The designer may now draw thumbnail dummies, visualizing roughly how the elements will fit together. From the small thumbnail, develop same-size roughs. Here the tonal value of the art is indicated by crayoning or penciling in various gray

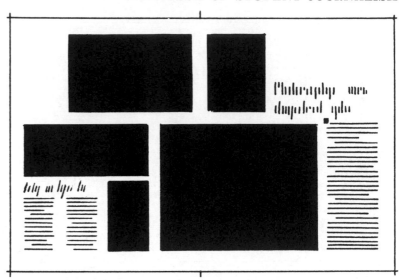

Oriented layout. Every element shares at least one axis with at least one other element. Most subtle alignment is left edge of picture in top left with margin of second column of body type.

areas. Another good device is to cut rectangles of gray drawing paper in the size, shape, and shade proposed for the pictures. These blocks are moved around until they're in pleasing balance. This, of course, indicates only the weight of the elements; the designer must be conscious of the lines of force within all the photos.

This will probably lead to applying the "hen-and-chick" principle—even though the designer may not know it by that name. A dominant element, usually a photo, is the big "hen" around which cluster the smaller "chicks." The dominant picture must be at least 50% larger than any other—and some designers want an even greater margin. But as it is not only the area but the tone that contributes to the weight and dominance of a photo, the ratio must be modified if the hen is unusually dark or light.

The "chicks" should vary as much as possible in shape and size. Either the hen or chicks may be tall and thin or shallow and wide for added dynamic thrust.

If the layout is truly organic, it will "grow" almost by itself and the designer will think of it only as "a layout that works." But there may be times when the problem is more pesky and the designer will deliberately seek to create a specific type of layout.

Oriented Layout

Almost all good layouts are *oriented* to some degree. This style has already been discussed in previous chapters. Just remember that the oriented layout is made up of elements that share common vertical and horizontal axes to make a strongly woven spread. White space is kept at the outside of the layout and trapped space is avoided. There are no "orphans."

Columnar Layout

In *columnar* layout, every element is in increments of the column. On a 3-column page then, they would be 1-, 2-, or 3-column widths, except those which bleed. Orientation is provided for all of them.

Mosaic Layout

Mosaic layouts stress the hen-and-chick technique. They follow principles of oriented layouts except that the designer doesn't place elements by mechanical alignment but relies on eye and instinct to create a pleasing relationship of shapes.

Mondrian Layout

To create a *Mondrian* layout, the designer divides the spread into rectangles of greatly varying shape and size by drawing a series of horizontal and vertical lines. Each sub-area is then filled with typographic elements

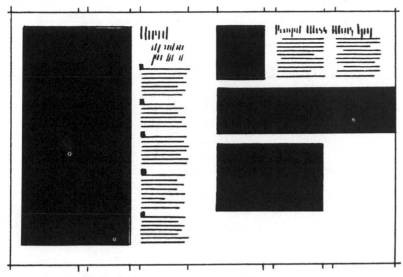

Columnar layout. Every element is in exact column-widths except those which bleed off page.

or left completely open.

Mondrian layouts that emphasize vertical masses are sometimes referred to as *skyline mosaics.*

Modular Layouts

Modular, also called *rectangular,* layouts are most generous with white space. A rectangle of usually two-thirds of the area of the spread is completely filled with typographic elements. The rest of the page is left blank. These layouts are usually well oriented.

There are other names for these layout styles and there are so many variations and combinations of them that they couldn't even be counted, much less named.

The student designer should remember, though, that these names are given here

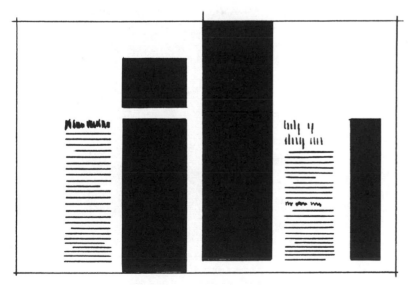

Skyline mosaic. Mosaic is variation of oriented layout with elements aligning optically but not necessarily physically. Skyline mosaic emphasizes vertical forms.

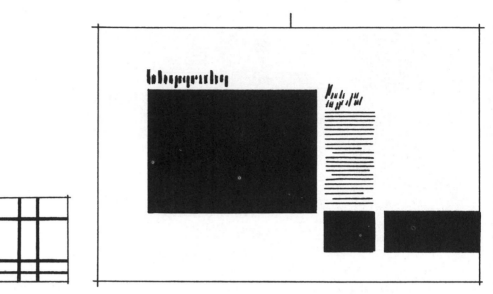

merely as a convenience in discussion. It is far more important that a layout be functional and organic than that it conform to one of these classifications.

Mondrian layout. As in small diagram, spread was divided by arbitrarily drawn vertical and horizontal lines. Areas were then either entirely filled with type elements or left blank. Basic lines should not be on obvious subdivisions of page such as half, thirds, or quarters.

Layout Harmony

In all these layouts, harmony is essential and, to bolster it, so is contrast.

Each spread must look as if it belongs to all those that precede or follow it. It is displeasing to the reader when there is no consistency from page to page or—a fre-

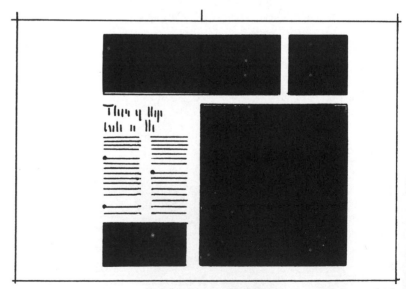

Modular layout. One portion of spread is completely filled with type elements; other, or others, are left completely blank. As in Mondrian layouts, divisions should not be obvious ones.

As senior year nears an end, we remember the good things

Running heads are effective unifying device in "Bellvilnois" of Belleville (Illinois) Township High West.

quent weakness—from section to section.

Much of this unity comes from the use of the same typeface and line lengths throughout the book. But there must be a consistency that is harder to define on the editorial viewpoint of a book.

Is your book formal or causal? Is the copy breezy, chatty, or more third-personish? Are your photos generally candid or more formally posed? Are most pages well filled or is white space used lavishly? Are bleeds rare or many? Is hand art used often or little? Is the whole effect of the book lively and dynamic or conservative and traditional?

Because on the typical yearbook several people may be doing layouts, it is the job of the editor-in-chief to inspect each spread before it goes to the printer and make sure that the necessary harmony has been maintained.

Tonal consistency is especially important. That means that, by and large, each spread has as much ink on it as each of the others. If a very dark picture is used on one spread, the next may have two larger but lighter photos, to maintain the same overall tone.

☆ Consistency does not mean monotony. Contrast is deliberately provided. If pages have been consistently light in key, a very dark full-page photo may be used as a change of pace. But all contrast must be deliberate and controlled. The dominant style must be established and maintained before a contrast is possible. If you have ten white rectangles, a black one will be striking accent. But if you have five black ones and five white ones, or four blacks and four whites and four grays, you'll have just a hodgepodge without consistency, harmony, or contrast.

Contrast is pleasant within an individual spread, also. Many useful techniques were discussed in the chapter just before this one and are worth reviewing now.

Balance

All layouts must be in balance; a page or spread that is not balanced is uncomfortable to the reader. *Formal balance* is too staid for most contemporary audiences, especially younger ones. So it is only a rare page— and usually a very serious one such as a record of student or faculty deaths—that is balanced in perfect symmetry. Other pages are in *dynamic balance*.

Note again that a little imbalance—a page that "leans" a bit—is alive and exciting.

Informal balance is similar to that of a teeter-totter. A chubby kid has to be closer to the center so the skinny one at the far end of the plank can balance him. Or two tiny folks can balance their mother. Of

Amid the 5,349 points scored by UNC varsity teams this year in competition sits inconspicuously the single point credited to the soccer team for a goal scored against Maryland.

That single point was a full fifteen years coming. It came on a penalty kick with a scant 4:47 left to play. One penalty kick had already been attempted and stopped, but the referee ruled that Terp goalie Ayasun had moved before the kick. Louis Bush slammed the repeat shot past the flailing fingers of a substitute goalie, Ayasun having been ejected for disputing the call.

Maryland was beaten for the first time in its fifteen years of ACC soccer competition. It was a finale in marked contrast to the preceding games. Highly rated from the season's start, the Tar Heels ran into a flurry of penalty kicks and an inconsistent offense, dropping four close matches. Despite the dogged

defense of [illegible] Van Allen and goalie Tim Haigh, the heart-breaks at the hands of Virginia and Duke pointed towards similar results at the feet of Maryland.

But the offense was now playing to its home gallery, spectators who had shared the years of frustration with their team. A follow shot by Mark Packard evened the score once, and Tim Moore headed the Heels into the lead, which held until halftime. Maryland tied the game itself as its bench chanted "San Jose, San Jose," site of the year's NCAA finals. Then Mr. Bush prevailed.

The hysterical fans, numbering close to 1,000, flooded Fetzer Field, surrounding Coach Allen who was thanking each player individually, then was himself lifted upon their shoulders.

It is seldom a sportsman finds himself in tears. A superior team takes its

wins in stride. The underdogs greet victory with surprise moreso than exhultation. It is only when that sportsman yearns, has yearned for longer than he would prefer to remember, that he merges with the ground he has worn down, the ball he has pushed around so often, the sportsmen he works with, and can replace the bitterness of the "almost", the despondance over the "if only", with an emotion rarely permitted the undedicated.

In that is the saving grace of sports. This 1969 soccer team fashioned for themselves and those who followed them something worth remembering. The fact that Man has a mouth and eyes does not distinguish him from rock and tree half so much as his ability to use them to laugh and cry.

And that's the point.

203

Jumping gutter—tying facing pages into integrated unit —is done here by aligning body type across top of page and pictures at bottom. This yearbook spread is unusual in that it doesn't have a headline; running copy is used. This weaving technique is useful for magazine pages, too.

course, a spread is more like a Ferris wheel because elements balance each other around an axis rather than on a simple fulcrum.

The optical weight of elements cannot be determined by a measuring device. Even a densitometer, which measures the tonal weight of a photo, cannot take into account the lines of force and the effect of varying shapes. The editor must rely on instinct and a trained, perceptive eye. But there are a few guidelines that can be used:

1. Dark pictures will outweigh those of equal size but lighter tone.

2. A picture at the top of the page will outweigh one of the same area at the bottom.

3. Circles outweigh squares.

4. Vertical rectangles will be heavier than horizontal ones of the same area.

5. Elements on the right half of a page or spread will outweigh equal ones at the left.

6. Headlines and copyblocks will weigh about a half of a middle-tone photo of the

same area.

7. Lines of force push weight in their directions. They change the "center of gravity" just as a person on a seesaw does by leaning toward or away from the balancing beam.

Yearbooks are always designed in 2-page spreads except, of course, for divider pages, which are singletons.

So the designer must jump the gutter as discussed in Chapter 18, and also define and defend the margins. Bleeds should be used only for their expanding effect and bleeds to the gutter should be minimized.

A picture that runs on facing pages, in effect, consists of two photos that bleed to the same point on the gutter. Great care must be taken that no salient part of the picture is in the bleed area. For there it may become lost in the binding with sad results.

Some designers believe that a bleed in the lower right corner of a spread will encourage the reader to flip the page to the next spread. Others will deliberately have a picture in this area face off the page as a guide to page-turning. There is no evidence that this is valid; the reader will instinctively turn a page after finishing a spread.

Strong lines of force may even persuade him to turn before finishing the pages.

Often it is most efficient to perform duties in a set routine. A good checklist for doing a layout goes something like this:

1. Inspect all materials for the layout. Read the copy and the headlines. Determine "the essence of communication" for the spread.

2. Determine the dominant element on the spread.

3. Find the lines of force within each picture.

4. Place pictures in the relative position they will occupy so that the lines of force lead the eye functionally and pleasantly.

5. Crop and scale each picture.

6. Dummy in the pictures.

7. Place captions.

8. Place the headline and/or running heads.

9. Place the body type.

10. If the body copy hasn't been written yet, or hasn't been divided by pages in case of running copy, determine how many characters—or words—will go into the available copy block and notify the proper editor.

11. Check common axes to assure a well-woven spread.

12. Check especially the spread or spreads immediately before this one—and any later ones, if they've been prepared out of order—to make sure of overall harmony.

The twelfth step is one that the editor performs just before the spread goes to the printer. A checklist determines those factors which are the editor's final responsibility.

A list of common errors which too frequently mar yearbooks should be drawn up to reflect the basic style of the book. It would include culprits such as these:

1. Overcrowded pages. Margins may be skimpy or erratic; space between elements may be too miserly. (There ought to be a minimum of 1 pica—and preferably 1½—between pictures, for instance.)

2. Jumbled pages. Avoid the three-ring circus effect when many elements compete for the reader's attention. Keep every element as far as possible from direct competition and so arranged that the eye will logically move from one to another until the whole spread has been consumed.

3. Gimmicky pages. Many "clever" layouts pall quickly on the reader. Many beginning designers think that every spread must be a tour de force, "an adroit or ingenious performance" as the dictionary defines it. You might call it "dazzling 'em with fancy footwork," a tactic used by a boxer to hide the sad fact that he isn't possessed of a knockout punch.

Many gimmicks are momentary fads that seem to return in cycles of about 25 to 30 years. So there's a new crop for just about every generation in high school. "Art nouveau" and "deco art" have each enjoyed short revivals in recent years. They zoom to popularity and descend to oblivion just about as fast. They "date" a book lamentably.

Among the gimmicks are heavy borders, especially around an entire page or spread; boxes piled on boxes; photos cocked at an angle; fancy backgrounds that overshadow the art; circles; deep tint blocks of solids—color, gray, or black; manipulation of type into fancy shapes or running it vertically, sideways, upsidedown, or at an angle.

The worst gimmick is the overuse of any technique other than the most simple and basic ones.

4. Backgrounds that overwhelm the art they are supposed to enhance.

5. Nonfunctional elements.

6. Pages or elements that are titled or run sideways. (It is much better to run an extraordinary wide picture across the gutter—maybe even manipulating it to avoid losing detail in the binding—than to run it sideways on one page.)

7. Collages or montages.

8. Blank pages ostensibly left for autographs but which look as if the staff ran out of material, energy, enthusiasm, or time before the page was filled.

Just about now the *final* or *working dummy* is prepared. This is the painstakingly detailed blueprint that directs the pasting-up of every element and the preparation of words and pictures that make up the page.

Again a checklist is a useful device. For

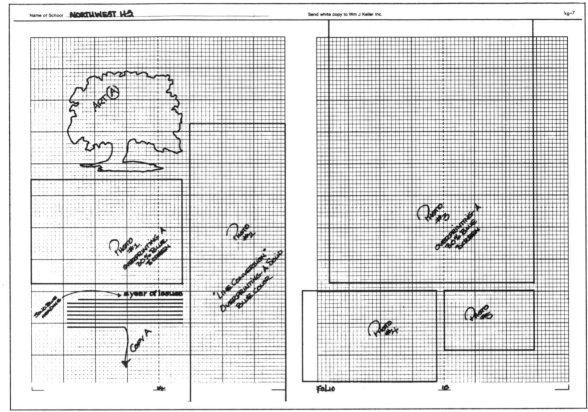

Name of School NORTHWEST H.S.   Send white copy to Wm J Keller Inc.   kg-7

Same-size yearbook dummy. Copy is designated by letters and photos by numbers. Directions for use of color are written in rectangles denoting photos. Irregular art, top left, is outlined so it will be positioned precisely. Page numbers and folios are indicated and name of school is always included. From this dummy . . .

it guards against those errors of commission, but especially of omission and ambiguity, that can be costly in effort and money and—most important at this stage of producing the book—in time.

1. Are the margins properly defined and defended?

The printer usually furnishes dummy sheets that are gridded in 1-pica increments, printed in light blue. Similarly gridded sheets are used for the actual pasteup, which, by using the grids as reference points, can quickly and accurately duplicate the dummy in the most minute detail.

2. Are all pictures shown in their proper size after cropping and scaling?

Discrepancies here can be annoying if not fatal. Suppose the dummy shows a photo of 8 x 4 inches at the top of a page. But when the reduction is made, its size is 8 x 4½ inches. What does the pasteup man do? If he sends it back and says, "Make this 4 inches deep," the new one will be only 7.1

inches wide. Or if the printer merely clips a half inch off the oversized picture, it may be the most important part of the photo which just wasn't recognized as such. In any case the result will be less than desirable.

So all scaling should be checked one last time.

3. Are all elements properly keyed?

Pictures are indicated on the dummy by a simple outline and are flagged "Photo #1," "Art #4," and the like. ("Art" refers to all hand art.) The corresponding picture, photo or hand, is labeled not only by the same number but also by page number: "Photo #3, Pg. 31." This key is written either on the back of the photo or on a projecting flap. Light blue grease pencil is

a year of issues

The past year raised issues that both inspired and discouraged the student body.

Students became more interested and involved in school policies and problems. Working with faculty and administration, students were instrumental in effecting major changes in rules and regulations.

Local, national, and international events continued to "turn off" many students. The disaffected and disillusioned developed a sense of frustration at being unable to right the wrongs that they observed.

14

Sagittarius

15

... is produced this spread. Photo at far left is in black, surprinted on 30% blue screen. Vertical picture is line conversion in black, printed on solid blue panel. Large picture on right is duotone. Color is over used here.

used because this color is invisible to the camera and smudges will not inadvertently appear on the plate. And the soft crayon, used with only a modicum of care, won't damage the fragile emulsion of photographs.

Copy blocks are flagged by letters to avoid confusion with the numbered pictures. Position is shown by a rectangle of the proper size and the original hard copy of the text is labeled: "Copy A, Pg. 12."

Headline position is shown by a rectangle and the head content is lettered in. The rectangle must be exact; the size of the handlettering need not correspond to that of the actual headletter.

4. Are color elements and tint block clearly indicated?

Instructions have already been given on the platemaker's copy in most instances. Specifications on the dummy repeat these and also designate proper positioning. A picture might be marked "Photo #2, Pg. 87, GREEN DUOTONE"; on the dummy the page reference would be eliminated.

A tint block is shown on the dummy as the proper rectangle and flagged, "Tint block, 50% GREEN." If the block is a rectangle, no further material is needed. If the block is in any other shape, the plate-maker is given a same-size piece of black paper or red plastic in the proper shape. It would be tagged, "Tint block, #1, Pg. 45, 40% BLUE."

Notice that pictures and copy are numbered only for the spread they are on. Thus every spread will have a "Photo #1" and a "Copy A." A senior page may go as high as "Photo #52" or higher.

5. Are folios specified?

The folios technically are page numbers. But the term is also used to designate the name of the book, perhaps the year, and sometimes the name of the section.

These elements should always go in ex-

251

actly the same position. If a bleed occupies the normal area, the folio is just eliminated; it is never moved.

Folios are most efficient at the bottom of the page, numbers at the outside corner, titles at the gutter.

A recurring fad is to place folios in the outside margin at about the half-way point vertically. This is awkward because they are hidden by the reader's thumbs as the book is held conventionally.

6. Is the name of your school on every dummy and piece of copy?

Most printers work on many yearbooks at the same time. Content of all books will have a strong similarity. Unidentified pieces of paper can all too easily be misplaced or mistaken for that of another school.

Printers have different systems for avoiding confusion. A general technique is to place all the material for one spread in a separate envelope. Often a checklist or "inventory" of contents is printed on the envelope. If not, the dispatch department should prepare such a "bill of lading." Typically, it might list:

> Central High
> FOOTPRINTS
> Pages 108-109
> Dummy
> 8 Photos
> 1 Art
> 3 sheets Text
> 1 sheet Heads
> 1 sheet Captions

The envelope used by one fine yearbook printer also asks:

1. Have you corrected your copy? Names, spelling, punctuation?

2. Have you keyed all pictures?

3. Have you written all heads and captions on separate sheets?

4. Have you keyed your layout (dummy)?

Always remember a very important point that is often overlooked:

☆ Write instructions on proper copy.

At least three departments work on the contents of each spread. The composing room sets all the type; the camera room prepares the pictures; the pasteup department assembles elements into pages. They may be separated by only a wall; they may be literally miles apart.

There is no point in specifying type on the dummy. The compositor who's supposed to set the type never sees the dummy; that's only for the pasteup department. So all instructions for the typesetter must be on the written copy. Those for the platemaker go on the art. Only instructions for the assembling of elements go on the dummy. All instructions must be on that particular piece of paper, no other.

Some staffs allow only the editor-in-chief to use a rubber stamp of the name of the school and book with which to stamp each piece of copy as the final act before the envelope is sealed and sent off. This not only makes sure all copy is properly identified but also says, in effect, "I, the editor, have checked all this material personally."

Some printers, wary of legal pitfalls, also ask that the advisor initial each piece of copy. This is to prevent immature staffers from smuggling out copy of dubious quality, suitability, and taste that they know the advisor and/or editor would scrap immediately. This will not happen with able, conscientious staff members. Unfortunately, even the finest basket will have an occasional rotten apple and the whole staff must suffer from such irresponsibility and insolence.

Single Pages

While most pages are made up in pairs, there are two kinds of singletons which stand alone. The *title page* is a most important one. As the first page of a book, it has only the end papers of the book facing it. Some staffs use this as the *half-title* page carrying only the name of the book and perhaps a little pictorial device. Then the first 2-page spread is the actual title page.

Whether it's a singleton or a spread, the title page sounds the opening note of the theme, usually with a strong pictorial element. Hand art is particularly useful in this case. The name of the book and its year, the name and city of the school, and perhaps the top editors' names are carried on the title page. In some instances the

PRODUCTION CHECKLIST

* WORK FOR FOLLOWING WEEK'S PAPER   ISSUE=

MONDAY

___ BEGIN PASTE-UP BY 11:15
___ PHOTO MASKS ON PAGES BY 11:30
___ PIX DUE BY 12:00
___ BEGIN PIX CROPPING   * ___ SOME ASSIGNM'TS MADE BY 12:30
___ DUMMIES DUE AT 11:15
* ___ STAFF CHECK FOR ASSIGNMENTS AT 12:30

TUES

___ HEADS DUE AT 11:15
___ FINISH PASTEUP
___ ASSIGN STORIES BY 12:00
* ___ ASSIGN PIX BY 12:00
* ___ STAFF CHECK ASSIGNMENTS BY 12:00

PIX DUE AT C-T TODAY

WED

___ GO OVER *FINISHED* PASTE-UP
___ CLEAN SURVEY AREA
* ___ SOME STORIES DUE
* ___ WORK ON STORIES

PAPER DUE AT C-T BY 12:15!

THUR

* ___ 12:30 STORIES TYPED   * ___ COPYREAD BY EDITORS
* ___ ADVISOR CRITIQUE STORIES   * ___ DRAW AD LINES
* ___ PRODUXN SET UP   * ___ COPY TO C-T AFTER SCHOOL

FRIDAY

* ___ EDITORS BEGIN DUMMIES
* ___ PASTE UP FLAG, FOLIOS,
* ___ PASTE UP ADS
___ FOLD PAPERS FOR MAILING
___ CRITIQUE + EVALUATION

COPY MUST BE AT C-T TODAY

SAT.

___ APPROVED LATE STORIES DUE
       TAKE TO SHARON OR DAVE

Production checklist is duplicated and given to every staffer of "Survey" of Marion (Indiana) High. Note that on this weekly, delivered Friday, work for current and next week's issues constantly overlaps.

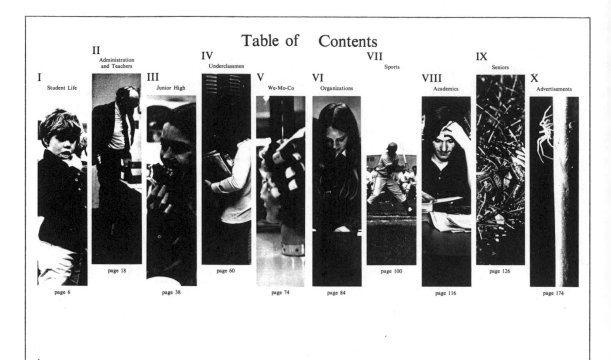

Table of Contents

I — Student Life — page 6
II — Administration and Teachers — page 18
III — Junior High — page 38
IV — Underclassmen — page 60
V — We-Mo-Co — page 74
VI — Organizations — page 84
VII — Sports — page 100
VIII — Academics — page 116
IX — Seniors — page 126
X — Advertisements — page 174

Table of contents for "Crest" of Churchville-Chili Central School in Churchville, New York, becomes interesting spread; photos in extreme vertical cropping give strong dynamic thrust.

complete masthead, listing all staff members' names, is also run here.

The last page of the book is also a singleton. Traditionally this carries some appropriate closing message, from the editor, class president or advisor, or the principal. It is a growing trend to run the masthead on this page.

Whatever the actual content, the last page is like the last chord of a good symphony. It should reiterate the theme; it should bring the book to a definite and logical conclusion; it should leave the reader with a feeling of satisfaction and reward.

Divider pages that introduce major sections are usually single pages, too. But these do have facing left-hand pages. Dividers are usually strong on art and light on text. The facing page ought to be as low key as possible, with little or even no art, so that it will not compete against the divider.

In some cases *subdividers* for secondary sections are also given a full right-hand page. More frequently, though, the signal for the subsection occupies only part of a page.

Single pages must be strong but actually they are easier to do than ordinary pages because you don't have to worry about jumping the gutter. In fact, the divisiveness of the gutter—a handicap on an ordinary spread—is an asset and therefore accentuated here.

Special Pages

The need for a *table of contents* is debatable—and debated. A logical case against such listing is that readers willingly go through the entire book; they do not seek out only a small section as they might in using a textbook, for instance.

If a table is used, it rarely needs a whole page. Many editors therefore make it part of the title page. Because the table is made up of only a few lines of type, care must be taken that these remain a cohesive whole and are not spread out excessively. Another danger is of excess space between the title

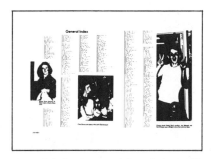

General index pages, left, which would otherwise be deadly dull, are enlivened by large candids. Page at right gains typographic color from large letters that signal alphabetical sections.

and the page number. A good rule of thumb is that such a gap can be no longer than four times the point size of the type used. So, if you were using 12-point type, four times 12, 48 points or 4 picas, is the widest gap the reading eye can effectively jump. If the space is wider than this, you should use *leaders*, a row of dots or dashes.

The *index* is also a debatable part of a book. If it is used, it should be set in 5½-point type, in 3 or 4 columns. The letter identifying each alphabetical division of the index should be at least 14-point. Sans Serifs make a good index letter. Index pages are visually dull and should be enlivened by good art. This is an excellent place to run a picture story or essay.

Indexing is a job dreaded not only by student staffs but by professionals as well. But yearbook indexing is simple and requires no great skill, only patience and great care.

The secret of painless indexing is to start early. As soon as a spread has been dummied, the editor—or some top-level and responsible associate editor—should go over the pages and, with a light blue pencil, underline every name or word that is to be indexed. Then that person teams with another staffer who has a sheet of paper for each letter of the alphabet. The editor reads

the item and page number and the teammate writes the entry on the proper sheet. After all pages have been handled this way, it is relatively simple to alphabetize the entries from each sheet.

Another way, taking a little longer and using more materials, is to write the dictated entry onto a 3×5 file card. Alphabetizing can be done every day by this method and the editor may dictate to two or three notemakers.

In either case, the copy for the printer must be carefully retyped from the working lists. When page proofs are returned, the index is checked one final time before the copy is sent to the printer.

Senior pages pose the hardest task for the staff. Because they require so much work by everyone involved, they usually have the earliest deadlines. There are countless chances for errors and errors involving names and pictures of individuals are the least forgivable. There isn't much chance to be spectacularly creative on these pages. Add it all up and it says: Much work, minimum fun.

But they are the most important section of a yearbook and deserve the best effort of the best staffers.

☆ All senior portraits should be the same size.

☆ All senior portraits should run in strict alphabetical order.

There can be absolutely no hint of favor-

ehs grapplers pin 4-5 record

After school practice was held in a new location this year — the cafeteria. Wrestling mats had to be moved to the cafeteria, daily since the wrestling room was occupied by the newly purchased universal gym. Wrestlers and coaches found the cafeteria to be spacious and ventilated, however, moving the mats from the gym to the cafeteria was a hassle.

Two wrestlers from Coach Bob Erland's Varsity were victorious in tournaments. Team Captain Rey San Juan placed 2nd in the 105 pound weight category at Monte Vista, Pacific, and Mt. Diablo. Mike Kenney placed 4th in the 135 pound weight division at the Monte Vista tournament. Final league record for Varsity was 4-5. JV coached by Dick Gorman ended the season with a 6-3 league record.

LEFT: STEVEN WEST attempts a breakdown on a Pinole wrestler.

TOP: VARSITY WRESTLING team, FRONT ROW: Vernon Garcia, Rey San Juan, Luis Mortes, Cayne, Jerry Bucklin, and Patrick Falls. ROW 2: Richard Servello, Rick Herex, Allen Woods, O Rickie, Steven West, and Mike Kenney. ABOVE: JV wrestling team, FRONT ROW: Dan Davis, J Francis, Rickie Bonino, Ken Inocencio, Steven Lozaro, Dalton Davis, and Dale Foster. ROW 2: Werk, Tom Fleming, Don McGarvey, Nick Lum, Mike Portahak, Bob Lewis, Ceferino Vaca, David ' and Trygve Sr

ABOVE: REY SAN JUAN grapples to attain a reversal. LEFT: Coach Bob Erbland gives Rey a warm-up talk before the match.

Class pages, often monotonous with scores of small portraits, are assured readership by being divided into smaller units which then are placed on other pages of "Horizon" of Encinal (Texas) High. Approximately a quarter of each spread, throughout most of book, is devoted to portraits.

itism in this section. If all students are created equal, this is the place to demonstrate that.

If only portraits are run on these pages, the checkerboard effect should be broken occasionally to reduce monotony. If space is not too severely limited, variety can be created by grouping portraits into an irregular shape instead of a full rectangle. Or occasionally a portrait can be left out of such a rectangle and replaced by a pictorial device, the insignia or seal of the school, a drawing, or the class year in display type. Even simpler is the occasional placing of the identification above instead of below the picture.

More spectacular is the combining of two sections, senior portraits with those of academics or faculty. Pictures from the other sections can be run larger as the dominant photo and subject matter will be variety from the mass of portraits.

Wild pictures, totally unrelated to the seniors section, may also be used for variety, either singly or as part of a picture essay or story. Hand art, especially line art, is particularly charming and refreshing on these pages.

Running heads are effective on these pages and an intriguing technique is to use the bottom quarter of the spread for running copy that recounts the events of the school year in prose. This content, which may or may not be illustrated, will run for many pages, usually at the foot of every spread of portraits.

In smaller yearbooks, the *senior index* or *directory* is combined with the portraits. This copy tells something about the senior and his school activities. In larger books, this written copy is presented as a separate section rather than with the portraits.

Combining portraits and the directory is a difficult job and requires more space because, while the portraits are all the same size, listings for a very active student will take more space than one who participated little in school activities and so you can't achieve a neat checkerboard of equal ele-

The first
hectic days
of school . . .

Confusion — Setting up workable school bus schedules and routes. Orientation of bewildered sophomores. Balancing overcrowded lunches. Making necessary schedule changes. Endless forms to be signed and filled out. A whole new set of room numbers and locker combinations to learn .

Changes — Removal of homeroom and a more compact school day. A new gym floor and roof work on the dome. A revised code of conduct. All sports activity after school. A "new" principal with a familiar face. A former biology teacher taking a new position in the guidance office and the addition of a new secretary . . .

LEFT: Greg Hurt, Darrell Hunley, and Freddie Hamm board the bus after a long day at school. **BELOW:** Mr. Ingram transfers from the science department to become the new head of the guidance office. **BOTTOM:** During the first days of school the halls are filled with confusion.

RIGHT: Carol Carmack signs a sheet that shows she understands the new code of conduct. **ABOVE:** Sophomore Nancy Robertson wanders aimlessly through the halls in search of her class. **TOP:** Mr. Atkins, temporary principal, converses with Leslie Hale during lunch.

38/Fall '73   Fall '73/39

Ganging captions creates handicaps for reader. First captions must be separated into sections, then each must be connected, by complicated route, to proper picture as broken lines indicate.

ments. Most observers believe separating the two contents is the most practical technique although many think that combining them gives a better package for the reader.

Pages of senior directory need the relief of large art elements.

If portraits are to be placed in irregular patterns, a useful technique is to cut out rectangles of gray construction paper in the same size and number as those of the portraits that must be carried on the page or spread. These are then moved around to create a pleasant mosaic. Then the portraits themselves are placed in that pattern to determine that no picture is facing off the page. If it is, it must be moved to the next row and the whole pattern rearranged. This is easy with an irregular pattern; it is virtually impossible in a full rectangle. This is another reason why the portrait photog-

rapher should be instructed to avoid profile shots that create such problems.

In all instances identification should be placed as close as possible—and preferably directly under—the picture. Avoid ganging idents in a block removed from the portraits themselves.

Color

Color is like a scoop of ice cream on a slab of cherry pie. It's very nice but it's not essential.

Color is expensive and so it's a luxury some staffs just can't afford. If you can't, don't cry over spilt printer's ink. For some of the most effective and handsome yearbooks are in plain old black and white.

For, while color can make a good yearbook better, it can't make a poor book good.

☆ Color must be used functionally.

1. The primary function of color is to improve communication by saying something that words alone cannot say as well—or cannot say at all. It's impossible for

words to describe the fall foliage around your school, the drama of a lightning storm that breaks up a track meet, or the gayety of folk costumes at an ethnic festival. Color can.

2. Color leads the eye through a page. Even a tiny spot of color has so much optical magnetism that judicious placement of such elements can lure the reading eye into every area of a page.

3. Color creates a mood that enhances the pleasure of the reader and makes him more receptive to the written word.

Unless color does at least one of these functions, it should not be used.

☆ Color must be used sparingly.

Surcharges for color are a fixed cost. It's much like a restaurant that, for an unchanging price, let's you eat all you can. The student designer—too many professionals, too—often is overtempted. To have an extra helping of this and two servings of that, just because it doesn't cost any more than a single portion, soon results in stomach ache. So overindulgence in color—because it doesn't cost any more—can bring on typographic dyspepsia.

Color might be considered a spice. Like all spices, it is most effective when used in pinches instead of in spoonfuls.

Spot Color

Spot or *flat color* is the simplest and least expensive way to add this pleasant spice. Usually only one color is used in this technique and almost any hue may be used effectively.

Usually a hue other than the primary or secondary one is most pleasing to the reader. So instead of ordinary green, use olive; instead of red, use a reddish orange or brown, etc.

Spot color may be used in its normal tone; it may be peppered by tiny white spots as a tint; it may be surprinted by minute black spots as a shade.

Spot color is effective as a tint block or to accent areas of hand art, especially line. Large areas of solid color should be avoided. A uniform monotone is difficult to print and

it will often smudge from the reader's fingers long after it is supposedly dry.

☆ Don't run type in color.

☆ Don't run halftones in color.

☆ Duotones are effective use of spot color.

All these principles have been looked at in Chapter 18 and the same techniques of using spot color in magazines are applicable to the yearbook. So is the use of mechanical separations, also discussed there.

Process Color

Process color is a grand illusion, an optical sleight of hand. Through a process called *color separation*, an original full-color piece of art is broken down into the three primary colors: Red, blue, and yellow. (Actually, they're magenta, cyan, and lemon if you want to be technical.)

When a bunch of these tiny yellow dots,

Staples Night Game A First for N.C. And a Lasting Memory for Players

"Right Side!" I yelled back and took the seat next to him. "Right side" was a little saying we had made up because he played right tackle and I played right guard and along with half of the center, we made up the right side of the offensive line.

"Pass back some cokes, will ya," I screamed and someone in the front of the bus, near the cooler, started the chain of cokes that finally reached me. As I drank my coke, I heard someone banging on the window of the bus and looked out to see who was there, but I couldn't see anyone because the windows were all fogged up. My mind went back to the game.

I was looking up at the scoreboard and we were behind 21-20 with less than two minutes left. It was third down with 24 yards to go. Kirk Shouvlin got the call, stepped into the huddle and pronounced, "I-right, short-trap left on two, ready, break!" It was a running play which in this situation could have gone for either one yard or fifteen yards, depending on the blocking. I had the key block. It went for one yard. After an illegal procedure penalty we then had a fourth down with 28 yards to go. Kirk again stepped into the huddle and with amazing coolness, considering it was only his second varsity game, said, "All right, guys, this is it. This is the whole season, right here. Flank left deep curl-in to Savoye on two, ready break!" We went up to the line and before I knew it, Kirk had the ball and was going back to pass. I had blown the last play, but this time there was no way that my man was going to wreck the play by getting to the quarterback. When I saw the ball go flying over my head, I realized that the other lineman had been thinking the same thing. Craig made the catch, 29 yards from the line of scrimmage — a first down. Some plays later Dennis got the ball and as he was crossing the goal line, someone yealled "Hey, right side, number one!"

As I climbed into the bus I could just begin to hear those sounds that anyone who has ever played a sport longs for.

"Hey, great game, baby!"

"Number one, number one, way to go!"

"How to run Dennis!"

"Great catch Craig! How you throw Kirk, baby!"

"Number one, number one!"

"This means Championship game, you know!"

"Number one, number one!"

And then I could make out the distinctive voice of my linemate.

"Hey, right side, back here!"

"Yea, number one!"

And there we were, the game over, still on top, homeward bound on the bus.

75

Sports page returns to technique of original, all-type yearbooks of past century. Big game is reported as reminiscence of athlete, written in excellent literary style.

let's say, run right alongside a batch of blue ones, the eye is fooled into thinking it sees green. By changing the ratios of these dots, all the colors and all their gradations that can be discerned by the human eye, can be reproduced.

Original art may be hand or photo. The latter may be a colored photo or a transparency such as the slides you project onto a screen.

Process color is expensive. For one thing, you need four plates instead of one to print it and the paper must be printed four separate times, once for each color. Color photographs, from film to print, are considerably more costly than black and white, of course.

But new technology constantly reduces the cost and only consultation with your printer can determine whether process color can be squeezed out of your budget. Many printers offer color at greatly reduced costs or even free as a bonus for meeting early deadlines.

As already noted, yearbooks are printed in signatures. If color is available on any page, it is available on all other pages of that signature. The copy control chart should show the pages where color can be used at no extra cost.

A recurring weakness in yearbooks is the use of poor color copy apparently just because it was available. Photographic quality of color art must be high; for the reproduction can be no better than, and is usually at least a little poorer than, that of the original. Learn to throw out poor color just as ruthlessly as you discard b & w photos of poor quality.

☆ Process color and black and white can be used on the same spread.

As a matter of fact, mixing full color and monochrome enhances both by the pleasant and dramatic contrasts between them.

If student work—especially photography —is to be used for process color, it requires additional advance planning.

Scheduling demands more advance time for color than for b & w. In most parts of the country, spring and fall are the most colorful seasons and much color shooting should be done then. On outdoor shots, late afternoon or early morning lighting causes an unpleasant, distorting ruddy or bluish coloration. The schedule must also provide enough cushion to make up for rainy or cloudy days that preclude color shooting.

Backgrounds must be selected with care and the subjects should be told what color clothing to wear; uncoordinated colors of clothing may clash painfully.

Be sure the photog knows exactly what the editor has in mind for any given color shot.

Inspect color work—it will usually be in the form of slides—under conditions that will not distort the hues. A *color viewer*— slanted frosted glass with light behind it —is an inexpensive, and probably the best, device. But good results can be obtained by ordinary desk lamp. Place a piece of white paper on the desk. Put a light source of at least 100 watts as far behind the paper as your eyes are in front of it. Shade the light so it doesn't shine in your eyes and view the slide with the light reflecting off the paper. Never hold a transparency directly to the

STREAKING, CHECKING, SCORING —

Raider skaters tune-up for upcoming game.

ST. FRANCIS		OPPONENTS
2	ORCHARD PARK	7
4	HAMBURG	3
0	FRONTIER	6
9	EDEN	0
1	BAKER	4
1	ORCHARD PARK	9
0	HAMBURG	1
0	FRONTIER	2
3	EDEN	3

110

Season's record for hockey team is recorded in tabular form in "Crusader" of St. Francis High, Athol Springs, New York.

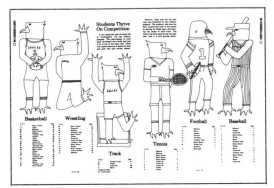

Year's complete athletic record is recorded in interesting chart from "Aerie" of Northwestern High in Elizabeth City, North Carolina. Teams' nickname is "Eagles"—as one might gather.

light; the color will be distorted unless you have a special light bulb.

Cropping slides is a little trickier than ordinary photos. A good way is to make an 8×10 b & w print using the slide as the negative. The result will be just horrendific to look at. It will be a negative print; all the whites come out black and vice versa. The colors will all be reduced to muddy grays. But it will show all the elements, and crop marks will do their job properly.

The other way is to lay tracing paper over the slide and with a very soft pencil— and using great care not to dent the emulsion—trace that area of the slide that you want to be used.

Of course, the best of all is to compose the picture with so much care and skill that the whole slide can be used. This is asking a bit much. But the more tightly the photo is composed, the less glaring will be those mistakes which are so easy to make in cropping slides.

In planning layouts using color, pieces of paper that duplicate the major hues and values of the pictures may be used along with the gray and black paper rectangles for regular work.

Color may be used effectively for theme elements. But because color usually is not available for all pages which might carry the theme, this technique will require intense and creative planning.

Never let the amount of money that color costs be used as an indicator of effectiveness.

Usually a bad expensive job is worse than a bad inexpensive one. For it's regrettable to see money wasted in any way.

Yearbook Covers

The cover of a yearbook usually represents a fifth of the total cost of the volume. That's a lot of money and it ought to be spent in the wisest possible way.

A cover must protect the book through the whole long life you hope for it. The cover must be attractive and appropriate to the rest of the book. The cover must fit the budget.

The budget is the first determinant and demands the first decision: What kind of cover should you choose? Only then can you get specific about the details of design.

There are many materials available for covers and all are good when well used. Most yearbooks are bound in plastic that simulates leather of any kind and any color you can imagine. Covers are coated with Pyroxylin which makes them durable and washable. The same substance is used to impregnate *buckram, monk's cloth,* and other *book cloth,* which are also highly popular. This makes the fabric impervious to soiling, especially by fingerprints. *Cover papers* come in a wide and functional variety.

These materials are usually used with *sewn-round and back* binding. This is the style of this book, for instance. Sixteen-page signatures are sewn, with thread, down the inside fold and then onto the sig before and after it. The back, or *spine,* is rounded and glued to a piece of fabric. This is now the "book" itself. It is attached to the cover by being pasted to the end papers which then are pasted onto the *boards,* the cover itself. The deep grooves at the sides of the spine do not clamp the book as many people believe. They merely allow the cover to swing freely as on a hinge.

Smaller books of 80 pages or less are simply sewn or *stitched,* using staples, into a single signature of which the cover becomes an integral part. Sometimes a separate cover is pasted on to hide the staples.

Less frequent is the use of *mechanical*

Photographic cover, left, wraps around entire book. Lithographed on cloth, it is posterized in yellow and brown. Cover at right is stamped in three colors. Background and two signal lights are red, arrow is black, GO signal in green.

bindings. This may be as simple as a loose-leaf notebook. More frequently a *comb* of plastic is used; its teeth are inserted into prepunched holes in the pages of the book and the "handle" of the comb then curls tightly to make a cylindrical fastening. A major advantage is that the machinery to do this job is inexpensive and the binding can be done by students themselves.

Cover Styles

Hard covers are most respected and are basic for yearbooks. Pieces of sturdy cardboard are covered with one of the materials just discussed to give good and lasting protection to the book.

For *padded covers,* a layer of soft material is placed between the stiff boards and the cover fabric. The effect is one of richness and luxury.

Paper covers can be used for saddle and mechanical bindings. As already noted, these come in a wide variety and should not be considered an inferior substance.

Cover Printing

All printing methods are used for book covers. Offset, because it adapts so nicely to strongly textured materials, is excellent for book cloth. It's particularly effective when the cover design is a *wraparound* photo that covers both front and back without a break.

Silk screen printing uses a stencil and either ink or paint to create the image. The paint can be applied thickly enough so this is the only feasible method of putting a light image on a dark background, the typical book cloth. The ink is brilliant and is highly appealing on lighter backgrounds. Although the stencils are prepared photographically, this method is not very good for halftones. But it is ideal for hand art, posterized photos, or line conversion.

Use of letterpress is infrequent.

Any of these methods can use color: Offset for process or flat; letterpress or silk screen for flat.

Color can also be applied by an airbrush, also using a stencil, that gives a *halo effect* around an element printed by any process. An *overtone rub* is applied by hand. Pigment is applied to the entire cover; then further rubbing with a clean cloth removes the color from raised areas, leaving it only in the deep grain. This is rather costly—as most hand work is—but the effect is sumptuous.

For tighter budgets, a picture may be printed in color on ordinary paper which is then *tipped on,* pasted onto the cover. To protect the picture, a sheet of clear plastic may be laminated to either the front or the whole cover.

Not quite printing—because they don't use ink—are *embossing* and *stamping.* In embossing the image is raised from the surface of the cover material by forcing it between two dies, concave and convex. This is the same method used to mold a notary public's seal onto a document.

Plane embossing is plain embossing—no pun intended. The image is raised onto a single plane, like a broad level plateau. Sometimes this is merely a background for an image printed by another process.

In *modeled* embossing, the image is in *bas relief,* like that on a coin. There are many, rounded planes. This is the most expensive method, for the dies must be prepared by a sculptor. Those for plane embossing can be made photographically.

Stamping is also called *debossing,* the opposite of embossing. The stamped image is impressed downward into the cover fabric. Relief or type photographically made dies are used and ink or metal can be applied at the same time the debossing is done.

That done without ink is called *blind stamping.* When ink is used to enhance the relief image, it's *brilliant* stamping. For brilliant embossing, the image must first be printed onto the fabric before it is pressed between the dies.

Probably the most spectacular method is *metal appliqué.* A sheet of brilliant metal foil is, in a single operation, embossed and fastened onto the cover fabric. The metal never tarnishes and remains brilliant indefinitely. It is especially effective for reproducing the school seal or simple insignia.

The various printing methods can be used in many striking combinations. Usually the covers are manufactured by a specializing company, rather than the printer. The representative of a cover company usually works closely with the printer's representative and the latter will be glad to set up an appointment for you.

Cover Design

The cover design must tie together two separate panels, the front of the book and the *backbone* or spine. The spine carries the name of the book and the year; the front cover can carry either or both and sometimes the name of the school is added.

Color is rubbed into markedly grained surface of cover at left; illustration—ancient wood block—is printed on foil and sealed onto cover.

"Gleam" cover is embossed and silk-screened in brown and orange. "Pelican" cover is grained, embossed and silk-screened in two colors, yellow for title and light blue for Script background.

Cover at right has background of oldtime advertisements printed in brown. Title is surprinted on red oval.

Bishop Turner Crozier 1974

BUFFALO N.Y. PM JUNE 1974

TOP SECRET

To Parents Of

Return Requested

"Crozier" of Bishop Turner High in Buffalo, New York, is packaged like national Turner Factor scholastic exam. Body of book closed with gold seal and all theme headings were in computer-readout type used for reporting such test results.

Unless the name is unusually short, the best way to carry it on the spine is to run it sideways from top to bottom; this puts it into reading position when it lies face up on a desk or table. Hyphenating a long name so it appears horizontally when in a bookshelf is generally unsatisfactory although it is not impossible.

Cover type should be legible and echo that used for display within the book. Art work may reiterate the theme or be nonrelated but appropriate. The seal or initials of the school, especially in metal appliqué, are so handsome that some staffs use only that, the name of the book, and the year, in volume after volume. By using these elements in different styles and colors and, of course, on various colors and materials of cover fabric, there is good variety along with tradition-building continuity.

Original art for most cover designs is hand work done in black and white. Both surface images and those in planes are reproduced from such original art. Relief sculpture can be used for modeled embossing but this is rarely done; b & w drawings alone will suffice.

If more than one color is used, the staff artist may do a single drawing or prepare mechanical separations.

If the cover is photographic, a single b & w glossy is the copy. An overlay shows where type elements are to be placed. For process color, the art is a transparency. Although a normal slide may be used, many printers prefer at least 3 x 5 inch original copy.

If the photographic cover is to wrap around the spine, an overlay or markings on a negative photo image should show where the division between spine and covers occurs.

End Papers

End papers should be considered as a bridge between the cover and the book itself. They should either harmonize or contrast with the color of the cover.

As long as the end papers are sturdy enough to link the book to the cover, any color or texture may be used and a wide variety is available. They may or may not be printed.

If the cover design is rather ornate, unprinted end papers seem to be most pleasing. If the cover is simple and especially when color is not feasible in the book, the end papers may use color photography effectively and usually at relatively slight cost. A picture of the school itself is a favorite subject. Another effective but simple device is to have the entire papers covered with a repetitive design, like wallpaper. Here the school seal or other insignia is pleasant. Only a single piece of copy need be furnished to the printer; he creates the pattern by the *step-and-repeat* method.

Some printers offer end papers as a collage of news events of the year, in full color, at little, if any, extra cost. This is colorful and timely. But it must, of course, cover events far removed from the campus and usually unrelated to the theme.

Stock Covers

For staffs on a tight budget, the *stock cover* design can be a godsend. Cover manufacturers have a large assortment of dies that can be used for embossing or stamping with no extra cost of making them from original art. There are literally thousands of such designs ranging from Vikings to floral designs, from coats of arms to armadillos.

One manufacturer estimates that stock elements can produce more than 50,000 possible variations using one of more than 50 colors, at least that many for overtone rubs, 30 textures of fabric, uncounted colors of ink plus the many designs, just mentioned, for plane or printed images.

Usually the staff that has to consider stock covers fears that another school just crosstown or up the highway will come up with an identical cover. But the odds are so slim that no one ought to lose sleep worrying about such coincidence.

In any case the name of the books will be different and the typical yearbook reader and owner doesn't even have another book with a similar cover against which to compare your own.

Cover manufacturers have highly skilled artists who will produce any needed art work from simple sketches submitted by the staff.

By reusing their own existing dies or stamps, the staff can save substantial amounts and yet avoid monotony and repetition by varying color, texture, and position.

Slip Covers

In recent years, as new materials make it practical, light-colored covers have grown in popularity. To protect them, *slip jackets* are often used. These are envelopes of sturdy, transparent material into which the book boards are slipped. They fit smoothly and the plastic is so clear that it doesn't detract from the cover design. They are sold separately so that no student is forced to buy one.

Cover designs should be simple. As has been said so many times in this book, simplicity wears well and is always in good style and good taste.

Good typography is a mirror of the culture in which it was produced. If you'll go to the public library and find a regular trade book that was printed in the 1920s, you'll notice that it is different in design from that of any other decade. And you'll notice that the yearbooks from your school show the same difference created by their eras.

But although they differ in detail, good books will always share common characteristics. They are simple; they are always examples of disciplined creativity.

School .... SAM HOUSTON, La Gorda .... Page No. __108__

Typing to guide lines helps save time fitting copy blocks to your layout. After checking rough notes for spelling and punctuation, typewrite (double-spaced) to width indicated. Six lines of typing will make one inch of printer's type.

Make all corrections in style, spelling and punctuation BEFORE final typing. Eliminate waste and assure on-time delivery of your book by making changes now instead of later on.

I have personally read and corrected the both copy for accurate spelling and good grammar.
SIGNED _Glen McKay_
Faculty Advisor or Editor

Copy Sheet For WRITE-UPS
10 Point Type

All type copy must be typewritten double-spaced on these sheets, starting at line number one.

Figures show width of copy block on layout when typing is set in 10 pt. printer's type. ➡

1¾" 2½" 3¼" 4⅛" 5"

1   Can you imagine attending a whole day of school
2   at Central without saying a word of English?
3   Members of <u>Los Pueblos Nuevos</u>, the club for
4   Spanish students, do so every February 18. This
5   is the anniversary of the raising of the Spanish
6   flag at the junction of the Gallos and Red Rivers
7   by Pascual de Verros in 1659.
8   Club members may speak only Spanish throughout
9   the day. In most classes, teachers allow written
10 answers ---in English--- or give special assignments
11 to do outside of class. It used to create some
12 problems in the cafeteria line. But this year
13 Mrs. Luisa McMillan, a native of Ecuador who works
14 for food service, acts as a willing translator.
15   Many students wear some distinctive piece of
16 clothing for the occasion and this year Sally Ann
17 Gregory's black lace mantilla caught all eyes. It
18 was a gift from Dominica Guitterrez of Argentina,
19 a foreign exchange student who lived with the Gre-
20 gory family this year.
21
22
23
24
25

IMPORTANT: 6 lines of typewritten copy double-spaced equals 1" depth of printer's type.

FOR KELLER USE

WM J KELLER INC • BOX 1052 BUFFALO, NEW YORK 14240

Form 10A

Printed copy sheets make it easy to determine space that type will occupy. When typewritten lines are length indicated here, line of 10-point type will be 3½ inches long. Six lines of double-spaced typing equals one vertical inch of type. Many printers furnish such sheets but they can easily be made by staff or individual writer.

25 Yearbook Typography

Although there isn't much type in a year-book—as compared to a novel or a textbook—it has a big job of communicating to do. So the editor must choose it carefully and use it wisely.

Along with selection of the faces for the book, the editor must also set the style in which it will be used.

Principles of good typography already discussed in Chapters 11 and 24 apply to all printed media, newspapers, magazines, advertising and yearbooks, and the yearbook typographer ought to review them regularly. This chapter, although it may seem to be somewhat repetitive, will emphasize those aspects of typography that especially apply to yearbooks.

Body Type

Body type deserves more attention than it often gets. Its choice will be made from the printer's type specimen book and there will usually be selection enough to satisfy both functional needs and the staff's esthetic desires. Don't feel badly if your printer doesn't offer you Valkyrie Medium; your book won't suffer if your choice is among Caledonia, Electra, Century Schoolbook, or Times Roman. The differences between well-designed typefaces are too slight to make any substantial difference as far as the reader is concerned.

It is interesting to note that—at least at the time this is being written—it isn't possible to copyright any typeface except a highly eccentric one. But the name can be copyrighted. So you'll find the same design but with each manufacturer tagging it with a different label. Many type specimen books even have charts which say: "Highland is the equivalent of Caledonia" or "English is similar to Times Roman." And obviously there can't, even by semantics, be much difference between the classic old Century Schoolbook and the more newly named Century Textbook.

This chapter uses the names of the original designs; you can readily translate these into the names your printer uses.

Body type should be Roman because of its high readability. It should be big on the slug and with nicely rounded curves as already noted.

Among fine Roman body types are Bodoni, Caledonia, Electra, Fairfield, Garamond, Primer, Century Schoolbook, and Times Roman. This is by no means a complete list; if the face you choose, or its equivalent, isn't listed here, do not despair—at least not if you have met the requirements of readability.

School editors are often intrigued by Sans Serifs and choose it for body type. The decision isn't wise. For the Sans have abysmally low readability.

Ten-point is probably the best size for body use and usually it should be ledded 1 point.

Also in body sizes is the face used for captions. This should be a contrasting design so distinction between text and captions is always obvious. The boldface of your body type may be chosen although most professionals think that this is the place to use Sans Serifs. If you do choose a Sans, be sure to check out its x-height (as noted in Chapter 11) because there is unusually wide variance in the height of primary letters in this type race.

Genuine Italics—of the Roman race—don't make very good caption letters; their tone is too light in comparison with that of the halftone pictures.

A possible third body type may be used for the senior directory and index, if you use either or both of these. Again the Sans are excellent for such usage as they are for tabular material such as scores in the sports section.

☆ Body type should never be set narrower than 12 picas or wider than 24.

It's a wise decision—and one of the very earliest ones to make—to establish basic line lengths for your book. Two lengths will usually be adequate for the main part of your book: A third and a half of the page width. A shorter measure—a quarter of the page width—works well for the directory, index, and perhaps captions.

Sticking to these consistent line lengths makes it much easier for the layout editor as well as for the typesetter, and is economical of money and time.

Unthinking editors sometimes say, "Look! We've got a firm contract. It isn't going to cost me a penny more if I change the length of every line of type." This may be partially true.

But the printer must make a profit or go out of business. If his contract with your yearbook didn't make a satisfactory profit because of excessively extravagant type use, you can make a sure bet that this will be remembered when it comes time to negotiate next year's contract. Even if you change printers, a school that has a reputation for typographic excesses will pay a heavier price.

But even if there is no immediate financial penalty for poor type specifying, there is a loss of time. Any variation in setting takes time. So if too many hours have been wasted in the setting of type, that time will have to be made up somewhere else en route and the end result is that other portions of the book-manufacturing process must be skimped or the delivery date can't be met.

Captions may be set in these two or three measures also, although you may come up with three altogether different line lengths. Changing length is practical when the typeface changes.

Captions should either align precisely with the edges of a picture or be markedly narrower. Set flush left or right, they should be at least 3 picas narrower than the picture and if they are centered—not a very good style—they must be indented at least 2 picas on each side.

For a page 7¾ x 10½, the settings would be: 12 picas, with 3 columns on the page; 18 picas, with 2 columns per page, and 24 picas which would be used in a single column.

For 8½ x 11 and 9 x 12 pages, settings are: 13 picas, 18 picas, and 24 picas. In all sizes this provides adequate alleys and margins although slight adjustments may be made on any of these dimensions.

Typographic Styles

Specifications for composition should be decided well in advance of the actual typesetting and given to the printer in writing. Some decisions that must be included in this list are:

1. How will paragraphs be designated? The usual method—and best—is to indent 1 em, which is a square of the point size of the type. So a 10-point face would be indented 10 points. Sometimes the first graf is not indented but all others are. Sometimes no graf is indented, a blank line just above it marks the start of a paragraph.

2. Will initials be used? If so, what face will they be in? How big will they be? (Initials are designated by their size comparative to body type, as a "3-line initial," for instance. With a 10-point body face, a 3-line initial would be either 30-point or 36-point.) Will initials be stickups or sunken? Will words or phrases reading out of the initial be set in small caps, all-caps, or lowercase?

Poor typographic usage. INDUSTRIAL runs vertically—and nearly illegibly. EIGHTY-FIFTH ANNUAL is sideways, disoriented.

LIBERATION is in type so tightly spaced that *i* is lost between *l* and *b*. NOW YOU is stacked, with no interlineal spacing.

MUSIC and last line—NATIONAL—demonstrate that Written and extreme Novelties should never be set all-cap.

First FACULTY was done in transfer letters; *F* is broken and characters are out of alignment. Second FACULTY is set on wavy line.

COMMENCEMENT is broken without hyphens and GRADES LOWERED are stepped lines.

ADMINISTRATION on two different backgrounds. HALFTIME is staggered and RELIGION is negatively spaced—and achieves negative legibility.

3. Will decorative elements be used as paragraph starters or as gimcracks between grafs? What design shall they be?

4. Will Italics (preferably) or caps (not very good) be used to emphasize words in the text? Or will no such visual emphasis be used?

5. How will you handle titles of books, plays, etc? In Italics, boldface, or caps—or by placing them in quotes?

6. Will there be a period at the end of a short caption? When captions are only sentence fragments?

7. What style will you use for designating position of people in pictures? (Look at Chapter 12 for help to this one.)

8. Will you use middle initials in names? Will you abbreviate titles such as "President" or "Secretary," etc.?

9. How will names be set in the senior directory? "William B. Smith" or "Smith, William B."?

These decisions guide the copyreader as well as the printer. They must be committed to writing so that the consistency so necessary to good writing and good typography be strictly maintained.

Headline Type

If body type is like underwear, essential but inconspicuous, then headline letters are like dressup clothes. They are highly visible and they contribute greatly to the impression that the viewer has of the wearer.

So the headletters should be chosen with that factor in mind, to reinforce the personality—and theme—of this one specific book. Legibility and beauty are also important factors.

As with so many choices involving good taste, you'll never go far wrong by choosing a classic. Remember that only good things endure; they are old because they are good. And remember that the style, in anything, that is the newest of new today will become dated awfully fast.

Sans Serifs make excellent headletters. The most popular are Spartan, Tempo, and Vogue. Helvetica, Univers, and Venus are excellent contemporary Gothics. In the Roman race, popular faces are Bodoni, Palatino, Caledonia, Garamond, and Times Roman. The Square Serifs, Memphis and Stymie, are also popular and good.

Handlettering may be used but rarely does a student have enough skill to produce the quality you want. Stickon or transfer letters will widen your choice but it will take staff time—not a serious problem—and money, which might be compensated for by a lower typesetting charge. Check with your printer.

☆ All headlines should be from the same type family.

No more than five sizes of type will be needed even in the largest book.

Divider pages use 36- through 72-point, although it is simple to go to an even larger size if necessary.

Subdivider or *department* heads scale down to 24- through 42-point. The *main head* on a 2-page spread should be 18- or 24-point. *Subheads* on such a page are two steps in point size smaller, from 18-point to 12, and from 24 to 14.

☆ Don't use too large headlines.

The size of heads depends on the headletter chosen; the lighter the face, the larger the size. The overall typographic tone of body type and typical pictures will also help determine how much of the intensity must come from the heads.

Student editors often use heads too large. This can lure the reader from the message to the medium—and despite what Marshall

Fragment of yearbook page, reproduced in original size, shows how type—positive, or in reverse as here—becomes illegible on variegated background.

McLuhan says, that's neither good communicating nor good typography.

The fifth face, when used, is for *running heads*, a technique not yet universal but highly popular and growing in use. The running heads are a continuous piece of copy, in display-size type, that runs from page to page. If only that element were read on a page, there would be a smooth-flowing commentary proceeding from front to back of the book.

☆ Running heads should be set in a face that contrasts as markedly as possible to regular headlines.

The Italic of the regular headletter may be used. In this case it would be in 18-point type and subheads would not be used.

The running heads should be divided in such a way that the fragment that appears on each spread is reasonably self-contained and logical. Here is a typical progression in the *Academics* section:

Academics is the reason Central High exists . . .

(This on the divider page showing a group of students carrying armloads of books as they enter the school.)

. . . *they bring honor to the individual student and to the school.*

(A page showing academic awards being presented.)

Academic work demands concentration and discipline . . .

(Shots of study halls, libraries, and students cramming in unlikely places.)

Non-functional page layouts. Left, black background over-whelms too-small pictures. Lack of identification plus small sizes make them totally useless. Spread at right disinte-grates from huge area of trapped space. Pictures are far too small and unidentified.

Left and center, art background is too large in relation to photos. Placement of pictures at left disguises design; there is no identification. In center page, faculty portraits are identified only by autographs which often are difficult to decipher. Page at right lacks unity because four different typefaces are used. Again, there are no picture idents.

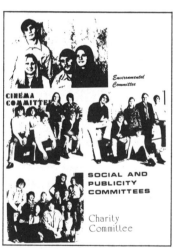

. . . it requires precision and accuracy.
(This section covered the labs, chem, phys-ics, zoo, and botany.)
. . . Academics bring alive the glorious works of the past . . .
(This spread covered art, music, and drama.)
. . . and the exciting creativity of con-temporary times . . .
(and this one English and journalism programs.)
. . . Academics are hard work . . .
(A full-page shot of students taking a final exam.)

. . . and Academics are fun.
(A group of candids of classes hugely en-joying some classroom joke.)
Notice the use of the *ellipsis,* the three little dots, which acts as a typographic chain to link the segments together.
So the running heads go, tying preceding and following pages into a satisfying whole. Because they are so conspicuous, running heads must be of highest literary quality. Assign them only to your best writer.
This same running technique may be used for captions on a spread:

FACULTY & STAFF

Left, collage is confusing, wasteful of space; identifications are lacking. Center, margins are too scanty, lines too long; lack of headline loses identity for page. Right, reverse type, especially in large masses, is difficult to read. Black pages smudge under reader's fingers long after ink has dried.

Left, pictures of almost identical shape and size make monotonous checkerboard, there is no nucleus for good page pattern. Neither players nor games are identified. Center, section-page heading runs vertically (bad typography) and was trimmed irregularly, common danger when type bleeds or runs too close to margin. Right, obtrusive pattern overlaid on photo is confusing; group is fragmented.

STUDENTS · CURRICULUM

While actors posture before the footlights . . .

. . . unseen but essential workers toil backstage . . .

. . . as the audience sits entranced . . .

. . . by the perennial magic of "Our Town."

Running captions cannot be used when identifications are required but some staffs have been fairly successful by setting the running captions in Italic and identifications in Sans Serifs. Consistency is im-

portant and this technique must be used throughout at least a section if not the whole book.

☆ Headlines should be road signs for the reader.

They should not be so conspicuous that they stop the reader. Rather, they should guide the eye throughout the spread. If you consider headlines as bait, to lure the reader into the text, then you'll logically avoid the malfunctional placement that sometimes plagues yearbooks.

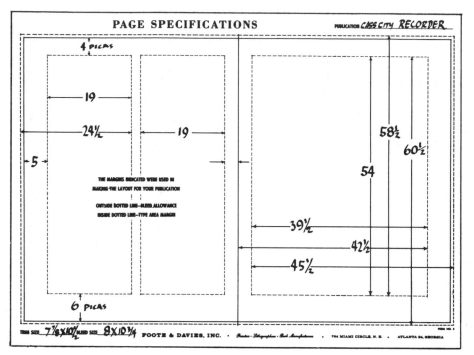

PAGE SPECIFICATIONS

PUBLICATION *CASS CITY RECORDER*

4 PICAS

19

24½   19

5

THE MARGINS INDICATED WERE USED IN
MAKING THE LAYOUT FOR YOUR PUBLICATION

OUTSIDE DOTTED LINE—BLEED ALLOWANCE
INSIDE DOTTED LINE—TYPE AREA MARGIN

58½
60½
54

39½
42½
45½

6 PICAS

TRIM SIZE _7⅞X10½_ BLEED SIZE _8X10¾_ **FOOTE & DAVIES, INC.** · *Printers · Lithographers · Book Manufacturers* · 764 MIAMI CIRCLE, N. E. · ATLANTA 24, GEORGIA

Specification chart. All measurements for page and spread are indicated here. Each layout is checked against it to assure consistency in margins, column, bleeds, etc.

☆ The head should never be lower than, or to the right of, the start of the article.

That would force the eye to go "backward" from the head into the type. There is one obvious exception to this: If the headline is in Column 1 and the story starts at the top of Column 2, the head may be lower than the start of the story because the eye naturally moves upward as it travels from one column to the other.

The longer the "backward" travel imposed by head placement, the greater the irritation to the reader. So it is extremely bad to have headlines at the bottom of the page or on the right-hand page if the article starts on the left page.

The path from the headline to the text should be as short and direct as possible. No barrier to the reading eye should be placed in that path.

☆ Headlines should be set only in straight lines.

Type that is set vertically, on a curve, sideways, or jumbled is difficult to read. It may be ornamental but that isn't the function of type; its sole purpose is to be read, easily, quickly, and accurately.

☆ Never set Script, Cursive, Text, or Ornamented letters all-cap. All-capital setting lowers legibility of all typefaces. In the case of ornate letterforms, legibility is destroyed.

Although limitations are not as severe as in newspapers, yearbook heads should be written tersely. They may be in "head-

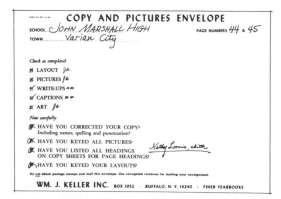

Envelope contains all material for spread. Printed checklist is initialed by sub-editors responsible for copy, captions, layout, etc. Editor-in-chief personally makes final check listed in lower left.

linese" or they may use ordinary English rules for tense and articles. But the chosen style must be used consistently throughout the book.

☆ Avoid placing type on dark or variegated backgrounds.

To read type we must see it; to see it there must be maximum tonal contrast between it and its background. So type printed on a gray background, or a colored one, loses much visibility.

☆ Type should be surprinted only on a solid background.

If type is placed over a halftone, let's say of the surface of a lake or river, the variegated background of highlights and shadows of the wave pattern will make it extremely difficult to distinguish the letterforms.

☆ Avoid all-capital setting.

We "read" words and phrases by recognizing their top silhouette. The more distinctive that outline, the more quickly we read. All-cap setting flattens out this silhouette to a straight line.

AS YOU READ THIS SHORT PARAGRAPH YOU NOTICE IMMEDIATELY THAT IT ISN'T NEARLY AS PLEASANT OR EFFICIENT TO DO SO AS IT HAS BEEN TO READ PREVIOUS BODY TYPE. WHILE WE AREN'T AS AWARE OF THIS DISABILITY IN READING THE FEW WORDS OF A HEADLINE, THE HANDICAP EXISTS THERE, TOO.

The Most Common Style For Setting Headlines Is Upper-And-Lower, Like This Sample. It Is Better Than All-Caps But Still Not As Good As What We'd Call "Regular" Setting.

The advantage of all-cap heads is that they are bolder, put more ink into a given area. Upper-and-lower is the style used by most newspapers today and so they say "headlines" just by that style.

But the most effective is downstyle. Here headlines are capped just as body type is: The first word and proper nouns are capped, all other words are lowercase.

☆ Headline style must be consistent throughout the book.

☆ The function of type is to be read.

As long as editors keep that in mind, as long as they use type to serve the reader, with the reader's wants and needs always in mind, they know that the typography of the book is sound.

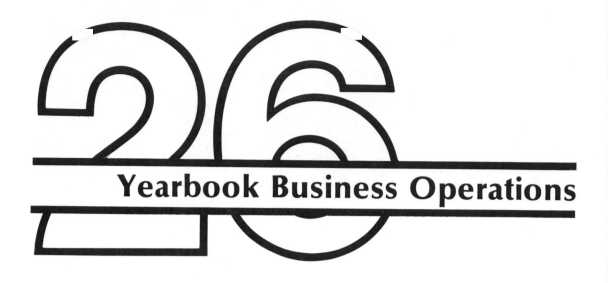

Yearbook Business Operations

Sound business procedures are as important for a yearbook's success as good editorial content. Combined, they can bring about a superior result in which staff and other students can take pride. Weakness in either can create a badly flawed product.

Mismanagement or sloppy handling of funds for a book's operations certainly can bring whirlwinds of trouble for the whole enterprise.

Like other scholastic publications, a yearbook can never be just an artistic success; it must be financially sound. This imposes substantial responsibilities upon the business staff.

The yearbook business manager faces the same problems in recruiting a good staff as any other publication and usually turns to journalism classes in the school during recruitment efforts. Also, announcements are made—either on the public address system or on official bulletin boards—telling office hours at the yearbook's assigned room when applicants can report to be interviewed for possible jobs. A fairly simple form should be made up, probably Mimeographed, for interested students to fill in. Information needed includes name, home address, home school room, telephone number for after-school hours, and possible times when the individual is available to work on selling subscriptions, soliciting advertising, or helping to keep records in the yearbook office.

Building a Budget

☆ The essential first step toward financial success is a good, sound budget.

An early decision must be made by the editor-in-chief and business manager on just what the financial limits will be for the emerging yearbook. The figures may shift slightly with sharper refinements of estimated expenditures and receipts. Without a tight budget-control system, costs may skyrocket while receipts decline sharply. That guarantees true financial troubles. Thus the business manager should make a re-examination during the Christmas vacation and several times during the months until the books are ready for distribution.

Best sources for data to draft a preliminary budget are past records of the yearbook's business staff, especially for the previous year's book. However, remember that in a shifting economy such figures may not reflect current prices with total accuracy. At best, budgeting represents educated guessing and as more information becomes available even better guesses can be made.

Points to consider in a preliminary budget include:

Receipts
Number of books sold (subject to revision after subscription campaign).

Price of the books (subject to updating after contract is negotiated with printer).

POINTS TO BE CHECKED IN SETTING UP YOUR BUDGET

PRODUCTION COSTS *These are the decisions which will affect your final production cost.*

Number of books...................		Text Pages	Number....................
			Grade (Name) of Paper............
Page Size	..........7¾ x 10½ inches		Weight ....
	..........8½ x 11 inches	Composition	Cost of Hand Set Type $..........
	..........9 x 12 inches		Machine Set Type $..........
	..........bleed pages	Artwork	Cost of artwork
	..........non-bleed pages		not done by staff $..........
Covers	Class...............	Plates	...............Letterpress
	..........Padded		...............Offset
	..........Other Factors		Number of photos to be
	Cost each		reproduced..............
			Number of separate
End Sheets	..........Plain		reductions..............
	..........Printed	Presswork	No. of pages.............color
	Number of colors...........		No. of pages.............color
Insert Pages	Printed in............colors	Binding	Type of Binding................
	Number.................		Special Folding, Cutting........
	Where in Book............	Estimated Printing Cost based on	
		these specifications $............	

NON-PRINTING COSTS

Photography:	Cost of Commercial		Art Supplies	$.............
	Contract	$.............		
	Film for Staff Use (Cost) $.........		Printed Forms (subscription blanks,	
			advertising contracts, etc.)	$...........
	Finishing of Staff Photos $...........		Car Expense	$...........
Shipping of Packing Cartons		$...........	Telephone Expense	$...........
Postage		$...........	Contingent Funds	$...........
Office Supplies		$...........	Non-Printing Costs	Total............

Add the Production Costs to the above items and here is your budget $...........

Checklist for setting up yearbook budget. This excellent aid was prepared by, and is used courtesy of, Mead Papers.

Advertising rates and revenues (subject of change when contracts have been signed with local merchants and others).

Appropriations by student government or allocation from school administration.

Sale of space to organizations.

Sale of pictures.

Contributions.

Expenditures

(Note that all the following are subject to change as further information becomes available.)

Printing costs.

Cover and binding costs.

Photography costs.

Office expenses.

Publicity costs.

Distribution costs, including mailing and express charges.

Miscellaneous costs and contingencies.

Let's examine these items in more detail.

The major portion of the book's revenues must come from its sale. This requires an aggressive subscription sales effort plus a price that most—if not all—students can afford and which they will be willing to pay. Thus establishing the price may decide, in part, a subscription campaign's success. The greater the number of yearbooks produced, the lower the cost per copy. This is the basis of all mass production. So a successful campaign can result in either a lower price to students or a better book for the money paid.

Some school administrations purchase a bulk quantity of yearbooks to use for promotion or public relations distribution. This is a boon in keeping per-page costs low.

Advertising, generally, is more important as a source of revenue for yearbooks than for newspapers and magazines. In some cases, a school administration allows the newspaper and magazine a grant from the student governing organization or local Board of Education. This is less frequently done for yearbooks.

The business staff should set a fair rate for advertising and conduct a conscientious selling job. Obviously, the lower the rate, the easier it is to sell space for ads.

When funds come from the student governing organization or local board, the money frequently is called a "subsidy." Actually in the strictest sense, that is not true. Rather, it is a hidden sale. Students' dues are split among various activities including funds to help finance the yearbook at a slightly lower price.

Many yearbook staffs charge student groups and clubs for pages showing their activities. While this is widely used to raise funds, the size of an organization's budget may easily determine the amount of space bought. This is blatantly unfair to a group with a highly useful program and which has other things to do with funds which might have provided ego trips in yearbook photographs.

Whether to solicit contributions arouses varying reactions. Where such requests have been successful over the years, there is plenty of reason to try again. When this approach is first introduced today, however, some contributors resent what they think has a touch of "blackmail." Gift solicitation may be done by mail and thus avoid any semblance of pressure by personal contact. Some donors regard their contributions as deferred payments on the pleasure they received from yearbooks in their own school days.

Charges against the budget may be handled in many ways. The printers' and binders' payments are outlined in the contract. Those involving student work can become sticky. What about mileage for taking to the post office a package for the out-of-town printer? What about Saturday work to print up photographs for sale?

☆ Out-of-pocket expenses should be promptly reimbursed; extra hours of work should not be.

Senior editors repeatedly work late at night and over a weekend. They do not expect payment. The same rule applies for other staff members. Also athletes do not expect payments for practice training and Saturday performances.

Don't forget that a lot of small items are needed to put out a good yearbook. Postage, especially if the printer is out of town and you have to send a lot of material by first-class mail; long distance telephone calls; supplies for photography; stationery; copy paper; pencils; rubber cement; typewriter ribbons; and so forth—all have to be paid for and thus should be budgeted. No matter how carefully you try to estimate these, the chances are that you will omit something. That is why you include some money for contingencies. And always some unexpected emergency will come up during the year.

In building the preliminary budget and keeping it up to date when new data come in, the business manager works closely with the editor-in-chief and faculty advisor. An editor always wants more pages and more color for a more impressive book but the business manager has to be diplomatic enough to convince the staff that it should not buy champagne when it only has money for beer.

☆ Tight budget control is a must.

The editor-in-chief and business manager have to determine early the specifications on which suppliers will submit bids on printing and binding. The more detailed this infor-

Useful checklist for exploring all sources of revenue for yearbook. "Representation fees" are used by some staffs; in effect individuals and organizations are charged for space devoted to their activities.

mation, the more exactly the bidders can pinpoint their figures.

☆ A precise, detailed contract with a printer helps to reduce potential frictions.

Details of preparing invitations to bid, drawing up specifications, and negotiating the contract are given in Chapter 28. It might be a good idea to read that chapter right now.

Subscriptions

Undoubtedly the easiest way for the business staff to balance the budget would be to have the student government appropriate funds so that every student would receive a free copy. However, to compel all students thus to buy books could be unfair, especially to the less than affluent pupils. Some schools include the yearbook as part of a "package" for graduating seniors; this still requires a sales campaign for all other students, faculty, alumni, and friends of the school.

If there is no appropriation or if it is only a supplement to sales revenues, the campaign must be well planned and conducted zealously.

☆ Set a sales goal.

Usually 80% to 85% of a student body is considered good coverage.

☆ Decide whether sales shall be cash or may be paid in several installments.

The installment plan entails extra work in collecting the installments and more bookkeeping.

A sales campaign should begin soon after the school opens in the fall. The sales staff should be briefed and inspired at pep meetings. Each sales person should know the reasons why a student should buy a yearbook:

1. As a permanent record of an important school year;

2. As a way to remember friends in the years ahead;

3. As a pleasant package to preserve a student's picture;

4. As an attractive addition to one's library at a low cost since a typical yearbook is strikingly less expensive than a similar commercial book; and

5. As a demonstration of loyalty to school and class.

For all practical purposes, the fall sales campaign is the only chance students have to buy a book. This should be stressed during the selling. A yearbook staff can't afford to order books on speculation that they will be sold in the spring. Any copies that turn up in the spring semester should be sold at

Yearbook sales receipt. Student's name on stub need not be on portion given purchaser.

a premium, which is $1 more in many schools.

If the sales efforts coincide with those for the school newspaper, business managers of the two publications should coordinate their campaigns. Competition should be played down and efforts made to sell both. Techniques discussed in Chapter 16 for newspapers apply generally for yearbooks. Good "show biz" devices maximize sales aspects to attract student and faculty attention: A kickoff assembly, a musical group or band concert during a noontime break, signs, bulletin board announcements, and commercials on the school loudspeaker system. Don't forget that news in the local newspaper and on broadcast stations also stimulates interest.

To identify those who have subscribed, buttons, ribbons, or just a plain feather pinned to shirt or sweater will create conversation and build a bandwagon effect among those who have not yet purchased.

Direct mail should be used to reach nonstudent prospects such as recent graduates and community patrons interested in what is happening in the local high school. Always enclose an order form, preferably a reply postcard so the prospect needn't write a letter.

☆ Conduct a cleanup campaign before Thanksgiving vacation.

This allows a final chance for sales before you have to give the printer the total figure for the press run. It also allows business representatives to check students who may have permitted their installment payments to lapse and to appeal one last time to those who hesitated earlier about buying.

In some larger urban high schools, editors

Receipt form for yearbook sales in installment payments. Forms are filled out in duplicate. Buyer gets coupon each time payment is made; carbon shows date of each; stub shows total payment.

Edie Adams	William H. Hubler	Pearl P. Schrack
Kathy Arton	Jody and Phil	Robin Slau
Astor Diner	Mr. Anthony Kinkay	Smaug
Sue Bieling	Mrs. Raymond G. Knaefler	Audrey Smith
Mrs. Beverly Clark	Jan Kratz	Mr. and Mrs. H. R. Smith
Clops	Ann Lau	Soft Pebble
Crickett	Lisa	Albert Stewart
Tricia Cruse	Janet Martin	Suzy's Violin
Theresa Daneman	Mr. and Mrs. Henry F. Mazaleski	Liz Teed
Discovery Days	Miss Mary Ann Mazaleski	Terry
Tim Dixon	Micky-the Terçible	Ginny Ward
Mrs. Gloria Dreisbach	John Myers	Mrs. Ruth Wardlow
Scott Dressel	Myot	N. B. Watton
enaj	Nikki the groat	Mr. and Mrs. Charles Wilcox
Mr. and Mrs. Richard Gilbert	Kathy Nuss	Doris Wilcox
Donna Jo Gerber	Oogie and dEdthumbe	Paul R. Winsch
Jon and Carole Haas	Mr. and Mrs. John F. Pauls	Sylvia Veneziale
Mr. and Mrs. W. I. Haas	Mr. and Mrs. A. Charles Roger	James Visser
Bertha M. Hirzel	RSQ	Holly Breuninger
Marina Hollenshead	Mr. and Mrs. Douglas Santos	

Patrons are pleasantly acknowledged in this spread from "Troubadour" of North Penn High, Lansdale, Pennsylvania. Although this is literary magazine, technique is equally useful in yearbook.

have tried with success a *two-edition year-book,* one in hard cover, the other in soft. Seniors, who generally keep the book and will pay more for permanence, purchase the hard-cover version while the other classes buy the soft covers since they are less likely to save the book for years and years. Since hard covers are an expensive item in costs, the soft-cover edition is cheaper and thus more salable. One caution: Putting out two editions adds extra record-keeping for business staff members but wider distribution can make the additional work well worthwhile.

Advertising

Because yearbooks are far more permanent than student newspapers and magazines, they have a built-in advantage and appeal for those who want to sell their products or services. This means that these ads must be written for long-term exposure and so tend to be institutional in tone. The message sells the store as a place to do business rather than individual items of merchandise that happen to be good buys this month or this season.

However, since some rules for selling ads and writing good copy are constant, much of the information in Chapter 14 is worthwhile to yearbook business staff members, especially statements about the teen-age market and its potentiality.

Advertising sales personnel should be organized for "beat" coverage just as reporters are assigned to cover news sources. Business and advertising managers make up a list of prospects, each one on a file card. On each card are at least the name of the store, address, telephone number, name of manager or the individual in charge of buying advertising, kind of products or services, and percentage of total sales that are made to teen-agers. This supplies sales personnel with individualized data which can give a shove toward signing a contract. Points that should be known and mentioned during the sales presentation include:

1. Yearbook ads are permanent and they will be viewed for years.

2. Such ads are well read, probably as much as editorial content.

3. Readers, because of pleasure with the yearbook, will see the ad in a receptive environment.

4. Yearbook advertising reaches a wide audience since students' family, relatives, and friends also will see the book. Minimum readership is considered six persons.

5. Ads in a fine yearbook build a merchant's prestige and give the store a quality image.

YEARBOOK ADVERTISING CONTRACT

Advertiser (Name of Business) **THE PIZZA PLAZA**

Advertiser's Address **417 So. Lafayette street**

Agree to take **½** page(s) of advertising at $ **80.** in the advertising section of

Name of Book **"The Saga"** Annual. Date **September 14 '77**

Name of School **St. John's** Address **Middleville** City Town **Iowa** State

Payment will be made (Date) **on publication**

Please make checks payable to **"The Saga"**

ADVERTISING SPECIFICATIONS	APPROVED SIGNATURES
Size of Advertisement (Circle One)	Advertiser *Ed Gregory*
⅛ ¼ ⅓ (½) Full Page Other	Faculty Advisor *Susan Peters*
Copy For Advertisement X Attached	School Representative *Bob Blake*
	FOR STAFF USE ONLY

Special Instructions *Horizontal half page*

WM J KELLER INC · FINER YEARBOOKS

Yearbook advertising contract. (Courtesy Wm J Keller Inc.)

Advertising rates depend on a wide range of factors such as the size of the book's circulation, previous ad results, the community's overall attitude toward advertising, and—to a considerable degree—the effectiveness of the advertising sales presentation. Generally, the basic advertising rate should be at least two times the cost of the page that is being sold, including not just the printing bill but also cover, binding, and overhead costs that the staff incurred. In other words, a page rate would be set by dividing the entire budget for total yearbook costs by half the total number of pages. Some yearbook staffs that have brought a lot of teen-age business as a result of yearbook ads charge two and a half or three times the costs.

To encourage larger space sale, you can graduate your rates. For instance, if a full page costs $200, you might set the following for smaller size ads:

Half page	$125
Quarter page	$75
Eighth page	$40

These rates should be presented as giving the larger purchaser a bonus, never as penalizing the small space user.

☆ Never sell less than an eighth-page ad. Ads smaller than that are useless for the merchant and they fail to provide a profit for the book. Stores that don't want or can't afford at least an eighth-page ad may be grouped with others in the same category into a single, large *cooperative ad*. Such co-op ads carry several signatures, instead of only one.

Chain stores, as a rule, do not buy school publication space locally. The business manager should find out the name of the advertising agency for the whole group and write a sales letter to it, providing ad rates and other information needed for a decision.

When an advertising sale is completed, you should fill out the contract that gives all the details: Ad size, total cost, date payment is due or amount of money collected at time of sale, deadline for copy, whether pictures will be furnished by advertiser or staff, and if additional charge—how much —will be made for engravings.

The original contract goes to the advertising merchant and a copy is kept in the yearbook files after being entered in the ad log. An entry also is made by the bookkeeper so payments will be recorded in the ledger and bills will be sent out at the proper time.

☆ Don't accept charity ads. Running an "ad" which reads, "Compliments of a Friend" has no justification and

All ads on page are student produced. From "Maroon" of Kingston (New York) High.

only slightly more exists for one of "Best Wishes to the Graduates" along with the advertiser's name and address. A "compliments" ad does the buyer no good; a congratulatory one does just slightly more. The merchant could far better make an outright gift and have it listed as such.

The custom of soliciting yearbook patrons has grown in recent years. As contributors of cash gifts, they publicly acknowledge a student activity that they think is worthy. Professional men whose ethics codes prevent advertising outright, school PTA, service clubs, church societies, and other organizations are potential patrons. Those who contribute are given printed certificates of appreciation, signed by a yearbook representative: Business manager or editor-in-chief. Patrons are neatly listed alphabetically on a specially designed yearbook page.

Solicitation of patrons should be made in a dignified manner and should never have overtones of a tin-cup approach or of a squeeze play. Solicitors of possible patrons should carefully point out that the contribution does not include a free copy of the yearbook itself. Contributions should be acknowledged promptly by a personal letter signed by the business manager or editor. In some schools the principal writes a note, too.

By tradition or necessity, some school staffs conduct special fund-raising activities. This is done by both small schools and large urban ones. While such special events are legitimate, there is always a danger that students will spend time and energy that might better have been devoted to producing a better yearbook.

Groups of students may form a Booster's Auxiliary to contribute to the book's success. Obviously, staff members may direct recruitment for this organization but should save other time for the annual. The Honor Society or other high school service clubs may take on support of the yearbook as a main activity.

Candy sales, baked goods tables, Christmas bazaars, book fairs, and rights to a vending-machine concession have been utilized to provide yearbook funds. While these raise money, they have little, if anything, to do with journalism or the main thrust of putting out a yearbook. All should be viewed with some skepticism—unless they are absolutely required to balance the annual's budget.

Sale of pictures taken by yearbook staffers can be a lucrative activity that has journalistic connections. Usually, if students know that they can buy photographs, they seize the opportunity. Glossies may sell for at least $1 apiece with reduced rates for quantity purchases. Some staffs auction off unused glossy prints with several students acting as auctioneers and this provides a gala atmosphere. Since the cost of these unused prints already has been absorbed in the budget, profits are 100%. However, this sideline should never grow so that it interferes with the basic job of taking pictures for the book. After all regular work is completed, an auction can be held or the photo staff may complete those special orders that were taken earlier.

One school swelled the yearbook treasury by scheduling a "dance" in the gym five minutes after the books were distributed in home rooms at the end of the school day. By custom, this was the time when autographs were exchanged. Although there was phonograph music, little dancing took place as autographs were exchanged. A small admission brought in some funds and the student body had a good time. Of course, advance arrangements would have to be made with the school administration.

Among the many methods of raising money, the school should choose the ones that render a real service, will be fun to carry on, will not demand too much of participants or staff, and will show a profit. Above all, it must be an activity that does not reflect unfavorably on either yearbook or school.

Student-produced ads—especially student art—have great appeal to young audience.

Bookkeeping

All the efforts on selling subscriptions and advertising may be wasted unless the business manager and staff maintain an adequate and accurate system of records.

The ledger is a permanent record, one that next year's staff will often consult. In it is written, neatly and legibly, each transaction. It should be itemized in rather fine detail. A teacher of business subjects may help set it up and tell how to maintain it.

You should have duplicate receipt forms for sales of books, advertising, photographs, and contributions from patrons. You may use one basic form with boxes to check for the specific items involved. The customer gets the original copy; the carbon is filed for rechecking and transfer to the ledger.

There must be a detailed record of ex-

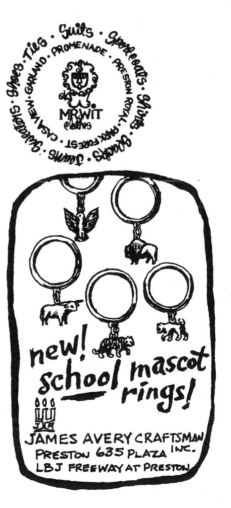

penditures, too. If you take care of the small items, the big costs will take care themselves—or so various surveys show.

A wise business manager is a penny-watcher. Too many small diversions may deplete money for budget items.

Supplies will account for many a figure in the expenditures column. In the dark-room, a photographer should cut a small test strip instead of using an 8 x 10 piece. Get maximum use out of developing chemicals but don't attempt to use them when they're so weak they'll only waste good paper. Writers should conserve copy paper by using spoiled sheets for scratch paper. Save paperclips—and watch that staffers do not pocket a few each week for their own personal use.

Establish an inflexible policy for purchase of supplies only upon authorization given in writing. It's easy to spend money when it isn't yours; students have gone on spending sprees and bought materials that were unneeded. Tell all suppliers that the yearbook will disallow any charges to its account that lack proper authorization.

☆ The business manager should control petty cash and not reimburse unauthorized expenditures.

This may seem hard-hearted but it is the only way to maintain effective control. Most expenses should be charged. The cash box should be kept nearly bare as a constant reminder to watch pennies.

Distributing the Books

The most pleasant task of a business staff is delivering the finished product. This, too, must be carried out in a businesslike way.

The printer is instructed—frequently in the contract but sometimes in a supplementary letter—where and how to deliver the yearbooks. The circulation manager should arrange, well in advance, for a suitable "receiving room." This space should be:

1. Large enough to hold the cartons and people who'll be working on them;

2. Clean, so dust and dirt won't wreak damage;

3. Convenient to the point of actual distribution; and

4. Securely locked.

It's a sad fact that many individuals who sneer when asked to buy a book in the fall will go to almost any length to obtain one in the spring—except paying for it.

Books should be checked after arrival to determine that the number of copies is correct. It is fairly easy for a printer to overlook a carton or two in the shipping room or to deliver some to another customer.

Have the proper tools to open cartons, since you may damage books or knuckles using makeshift instruments.

Utilize all the school's communications systems to announce where and when books will be distributed. Some schools permit a break in the regular class schedule for distribution but that, of course, has to be arranged with the principal.

If the receiving room is adequate, you can pass out books there or from tables set just outside the door. The staff room or part of the yearbook office may be convenient. If the main supply of books is distant from the distribution point, make sure a battalion of runners will keep the supply adequate at all times.

Rehearse procedure before the actual delivery. A student must have a receipt or final stub, if payment was in installments. The circulation manager should be on hand at all times to supervise proceedings and the business manager should be there as a trouble-shooter. If a dispute arises, the person in charge should settle it at once. To do this, it's necessary to have ready access to all records. A student, entitled to an annual, wants it without delay.

If you have extra books, the day of distribution is the time to sell them. Don't forget that such students pay more money as penalty for not purchasing during the fall campaign. Also have money on hand to make change for such sales. Safeguard the receipts of these purchases as you did others earlier. They, too, are part of the yearbook business records and should be so treated.

The vast percentage of all copies will go like hot cakes but a few unfilled subscriptions will always remain. If a student is home sick, have a staff member deliver the annual. For other absent students, send word to their home rooms where they can pick up their copies.

Distribution should be in person, wherever feasible. If books must be mailed, do so with care, in mailing boxes or corrugated board wrapping. Include a return address for such packages. Since the book will move at a special low (and slower) postal rate, notify the cusomer by first-class mail that it's on the way.

The circulation manager also distributes yearbooks on the complimentary list, such as the principal, school library, and local Board of Education members. Business manager and editor-in-chief should prepare this list of free distribution well in advance and should be properly appreciative—but not overly generous.

Finishing Off the Job

The advertising manager checks to see that all ads contracted for actually were printed and without errors. If human error

Ten Reasons for Buying Yearbook Ads

1. The yearbook is for teenagers and their parents and covers that market in depth.
2. Teenagers deeply appreciate recognition of their book and will respond to an ad.
3. Three-fourths of all parents read their students' yearbook and will see the ad.
4. Having an ad means school endorsement. Not every business can be in the book.
5. Yearbooks are preserved, so these ads are looked at again and again.
6. Ad rates are low because the yearbook is a non-profit school enterprise.
7. Pictures in the ad section will draw the attention of readers as never before.
8. Students will establish homes in the near future and will be permanent customers.
9. Students influence the purchases of their parents. The yearbook reaches them.
10. The book also reaches buyers like the teachers, administrators and the alumni.

KNOW THESE REASONS FOR BUYING YEARBOOK ADS SO YOU CAN QUICKLY ANSWER ANY QUESTIONS RAISED BY BUSINESSMEN YOU MEET.

Reminder card carried by yearbook ad reps lists 10 strong reasons why yearbook advertising is beneficial to merchants. (Courtesy R. Wallace Pischel, Inc.)

crept in, the ad manager should immediately make both a refund and a sincere apology. An apology promptly made—never excuses or phony explanations—just may smooth out these troubles.

The bookkeeper should check all ads and if there was no prepayment, bill the advertiser. This may be sent by mail but it is better for an ad staffer to deliver it by hand. These statements should be accompanied by either a tearsheet of the ad or a duplicate copy of the page. No advertiser should expect to receive an entire yearbook but is entitled to a copy of the ad as proof of publication. If payment is not received a week or two before the end of the school year, a polite reminder should be sent to the delinquent advertiser.

Payments should be made to the photographer, printer, and bindery, if separately billed, as soon as possible.

After the excitement of delivery and actually viewing the completed annual, business side staffers should double-check ads for errors, just as the editorial workers check other text. Any mistakes should be noted; apologies promptly made, preferably by the business manager in person; and corrections made neatly in India ink in several books. One, obviously, is kept in the office for future staffs' use—so that a mistake does not go echoing for all time.

Advertising is not ganged at end of book in "Perannos" of New Canaan (Connecticut) High. Staff treats book like magazine; first ads appear as early as Page 9 and then throughout book. This ad on Page 34, designed and drawn by student, certainly does not detract from Seniors page; indeed, variety is pleasant.

Another corrected copy may be filed in the principal's office and a third with the school library.

Before taking off for the summer, the business manager should get all the yearbook finances in shape and have them audited by an expert not associated with the staff. This might be a teacher of commercial courses, the school administration accountant, or even someone from outside the school system.

Finally, the whole staff comes out, usually on a Saturday, to clean house for the incoming staffers. Throw out material that is no longer needed but don't discard stuff that will aid your successors the next year. In fact, retiring and incoming staffs may want

New Buggy Belle Tracey Horn finds "separates" the wearable way to welcome spring.

Student model makes appealing small-space ad in "Shield" of Northwest Classen High, Oklahoma City, Oklahoma.

to work together in this job. In any case, close liaison must be maintained between the two groups so that continuity is maintained.

Now the outgoing staff members have completed the big job and left behind a properly indoctrinated new group—and a yearbook in which they and their fellow students can take great pride.

BOOK

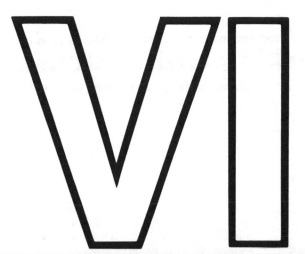

VI

THE PEOPLE IN JOURNALISM

Faces are of Ornamented race

27 Working with Teachers

"Some of my best friends are teachers."

When a scholastic publication's staff member makes such a remark, it is not necessarily apple-polishing, unrestrainted flattery, or sarcasm. A successful high school editor and business manager almost always get along well with the advisor. Other teachers, too, may give great assistance which is reciprocated in friendly admiration.

If you polled editors or managers from highly rated newspapers, magazines, or yearbooks, the overwhelming majority would say that this was true.

Faculty advisors can show you shortcuts in journalistic procedures that will save time and allow you to do a better job. They help fill in gaps in your limited training. Teachers usually know more about the school "world" since most of them have been around longer than any of the students. Thus they know its history, traditions, and other background that could be obtained nowhere else. They can help solve ticklish questions of what is good taste and what is good for staff morale. They may help in obtaining better office space, typewriters, and other conveniences that will permit a better publication.

Other teachers and administrators also are important to a successful operation. Much news comes from the faculty. Enrollment statistics, class schedules, announcements of forthcoming assembly programs, lists of awards and honors all may be obtained at the principal's office. Plans for a school play are released by the drama coach. Details on next week's football game come from the athletic director or coach. The program for a Latin Club festival might be told by a Latin teacher instead of club officers.

The school librarian should rate an especially high position on an editor's list because all kinds of reference books and idea sources are in a school library for staff members to use and peruse.

The Faculty Advisor

A generation ago high school advisors were known to rewrite students' copy, revise headlines they didn't like, and spike material that they thought inappropriate for publication. Much of this has changed, due, in a considerable degree, to recent court decisions about student rights for freedom of speech and freedom of the press. Also increasing emphasis has been put on the concept that the scholastic press is a valuable learning tool and educational resource whose effectiveness can be substantially impaired if student editors must function under imminent fear of discipline for errors in judgment. An oftquoted comment in such discussion is:

> The right to freedom of expression carries with it the right to make mistakes on occasion.

Discussing all extracurricular activities, including the student press, the New York

State Education Department said this about advisors' responsibilities:

> If a student organization decides or is required to have an advisor, the function of the advisor is to counsel, not to control or censor, and he should not be held responsible for the action of the student group if it rejects his counsel.
>
> *"Guidelines for Students*
> *Rights and Responsibilities."*

Since they were first prepared in 1972, the New York guidelines have formed the basis for similar rules in other states.

The faculty advisor should be considered an honorary member of the staff or an older brother or sister who can be consulted, with profit, about a ticklish problem or when in search of advice. An editor who has a good working relation with the advisor might turn for help when the questions comes up, "Should we print this material?" or "How can we get that news?"

Several advantages exist for consulting the teacher:

1. The advisor may have had previous comparable experiences and thus know a good solution.

2. The teacher has greater knowledge of the legal responsibilities in cases of possible libel and obscenity and probably a greater sophistication in cases of possible poor or bad taste; and

3. The advisor should be able to bring an impersonal attitude to the discussion whereas students may be emotionally involved in an argument or situation.

The advisor is a source for useful news tips, background, academic information, and journalistic know-how. Valuable historical information and traditions in a school may be obtained from teachers. For instance, is this year the first time that a basketball team elected co-captains? Or how many times in recent years have twins—or any other pair of students—won identical scholastic honors because their grades were the same for four full years? Is there some way to get a principal to tell some information to the editor-in-chief in confidence? An experienced advisor may know.

Advisors often serve as official liaison with the school administration and superintendent. When students do not accept and assume their responsibilities for good, sound journalism, then teachers point out these deficiencies and help students to correct them. Advisors may need to stress that student editors, like their professional counterparts, have obligations to be governed by standards of responsible journalism, such as avoidance of libel, obscenity, and defamation, and to provide as much opportunity as possible for sincere expressions of all shades of student opinion.

If a staff has a legitimate request to make of the school administration or the student governing organization, a faculty advisor can help in planning and drafting the petition and supporting arguments. You may desire more space for an enlarged staff, more filing cabinets in which to store records of advertisements and subscriptions, or permission for key editors to meet during a free period for the next month for planning. The idea may be good, but unless the presentation is effective, approval may not be forthcoming. Here, again, a faculty advisor should be considered as a helping, knowledgeable friend—not as a fellow conspirator who can win you and your staff colleagues something that you would like but which you really don't deserve.

☆ Be sure you deserve support before you involve the advisor.

Advisors can help an enterprising staff to protect its "scoops" by explaining to the principal and other teachers who are news sources how journalistic deadlines work. School administrators, especially the principal, should be told that when a school staff uncovers a feature article or other news by its own enterprise, faculty members are under special obligation to respect the students' initiative. Teachers should not accidentally give the same information to a regular reporter from the local daily which can get it into print promptly. If the daily's staffer stumbles onto the same idea, then students should be told that the local paper is working on the story, too.

Faculty also may help in releasing some

news stories at times favorable to the school paper's deadlines. Obviously, spot news, such as an accident or sudden resignation of the football coach, can't be delayed to favor the student press. However, many events can be controlled by administrative officers. For instance, release of the names of honor students could be held up so that both school and community papers print the news the same day.

Even if they might be tempted to do so, staff members should not run to teacher every time something goes wrong. Student editors and staffers should try to solve their own problems—at least the first time around. The initial responsibility on any school publication belongs to the students, and properly so.

One place where an advisor's counseling might be especially helpful is when awards and recognitions are being given. A teacher can bring an informed and possibly less emotional or biased viewpoint to evaluating.

☆ In making awards and granting recognition such as masthead listings and issuance of press cards, be generous but impeccably fair and just.

Some editors and advisors have found it useful to have *press cards* printed. When students are recognized as regular staff members, they are presented with their individual cards. Such a card might read:

☆ Holding a press card always should be a privilege that has to be earned through effective work on the staff, either editorial or business.

Many advisors mark up a copy of each issue of the student paper, pointing out superior work and poor performance. This notes students' errors so that not only they but fellow staff members may benefit—and, with luck, none will make them again. Of course, a teacher's comments should not be caustic, unless the student has been stupid or stubborn.

A highly competent editor-in-chief may do this analysis adequately. If an editor has sufficient expertise, naturally the advisor defers and lets the editor do the commenting.

An advisor may contribute much by directing efforts of students to evaluate their own performances. One school uses a form to have staff members rate themselves and then turn in copies to the editor-in-chief and advisor:

Staff Member's Self-Evaluation Sheet

Name: Issue No.

(Collect your stale copy, evaluate it by filling out this form, and staple your copy together with this form on top. Place your folder in filing cabinet.)

Best thing I did in preparation of this issue:

Worst thing I did in preparation of this issue:

Grade I think I deserve for my work on this issue:

Circle "Yes" or "No" before each question:

Yes   No   1. Did I meet the deadline on each story?

Yes   No   2. Was the copy clean when I turned it in?

Yes   No   3. Did I prepare my copy according to the style sheet?

Yes   No   4. Did I find a feature and play it up in the lead?

Yes   No   5. Did I avoid grammatical errors?

Yes   No   6. Did I avoid wasting words in my lead(s)?

Yes   No   7. Did I include only facts, stating sources for any opinions?

Yes   No   8. Was my copy clear?

Yes   No   9. Was my copy concise?

Yes   No 10. Was my copy accurate?

Yes No 11. Did I follow the style sheet for names and identities?

Yes No 12. Did I avoid editorializing?

Yes No 13. Did I stick to the third person except in quotations?

Yes No 14. Did I avoid a "will be held" expression?

Yes No 15. Did I write with the publication date in mind?

Yes No 16. Did I avoid using passive voice?

Yes No 17. Did I use "tomorrow," "last Friday," in preference to dates of the month?

Yes No 18. Am I proud of the contribution I made to this issue?

My contributions to this issue included (be specific):

☆ Expert evaluation should be helpful to all the staff.

Such careful study of performance is no childish action. Theodore M. Bernstein, former assistant managing editor of the *New York Times*, compiled a comparable analysis called "Winners & Sinners: A bulletin of second guessing issued occasionally from the southeast corner of The New York Times News Room." Here were bouquets for good work with staff members frequently mentioned by name, and adverse remarks on unidentified writers and copyreaders. So popular were Mr. Bernstein's sharp comments that many of them were collected into two books: *Watch Your Language* and *More Language That Needs Watching*. Both books should interest scholastic editors and advisors who seek hints on how to critique a publication staff's work.

A knowledgeable advisor will be able to supply guidance on staff relations. Every organization has its personnel problems, and high school publications, since they pay off in glory and status rather than dollars and cents, have their full share. As most stu-dents have little experience in managing people, even their contemporaries, an advisor who can give quiet but effective counsel is extraordinarily helpful to an editor.

Advisors should introduce themselves to staff members at local newspapers and broadcasting station. Early in the fall term, a visit to a newspaper office will provide beginners with useful information on how a daily is published. Some of this information should make them better staff workers; all will broaden their background about modern communications.

Professional journalists usually are willing to talk to the school staff and pass on valuable hints. A local reporter may be willing to tell some personal experiences about gathering news, an editor to discuss copy reading and headline writing, an editorial writer to tell how the paper's policy is set, and the business manager to explain handling records of subscriptions and advertising.

Students on the business staff turn to the commercial, business practices, or accounting teacher for help in setting up account books, establishing proper procedures for selling and writing advertising, and for keeping track of subscriptions. Although an English or journalism teacher traditionally is given the assignment as advisor, commercially oriented faculty members can be of great help for staffers on the business side. What business records should be set up and maintained was discussed in earlier chapters, but your teacher in charge of business training courses should be consulted for help in inaugurating the system most useful for your publication.

Faculty advisors should be appointed by a principal only after consultation with various students, especially key editors, business manager, and senior staff members. If an administrator wants a periodical to serve as an effective educational device, then a teacher should never be imposed arbitrarily upon a staff.

Some advisors have worked on newspapers, magazines, or at broadcasting stations and bring that experience to their counseling. Others have undertaken extensive preparation by independent studying. Many faculty advisors with years of experience have picked up valuable information from previous publication staffs that they happily and unselfishly share with current editors. These tips will involve not only writing and preparation of editorial copy and pictures but also valuable suggestions on how to work with printers, commercial photographers, and business leaders in the community who purchase advertisements in scholastic publications.

Among present faculty advisors are many who took college courses in journalism and communications, attended special workshops after graduation, or participated in summer training especially in publication supervision. Increasingly state education departments and professional teachers' organizations have approved specializations for teaching journalism in high schools or for supervising student publications.

To expand such training, The Newspaper Fund, Inc. has brought more than 6,500 school-paper advisors back to college campuses for practical journalism training.

In a few schools, the same teacher has served as advisor to both the so-called official paper and an underground publication. This comes close to the ultimate in objectivity—as far as publication counseling is concerned.

Faculty as News Services

Teachers are important sources for both news tips and facts. They should be organized into a series of news-beat assignments just as are other informational sources.

The No. 1 news source is the principal's office. Some principals like to do all their own talking; others authorize an assistant or secretary to give out information on their behalf.

☆ Find out the administration's ground rules, then follow them.

A principal's office keeps many records on school administration and thus it may be used to check all kinds of information. If the principal is willing, you could obtain, for instance, home addresses of students

you wish to contact outside of classes, statistics to be used for historical comparisons, and biographical material on faculty members.

This office probably could provide information about education beyond your own school, too. Most state education departments issue a statewide directory of teachers. This could be used to check the spelling of faculty names in other towns, such as debating or basketball coaches at a distant school. Practically all school districts and county teachers' associations print and distribute rosters of teachers in their areas.

An alert editor arranges with the principal for senior staff members to use these source materials; or, better still, an editor orders the publication's own copies if they prove valuable enough. Despite new federal guidelines for individual student access to their own records, staff members can never be allowed to shuffle through every personnel file in the principal's office.

Another key news source is the spokesman for athletic activities. This may be the sports director, a specific coach, or some other individual on the sports staff.

☆ Find out who is authorized to make sports announcements and go to that person for them.

The same applies to all the variety of school activities. At the start of the school year, compile a list of officers and faculty advisors for clubs and other outside activities. If students are not available, then news may be obtained from the teacher concerned.

Also make a list of home-room teachers because they, too, may become news sources.

Here are some suggestions for interviewing teachers as news sources:

1. Always be polite and courteous to teachers you interview for possible news items.

2. Remember there is nothing wrong in trying to obtain all necessary facts involved in a news item. So ask, ask, and ask questions.

3. If you don't get all the information you think is needed, ask if some other teacher—or student—can provide the facts.

4. Don't be bashful, flustered, or intimidated because you are receiving news from a teacher instead of a student.

The School Library

A good school librarian deserves special affection from any publication's staff. Among the volumes may be the only complete files of school publications, including your own, that are available anywhere. Despite careful efforts, office copies of back issues of school papers, magazines, and yearbooks somehow seem to vanish or to be mutilated. Possibly the library's are in better shape because librarians make borrowers sign up when they take out any material and require that it be returned promptly.

Editors will be doing their successors a favor and making them less dependent on library files if they preserve at least two bound sets of complete copies of the newspaper or magazine each year for their own morgue. Each should have errors corrected so next year's staff won't make the same mistakes again.

☆ Scissors are *never* to be used on these bound files.

Such thoughtless action is ground for immediate murder—almost.

A school library also contains many standard reference books that a staffer needs to check facts, although some references should be available in the publication office, as suggested in Chapter 9.

Standard references in a school library contain this vital information:

1. Local city directory—names and addresses for all those living in the community. More complete than a telephone book (which should be on hand in the office) but generally more dated. Larger metropolitan areas issue directories of city officials, their addresses, telephone numbers, and a brief summary of their duties. When coverage extends beyond the school yard, this city listing may be especially useful.

2. Almanacs and yearbooks—general compendiums of statistics, history, and biography for earlier years.

Yearbook advertisers do not receive copy of publication as do those in newspapers or magazines. So, as proof of publication, this form is signed by ad rep and certified by printing firm. Page number where ad ran might usefully be included.

3. Encyclopedias—range from single-volume *Columbia Encyclopedia* to the multivolume *Encyclopaedia Britannica*, which is printed for American audiences despite its centuries-old title. Others widely used include *Collier's Encyclopedia*, *Encyclopedia Americana*, *New International Encyclopedia*, *Merit Students Encyclopedia*, and *World Book*. The latter two are designed especially for students. For a writer seeking extensive general background, any of them is a rewarding storehouse of facts.

4. Biographical information. *Who's Who in America* is an outstanding source for biographical material. Issued every other year, these volumes would supply facts on guest speakers, visitors, and so forth. Regional and vocational references include, among others, *Who's Who in the East* and *American Men of Science*. *Current Biographies* supplies more extensive biographical information on a far fewer number of prominent Americans. Issued monthly and cumulated annually, these are biographies in depth. The *New York Times Biographical Edition* weekly reprints profiles and biographies of individuals who have been written up in that metropolitan daily. This includes obituaries plus sketches of personalities in the current news.

5. *Readers' Guide to Periodical Literature*—cumulative publication that lists contemporary magazine articles by topic, title, and author. If you want to learn what has been printed on, say, shifting college-

admission standards, you look under the appropriate topical listings and find listed recent articles in a representative cross-section of mass circulation magazines and some specialized periodicals.

6. The *New York Times Index*—listing of every news story that appears in that paper. This semimonthly and cumulative annual index provides the dates, pages, and columns for stories on a desired subject. Many libraries keep files of the *New York Times.* But even if your library does not, the date in the *Index* will tell you in which of your local paper's editions to look. *Facts on File* is another source for contemporary facts.

Reference books, either in the publication office or in the library, make it possible to get the facts right for whatever news you have uncovered.

Working with teachers, whether they are advisors, news sources, or librarians, is a two-way street that makes it possible for publication staff members to perform professionally while still learning. Also they will be making friends that they will remember throughout the years.

Certificate of award gives tangible recognition for good staff work. (Courtesy R. Wallace Pischel, Inc.)

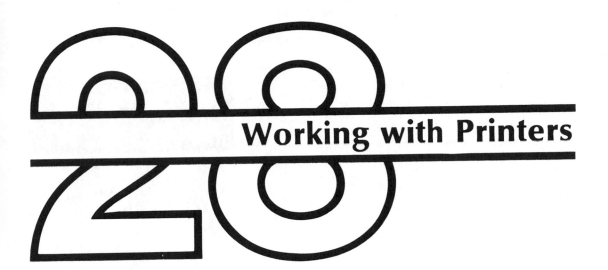

Working with Printers

I hate the printer when he snarls
"This head's too long!
"This pic won't fit!"
But I contemplate murder
When he screams
For copy that's not yet been writ.

But when he finds
Type we'd thought lost,
Or spots what might a libel been,
Or finds a typo that I missed . . .
I love him like a brother, then.

That newsroom doggerel has been echoed by uncounted editors, scholastic and professional. While it doesn't challenge Wordsworth or Browning, it points out the unusual relationship between the editorial and mechanical departments of a publication.

Printers and editors normally meet only at times of tension. When deadlines approach—not on little cat's feet, but with the clomp of a charging rhino—there isn't time for idle small talk. Conversation becomes terse and brusque and this may be interpreted as unfriendly. Printers can do nothing on their own; all their actions are directed by editors or advertising people. And often those directions seem irrational or are impossible to execute.

So it's no wonder that at times not only the editor but the printer "contemplates murder."

But the printer also deserves to be "loved like a brother." Many times the printer meets deadlines only by minor miracles.

And many's the time the backshop has saved the news staff from embarrassment. (Imagine the red faces of the staff of a well-known daily if the composing room had not pointed out that it's impossible to print the 47-page edition the dummy called for!)

Some student staffs fear and resent the printer because it is in the printshop that their errors come home to roost. But actually the printer is your ally—by the very fact of being your printer.

The shop is just as interested as you in producing a good publication. For it is an example—not only of your skill and pride of craft—but of the shop's as well.

Remember this in all your contacts with the craftsman, not only on the rare ones when the sun is shining but those when incipient calamity hangs like a low storm cloud.

Get to know your printer as a human being. You'll find printers, because of their work as preservers of all human knowledge, to be well-informed people. And because of a long tradition of their craft, they live up to the motto of the International Club of Printing House Craftsmen: "Share your knowledge." They can be fine teachers for young journalists.

Publication staffs ought to meet with their printer in the spring or late winter to discuss aims for the coming year, find out what help the printer can give—and begin the nitty-gritty of talking about deadlines, standards, and prices.

293

Speak up freely at these conferences. Many students fear being thought of as "hagglers"; others think that because they are inexperienced, they are being "taken" by a sharp operator. Neither is correct.

Purveyors who serve student publications are reputable business organizations; they aren't selling gold bricks. At the same time, they are used to the give-and-take of commercial bargaining. There's nothing disgraceful or petty in the staff getting the most for its money—or for the printer to get the best price for a product.

☆ A good transaction is one that is mutually satisfactory.

Discussions carried out with courtesy and good faith reach that mutual satisfaction in the most expeditious and pleasant manner.

Yearbook Contracts

Because of the substantial amounts of money involved, yearbook production is always covered by a contract. Newspaper and magazine are more usually produced under a less formal letter or even just a word-of-mouth agreement.

The students' actual participation in contract signing will vary according to the laws of their state. The trend to lowering the age of majority permits many high school students full legal rights, which includes signing contracts.

In some states a minor student may sign but the contract must be countersigned by an adult. Many school districts permit only their purchasing agent or the advisor to sign. But in all cases, it is *your* contract, a binding moral—even if not legal—obligation.

This is probably the first formal business transaction that staff members have taken part in and is often an occasion of some solemnity. In most cultures the importance of a contract is second only to that of an oath taken in court. It is not to be taken lightly. It implies not only an obligation to the business firms involved but also to the school and the staffers' classmates.

But the contract is not to be feared, either. It protects the staff as much as it

Color is well used on magtab cover of "Story" of West High, Iowa City, Iowa. Stars panel is blue; voting-machine handles, red; nameplate and type, black. Bold spot color is well adapted to newsprint.

does the supplier. And it formalizes deadlines and stresses again their very great importance.

There are preliminaries to signing a contract. First the staff must tentatively decide what it wants and then what it can afford. Final decisions, though, often cannot be made until the actual formalization of the contract.

The editor-in-chief and business manager must discuss a contract with printers early, even if the one who handled last year's book was entirely satisfactory for both production quality and costs. Many school districts require estimates from two or three printers before signing a contract simply as standard business procedure. Considerable money is involved, as much as a modest residence for most of the medium- or larger-size metropolitan high schools. Thus some assurance must be gained that the price is right in a period of rapidly shifting costs. Last year's estimates may be entirely unrealistic for this year.

Specifications or detailed instructions on varieties and sizes of type to be used must be drafted exactingly because a printer requires accurate, complete information in order to figure a firm price. This demands that key editors and business manager determine early:

1. At least a fairly firm estimate of total number of pages;

2. How many will have more than one color (plus an estimate for 4-color pages, if any); and

3. Minimum number of yearbooks to be delivered; forward-looking editors and business managers usually request prices for additional copies in units of 100 or 500— just in case actual sales exceed initial guesses.

Scholastic press association executives report a rising number of complaints by yearbook staffs that some printing companies are insisting on absolute standardization of all typographic specifications. These printers want the type on every yearbook they manufacture to be set at a few standard widths and styles. Some go so far as to furnish a set of dummies and insist that only these arbitrary page patterns be used by the staff regardless of the pictures that are available.

Standardization within a book is, of course, not only good but essential. Such standardization is established by the staff itself as a matter of consistency and style. But assembly-line conformity, set by the manufacturer, is not good and benefits no one but the insistent printer.

Fortunately most printers do not have such restrictions. Before the contract is signed, the staff must have assurances that the manufacturer's convenience will not supersede the creativity and legitimate wishes of the student editors. There are plenty of printers who are eager to serve you; just don't have anything to do with those who think they are calling the tune.

Then the *purveyor* or *supplier* must be chosen. Many factors are involved in this decision.

Price is always a major consideration but it cannot be the only one. Laws that cover contracts by governmental units say that the business shall be given to "the lowest or best bid." That means, of course, that "lowest" and "best" are not synonymous.

☆ Past performance is a good indicator of a "best" bid.

Businesses become old and established because they have, over a long period, given good service at a fair price. Their bid may not always have been the lowest but consistently they must have been the best.

That doesn't mean that new businesses must automatically be written off. Every business has to start out at some time. But, like a rookie competing against a veteran athlete, it must prove itself without the benefit of last season's record book.

☆ Purveyors must be equipped to fulfill the contract.

Sometimes a company will bid on a job it's just not able to produce. An awful example is one that still haunts school officials in a midwest city. A photographer, just establishing his business, offered to shoot senior pictures at just a little above cost because it gave him a chance to show his work to the community. This is a legitimate device, of course. Unfortunately, just after he had shot all the portraits but before he had printed them, he was taken seriously ill. In his one-man operation there was no one to step in and finish the job. The yearbook was three months late!

Sometimes a printer will shave the bid to get a contract, then will cut corners in production in order to make a profit. So the staff should look at books the printer has produced to be sure that the printer maintains high quality on small jobs as well as big ones.

☆ Purveyors should be chosen on the basis of convenience.

Most yearbooks are printed at distant plants and materials travel from staff to printer and back by United States mail. It doesn't take any longer just to mail a letter across the continent than across town. But there is a substantial difference, obviously, in the time the trip itself takes. This is not only a factor of distance; the routing through local and regional distribution centers can make the difference of as much as two days in a trip of the same mileage.

☆ Purveyors should be chosen on some basis of personality.

The yearbook staff will work very closely with the printer's representative. A staunch ally, with long experience, who knows the best way to get a good job done, the rep travels among scores of schools and colleges and is aware of current trends and bright ideas that are hatched by many staffs. Staffers should make sure that the rep and they are *muy simpatico*, it makes everyone's work easier.

There will be telephone contacts with people at the printing plant whom the staff will never see. But warm friendships can—and do—develop from these. Again, you want a sympathetic friend at the end of that long-distance line.

☆ Local firms can produce good yearbooks.

Just because most yearbooks are produced by specialists—who are usually some distance from the schools served—doesn't

mean that a local printer can't do a book—and a good one. But often the equipment of a local firm is not geared to book production. Or the plant may have regular customers whose work can't be postponed to get the book out on deadline. Or the yearbook may come at a busy season when the printer just can't take on extra jobs.

But the local printing company deserves the courtesy of being asked whether it's interested in bidding. It is part of the business community that supports your school system through taxes and supports school activities in many ways—by gifts, contributions, manpower, leadership, and attendance at school events. In smaller towns especially, there may be only one printshop and it may print the school paper. In that case it has already demonstrated its friendship to and interest in scholastic journalism.

When the list of possible purveyors has been compiled, they are asked to "bid the job." This takes time and costs money and so no company should be asked to bid unless it has a fighting chance of getting the contract. It is unethical to ask for several bids when the decision has already been made, just to imitate the legality of true competition.

Contract Details

Specifications included in the tender to bid are almost a duplicate of the final contract. Only minor variations will be made

"Plaid," much imitated landscaped magazine of Upland (California) High, is known for strong covers, in-depth reporting. Although this weekly can cover news promptly, all but most important items run as briefs with only subheads.

between the two documents. Here are the many basic points that must be covered in both:

1. Dimensions: page size, number of pages.

2. Number of books. As this can't be determined until the later subscription campaign, a base figure is chosen. Then a date is set when the tentative number must be made a firm one. The change in cost of the basic number when revised upward or downward is also given here.

3. Number of pictures to be handled in special screens, linear definition, or other techniques such as silhouetting.

4. Total area for pictures. This is important for letterpress printing but non-essential for offset. So this point will probably be eliminated in most contracts.

5. Total galleys of type. Often the printer will not ask for either Point 4 or 5 because experience predicts the amount of art and type a typical book will take. But these points should be raised with the printer even if they are finally not included in the formal contract.

6. Number of divider pages and other inserts. The kind of paper for special pages and the use, if any, of color there is also specified.

7. Summer inserts. All printing and photographic specifications are detailed for these. So are procedures for delivery to the school or for mailing by the printer. In the latter instance, it must be specified how addresses will be furnished him. The final date when the staff can decide on an insert —and for notifying the cover manufacturer—is also set.

8. Kind of paper. This is usually designated by a trade name: for instance, "Tamarak Book, 60 pound." The phrase "or equivalent" is usually added. In recent years the paper market has fluctuated so widely that sometimes a printer was just unable to buy a specific brand of paper. This phrase allows necessary substitutions.

Because "equivalent" means different things to different people—are root beer and orange soda "equivalent"?—this phrase can create problems. The integrity of the purveyor is the best assurance that the firm

won't use this device to substitute an inferior quality. There may be added to the contract the phrase "the purchaser shall specifically approve any substitutions." Even without that, the printer typically will seek such approval.

9. The estimated number of pages of advertising. Composition of ads varies from that of editorial pages and the printer may need this information to make a good estimate of cost and time. Often, though, this is not included in the contract though it ought to be in the request for bids.

10. Use of color. Here is specified the number of signatures that use color and whether it will be flat—and in how many colors—or process.

11. Cover. Method of binding, style and material of cover, embossing, stamping, printed elements, or combinations thereof are spelled out. Use and number of colors also are specified.

12. Deadlines. In invitations to bid, the staff sets up its tentative schedule for submitting copy. Firm deadlines are then stated in the contract after consultation between staff and purveyor.

13. Delivery date. This binds the purveyor to a date when the book must be delivered to the staff. This is usually a day or two before the students get their copies. Sometimes the contract will call for a penalty to be paid by the purveyor if books are late and must be sent out at the extra postage expense. Penalties are collectible only if the staff has met all its deadlines.

14. Method of delivery. Usually this is indicated in the contract only as "the best way." Because the printing company ships out thousands of books, it knows better than the staff what is the most advantageous route and carrier. Because insurance covers damage en route, there is no need to specify the kind of packaging that should be used. These should be discussed informally, though, to make sure that such containers will be convenient to handle and unpack in the school.

15. Payment. Because the purveyor must meet the payroll and other bills on a weekly basis, there can be no wait until the end of a long job to collect the money. So payment

for yearbooks is usually tied to the deadline schedule and the total is paid in two to four installments.

16. Footnotes. Additions or exceptions to customary procedures are also noted in the contract.

If the staff plans to set some of its own type, body or headletters, this should be noted; it may reduce the cost a bit.

If the staff plans to use artists on the printer's staff, this should be noted even though this is usually included in the basic cost.

Some printers will insist on a clause that says, in effect, "No material will be accepted by the printer unless the advisor has signed it." This is a protection for everyone—not only the printer—against unfunny practical jokes by irresponsible staffers.

The printer of last year's book should be consulted before the invitations to bid are drawn up. Printers know from their side of the fence—as the advisor or senior staffers do from theirs—what problems have arisen in the past that ought to be foreseen in future contracts.

Covers may be contracted for separately or contained in the basic agreement with the printer. In either case, the printer will usually handle the details and accept payment for the covers. There will be separate deadlines for the cover. An important one is the date when the staff must notify the manufacturer whether a summer insert must be provided for.

It should be stressed again that not all the above points need actually appear in the contract. But each one may be important and should be well considered before it is deleted.

Photography Contracts

Contracts with the professional photographer should follow another lengthy checklist:

1. Senior portraits. (For those books that use portraits of underclassmen, the same procedures apply to them.) Where and when portraits will be taken, when proofs will be shown, and when returned, and when finished glossies will be delivered—all this must be spelled out.

2. Portrait approval. How many shots the photographer will make of each subject is specified. So are the number of retakes if the student is dissatisfied with the original proofs.

3. Portrait costs. How much—if anything—must the staff pay for the glossies it uses? What prices are offered the student for the customary wallet-sized portraits, 5x7's for family and special friends and, perhaps, an enlargement or two, or some in color?

Because the student is, in effect, a captive prospect, entree to whom may be bought by providing free glossies to the staff, it is essential that this price list be spelled out and made known in advance to the senior class.

4. Other sources for portraits. Some schools refuse to give a studio such a monopoly. In such instances, it must be spelled out how a senior may have a portrait taken at some other photographer's. Standards of acceptability in photographic quality, pose, and lighting, and size of glossies, and deadlines for their delivery must be specified. In such cases the student himself is expected to provide a suitable glossy at no cost to the yearbook.

Will portraits be retouched? They should be. It should also be specified that all will be in sharp focus—not diffused, that all poses be conventional, that all dress meet specified standards, and that all glossies be of the same overall size and with the same head size and margins.

5. Group portraits. How many, where, and when will such pictures be taken? How long will the photographer wait for a group —or they for him? If reshooting is necessary, how will it be handled? When will proofs be shown the staff and when must they be returned? When must glossies be delivered?

6. News shots. Specifications should be the same as for group portraits.

7. Size of glossies. It is not practical to have the studio make glossies the same size as they'll be used. Usually they are provided in one of four standard sizes: 2½ x 3½, 4 x 5, 5 x 7, or 8 x 10. The platemaker always wants to shoot down and so

"Echo" of Rincon High of Tucson, Arizona, is pioneer among high school news magazines. All news is carried as short items on roundup page. Page size is 8x10. Nameplate is black, cover design in bright purple, almost magenta.

the glossy should be larger than the reproduced picture will be.

If the studio needs this clause in the contract, it is usually covered by the phrase: "Glossy prints shall be furnished only in standard sizes, cropped according to instructions."

8. Cost of group and news shots. Charges must be specified in detail. Sometimes the studio will agree to take up to a certain number of these shots either at a flat fee or even without charge—for the privilege of taking senior portraits. If shots will be charged for individually, either to the staff or to students in the picture, the rates should be spelled out.

As with printing contracts, this is just a checklist which should be considered in detail, then modified to meet actual needs of both staff and purveyor.

Newspaper and Magazine Contracts

Newspaper and magazine production are so alike that we can look at both procedures at the same time. Because these publications have few, if any, variables, it is easy to set specifications. Usually the printer is handed an old issue and told: "This is what we want." All pages have the same number of columns of the same length, and paper quality rarely changes.

Typically, no contract is executed for such printing; the agreement is oral. But some staffs—and printers—prefer something in writing. So they set forth the agreement in a letter, a *memorandum agreement*, which both parties sign. This covers specifications, deadlines, and price.

There are two basic ways of determining price. The printer may offer a *flat price*, a fixed price per page, per issue, or per academic year. The latter two will be for a specified number of pages and issues; then the price of extra pages must be specified.

Or the printer may offer a *cost-plus* contract. An accurate record of time and materials used to produce an issue is kept. To it is added an agreed-upon percentage for profit. A bill is submitted for every issue as it is printed.

The cost-plus system offers the greatest advantages to the staff; it can effect substantial savings by efficiency and discipline. Although the cost per issue may vary considerably under this arrangement, the total for the year will probably be well below that of a flat price.

If for one issue you have a lot of *overset*, more type than you can use, the cost will be higher. But if you can print that material in the next issue, your bill will reflect the smaller amount of typesetting this time. So the staff will be encouraged to control copy very closely and avoid that costly overset which cannot be used in the future.

Late copy or proofs, too many author's alterations, and tricky ad layouts are all items which increase costs but are under control of the staff.

A flat price has a cushion for contingencies. Things may go wrong anywhere in the long and complex production chain. As insurance against such misfortune, much of its possible cost becomes part of the contingency item. On a cost-plus basis, the staff pays only when such misfortunes occur and when they are the fault of the staff. There is the risk, then, that the staff might have to pay for a rare but major catastrophe. The risk is slight but it cannot be entirely ignored.

Deadlines are always a critical factor in determining cost and price. If you miss a deadline for return of proofs, your paper or magazine can't go to press at the scheduled time. So some other job is put on the press, for printing machinery is very costly and when it stands idle it costs the printer money. Now your publication has to await its turn and may be a day or two late. Or it must be produced during overtime at a substantial increase in cost.

☆ Discuss deadlines thoroughly with your printer.

☆ Deadlines must be realistic.

There's no point in setting a Friday-noon deadline when you know you will want to get scores of games that evening or Saturday in the paper. There's no sense in agreeing to return proofs in 12 hours when you

know the staff just can't get that job done in that time.

☆ Changing days and dates of publication can affect costs.

If, let's say, Wednesday is a very busy day for your printer, there may be only a narrow margin of time for your job. If anything at all goes wrong, you may be forced into overtime. By moving your deadline 24 hours one way or another, you may avoid this time squeeze and the often attendant extra costs.

Sometimes the printer may say, "I have open time on my press Tuesday. If you can use it, I'll make you a good price." This can avoid having the press stand idle. For it's better to run machinery at only a small profit than to keep it motionless at a loss.

☆ Changes in page size may reduce costs.

Reducing the page size only a little may enable printing of four pages instead of two at a time and thus halve presstime and costs. Increasing the page a bit may enable use of a web-fed press and again save time as well as money.

In the case of magazines, changing the kind of paper can effect cost savings or increase quality.

If a magazine uses color, it can often save money by accepting a hue other than its first choice. Each time a different color is used on a press, all that ink must be taken out of the fountain and all the many rollers washed. If your job can run without such washup, you save the cost. So the printer may say, "I'm running a job in blue next week. If you can run your cover in blue instead of orange, you'll save the washup."

In many instances that change in color is immaterial to the quality of the cover design. If you have a jack-o-lantern on the cover, it won't look so good in blue. But the difference between an orange pumpkin face and a red one is insignificant.

Many staffs now paste up their own pages and more than a few schools even set their own type. (Of course, many excellent publications are produced entirely by students in the printing or graphic arts departments of their schools.) As the cost of typesetting and pasteup is substantial, the cost of the printing job should reflect this student effort.

☆ Another factor of cost and time is the method of delivery.

If the staff picks up the publication at the printer, it saves the delivery truck a run and may save several hours' time in those cases when the school is the last stop on a long route.

☆ Establish whether the staff can work in the print shop.

Many printers allow the student staff to supervise pasteup just as the professional makeup editor does, telling the craftsman what to do if any problems arise that haven't been anticipated in the dummy. Working "on the stone" is lots of fun and valuable experience. Student editors shouldn't abuse the privilege by interfering with the craftman's work or making capricious demands.

Usually the number of students in the shop must be limited. Space is often small and too many bodies cluttering the aisles will make the printers' work more difficult. And as carelessness increases in direct ratio to the number of people in a given area, hazards arise from all the machinery that can be dangerous to careless people.

In union shops, a nonunion person can't as much as touch a piece of type. You can tell the pasteup man that the story he's looking for is on this galley but you can't hand it to him even if it means he must walk clear around the table to get it.

Many union rules appear ridiculous and some of them are. And their enforcement is usually a matter of union politics or momentary caprice. But the rules are there, written in a contract. So student editors must learn to obey them just as they will when they're professional editors.

Several printers who produce student periodicals were asked: What makes it difficult to work with student staffs?

"They don't make their deadlines." This was mentioned by every printer surveyed.

"They know it all; they never take advice."

"They change their minds too often."

"They make unnecessary changes."

"They don't know the cost of things they want, then complain when they get the bill."

"Their dummies aren't clear."

"They want things done that can't be done. Or can't be done in the time or budget available."

"They're discourteous."

"They horse around too much. This distracts our craftsmen from their jobs. And I'm always afraid some wise guy will stick his fingers into the gears of some machinery."

The same complaints could be—and are—made of adults, too. But the wise editor—student or pro—will make sure that at least this one staff isn't guilty of these annoyances.

Many a staff has found that its behavior causes the printer to refuse to print their publication any more. "It's just too much hassling," more than one printer has told the authors.

But at the same time, many printers find great satisfaction in working with student staffs. Says one of them, who has printed high school, junior college, and university periodicals for a couple of decades:

"I like to work with these kids. They're bright and eager and often come up with ideas that I can use myself. The bad apples are few—but I worry that the good staffers are penalized for what the goof-offs do. I want to put out the best publication possible and so do they. So we make a pretty darn good team."

And with this he lit up a cigarette with a lighter that he proudly displayed—engraved with a thank-you from a previous staff.

The editor and staff who consider the printer a member of their team, who treat him fairly and courteously, who respect his experience and skill, will find that the phrase is "the printer's devil"—not "the printer's a devil."

Working in Professional Journalism

Professional journalists often say that they enjoy their work because "you meet such interesting people."

A wry addition often heard is, "Yeah, other newspaper people."

Both statements are true. And the general public also shares some of the same feeling. Ways in which news is gathered and the individuals who do the assignments fascinate the mass audience more than ever before. Attention—and some concern, too, in quite a few quarters—has concentrated on all phases of communication during the 1970s. Many, many readers and listeners want to learn more about what goes on in high places of government, business, entertainment, sports, and society's jet set—the behind-the-scenes stories—as well as about the men and women who dig up and process the information. Yet why would one consider going into a journalism for a career?

There are many motivations but a few are heard repeatedly:

1. Journalism is challenging.

2. It's a chance to serve the public. In a democracy, the people need to know—they *must* know.

3. Journalists enjoy what they are doing more than most other professionals. They have fun while being paid for working, an experience not always attained.

4. Communications is rewarding in satisfactions, status, and salary.

How to gather news when officials may not wish to tell, how to write events so that readers and listeners can relive them, how to attract the largest possible audience, and how to snap an action-packed photograph that tells the whole story—these intrigue any intelligent and alert person who wants to take a place in the communications field. The challenges are there for both print and broadcast journalists.

After the news people have obtained facts, the exacting requirement of translating them into words still remains. The requirement is to pick those graphic, precise words that will make readers and listeners smile or cry—and better comprehend the world in which they live.

The photographer's challenge is to preserve visually an event that may defy description by words alone. A cartoonist seeks to epitomize with a few bold strokes what would require many words of comment.

And for all this, editors and broadcast program managers strive to package it so readers and listeners will stop, read, or listen to get the news they truly need.

Change of pace and humor are important and necessary, too. It is an exacting assignment to capture the reality of grim news and still balance it with light items.

For the business staff, the job is to promote and sell this news "product" so that it will attract and serve the largest possible audience. The people concerned with subscriptions, circulation, and promotion face special responsibilities to let the public know about the "product."

Vitally important are those staff members who persuade individuals and concerns to buy space or time and thus produce the revenue that keeps the media alive.

Any reporter has entree to places that ordinary citizens never see. Correspondents travel to faraway places in Africa, Asia, and Latin America. Washington correspondents meet the president of the United States at news conferences and in his office. Important personages, who are protected from contacts with the general public, will give constant access to news staffers. Investigative reporters unearth information about national scandals that those who know might not even tell their wives.

Editors and commentators express their own opinions and explanations. Background, interpretation, and analysis, grounded on a foundation of facts, can help the mass audience understand what is going on and what the alternative choices are. The media are an essential channel in the exercise of a truly democratic process. World history is stained with examples of dictators—real or potential—who attack the press as an initial, essential step toward their authoritarian control.

Listen to the "shop talk" of journalists swapping stories of their experiences or read their reminiscences in books or magazine articles and you will soon learn that they have moments of high drama plus a lot of fun, too.

Going behind the scenes, obviously, is a satisfying experience. That the nation's leaders, political and otherwise, pay so much attention to reporters is flattering to members of the Fourth Estate. In fact, some media critics charge that this flattery can erode the rigor of high journalistic standards. Unfortunately, they are right—in some few cases.

☆ Professional journalists have a chance to stand up and be counted.

An opportunity to move the public conscience isn't always available but it happens often enough to make journalism an attractive field for a large number of young people who have made up their minds about today's world and want to do something about it. News should not be loaded with bias and prejudices, as was emphasized earlier, but

editorial influence can be a powerful journalistic device.

To illustrate, two famous journalistic credos—the ideals of two great publishers —provide the cornerstones for two daily newspapers that are respected around the world.

The policy of Adolph S. Ochs, then the owner of the *New York Times,* was summarized in 1896 as:

It will be my earnest aim that THE NEW-YORK TIMES give the news, all the news, in concise and attractive form, in language that is parliamentary in good society, and give it as early, if not earlier, than it can be learned through any other reliable medium; to give the news impartially, without fear or favor, regardless of any party, sect or interests involved; to make the columns of THE NEW-YORK TIMES a forum for the consideration of all questions of public importance, and to that end to invite intelligent discussion from all shades of opinion.

(Note how the paper's name has lost its hyphen.)

A statement by Joseph Pulitzer to his staff when he stepped down from active control of the *New York World* in 1907 is still printed on the editorial page of the *St. Louis Post-Dispatch,* managed by his heirs.

I know that my retirement will make no difference in its cardinal principles, that it will always fight for progress and reform, never tolerate injustice or corruption, always fight demagogues of all parties, never belong to any party, always oppose privileged classes and public plunderers, never lack sympathy with the poor, always remain devoted to the public welfare, never be satisfied with merely printing news, always be drastically independent, never be afraid to attack wrong, whether by predatory plutocracy or predatory poverty.

Along with status and ideals, money plays a role in vocation choices. So let's look at the range of salaries in media jobs.

Most college graduates with journalism

training and experience on their campus papers are now starting their first professional positions with at least $150 a week. Those with special qualifications begin at even higher levels. Others in smaller communities, where living costs are not so high as in the larger cities, get somewhat less.

The Newspaper Guild, union of workers in print news media, has campaigned since its founding during the 1930s depression for higher wages and better working conditions. Contracts covering thousands of news personnel set minimum annual salaries after five years at $20,000 or higher. Many veteran staff members on affluent papers get well above that figure.

Usually higher salaries are paid broadcast newscasters, those who write scripts, and station executives. Most salaries in advertising, public relations, and industrial journalism result from individual arrangements and thus are geared to the accounts or assignments handled.

Top salaries may run upwards to a quarter or half million dollars a year for the exceptional newspaper owner-publisher, broadcast network executive or commentator, public relations counsel, advertising agency head, widely syndicated columnist, or successful comic-strip artist. A handful of individuals at the very top of the media employment ladder reportedly receive a million dollars a year.

One thing to keep in mind about cub reporters' and junior editors' pay is that while some professions have higher starting salaries quite a few see the pay scale plateau after a few years, whereas journalists' salaries move up fairly steadily throughout their careers.

Regardless of what one may do in professional journalism for newspapers, magazines, radio, television, advertising, public relations, or communication research, the work will differ only slightly from the basics learned on a school publication or broadcast station.

☆ Scholastic journalism is one extracurricular activity with built-in future usefulness.

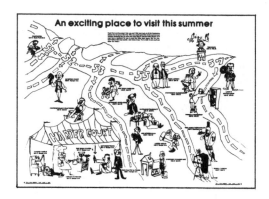

Freely-drawn map of area around University High in Chicago has great pulling power and is highly saleable to merchants involved. This is center spread in "Midway", school's compact-format paper.

Few football, basketball, or baseball players join professional teams after they finish their education. Fewer actors in a school play find their ways to success in Broadway plays, Hollywood motion pictures, or broadcast programs. But high school journalists quite often do go into commercial communications. In fact, most surveys show that a job on a high school or college publication's staff is one of the important factors in determining whether a student enters journalism when picking a vocation.

Even those who do not become communicators find their publication or broadcast experience of value. For instance, law schools want students who can ask good, probing questions, a trait useful for reporters and cross-examining attorneys.

Journalism can be a fine springboard to other careers. Many politicians started as reporters and smaller-town editors. The same is true of civil servants and business executives.

News personnel have entree to levels of management that are totally closed to people of the same age in other kinds of work. The young editor of a house magazine meets the president and top company officers almost daily. A young accountant, sales clerk, or secretary may never lay eyes on these officials. A reporter of 25 years of age meets the mayor and governor person-to-person.

And since all adults are "news consumers" as they get information and ideas from the mass media, anyone with even limited news experience can make better judgments on what is printed and heard. An informed "news consumer" knows about the workings of media and the goals that they strive for and then can insist—quite properly—that high standards be met.

When one considers journalism as a possible vocation, what are the major careers to choose from?

The list is long and each segment has its own combination of qualifications and requirements. This chart gives an overview of opportunities in various major fields:

	Writing	Copy Editing	Commenting Opinions Editorials Columns	Business Distribution Advertising Promotion	Mechanical/ Production	Research
Newspapers						
Daily	Yes	Yes	Yes	Yes	Yes	Yes
Weekly	Yes	Yes	Yes	Yes	Yes	Seldom
Press Associations/ News Syndicates	Yes	Yes	Yes	Promotion/ Sales	Transmission only	Sometimes
Consumer or Mass Magazines	Yes	Yes	Yes	Yes	Yes	Yes
Industrial Journalism						
Trade	Yes	Yes	Yes	Yes	Yes	Yes
House	Yes	Yes	Sometimes	Distribution	Yes	Seldom
Religious Journalism	Yes	Yes	Yes	Yes	Yes	Yes
Advertising						
Media Staff	Yes	Yes	Seldom	Yes	Sometimes	Yes
Agency	Yes	Yes	Seldom	Promotion/ Sales	Sometimes	Yes
Radio	Yes	Yes	Yes	Yes	Yes	Yes
Television						
Network	Yes	Yes	Yes	Yes	Yes	Yes
Station	Yes	Yes	Sometimes	Yes	Yes	Yes
News films	Yes	Yes	Sometimes	Promotion/ Sales	Yes	Seldom
Public Relations	Yes	Yes	Sometimes	Yes	Seldom	Yes
Free-Lance Writing	Yes	One's own writing	Seldom	Sales	No	For one's own writing

Individuals who pick journalism for a career may possess diverse talents that qualify them for a place among an exceedingly broad variety of possible assignments. They must assess their own training, talents, and predispositions and made carefully considered choices.

To make this assessment as realistic as possible, a student who is considering any field of communications would be wise to talk to a journalism teacher, advisor, or—when a chance is offered—professionals in the community. These individuals are more likely to have details at hand than a vocational guidance counselor, who would have to look up facts in reference books or other sources. The counselor can't possibly remember details for hundreds of various vocations.

Some students may choose to go into gathering and writing news and features. Others may handle the editing and preparation of copy and pictures.

Those with an artistic aptitude may join an art department. They may become nationally known cartoonists for editorial or sports pages or even more widely recognized if they create popular comic strips. A highly successful comic strip can yield more financial return than a syndicated opinion column.

For those interested in the new newsroom technology there are opportunities to participate in the tremendous advances that are now being made in the mechanics of newspaper and magazine production. New developments have been innovative and extensive during the past decade. Working out how to use them effectively for a better product at lower costs requires ingenuity and intelligence. Now engineers are needed where formerly only mechanics served. Original ideas here pay rich premiums.

Those with a commercial bent may join a business staff and be concerned with circulation, promotion, and advertising. Those who go into advertising and promotion may do such varied jobs as sell groceries in a supermarket to study consumer buying habits, manage an annual Golden Gloves boxing tournament, or lay out double-page advertising spreads.

Still others may go into the service activities of advertising agencies and public relations counseling with industrial firms, nonprofit institutions, or specialized groups.

Some individuals may elect to work on specialized publications of such a diverse range as employee magazines for industry, journals for labor unions, and religious or fraternal periodicals. Those employed by

Professional journalists are eager to recruit good young people into industry. Comic books, such as this one featuring Popeye, are used to reach prospects as early as elementary and junior high schools. King Features Syndicate, through whose courtesy this is used, furnishes career books for distribution by daily newspapers.

industry have a good chance to work their way into top management, as witness the many former employee-magazine editors who now hold positions as vice-presidents and even corporation presidents. While salaries in religious journalism are not as high as those on most commercial publications, status is particularly high; some editors of religious periodicals get the same respectful treatment accorded ministers, priests, and rabbis.

Others may become public information officers for corporations, unions, government at any level, schools, or research institutions.

Still others may combine journalistic background with social science training to become communication research specialists and market analysts for media, advertising agencies, government, or independent groups.

A few may become free-lance authors who sell their work to high-paying publications.

Others may go into teaching journalism in colleges and high schools.

Despite this wide spectrum of journalistic opportunities, what about hiring prejudices, say, against employing women?

Most doors are open to both sexes. Opportunities for women in media have been greater during the 1970s, as they have in many other vocations. For instance, it is no longer unusual for women to cover sports, even including postgame dressing-room interviewing of professional players. Although women have encountered occasional bias, they have advantages over their male colleagues on some assignments. Positions on women's-interest magazines, accounts of women's products handled by advertising and public relations people, and editorships of food and fashion sections of newspapers and networks seem to be a special—but not exclusive—province for female workers. More than 20,000 women rated sufficiently high media positions to rank as "image-makers," according to one survey in the mid-1970s.

Women have served as publishers, editors, and war correspondents. One won a Pulitzer Prize for her Korean War coverage, including front-line action, and another received that prize for foreign correspondence and commentary. Katharine Graham, publisher of the *Washington Post,* made final decisions for that paper's publishing the Pentagon Papers and for pursuing the Watergate exposés despite White House opposition.

What are the media opportunities for minorities such as Blacks, Spanish-speaking, American Indians, and Orientals?

During the late 1960s and 1970s, special efforts were instituted to hire more qualified journalists from minority groups. This was particularly true for the broadcast networks, stations in urban centers, and larger metropolitan dailies. The largest percentage of minority members employed in "image-maker" positions was in broadcasting, followed in descending order by advertising,

periodicals, and newspapers. Some of this expansion in hiring minority representatives came after the report of the National Advisory Commission on Civil Disorders in 1968 said that media, like the country as a whole, have "too long basked in a white world, looking out of it, if at all, with white men's eyes and a white perspective."

What preparation should one make for a professional journalism career?

☆ Learn to typewrite.

Granted that this is just a simple, mechanical skill, it is essential preparation that any high school student must make who is serious about communications work. A staff member on a school newspaper, magazine, or yearbook who does not type is so handicapped that chances for promotion are small. In any case, the individual will have to learn later—without benefit of much scholastic journalism experience for a job résumé. Employers on commercial periodicals and broadcast stations are refusing to hire potential employees unless they can type—and fairly well, at that. The new electronic newsroom requires that reporters use a typewriter, and already some news writers are, for all practical purposes, "setting" type that goes into print as their fingers hit the keys.

Shorthand is a useful, but not required, skill for newsgathers. One of the distinct differences between British and American journalists is that the former must learn how to take shorthand as part of their job training while those in this country do not. Knowledge of shorthand symbols is of little aid, however, when a journalist has to concentrate on these mechanical details instead of thinking about important points of an interview or of a speech.

More and more today the young people going into communications are college and university graduates. Many of the more successful ones have majors or minors in journalism. Employers seek individuals who have broadly based backgrounds, such as journalism majors now receive in all recognized schools and departments of journalism. For instance, the *American Council on Education for Journalism* (*ACEJ*), the accrediting agency in this field, advocates that students devote not more than 25% of their college courses to journalism or mass communication; the rest should be in the liberal arts or related departments. For editorial assignments with any of the media, a free-ranging knowledge of liberal arts and sciences is needed. Those who have that education receive favorable consideration by those who hire.

For jobs on the business side of the mass media, public relations, advertising, and industrial journalism, attention is given to training in economics, marketing, business management, and general commercial orientation. However, broad liberal arts and sciences should not be neglected by those planning to enter these communication specialities.

For those expecting to teach or perform communication research, training in education and social sciences is desirable along with a wide range of humanities and sciences.

After obtaining a college degree, you should consider carefully whether to join a large organization and learn a small job with a wider future or whether to take a job with a smaller concern—be it publication, station, or agency—where you will do a variety of assignments. There are impressive arguments for each approach. Pick the one that you honestly think will fit you better.

In considering the future, a student should keep in mind that many a weekly publisher or small-town station manager attains satisfactions and status that are unknown to the sometimes frustrated and harried public relations counsel, advertising agency vice-president, metropolitan daily's promotion manager, or copy-reader on a news magazine. Running a successful weekly is not the one-horse operation of half a century ago and the rise of suburban weekly papers during the past generation has upset small-town journalistic traditions with hurricane force. Except for those in the very top positions, a metropolitan daily's staff member may be far less highly regarded than those on a respected weekly.

The students with the greatest chance of success, no matter where they work or what they attain in dollars, respect, or service, will bring these characteristics:

1. A high level of technical skills for communications: The ability to dig out information no matter how difficult, the capacity to write clearly and concisely, and the ingenuity to present complex ideas in attractive and understandable terms;

2. A natural curiosity with a vein of skepticism but without the flaw of cynicism;

3. A respect and dedication for the truth, even when unpleasant for readers and listeners; and

4. An intelligence and determination that is willing to challenge the status quo when its underpinnings are soft and rotten.

If you think you have these capabilities when you take a cruelly honest appraisal of your talents, then welcome to one of the most stimulating and rewarding vocations— one that offers opportunities to help your fellow habitants in this world while having some fun and being paid for it.

Glossary

A

AA's: abbreviation for author's alterations, which see.

accent face: type of markedly different design or weight used to contrast against basic letters used in ad or page.

add: new material to include at end of story already written or already set in type.

advance: story about event which will take place in future. Also, copy of speech, resolution, etc., given to reporter before it is actually presented.

advertising manager: executive in charge of ads.

advocacy journalism: term applied to special-pleading, nonobjective news stories. Sometimes confused with "new journalism."

agate: $5\frac{1}{2}$-point type. Also, as agate line, unit of measuring advertising, 1 column wide by $\frac{1}{14}$-inch deep.

all-cap: caps, material set entirely in upper case.

American: ethnic group of Square Serifs race.

anchor the corners: layout technique that places strong display elements in or near the corners of page.

anchorman: person who speaks material which ties together segments of news broadcasts.

angle: variation on letterform creating Italic and Oblique.

announcer: person who presents spoken word on television and radio broadcasts.

A/O: axis of orientation; imaginary line at left of type element to which reader returns to start following line.

AP: Associated Press, major wire service.

Arabic numerals: 1, 2, 3, etc.

armpit: undesirable layout technique of placing narrow headline immediately under wider one.

art: illustrative material of all kinds in publication: photography and hand art, prepared by artist.

art head: unchanging label heading containing pictorial element.

ascender: portion of letter that extends above meanline. Also, those letters which have such extensions, such as b, d, h.

assignment: reporter's designated job.

assignment book or sheet: editor's record and announcement of jobs given to staff reporters.

assignment editor: staff member responsible for giving reporters assignments.

attention compeller: element of strong visual appeal.

author's alterations: AA's, changes made in set type, not to correct typographical errors but to revise content.

B

backbone: bound side of book; spine.

background: supplemental stories, frequently historical or explanatory.

backing up: printing second side of sheet of paper.

backshop: mechanical departments of newspaper.

backslant: letterform slanted to left.

bank: one line of headline. Also, that surface on which typographic material is stored before it is made up.

banner: streamer, headline that extends across width of page. Also, largest head on front page.

baseline: imaginary line on which primary letters align at bottom.

basement: lower half of front page of newspaper.

bay: mortice surrounded on three sides by picture.

beat: run, regularly assigned area covered by reporter. Also, exclusive story.

beat reporter: one who covers same territory regularly, in contrast to general assignment reporter who covers specific and changing events.

Ben Day: process of placing shading pattern on line engravings or type; named for inventor.

billboard cover: that of magazine which uses all-type to call attention to several inside stories.

bimo: pronounced *buy*-mow, bimodular. Headlines with two elements such as kicker, hammer, tripod, and wicket.

binding: fastening paper together to create book or magazine.

Black Letter: Text, race of type, usually only thick and thin strokes with no curves. Erroneously called Old English.

blanket: rubber sheet on which lithographic printing is transferred from plate to paper.

bleed: to extend picture off one or more margins of page.

blind stamping: that in which type characters are defined only by depression into paper or fabric with no ink used.

block letters: variety of Gothic letterform.

boards: stiff material covered with paper or fabric to make book cover.

body: regular reading matter in newspaper as contrasted to display lines.

body type: that style and size in which most nonadvertising material is set.

boldface: form of alphabet in which size remains constant but strokes are heavier. Abbreviated bf.

bold graf: paragraph of news story set in boldface to change color of mass.

boldline: boldface type used for first line of random paragraphs, used in place of subhead.

bond: kind of paper usually used for letterheads.

book: name for magazine frequently used in trade. Also, yearbooks. Also, prepared set of two sheets of copy paper and one of carbon paper used by reporters in writing story.

book method: proofreading technique which uses two marks for each error, one at point of error and correction in margin.

book plate: label bearing owner's name printed or pasted on end papers of book.

bowl: that area of a type character enclosed entirely or partially by curved lines such as interior of o, a, b.

box: unit of type enclosed by border. Sideless boxes use such border only at top and bottom.

bracketed: serifs joined to main stroke by curves, distinguishing Old Style Roman ethnic.

brayer: roller for applying ink to type.

breaker head: subhead set in display type.

bright: humorous or human interest news item, almost always short in length.

brilliant: form of stamping or embossing combining image in ink with one in relief.

broadsheet: newspaper page approximately 15 inches x 20 inches.

buddy system: oriented layout.

budget: total amount of editorial copy and art available for one issue of newspaper or news magazine.

bullet: large period used for decoration or typographic color.

bumping head: jammed; one headline actually or almost touching another.

bureau: out-of-town news-gathering office of newspaper.

burnish: to smooth down; to polish.

business department: staff of publication concerned with circulation, advertising, and accounting. Usually headed by business manager. Other departments include news, editorial writing, and mechanical.

by-line: writer's or photographer's name above story or under picture.

C

calligraphy: beautiful writing, letterform often used for nameplates or column heads.

camera-fresh copy: clean matter direct from typesetter or artist for use in pasteup.

canopy: headline which runs across related picture and story.

caption: descriptive material accompanying pictures in a yearbook. Erroneously used instead of cutlines in newspaper usage.

carrier-current: system in which radio signals emanate from existing electric power lines instead of being broadcast conventionally from towers.

catchline: line of large type between picture and cutlines.

chase: rectangular metal frame in which typographic elements are assembled for printing.

circulation manager: C.M., executive in charge of subscriptions and other distribution.

circus makeup: razzle-dazzle, that which uses strong and sensational display patterns.

city editor: executive in charge of publication's coverage of local news and director of local staff.

city room: area in newspaper office where local or city news is written and edited. On many newspapers called news room, where all copy is processed.

clamshell: platen press.

clapper: platen press.

classical: layout pattern in which elements are placed in patterns generally resembling certain letters of alphabet.

clean copy: material relatively free of errors and corrections.

clip: clipping, cutting from periodical, especially one filed for future use.

clip book: collection of reproduction proofs of art to be used for offset work.

closed-circuit: system of carrying television signals by wire instead of being broadcast by conventional methods.

coated: smooth paper often used for books and quality magazines.

cold type: that produced photographically, by typewriting, or by preprinted characters; as opposed to hot metal.

collage: art produced by pasting together various elements into single composition.

color: typographic device used to change overall tone of masses of type. Apparent tone or density of a page as affected by varying type faces, borders, decorations, etc. ROP color is use in newspapers of inks of hues different from black.

color, flat: use of additional hue or hues without attempting to create spectrum of nature. In newspaper usage, commonly referred to as "spot" or "ROP" color. ROP (run of the press) designates that color, flat or process, produced on a regular, instead of specialized, press and on any page.

color separations: screened negatives, each recording one primary color, from which are made printing plates which later combine to reproduce full spectrum of hues.

color, typographic: variations in tonal value of masses of type; created by using boldface, Italic, white space, or ornaments.

columnar layout: yearbook page pattern in which every element is in increments of basic column-width.

column inch: unit for measuring advertising space, 1 column wide (this dimension varies among publications) by 1 inch deep.

column rule: vertical line separating type masses.

comb: plastic device for binding books.

combination plate: printing element with halftone and line elements.

communication theory: application of social science research findings to transmitting information.

compact: format of newspaper with pages approximately 11 x 15 inches. This is also called tabloid format, but compact format uses more conservative layout, and pages become smaller versions of conventional, full-format papers.

composed: set in type; typographic elements arranged in form for printing.

composing room: part of printing establishment or plant where type is set, then assembled into ads and pages.

composition: type set manually or by machine. Also, act of typesetting.

compositor: person who arranges typographic elements into pages, ads, etc.

comprehensive: detailed, same-size dummy almost a replica of finished printing job.

compres: pronounced com-preez; comprehensives. Cutlines so long no accompanying story is needed.

Condensed: form of alphabet in which characters retain their height but are narrower than normal.

connotative: teaser headline. One that piques curiosity rather than summarizing story.

consequence angle: emphasis on importance of news development.

constants: those elements which appear in every issue of publication, such as nameplate, masthead, folio lines, etc.

contact print: uncropped, same-size photographic print made from negative without use of enlarger.

continuous tone: picture in black, white, and intermediate tones of gray, or their equivalent in color, without screen dots.

contrast: introduction of markedly different typographic or art element into layout for emphasis or interest.

copy: material written for possible publication. Also, materials from which printing plates are made.

copy block: persuasive copy in ad, set in body type.

copy desk: location, usually U-shaped desk, where copyreaders edit copy. Also, collective group that staffs that desk. Also, general term for news-room management.

copy editor: copyreader, which see.

copyfilling: determining by mathematics how much space manuscript will occupy when set in type.

copyreader: staff member who edits copy, sometimes writes headlines and dummies-up pages.

copyright: formal legal procedure for protecting "exclusive use" to authors, photographers, and other artists of their creative work. Applies specifically to style of presentation.

copywriter: creator of verbal portion of advertising messages.

correction: publication of correct information after mistake. Also, process of repairing typographical errors.

cost-plus: system for determining price of printing job by adding agreed-upon profit to all expenses involved.

counter: areas within and around printing surface of type.

cover: to gather information.

criticism: broadly, report on some performance in arts, books, drama, etc.; frequently evaluation and sometimes including subjective, opinionated comments. See review.

crop: to eliminate unwanted areas of picture. These are not actually cut away; desired portion is indicated by marginal crop marks.

crop marks: indicators that show areas of

a photograph to be eliminated in printing plates.

cropper's L's: pair of L-shaped cardboard pieces that are manipulated to find most effective area in picture before cropping.

CRT: cathode-ray tube, television-type scanning method used to set photographic type.

CSPA: Columbia Scholastic Press Association with headquarters at Columbia University, New York City.

Cursive: letterform resembling handwriting but with unconnected characters. See Script.

cursor: moveable spot of light to indicate on screen where changes are to be made in electronic editing of copy.

cut: photoengraving. Also, used for pictures in publications printed by offset or gravure. Also, to compress story in length.

cutlines: explanatory copy that runs with pictures. In yearbooks, called captions.

cutoff rule: thin line used for horizontal separation on newspaper pages.

cut to waste: large, unused, and useless paper left at margins of printed page.

cylinder press: printing machine on which paper is impressed upon flat typographic surface by cylinder. Also called flatbed.

D

dateline: phrase showing origin and date of filing of out-of-town news story.

deadhead: label headline; one not written as active sentence.

deadline: time when reporter has to submit copy, when copy must go to composing room, or when publication goes to press.

debossing: design depressed into paper or fabric.

deck: that section of multi-unit headline composed of one or more lines in same face and size. When deck is subordinate to banner, it is called readout or, more rarely, drop.

definitive head: one summarizing its news story.

delayed broadcast: that recorded for later release.

delete sign: stylized medieval *d*, to indicate on proof removal of unwanted typographic matter.

density: quality of negative or picture which gives well-defined gradation from black, through gray, into white.

departmentalize: to group news content of paper by subject matter.

descender: portion of letter that extends beneath baseline. Also those letters which have such extensions, as g, p, q.

desk: that place in news room where copy-reading is done. Usually city desk or news desk. Also, that broad definition of duties which distinguishes editors from writers. Also, the administration of special departments such as sports, financial, etc. Also, general term to designate executive levels of news staff.

diagonal, common: system for determining size of printing plate smaller or larger than original art.

direct quote: verbatim quotation from interview, speech, or text.

dirty copy: written material with many mistakes and corrections.

display: that size of type larger than body type which is used to attract attention. Use, rather than size, determines difference between body and display types.

divider page: page or pages in yearbook that introduce major division of contents.

documentary photography: that form of art which concerns itself with recording facts rather than primarily or only with form and composition.

dominant head: strongest one on newspaper page, acting as nucleus for page pattern.

downstairs: lower half of front page of newspaper.

downstyle: copy or headlines set with minimum of capitals. In body type, only key words of titles are capitalized, as in Central high school or Middletown Athletic association. In headlines only first word and proper nouns are capped.

dulling spray: plastic substance to eliminate glossiness of still photographs used on television broadcasts.

dummy: drawing showing arrangement of elements of printed page or ad. Thumbnails are small, sketchy preliminaries. Roughs are larger but with little detail. Comprehensives are same size and in detail. Mechanicals or comprehensives are exact replicas of finished printed job.

dummy-up: to arrange news material in page form by preparing rough dummy.

duotone: printing process in which dark and light color are combined to produce third color, only visible one.

duplex: usual combination of body type such as light and bold or Roman and Italic.

dynamic balance: layout pattern balancing elements optically rather than mathematically.

dynamic thrust: motion added to printed page by pictures differing markedly from 3-x-5 proportions.

E

ear: small block of type that runs alongside newspaper flag.

edit: to check copy for mistakes of any kind, including facts, style, spelling, grammar, and libel, and to improve it as communication. Also, abbreviation for editorial.

editor: staff member who edits news copy, in contrast with gathering and writing news for publication. Also, executive in charge of specialized department of a publication, as sports, business, etc.

editorial page: edit page, that devoted to opinion and comment.

editorial side: news department.

editorial writing: department of publication concerned with expressing opinions, usually through editorials. Also function of periodical sometimes known as opinion function. Usually directed by editor of editorial page or chief editorial writer.

editor-in-chief: senior editorial staffer.

Egyptian: ethnic group of Square Serifs race.

electrical transcriptions: phonograph records used in broadcasting.

electronic editing: processing copy by electronic means, usually involving a computer.

embossing: process of pressing design into reverse side of paper or fabric, especially book covers, to create raised image on front side. Opposite side of paper is debossed.

end mark: 30-mark, symbol that shows end of story in copy or print.

engineer: person who handles mechanical details of broadcasting.

engraving: photoengraving, process of converting photograph or art work into relief printing plate by photochemistry. Also, plate so made. Also called cut.

entertainment function: lighter, amusing side of journalistic coverage.

equal time provision: legal guarantee of equal distribution of air time to candidates for same political office.

ethnic group: first subdivision of type race.

evergreen matter: stories or pictures that are not subject to rapid obsolescence or "aging" after specific date.

exchange editor: staffer in charge of exchange subscriptions.

exchange subscriptions: complimentary copies exchanged with other publications. Part or sometimes all of free list.

Extended: form of alphabet in which characters retain their height but are wider than normal.

eyeball: to trust to visual perception rather than mechanical aids in aligning matter in pasteup.

F

fairness doctrine: concept of broadcasters' responsibilities to opposing viewpoints when expressing their own opinions over airwaves.

fallow corner: top right or lower left of printed page or advertisement.

family: subdivision of type race identified by trade name and made up of various sizes and forms of basic design.

FCC: Federal Communications Commission.

feature, news: material developed out of current happenings as background information or "with" story.

feature editor: editorial staffer in charge of features.

filler: short item used to fill space.

5 W's: who, what, when, where, why; term to denote possible elements that may be included in summary lead paragraph. Also called 5 W's and H, to include how.

FJA: Future Journalists of America with headquarters at University of Oklahoma, Norman, Okla.

flag: nameplate, formal identification of newspaper on its front page. Often but erroneously called masthead. Sometimes called logo.

flatbed press: cylinder press.

flat color: spot color; one that in printed form does not reproduce natural spectrum of nature.

flat embossing: design impressed into paper or fabric by only single-plane, flat plate.

flatout: one-up; arrangement of story in one more column of space than there are legs of type.

flitjays: f, l, i, t, and j; used in counting headline units.

floating flag: short newspaper nameplate that may be placed other than at top of page one.

flong: stereotype matrix, mold of papier-mâché from which printing plate is cast.

floret: typographic ornament, usually in form of stylized flower.

flush left: type of headline set so all lines are against left-hand column rule. Also, any other type so set.

flush right: headline style which is set so all lines are even at right and ragged at left. Also, any other type so set.

folio lines: small type which gives newspaper or magazine name, date, and page number. Erroneously, datelines.

follow copy: instructions to printer to set copy as written. Used to indicate unusual spelling, type arrangement, etc.

follow-up or folo-up: instructions to gather additional information on event. Also, story about event that has been forecast in advance story.

font: collection of letters, numbers, and characters in one type family and of one size.

forced circulation: system in which subscription to publication is included in another fee such as membership dues.

form: relief type and engravings, assembled in a chase, from which a page is printed or stereotyped.

formal balance: symmetrical layout.

format: shape, size, and general physical appearance of publication. Full format is usually newspaper in 8 columns of about 21 inches deep; tabloid, or compact, format is approximately half that size.

foundry type: reusable metal printing characters used in letterpress.

four-color process: printing method that combines three primary colors with black to reproduce full color spectrum of nature.

4 C's: correctness, clarity, conciseness, and color; guidelines for broadcast news writers.

Fourth Estate: term applied to journalism, the press, newsmen. In feudal Europe, three estates were nobles, clergy, and commons; fourth was not official but so named in deference to influence of press.

frame: page pattern with strong pictorial elements arranged on outside.

free form: one not describable in geometric terms.

free list: complimentary and/or exchange subscriptions of publication.

frequency: clear channel for broadcast purposes determined by oscillation rate of electronic signals.

fresh air: white space injected into layout.

fullface: normal design of letters as opposed to Condensed and Extended and normal weight as opposed to boldface or light. Lightface is often used as a synonym of fullface but confusion is possible when there is a weight lighter than normal.

full format: that of newspapers of 7 to 9 columns of approximately 21 inches in depth.

functionalism: philosophy that demands that every printing element perform useful, necessary job of communication.

furniture: wood or metal rectangles used to create white space in printing forms.

future book: editor's listing, under dates, of forthcoming events that should be covered.

G

gallery cover: that of magazine which uses one picture, usually not related to any inside story.

galley: long, narrow, shallow tray in which type is stored after being set and before

One-up technique used in "Chieftain" of Pocatello (Idaho) High. Skyline story is displayed 4-across-5, tied together with Ben Day rules at top and bottom.

it is assembled. Also short for galley proof.

galley proof: first printing of type to detect errors.

gatekeeper principle: concept of determining what gets into print or on air.

gathered: (printed sheets) assembled in proper order before binding.

general assignment reporter: one who covers specific event or meeting, in contrast to beat reporter who has specific territory to cover regularly.

geometric layout: one in which typographic elements are arranged to form definite patterns of lines and areas.

gimcrack: typographic decoration, usually small, used to break up masses of type.

glossy: photograph with shiny finish. Often used as synonym for all photos.

Gothic: ethnic of monotonal race. In its earlier form it was ungainly and compressed, with heavy strokes and squared-off curves.

go up: to use flatout technique, one more column of space than type.

graf: paragraph.

graphic arts director: executive in charge of all nonverbal communication of periodical.

gravure: intaglio printing. Method in which printed image is incised into metal plate. Rotogravure is common commercial application most frequently used for Sunday newspaper magazine sections.

Greek: to indicate blocks of body type in dummy by penciled lines.

Grotesk: European name for Gothic type.

guideline: proofreading method in which error is circled and line drawn from it to margin where correction is noted. See book method.

gutter: two margins of book and magazine pages that meet at fold. Single margin there is called inside or gutter margin.

H

hairline: thin stroke in type character. Also, thinnest rule used by newspapers.

half-title page: often first printed page in book carrying only its name.

halftone: printing plate which reproduces continuous-tone art by use of screen.

hammer: reverse kicker. Headline form of short line of large type above two lines of smaller type.

hand art: all pictures and decorations produced by artist, in contrast to photographs.

handout: press release.

hanging indent: headline style in which first line is set flush left-and-right and each succeeding line is indented specified, identical amount at left.

hard copy: typewritten copy, usually produced at same time tape for automatic typesetting is perforated or fed into OCR.

harmony: arrangement of typographic elements to lead reading eye pleasantly throughout whole area.

head: short for headline.

headletter: type used for headlines.

headline: heading, label, or caption placed over news, columns, etc.

headline schedule: collection of all headline forms and sizes used by one newspaper.

hellbox: depository for discarded type, slugs, or other material, often even including editorial.

H.I.: human interest, feature or news material with high emotional or dramatic appeal.

highlight dot: tiny specks in white and light areas of halftone picture.

hold copy: material which is to be kept and not used until notification, or at specified later time or date.

hood: rules around top and sides of headline.

horizontal makeup: typographic technique of disposing type in wide, flat areas to make it appear easier to read.

hot metal or hot type: linecaster slugs and foundry type as contrasted to cold type.

house publication: newspaper or magazine printed by business organization or institution, generally wholly subsidized and distributed free or for small fee to convey special message for its publisher.

HTC: head to come (or HTK, hed to kum), indication to printer that headline will follow but to set copy at once.

human interest: news with emotional impact about individuals or animals. May be fairly short items, such as brights, or longer features.

I

i & e lines: identification and expository. Name of person, on one, i-line, and descriptive phrase, e-line, on second, as title for printed portrait.

ident: identification. Simplest of picture captions.

ideogram: symbol used in early writing to represent abstraction.

imposition chart: diagram showing placement of various pages printed as signature on same sheet of paper.

impression: product of one cycle of printing press. Also, clearness of printed sheet. Also, force with which paper and type meet.

in-depth reporting: news items with explanation, background, interpretation.

index: alphabetical listing of topics in book or magazine.

index, senior: list of names of graduates and their school activities.

informal balance: layout pattern in which elements are balanced by optical weight rather than by mathematical placement.

information function: factual presentation of news as contrasted with opinion function.

initial: first letter of paragraph set in type larger than body type for decoration or emphasis. Its size is indicated by number of lines of body type it occupies, as 3-line initial. Those aligned at bottom of body type and projecting upward are rising or stickup initials; those that occupy corner cut out of type block are inset or sunken.

insert: new material that is to be inserted into copy already written or type already set. Also, section of yearbook printed after main book is complete and so designed that it may later be fastened into cover with earlier material. Also, small picture or type placed in opening created by narrowing some lines of block of type.

inset head: headline, used especially with typewritten copy, which occupies corner within mass of body type.

insurance shot: extra ones taken to assure usable photo of event that cannot be duplicated.

intaglio: pronounced in-*tahl*-yo. Printing from incised plates. Rotogravure is that variation used by newspapers and magazines.

internal silhouette: tint block with area removed so silhouette halftone will print on white background but be surrounded by color.

interpretation: explanation, background, in-depth reporting, attempt to get below surface in news reporting without becoming subjective.

interview: story obtained by talking with individual. Also, act of such talking.

inverted pyramid: style of newswriting starting with most important facts first and following paragraphs containing information in descending order of interest.

Italic: Itlx, variation of Roman type which slants to right and is often more decorative. Also, erroneously, but commonly, used to designate slanting form of non-Roman faces, which are correctly designated as Oblique.

J

jam: to place two or more headlines on page so they touch.

jazz: layout pattern in which each margin of layout is suggested but not entirely defined.

journal: working daybook record of business transactions.

jump: to continue story from one page to another. Also, story so continued, especially that portion on following page.

jump the gutter: to combine two facing pages in book or magazine into single visual unit by minimizing division between them.

justify: to set type so it fills line completely. Also, to space type so column is exactly filled vertically.

K

key page: one without advertising.

key plate: that carrying black or major image in multi-color printing.

key word: one in headline on page one that is repeated on jumped story.

kicker: small headline that rides above main headline.

kill: to eliminate material, either in part, as within news report, or entirely. Mandatory kill, order from news service to its clients forbidding use of previously transmitted material.

L

label head: one without verb that indicates general story content or departmental classification. Also known as deadhead.

Latin alphabet: 26 letters used for writing English. Also called Roman alphabet, although that can create confusion with Roman type race.

layout: application of principles of typography to specific problem. Also, dummy.

lay the paper: to place advertising in page dummy.

lca: lowercase alphabet length, measure, in points, of all minuscules of font.

lead: pronounced leed, opening of news story. Pronounced ledd, any added space between lines of type.

ledger: record of all business transactions, including both receipts and expenditures.

leg: one column of type of several in story spread out in horizontal mass.

legibility: visibility, that quality in type that affects quickness of perception of single line or compact group such as headlines. Erroneously used instead of readability.

leg man: staff member who gathers news, then transmits information to rewrite man who does actual newswriting.

lettering guide: mechanical guide for producing characters on Mimeograph stencils or for cold type.

letterpress: method of printing from relief typographic elements.

libel: false and malicious defamation, includes type, pictures, cartoons, drawings.

lightface: fullface.

light table: translucent working surface, through which light shines from below, used for preparing stencils and pasteups.

linear definition: line conversion.

line art: art work in only lines and masses of black and white, that makes line engraving printing plate, as opposed to halftone.

linecaster: machine that produces a line of type. Lintoype, trade name, was first keyboard linecaster and name is used almost generically. Ludlow has no keyboard.

line conversion: black-and-white reproduction of continuous-tone copy, in which gray middle tones are eliminated.

line cut: printing plate which prints only lines and masses of black.

lines of force: lines within picture or created by type arrangement which act as directional guides to reading eye.

Linotype: first linecaster, machine which casts relief type in lines instead of as individual characters.

literary editor: staffer who handles creative writings of periodical.

lithography: writing with stone. Printing method that uses repulsion between ink and water to transfer image from stone surface to paper. Modern development, photolithography or offset, uses metal or paper plates prepared photographically instead of manually as in lithography, which today is used basically as fine-art form.

local angle: emphasis on nearby neighborhood in news writing.

locked up: (relief printing form) wedged tightly into chase and ready for printing.

log: record of advertising scheduled for future issues. Also, all material processed by copy desk.

logotype: heading which identifies section of newspaper or magazine, such as sports or activities. Abbreviated logo. Sometimes used for nameplate or advertiser's signature.

loose register: arrangement of images in two or more colors that can vary slightly in relative position without affecting quality of printed image.

lowercase: minuscules, small letters; so named because in old print shops these characters were kept in the lower of two cases.

M

magazine: a periodical publication, usually bound and smaller in format than a newspaper.

magtab: publication that combines magazine and newspaper formats.

mail room: location from which papers are distributed.

majuscules: capital letters.

makeup: assembling type, ads, and cuts in chase.

makeup editor: representative of news department who directs assembly of type and pictures in mechanical department. Not to be confused with makeup man, printer who actually handles typographic material.

makeup man: printer who assembles ads or pages in composing room, frequently under direction of makeup editor.

malapropisms: misuse of words that sound somewhat alike.

managing editor: M.E., executive in charge of all news functions of publication. Title varies; sometimes it is executive editor or news editor.

mandatory head: one without subject of sentence, giving effect of stern order, i.e.: STOP FIGHTING IN INDIA.

manipulated candid: photograph of unposed action in carefully arranged surrounding and conditions.

mass media: communications channels to general public. Generally considered to include newspapers, magazines, radio, television, newsreels, and, in some cases, nonfiction or informational books. Sometimes, but rarely, direct-mail and billboard advertising is included. Used in contrast to personalized approaches, such as individual letters or lectures to comparatively small groups.

masthead: that collection of data, usually appearing on editorial page, which lists publisher, editors, and staff of publication. Often but erroneously used to refer to flag.

matrix: mold from which type, decorative materials, advertisements, and illustrations are cast for letterpress use. Abbreviated to mat.

matte: photographic surface of tiny pebbling, usually used for studio portraits.

M.E.: abbreviation for managing editor.

meanline: imaginary line at top of primary letters.

measure: length of line of type.

mechanical: pasteup, cold-type material arranged for platemaking.

mechanical binding: one fastening book by rings, spiral wire, or plastic comb.

mechanical department: section of publication concerned with production of newspaper or magazine.

mechanical separation: art work, prepared by hand, for each plate to be used in multi-color printing.

mechanical shading: shading screen or sheet.

memorandum agreement: letter less formal than contract, outlining arrangement between printer and staff.

memory: storage for copy and instructions for electronic editing.

metal appliqué: shiny foil elements bonded onto book cover.

mezzotint: special halftone screen that reproduces photo in style of crayon drawing.

milline rate: cost of one agate line of advertising per million readers.

Mimeograph: stencil duplicating machine. This is trademark and should be capitalized, although, because machine was first of its kind, there is tendency to use name as generic term.

minuscule: lowercase letter.

modeled embossing: design in bas relief produced by pressing paper or fabric between two dies.

Modern: form of Roman letter with sharp, straight serifs, maximum difference between thick and thin strokes, and bowls on perpendicular axes.

modular: rectangular layout.

mold: matrix.

Mondrian: page pattern in which page is divided into rectangles of varying shape and size but each harmonious with all others.

monochrome: hand art done in various shades and tints of single color.

montage: picture produced by using portions of various negatives in single photographic print.

mood shot: photograph stimulating emotion rather than conveying information.

morgue: library of reference materials. Probably called that because it stores obituaries or "obits."

mortice: area removed from printed picture to allow type or other art to occupy that space. Most common is "notch," where rectangle is removed from one corner. Area removed within picture is internal mortice.

mosaic: page pattern using hen-and-chick principle.

mousetrap cover: that of magazine which lures reader to specific inside story by means of picture or type.

N

naked column: one without head or picture at top of page.

nameplate: flag.

"new journalism": using semifictional techniques in news stories to stimulate interest.

news: reports of anything timely which has importance, use, or interest to considerable number of persons in publication's audience.

news angles: aspects of event which make it of special interest to communicators and their audiences. Among most common are: today angle, local angle, prominence angle, consequence or importance angle, human interest, paper's policy, and good taste.

news budget: all nonadvertising available to newspaper for any given issue or edition.

news bureau: organization that furnishes news matter about school activities to community media.

news department: that organization of publication concerned with gathering, editing, and displaying of news items. Usually it is headed by either managing editor or news editor.

news editor: executive in charge of news department.

news hole: that area in newspaper devoted to editorial, as opposed to advertising, material.

newsprint: relatively inexpensive paper usually used to print newspapers.

news room: areas of publication office where news copy is written and edited. On smaller papers it combines with city room.

noise: interference in transmitting information. Applies to communication theory.

nonverbal communication: telling news through pictures, cartoons, drawing. Sometimes similarly applied to advertising.

no-orphan system: oriented layout.

no-run: advertisement which was not printed as scheduled.

notch: simplest form of mortice, rectangle cut out of one corner of printing plate.

Novelty: ethnic of Ornamented Letter.

NRM: next to reading matter, instructions given for placement of newspaper advertising.

NSPA: National Scholastic Press Association, organization for school journalists with headquarters at University of Minnesota, Minneapolis, Minn.

number: issue of magazine or newspaper within single year of publication.

O

obit: obituary, biographical materials used on death of individual. Often this is prepared in advance from material entered on printed obit form.

Oblique: those letterforms, of races other than Roman, which slant to right. Slanting Roman forms are Italics.

obscenity: material of prurient interest

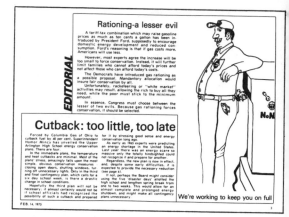

Editorial page in "Arlingtonian", news magazine of Upper Arlington (Ohio) High, proves that such pages can be as lively as any others in publication.

which offends community moral standards and has no redeeming social values.

OCR: optical character recognition machine, often called "scanner" which interprets letters and punches tape.

office manager: individual or group that maintains records, including ledger.

offset: planographic printing method in which image is lithographed from metal or paper plate onto rubber blanket, then "set off" onto paper. Technically this is offset lithography, although the second word is commonly dropped.

Old English: family of Text type race.

Old Style: ethnic of Roman letter with minimum difference between thick and thin strokes, bracketed serifs, and bowls that tilt to left.

one-theme spread: extensive display on single topic.

one-up: layout technique which uses one more column of space than of type, extra space being distributed between columns. When two more columns of space are used, technique is called two-up.

opaque: to remove, in negative, unwanted shadows and other defects before platemaking.

open-air: radio and television stations (usually those operated by schools) that broadcast on frequencies accessible by general public.

op (optimum) format: newspaper page using body type at optimum line length, usually in 6 columns on broadsheet, or 4 on tabloid page.

opinion function: one of aims of periodical. Others include information, entertainment, and service. Opinion function applies to editorials and columns that express opinions. Includes editorial writing.

opinion magazines: publications concentrating on subjective presentations, usually of contemporary issues.

optical center: that point at vertical center and 10% above horizontal center of a page or ad.

optimum line length: that width of line of type which is most easy and pleasant to read. Determined by multiplying lowercase alphabet length by 1.5.

oriented: buddy or no-orphan system, layout pattern in which each typographic element is arranged to align horizontally and/or vertically with at least one other.

Ornamented: type race with variations in shape or texture of strokes or additional elements around letter itself.

ornaments: those typographic elements other than characters of normal font. Most common are stars, florets, borders, and initials.

overlay: transparent paper or plastic laid over picture to create mechanical separations; to indicate cropping, especially of intricate shapes; or to give instructions to platemaker.

overline: line of display type over picture. Also, erroneously, called caption.

overset: composed type in excess of current available space. Usually such matter must be discarded because of loss of timeliness.

overtone rub: method of decorating book cover by rubbing contrasting paint over an embossed area.

P

padded cover: book covering that has soft material between fabric and heavy boards.

page proof: sample impression of whole page or form.

pagination dummy: rough, small folder showing number of pages and arrangement of magazine or yearbook.

paragraph starter: decorative element used instead of customary indenting of paragraph.

pasteup: assembling various cold-type elements into form from which printing plates are made. Also, pasteup dummy, guide for printer made by affixing duplicates of actual type and pictures to same-size sheet of paper.

pattern shot: photograph which repeats same shape of objects many times to create pleasant composition.

pebble: texture of paper with tiny hemispherical depressions.

performance sheet: visual representation of completed work, frequently comparisons of individual staffers or with previous years' activities.

personal: brief news item about individual or small group, frequently found on society page. Unlike brights, personals generally do not give humorous or amusing incidents.

photoengraving: relief printing plate that reproduces pictures. Also, process of converting photographs and art work into printing plates.

photo release: signed statement by person(s) in picture allowing it to be used for advertising and other commercial purposes.

pica: unit of printer's measurement, 12 points, $\frac{1}{6}$ inch. Also, larger of two standard typewriter faces.

pick up: instruction to composing room to add material indicated, usually already set type or available picture.

pictogram: earliest form of writing by simple drawings of objects.

picture editor: executive in charge of all pictures, local, mail, mat, and wirephoto. Generally assigns local photographers to cover local news events.

pinched: narrowed stroke of letterform, usually where curve meets straight line.

pix: pictures, plural of pic.

plane embossing: that in which image is raised in flat relief.

plastic bindings: method of binding using rings or spiral fastening of plastic or metal.

plate: piece of metal that carries printing image in relief, depression, or planographically.

platen press: letterpress printing press, also called clamshell or clapper press, which impresses flat typographic surface upon paper in hinged motion. Also, surface upon which the paper rests during printing and typewriting.

play: emphasis given to news and pictures. Also applies to extensive display given to a story or picture.

POA: primary optical area.

point: unit of printer's measurement, $\frac{1}{72}$ inch. Also, any punctuation mark.

poll: survey of attitudes or public opinion.

porkchop: half-column picture.

poster layout: that used in typical tabloid format for page one, consisting of one or two headlines (with stories inside) and large picture.

PR: public relations.

press associations: press services or wire services, organizations which supply regional, national, and world news and pictures. AP and UPI are two leading ones in United States.

press card: printed identification for staffers.

press release: information given to newsmen or sent to publication, usually as public relations function on behalf of organization anxious, or obliged, to have such news widely disseminated.

press room: location of printing presses.

primary letter: those lowercase letters without ascenders or descenders, such as a, c, m, r.

primary optical area: POA, that portion of written or printed page in upper-left corner where eye instinctively begins reading or inspection.

printing: production of multiple, repetitive images in ink on paper by use of plates or movable type on press of any variety.

prior restraint: prohibition, generally by court, on publication of news or comment thereon.

process color: that printing operation which combines halftones in two or more colors to create optical illusion of colors which are physically mixed, as in paint. Three-color (commonly used in newspapers) and 4-color process can duplicate all colors in the spectrum.

production chart: one showing status of preparatory steps of each page of yearbook.

production typist: one who produces final, perfect copy for platemaking.

profile: personality sketch.

progression: arrangement of total material in magazine or yearbook.

prominence angle: emphasis on well-known people and places in writing and evaluating news.

proof of publication: tearsheet or issue containing ad, given to space buyer.

proofreader: person who examines first impressions of printing to correct errors, primarily typographical, but also in fact and style.

proportional spacing: device giving different amounts of space to wide and narrow characters in typewriting.

publisher: top executive in charge of periodical's operations; on commercial papers, sometimes also owner.

punched tape: paper tape with holes that convey commands to typesetting machine.

put the paper to bed: complete work for publication; give final approval before publication is printed.

pyramid: ad pyramid, placement of advertising on newspaper page.

Q

Q and A: question and answer, used for transcript of court trials, hearings, etc.

quality magazine: journal which is concerned primarily with expressing opinions or subjective evaluations, usually on contemporary scene.

Quill and Scroll: honorary society for high school journalists with headquarters at University of Iowa, Iowa City, Iowa. Also name of society's bimonthly magazine.

quoin: metal wedge, used in pairs to fix typographical materials firmly into chase.

quotes: quotations used in story. Also quotation marks.

R

race: basic subdivision of type, Roman, Text, Monotonal, Square Serifs, Written, and Ornamented.

razzle-dazzle makeup: circus makeup.

readability: that quality of type which affords maximum ease and comfort in reading over sustained period.

reading diagonal: basic, instinctive motion of reading eye through printed page, from top left to lower right.

read-in head: one that is first part of sentence that then continues in body type.

rectangular layout: layout pattern in which area is subdivided into rectangles that harmonize with whole and each of its parts.

register: arranging position of impressions of different colors so they match properly on printed page.

reglet: letterpress spacing material, usually wood but often metal, 1 pica or more wide.

release: press release. Also, authorization to print material sent out to composing room to be set into type and marked to be held.

relief printing: letterpress, method of printing by applying ink to raised surfaces and impressing on paper.

reproduction proof: repro, carefully produced impression from relief type, used to make printing plates.

Resisto: trade name for water-resistant photographic paper.

retraction: correction of error in previously printed news story. Generally important as means of showing willingness to rectify mistake. Retraction may help establish lack of malice if libel action is taken.

reverse cut: printing plate which produces effect of white letters on black or gray background.

reverse kicker: large, short headline above a smaller main headline. So called because it reverses ratio of regular kicker to main head.

review: broadly, report on some performance in arts, books, drama, etc.; frequently comments resemble a news item in objectivity. See criticism.

revise: second proof of type in which errors discovered in first—or galley—proof have been corrected.

rewrite man: staff member who either writes information received from leg man or rewrites copy, already submitted, which needs major revisions.

rim: outside of U-shaped copy desk as opposed to slot.

rim man: regular copyreader who is under supervision of slot man.

Roman: race of type distinguished by thick and thin strokes, swelling and thinning of curved ones, and by serifs.

ROP: run of press, color work produced on regular newspaper press, not special one, and on any page.

rotary press: letterpress printing press in which paper—fed from endless roll—is impressed upon curved typographic surface by cylinder.

rough: same-size dummy showing elements without detail.

roundup: summary in one story of numerous news developments from different sources.

run: reporter's beat. Also number of copies of publication being printed.

runaround: narrowing column of type to provide room for insetting photo or display type.

rundown sheet: schedule used by broadcasters showing time when each segment of broadcast should go on air.

runners: messengers who deliver news matter to media for simultaneous release.

running head: material in display type that reads from one page to another. Also, name and number of book, and sometimes of chapter, that appears on every page.

S

saddle staple (and saddle stitching): binding method in which wire or thread is passed through fold.

salon shot: picture printed for its beauty rather than communication.

Sans Serifs: ethnic of Monotonal race.

scaling: determining size of printed picture when reduced or enlarged from original art work.

schedule: collection of headlines used by newspaper.

scoop: exclusive news story or one, covered by many reporters, printed and circulated first.

screen: device used by platemaker to reproduce continuous tone art work. Also, indication of fineness of engraving when combined with number—as 65-line screen —which indicates lines of halftone dots per lineal inch.

Script: ethnic of Written type race.

self-cover: magazine or booklet cover of same paper as that used for inside pages. Also, periodical so bound.

senior index: list of graduates and their scholastic activities.

sequence pictures: series of still pictures taken at close intervals during progressive action.

series: subdivision of type families that contains various sizes of one form of alphabet. Identified by size and family name.

serif: tiny finishing stroke at end of main strokes. Major distinguishing feature of Roman type.

service function: journalistic presentation of information of specific use, such as times of broadcasts and ads.

sewn-round and back: the most common permanent method of binding books, in which pages are sewn to each other for easy opening.

Shaded: ethnic of Ornamented type race in which ornamentation is added to face of letters.

shading sheet: regular pattern printed on transparent plastic sheets and pasted onto line drawings for equivalent of Ben Day.

shadow dot: tiny white specks in dark areas of halftone reproductions.

Shadowed: ethnic group of Ornamented type race in which decorative elements are added to outside of letterform.

shoot down: to make printing plate smaller than original picture.

shoppers: publications resembling newspapers but containing little, if any, news in addition to advertising.

short: any brief news story, but frequently used for humorous incident told in few words. See bright.

shotgun head: single headline over two or more separate stories.

sidebar: second story that goes with another. Also known as with story.

side head: one at side of, rather than above, its story.

sideless box: decorative rules used at top and bottom of type to create typographic color element.

sideline: display type under left side of printed picture, acting as transition to cutlines under right portion.

side staple: binding method in which fastener is inserted through side of sheets near the fold.

sig cut: signature, that typographic element which performs functions of trademark and identifies an advertisement. Also called logo.

signature: sig cut. Also group of pages printed on single sheet of paper.

silhouette: halftone plate from which background has been removed.

silhouette, modified: halftone plate with subject partially outlined but with one or more straight sides.

silk-screen: reproduction process using stencils, often used on yearbook covers.

singleton: line of display type used as caption material.

single wrap: copies of publication which are packaged and mailed individually.

sketch dummy: very simple diagram for assembling page of publication or advertisement.

skyline: any elements that run above nameplate on page one.

skyline mosaic: yearbook page pattern stressing vertical photos.

slip jacket: envelope of clear plastic into which book is placed to protect it from wear and soiling.

slipsheet: waste paper put between freshly printed sheets to avoid smudging.

slot: inside of U-shaped copy desk. Reserved for slot man.

slot man: staff member in charge of copy desk. So named because he sits on inside of U-shaped desk and directs activities of copyreaders on outside edge, or rim.

"Hi-Comet" of North Little Rock (Arkansas) High is in compact format. But center spread becomes broadsheet, always used for in-depth feature. Page 5 is over-designed with too many heavy, intricate borders.

slug: line of composition produced on a linecaster. Also, blank relief printing unit 6 or more points thick.

slug line: word or several words used to identify news copy.

small capitals: letterform of capitals but in size almost that of small letters.

solarization: photo with blacks and whites partially reversed by exposure to light during development process.

spec: specify, to instruct printer which types and sizes to use on page or ad.

specialized desk: copyreading arrangement that handles special types of copy such as wire, sports, local, etc. Distinguished from universal copy desk.

spec layout: speculative; advertisement prepared for presentation and possible sale to potential space buyer rather than done to order.

spike: to kill or eliminate copy. Also, hook in which such copy is placed.

spine: backbone, that portion of book where all folded edges are joined.

sports editor: executive responsible for sports coverage.

spot: small decorative art. May be hand or photographic.

spot a negative: to eliminate small defects in film with opaque paint.

spot color: flat color.

spread: two facing pages of book or magazine.

square halftone: halftone printing plate with 90-degree corners.

Square Serifs: race of type with letterform made with serifs of same weight as main stroke.

S/S: abbreviation for same size, instruction to engraver.

staff: group of people who produce a publication. Most commonly this refers to those performing editorial and writing functions, although business department personnel are also designated as business staff. Mechanical and circulation personnel are usually called crew.

staggered grafs: paragraphs set narrower than available space and alternating flush-left and -right.

stamping: impressing type into paper or fabric for debossed image.

standing head or stereotype head: heading on recurring feature used repeatedly without change.

station manager: executive in charge of broadcast operations.

stencil: sheet with various openings through which ink is forced to reproduce written, typed, or art material. Used in Mimeographing and silk-screen process.

step-and-repeat: process for covering large area with repetitive design made from single piece of art.

stereotype: process of making flongs from printing forms and casting printing plates from them. Also, plates thus made. Also, standing heads. Shortened to stereo.

stet: in proofreading, "let it stand," despite earlier markings.

stickon type: that used for pasteup by affixing letters to dummy.

stitched: book or magazine fastened with wire staples.

stock cover: book binding using available decoration rather than that drawn specifically.

stone: smooth surface upon which printer works. In old days actual marble-topped table.

streamer: banner.

strikeon: typesetting produced by typewriter-like machines.

stringer: area correspondent of newspaper. So called because in old days payment was made on amount of material which was printed, and which was pasted in long strip as proof of claim.

style book: handbook for publication's style in grammar, spelling, capitalization, etc. Less detailed instructions may be merely style sheet.

stylus: pointed instrument to produce stencils, or illustrations thereon, for Mimeograph and similar machines, or for cutting shading sheets and certain stickon type.

subdivider: page in yearbook that introduces subdivision of contents.

subhead: grafhead, displayed line, usually boldface and centered body type, within story.

summary head: definitive headline.

summary lead: initial paragraph which tells

highlights of news at beginning of story.

supplement: insert to yearbook.

supplier: commercial firm that sells printing and similar services to school staff.

supportive journalism: bulletin boards, news letters, public-address systems, etc., used to supplement conventional print and broadcast news media.

surprint: to overprint, especially on a photo or colored background.

survey: roundup of news on special theme or attitudes and public opinions.

swipe file: collection of pictures and ideas used by artists and layout men for their own guidance and inspiration.

symmetrical: layout pattern in which each half is mirror image of other.

syndicate: service organization which provides comics, features, pictures, columns, etc., to papers.

T

TA: terminal area; lower right corner of printed page or advertisement.

table of contents: list of material in book or magazine.

tabloid: tab, newspaper format with pages approximately 11 x 15 inches. Also, a philosophy of presenting news of sensational content and in circus form. The same format but with conventional typography is called compact.

tearsheet: single "torn-out" sheet of newspaper or magazine delivered to advertiser as proof that ad has been properly run.

teaser head: connotative headline.

telegraph editor: wire editor, executive in charge of copy originating outside locality of publication. Handles press association and syndicate copy.

Teletype: machine for sending electrical impulses which will print message simultaneously on typewriters at distant points.

Teletypesetter: development of Teletype permitting electrical impulses to punch paper tape at distant points, which tape then automatically actuates machine to set type.

Text: Black Letter. Second type race.

texture: surface quality of paper.

theme: unifying idea connecting various portions of yearbook.

Thermofax: photocopying process used to provide proofs of cold type.

thirty: symbol meaning "The End"; sometimes written "30" at end of story copy. As 30-dash, end mark.

thumbnail: first small, sketchy dummy drawn by layout man.

tie-in: advertising combining sales appeals for related items such as shoes and purse, or offering special inducements in sale of one item to purchaser of another, as movie tickets at half price with every purchase of restaurant meal.

time copy: material that is not directly under pressure of deadlines for immediate publication. Sometimes called "AOT copy" (Any Old Time).

tint block: background of color over which is printed type or picture.

tip-on: to paste smaller printed sheet onto page or cover of book.

title page: that at opening of book giving its name and that of author, publisher, date, etc.

today angle: emphasis on recentness in news writing.

tombstone: two or more heads touching horizontally.

tracing paper: sturdy but transparent paper used for making layouts.

traffic department: that which handles all material going to and from printer and advertisers.

transfer sheet: method for adding mechanical patterns to line art.

trend pieces: type of background articles.

trim: to cut or compress copy.

tripod: headline starting with short line of large type, then two lines of smaller size at its right.

turn rule: instructions to composing room to reverse slug so its blank, bottom edge will print and thus indicate some change is to be made in copy above or below.

two-digit code: system for marking headlines. First digit indicates column width and second weight of head in that width. Thus, 2-3 head is 2 columns wide and third heaviest in that width.

two-edition yearbook: annual printed in both hard cover and soft cover.

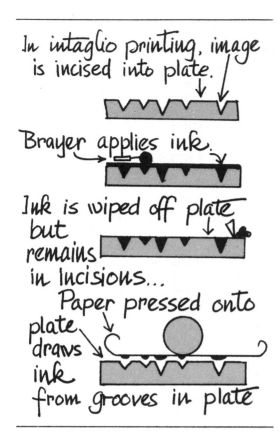

In intaglio printing, image is incised into plate.

Brayer applies ink.

Ink is wiped off plate but remains in Incisions...

Paper pressed onto plate, draws ink from grooves in plate

Schematic of intaglio printing.

type library: all faces available in print shop for publication use.

typemetal: alloy of lead, tin, and antimony used to cast movable type. Also, all relief printing elements.

typesetter: person who converts manuscript into hot or cold type.

typo: typographical error, mistake made in composing room.

typographical director: graphics arts director.

typography: basic plan for use of typographic elements.

U

unit count: method of determining number of specific letters which can be set in line of head.

universal copy desk: copy editing arrangement that handles all types of copy at same place. Distinguished from specialized desk.

UPI: United Press International, major press association.

upper-and-lower (u & lc) head: headline in style which capitalizes every major word.

upstyle: copy or headlines set with maximum of capitals. So called because of emphasis on capitals or upper-case letters. In headlines all words are capped; in body copy all words in phrases that are proper titles, as Central High School. In contrast to downstyle: Central high school.

V

VDT: video display terminal, television-type screen and typewriter keyboard. Basic newsroom tool in electronic editing.

vignette: printing plate which gives effect of picture blending almost imperceptibly into white of paper.

void: counter of type.

volume: number designating year of publication's life.

W

wammies: w and m, in counting headline units.

web: continuous roll of paper for printing by rotary process.

weight: variation of letterform to create series by changing thickness of strokes.

well: deep, narrow opening between advertising for editorial matter.

wicket: two-part headline with two lines of smaller type at the left of single line of larger size.

widow: last line of paragraph if not entirely filled.

width: variation of letterform to create series without changing height or eliminating family resemblance.

wild picture: one without accompanying story.

wire editor: telegraph editor executive in charge of copy originating outside locality of publication, from press association, syndicates, bureaus, and stringers.

woven: book page or advertisement in which all elements share common vertical and/or horizontal axes.

wrap: to continue type from one column to next.

Written: type race resembling informal cursive forms of everyday use.

X

Xerox: photocopying machine used to provide proofs of photocomposition.

x-height: height of primary letters, from baseline to meanline.

Z

zinc: engraving, especially line cut.

zinc etching: line cut. Sometimes erroneously applied to all photoengraving.

Zip-A-Tone: trade name for shading screen.

zoom lens: attachment for television camera that provides pictures from extremely long shot to very closeup without moving camera.

Index

Index of Publications